Journey through the Workbook of *A Course in Miracles*

Volume One

Lessons 1 through 60

Journey through the Workbook
of
A Course in Miracles

The Study and Practice of the 365 Lessons

Third Edition

Volume One

Lessons 1 through 60

KENNETH WAPNICK, Ph.D.

Foundation for A COURSE IN MIRACLES®

Foundation for A COURSE IN MIRACLES®
375 N Stephanie St, Suite 2311
Henderson NV 89014
www.facim.org

1st printing, 2005
2nd edition, 2011
3rd edition, 2020

CONTENTS BY VOLUME

Preface to the Third Edition

This new edition is reduced to seven volumes without a hardcover case. The appendix has been moved to Volume One, and each volume contains the Complete Index of References to *A Course in Miracles*.

Preface to the Second Edition

The notable revision in this new edition appears in Volume Eight, where we have replaced our catalog of publications with an appendix consisting of excerpts from a 1992 workshop I gave entitled "The Workbook of *A Course in Miracles*: Its Place in the Curriculum • Theory and Practice." The selections focus on several of the key themes I developed and wove into my commentary throughout the preceding seven volumes. These excerpts, which include discussions of questions asked by students, serve to reinforce some essential guidelines for students to keep in mind on their journey, not only with the workbook, but with *A Course in Miracles* itself. As is our practice with published transcriptions of workshops and classes, we have striven in our editing to maintain the informal nature of the actual workshop.

I especially want to thank Rosemarie LoSasso, our Publications Director, for editing the excerpts from the original workshop and putting them into a coherent whole. It was a challenging task, and one she fulfilled with her usual skill and loving dedication.

For this second edition we also have corrected typographical and numbering errors.

Preface to the First Edition

These eight volumes are the end product of a series of fifty-eight classes that I conducted at our Foundation's former location in Roscoe, New York, in 1998 and 1999. Each audio-taped lecture was approximately one hour, and consisted of a line-by-line analysis of the workbook: lessons, introductions, reviews, summaries, and the Epilogue. Time constraints necessitated omitting, or only briefly commenting upon some relatively minor passages. For this eight-volume book, however, I have included the passages omitted during the original classes. I have also considerably enlarged some of the discussion, supplying additional references to other relevant portions of *A Course in Miracles*, the Course's Preface, the two pamphlets *Psychotherapy* and *The Song of Prayer*, poems from *The Gifts of God*, and the prose poem "The Gifts of God"*—all of which amplify or parallel what had previously been discussed. These current volumes can thus be seen as a complete Course companion to accompany students on their own journey through the workbook.

My purpose in this book—as it was in the classes that inspired it—is to help students of *A Course in Miracles* better understand the meaning of the lessons and their place in the overall curriculum of the Course. Most of all, the purpose is to help students see the importance of applying the daily lessons to their everyday lives. Without such application, the brilliance of Jesus' words in *A Course in Miracles* is wasted, and they become simply a sterile system of intellectual teachings. Indeed, the stated purpose of the workbook is to help students apply the teachings of the text's theoretical framework:

> A theoretical foundation such as the text provides is necessary as a framework to make the exercises in this workbook meaningful. Yet it is doing the exercises that will make the goal of the course possible. An untrained mind can accomplish nothing. It is the purpose of this workbook to train your mind to think along the lines the text sets forth (W-in.1).

As any teacher knows, students learn by constant practice and repetition. While our memories may not extend that far back, that was how we all learned to read, write, and do arithmetic. Similarly, anyone who has ever learned to play a musical instrument remembers the daily practice and repetition of scales and exercises. So, too, with the text's principles of forgiveness. These must be practiced day in and day out, moment by moment if necessary. Jesus reminds us in the text that every encounter is a holy one (T-8.III.4:1), because each experience, regardless of its magnitude, provides an opportunity for the reversal of projection that allows us to examine the contents of our unconscious minds.

---

* The poems and prose poem were written down by Helen Schucman, scribe of *A Course in Miracles*. Throughout this book, I shall refer to her as "Helen," and her partner in the scribing, William Thetford, as "Bill." For an in-depth discussion of Helen, her scribing of *A Course in Miracles* and other material, and her relationship with Bill, please see my *Absence from Felicity: The Story of Helen Schucman and Her Scribing of A Course in Miracles*.

Without such awareness we can never truly choose again, the Course's ultimate goal. Moreover, when we learned our basic skills in elementary school, we did not learn each and every possible combination of words and numbers, but only the principles in specific examples, which we then generalized to all instances. Thus does our new Teacher—Jesus or the Holy Spirit—instruct us to forgive certain of our special relationships, helping us then to generalize the principle to all relationships:

> The purpose of the workbook is to train your mind in a systematic way to a different perception of everyone and everything in the world. The exercises are planned to help you generalize the lessons, so that you will understand that each of them is equally applicable to everyone and everything you see (W-in.4).

In case we missed it the first time, Jesus repeats his point two paragraphs later:

> The only general rules to be observed throughout, then, are: First, that the exercises be practiced with great specificity, as will be indicated. This will help you to generalize the ideas involved to every situation in which you find yourself, and to everyone and everything in it…. The overall aim of the exercises is to increase your ability to extend the ideas you will be practicing to include everything (W-in.6:1-2; 7:1).

We shall return to this essential point when we begin our journey through the workbook.

These volumes can be read in at least three ways: 1) straight through, as one would do with the text of *A Course in Miracles*; 2) different lessons at different times; or 3) one lesson at a time, as a companion to each lesson. I would urge students, however, if they are doing the workbook for the first time, to read the lessons as they are, without my commentary. In other words, as with all my other work on *A Course in Miracles*, this eight-volume book is meant to supplement a student's experience of the workbook, not to substitute for the workbook as it was given to us.

Before continuing, I should like to make a few comments about the nature and structure of this book. For those reading it straight through, please be advised that I do not explain *everything all the time.* To do so would make these volumes unbearably

cumbersome, and even longer than their current length. Thus, ideas or principles are often stated on the assumption that the reader has already read the material in the book that explains them in more depth. For example, I frequently mention the foundational ego principle of *one or the other*, without always explaining its ontological origin or full meaning. Below, I discuss the metaphorical use of language in *A Course in Miracles*, wherein, for example, the term *God* is sometimes used when the meaning is *the Holy Spirit*. While the reader is sometimes reminded of this, it is not always mentioned.

Because of the cyclical nature of the workbook, I from time to time repeat relevant quotations and citations from the text, manual, and other material. Here, too, I do not always indicate to the reader that I have done so. The index in any volume can be easily referenced to see where and how often passages from the Course, the pamphlets, and *The Gifts of God* have been cited. As mentioned above, I have also used Helen's poetry to augment my discussion of the lessons. I have done so not only because of its obvious relevance, but to introduce these wonderful poems to readers who may not be aware of their existence. Likewise with the prose poem, also entitled "The Gifts of God." This minor masterpiece is found at the end of the volume of Helen's poetry, and provides a powerfully succinct overview of *A Course in Miracles'* thought system. I hope those readers already familiar with these writings will enjoy their inclusion, and those making their acquaintance for the first time will be gladdened by still another source for the same teachings found in the Course itself. For further discussion of the origin of this material, the interested reader may consult my book on Helen and the Course's beginnings—*Absence from Felicity*—cited in a previous footnote.

In addition, not all scriptural references in the workbook have been mentioned. The interested reader can consult my *Glossary-Index for A Course in Miracles* for an exhaustive list of these many citations and allusions.

A word now about the use of language in *A Course in Miracles*. As I discuss in great detail in *Few Choose To Listen,* Volume Two of *The Message of A Course in Miracles*,* the Course is written in dualistic (or metaphorical) language. That is the meaning of Jesus' statement in the Introduction to the clarification of terms:

This course remains within the ego framework, where it is needed. It is not concerned with what is beyond all error because it is planned only to set the direction towards it. Therefore it uses words, which are symbolic, and cannot express what lies beyond symbols.... *The course is simple.* It has one function and one goal. Only in that does it remain wholly consistent because only that can *be* consistent (C-in.3:1-3,8-10).

Underscoring the symbolic, and therefore inherently illusory nature of words, Jesus makes these comments in the manual for teachers:

> God does not understand words, for they were made by separated minds to keep them in the illusion of separation. Words can be helpful, particularly for the beginner, in helping concentration and facilitating the exclusion, or at least the control, of extraneous thoughts. Let us not forget, however, that words are but symbols of symbols. They are thus twice removed from reality (M-21.1:7-10).

Therefore, because of our limited capacity to understand—identifying with the brain instead of the mind—Jesus' abstract or non-specific love needs to be expressed in a form we can understand and eventually accept. Thus he says in the text, concerning the Holy Spirit's teaching us how to experience the oneness of truth through forgiveness:

> All this takes note of time and place as if they were discrete, for while you think that part of you is separate, the concept of a Oneness joined as One is meaningless. It is apparent that a mind so split could never be the Teacher of a Oneness which unites all things within Itself. And so What is within this mind, and does unite all things together, must be its Teacher. *Yet must It use the language that this mind can understand, in the condition in which it thinks it is.* And It must use all learning to transfer illusions to the truth, taking all false ideas of what you are, and leading you beyond them to the truth that *is* beyond them (T-25.I.7:1-5; italics mine in sentence 4).

Thus God and the Holy Spirit (and Jesus) are spoken of as if they were persons, members of the species homo sapiens. They have gender, and speak, act, think, make plans, have reactions and feelings, and even have body parts—voices, arms, hands, and tear ducts. Yet how can a non-dualistic God be or do any of these things? Lesson 169 states that "God is," and nothing more can be said that is truly meaningful. It is essential, however, for the student of *A Course in Miracles* to understand that all such references for God, Christ, the Holy Spirit, and Jesus are not meant literally. On the level of symbol or metaphor, they simply meet us *in the condition in which we think we are.* Much of the workbook is written on this level, and I shall usually point out the *seeming* inconsistency between form and content, word and meaning, sometimes referring back to the passages I have just cited. When the use of symbol is properly understood, the problem of consistency will disappear. That is why Jesus cautions us in the text not to confuse symbol with source (T-19.IV-C.11:2).

In addition, there are notable inconsistencies in the use of words. For example, as mentioned above, the word *God* is used when it is obvious *the Holy Spirit* is the proper subject. One example comes in Lesson 193, "All things are lessons God would have me learn." The lesson itself makes clear that "God does not know of learning," while throughout all three books the Holy Spirit is referred to as our Teacher. In Lesson 29 we are told that "God is in everything I see," yet the lesson and the one following make it clear that it is the *purpose* of God that is meant, and we know from our study of *A Course in Miracles* that it is the Holy Spirit's function to hold that purpose of forgiveness in our minds. Other examples abound, and I shall for the most part point them out when they occur.

It is also important to point out the references to traditional Christian terms, such as *Atonement*, the *Second Coming*, and *Last Judgment*, not to mention lessons such as "I am the light of the world." This follows the same lines of reasoning I just discussed —Jesus' use of our Western and dualistic language as the *form*, within which he teaches us a different *content*. Therefore, it is extremely important to understand in the Course that most of the time Jesus uses the language of symbols with which we all have grown up. Both in Judaism and Christianity, God is seen as having plans and doing things for us, such as sending various kinds of help: natural phenomena, angels, His Son, even having the last

---

* See especially Chapters 2-3.

named killed on our behalf. A significant part of His plan includes special people with special parts in the special plan. Such obvious anthropomorphisms, when the symbols are taken literally, are red flags pointing to the voice of specialness and not the Voice of truth. Jesus does not speak directly of specialness in the workbook, but he does describe its dynamics. In an important line from the text, he says that we cannot even think of God without a body, or in some form we think we recognize (T-18.VIII.1:7). That is his way of explaining that because we believe we are bodies that are separate, he must talk to us about a God Who also seems to be separate—not that He is in truth, but that He *seems* to be. Again, this does not literally mean that God has put the remedy or the Holy Spirit in our minds, or that He even has a plan. When we fell asleep and began this insane dream, we took with us into the dream a memory—the Holy Spirit—from where we came. *We* did that—not God. The Holy Spirit is the memory and Presence of Love, and the reminder of who we are as Its children. We shall return to this below.

As one begins this journey through the workbook, some additional comments may be helpful. A student would have to be either heavily into denial or so highly advanced as not to recognize the concept, if resistance to the lessons is not experienced somewhere along the way. The workbook's stated purpose, reflecting that of *A Course in Miracles* itself, is to undo the ego's thought system of guilt—the foundation for our very existence as separated and individualized selves. One does not let such a foundation go easily or lightly. To do so would mean the end of existence as we know it. And so our selves—ruled by the ego—resist any incursion into the ego's bastion of defenses. Thus we speak of the process of learning and living the Course as a journey we take with the Holy Spirit as our Teacher. It is a journey through the far country of resistance—fear, guilt and projection—with the light of forgiveness our guide, and the light of Heaven our goal. That is also why we speak of the structure of *A Course in Miracles* as symphonic, wherein certain core themes are repeated, varied, set aside, and restated, until the stirring coda of redemption heralds the journey's end.

One of the many forms resistance takes, in addition to the more obvious ones such as forgetting the lesson title or the lesson itself, is using the titles or statements as affirmations. That is not their purpose, and their misuse reflects the ego's process of bringing the light to the darkness; this not only covers the darkness, *but the light as well.* Rather, the statements in question are meant as symbols of the light, to which we bring the darkness of our ego's guilt and judgment that are gently shined away.

ACKNOWLEDGMENTS

I should like to thank the many people who have made this book possible. I begin with the students of the original classes—Foundation staff as well as long-term (and occasional) students—at our Center in Roscoe. Their ongoing interest in *A Course in Miracles*, both in theory and practice, was the inspiration and stimulus for the series of lectures. Next I am grateful to the many people who graciously volunteered to transcribe the audio tapes, and those who did a preliminary edit to eliminate the obvious verbalisms, which, while normal for informal speech, make for very cumbersome reading. Rosemarie LoSasso, the Foundation's Director of Publications, took over from there. In addition to her performing the original taping and preparing the tapes for publication, Rosemarie was largely responsible for the huge task of putting the transcriptions into much more readable form, which she performed in her characteristic tireless and faithful manner. It was from her edit that I was able to thoroughly review and revise the entire manuscript until it reached its final form. Her help, as always, was invaluable. I am also grateful to the many people on the Foundation staff who worked so diligently in preparing the manuscript and book for its final form: Jennye Cooke, Jackie Futterman, Emmy Massengill, Loral Reeves, Elizabeth Schmit, and Virginia Tucker.

Finally, as with all my teaching, it is with deep and loving gratitude that I speak of my wife Gloria, who has always been by my side, inspiring and encouraging my work, and indeed, making it all possible.

PRELUDE

Introduction

We are about to embark on a journey of 365 steps. Our guide is the workbook for students of *A Course in Miracles*. We begin in the world of form, with hardly a clue as to the vistas that will unfold before us, as step by step we are led along the path by Jesus—teacher and guide, brother and friend—until we reach the gentle lawns that herald the last step in which we disappear forever into formlessness. We speak of steps—365 lessons—yet this is in truth a journey without distance, for we left our home only in dreams; we speak of time—one year—yet eternity is a constant state and linear time but part of a dream that never happened in reality. However, we need to begin, and our everyday world of aspirations and hopes, loves and hates, births and deaths is the classroom in which we learn the lessons that in the end teach us there is no world.

Indeed, rather than speak of a journey through time and space, we can speak of an experience of circularity, which ends at its beginning. With apologies to T.S. Eliot, I substitute *journeying* for *exploration* and *exploring* respectively in the following immortal verse from "Little Gidding" (the last of his *Four Quartets*):

> We shall not cease from journeying
> And the end of all our journeying
> Will be to arrive where we started
> And know the place for the first time.

Our journey is linked by a thread, as in a subtle musical theme that winds its way through a score, often unrecognized by all but the artistic cognoscenti. And yet without it, the work's thematic structure would fall apart. In our workbook symphony, there are two significant themes that recur throughout: 1) our identity within the illusion as a mind—wrong mind (the ego), right mind (the Holy Spirit), and the decision-making part that chooses between them; and 2) our ego's wish to be right and prove Jesus wrong. The foundational backdrop of these themes is the theoretical structure of the Course itself, most significantly expressed in the text.

Therefore, much like an operatic overture that presents the themes to be developed in the work to follow, this Prelude will present an overview of the thought system of *A Course in Miracles*. We have already quoted the workbook's Introduction, setting its lessons squarely within the text's theory. It is fitting, therefore, before we embark on our journey through the workbook that we set forth such a summary, to which we can refer throughout our discussion. While certainly not meant to be an in-depth presentation of the Course's principles, it will nonetheless highlight its central concepts, with particular emphasis placed on these aspects of Jesus' teachings in *A Course in Miracles* that are directly relevant to our journey. This discussion is organized around the two levels reflected in the Course's teachings: Level One distinguishes between truth and illusion, Oneness and separation, God and the ego. Level Two relates only to the ego's separated world of illusion, and contrasts the wrong-minded thought system of guilt, attack, and defense—the ego's world of special relationships—with the right-minded thought system of forgiveness—the Holy Spirit's world of holy relationships.

Level One: The Oneness of Heaven

The fundamental premise of *A Course in Miracles* is the Oneness of God:

> Heaven is not a place nor a condition. It is merely an awareness of perfect Oneness, and the knowledge that there is nothing else; nothing outside this Oneness, and nothing else within (T-18.VI.1:5-6).

This perfect Oneness is the prime characteristic of the Course's view of reality, what establishes it as a non-dualistic thought system. God and His Son are totally one, with no differentiation possible between them. Thus we read in the workbook:

> God…makes no distinctions in what is Himself and what is still Himself. What He

creates is not apart from Him, and nowhere does the Father end, the Son begin as something separate from Him (W-pI.132.12:3-4).

Since we believe we are dualistic creatures inhabiting a world of time and space, a non-spatial, non-temporal world without differentiations is inconceivable to us. Thus Jesus says of God's Oneness and ours:

> We cannot speak nor write nor even think of this at all.... There is no need to further clarify what no one in the world can understand. When revelation of your oneness comes, it will be known and fully understood (W-pI.169.6:1,10:1-2).

Within this Oneness, love continually extends itself: God extending His Self to His Self, called Christ. This is the Course's definition of creation.

Christ, being part of God, shares in His Creator's ability to create, and His extensions are known as creations. All this, of course, occurs in a reality that has no time or space, being totally at one within itself.

When we speak of the Course's metaphysical non-dualistic foundation, we speak of its ongoing contrast of truth and illusion: Level One. This treats the distinction between God and the ego, wherein only God's Oneness and Wholeness is reality, and everything else is unreal. No compromise is possible here, and there is no room for gradations: "...what is false is false, and what is true has never changed" (W-pII.10.1:1). Since eternity alone is true, what we know of as time—past, present, future—is illusory.

LEVEL ONE: THE EGO'S UNHOLY TRINITY

In words we shall cite frequently, *A Course in Miracles* states:

> Into eternity, where all is one, there crept a tiny, mad idea, at which the Son of God remembered not to laugh. In his forgetting did the thought become a serious idea, and possible of both accomplishment and real effects (T-27.VIII.6:2-3).

This insane idea was that God's Son could actually separate from his Creator and Source. In truth, of course, this could never happen, but in the illusory dream of the Son's mind it not only *could* happen, but *did* happen. This impossibility set into motion a cosmic drama of mythic proportions, consisting of three *dramatis personae*: the ego, the Holy Spirit, and the decision-making Son of God. This trio comprises the split mind, now seemingly separated from the Mind of Christ, God's true and undivided Son.

The drama unfolds in this way: The mind's decision maker must choose between two mutually exclusive perceptions of the tiny, mad idea. The ego—the Son's belief he is separate from God—speaks to the Son of the glories of separation, individuality, and freedom from the tyrannous yoke of the cruel authoritarian Creator. The Holy Spirit's response—the Son's memory of his Identity as Christ—echoed by Cordelia's in *King Lear*, is simply to love and be silent. To respond to a lie

merely reinforces it, and so the Holy Spirit's gentle smile reflects His principle of Atonement—the separation from God never happened. This reflects the principle that governs Heaven: *Ideas leave not their Source*—the Idea of God's Son has never left Its Source in the Mind of God. The ego, needless to say, argues the opposite: ideas *do* leave their source, and have indeed done so.

The decision maker—actually more in the role of judge at this point—is not impressed by the Holy Spirit's response, and chooses the ego's perception as truth. This is the beginning of the central and governing principle of the ego's now-burgeoning thought system: *one or the other*. By virtue of choosing the ego's separation, the Son effectively chose against the Holy Spirit's Atonement, thereby for all intents and purposes silencing His Voice of truth beneath the ego's lies.

The ego has won this first round, but immediately recognizes a tremendous threat hovering over its newly established horizon. It knows that it owes its existence to the Son's having chosen it. What if, the ego now considers to its horror, the Son should change his decision? Without the power of the Son's mind to believe in it, the ego could do nothing but disappear into nothing, since it is inherently nothing. This illusion of something, therefore, develops a plan whereby it can preserve its illusory existence in the Son's mind. Its strategy for survival is based upon the following logic:

> The ego's existence is predicated on the Son's belief in it, which it has already achieved by virtue of his mind's decision.

> Its extinction can come only when the Son changes his mind.

> Therefore, making the Son mindless—causing him to forget he even has a mind—ensures that he cannot change a mind he no longer remembers he has.

Thus, all that remains is for the ego to convince the Son it is in his own best interests to be mindless. Only then will the Son voluntarily choose to leave his mind and never return.

Now established in theory, the ego's plan needs implementation. It fleshes out for the Son the meaning of his having chosen against the Holy Spirit: a choice against God and His Love that obliterates Heaven's unity, sacrificing God so that he would live. The ego names this decision to oppose God *sin*. Thus the separation from God is not a silly dream at all, as maintained by the Atonement principle, but a sinful fact that has actually occurred—nothing less than the Son's taking life from God and investing it in himself. By the murder of the Father and crucifixion of Christ, the Son emerges from this blood-drenched battleground as an individual—separate, unique, and special—the possessor of the life that God now lacks. But at a price, for the Son's separation and individual self is forevermore equated with sin. He exists not only as an individual, but a sinful individual.

To briefly digress, as our myth progresses, keep in mind that from the point when the Son's decision maker chooses for the ego and against the Holy Spirit, he hears only the voice of separation and no longer the Voice of Atonement. Therefore, hearing only the ego's voice, the Son must perforce believe the ego's voice is God; its words must be true because there is no other voice that offers a contrasting view. The Son thus knows nothing but what the ego tells him, which alone can explain our collective belief in the ego's insanity.

Therefore, when the ego tells the Son he has separated from God and is sinful, this becomes his reality, which leads to the guilt that is the psychological experience of sinfulness: "I have not only *done* a terrible thing, I *am* a terrible thing. My identity as a separated self is inherently sinful, for I have become what I did: I sinned, and am now, incontrovertibly, a sinner." Remember, this is the ego's myth, its purpose being to induce the Son to leave his mind—literally and figuratively.

The first step toward achieving the ego's aim, therefore, is to convince God's Son he is a separated, sinful, and guilty entity. His very existence now proves his sin, because the ego told him he could exist only through the sin of selfishly destroying God. Thus has the Son's self-concept gone from decision maker, to separated self, to sinful, guilty self—all accepted as gospel because, again, the ego's is the only voice he hears within his dream of separation.

The ego continues to weave its evil magic, telling the Son: "Despite your murderous sin against your Creator, God was not completely obliterated. In fact, being very much alive, He is vengefully coming for you to take back the life you stole from Him." In the Course's words:

> "You have usurped the place of God. Think not He has forgotten."... And now there is no hope. Except to kill. Here is salvation now. An angry father pursues his guilty son. Kill or be killed, for here alone is choice. Beyond this there is none, for what was done cannot be done without. The stain of blood can never be removed, and anyone who bears this stain on him must meet with death (M-17.7:3-4,7-13).

The ego's myth has thus rapidly become a nightmare—totally unreal, but hardly so in our awareness—in which we see the birth of its principle that sin and guilt demand punishment. The Son has sinned against God, witnessed to by his guilt that tells him of the punishment he deserves. Since God is the object of his sin, He becomes the avenging agent of his punishment, which inevitably gives rise to fear: If the Son does not act quickly, therefore, God will certainly destroy him—the origin of the belief in death that is the justified conclusion of a life of sin. I stole life from God, and so it is only right He steal that life from me, leaving me life-less.

When God takes away my life, He has it and I do not—the principle of *one or the other*: in order to gain, something or someone has to be sacrificed. Thus the choice is between a separated Son or a living God of Oneness. If God has life, there is no ego;

if the ego has life, there is no God. The ego has therefore cleverly orchestrated its plan so that the mind of the Son has become a battleground in which he is helplessly pitted against his Creator. Within the ego's story, of course, the Son is no match for this avenging, maniacal, and destructive deity, which means that having listened to the lies of the ego he is in serious trouble. If he remains in his now terrified mind, the home of his sinful separation and guilt-ridden individuality, he will surely be destroyed, for, given his Enemy, annihilation is certain. He will not disappear into the Heart of God; he will just disappear. In other words, the ego has the Son of God exactly where it wants him. Remember, the purpose of the ego's machinations was to convince the Son voluntarily to leave his mind and never, ever return, thus rendering himself mindless. If he does return, he will meet with certain death as a result of his sin, born of the separation from God.

Therefore, the principal characteristics of the separated mind now include sin, guilt, and fear of death. The Son now has no choice but to say to the ego, his only "friend": "I believe in all you say. Please help, for if I remain an instant longer in the mind, my existence is over." The ego, its words dripping sweetness and concern, replies: "I have a wonderful plan to save you. Just continue to trust me." The Son has no choice—the Voice for God has been effectively silenced—and thus the ego is allowed to continue weaving its web: "The way you escape to safety is simply to leave the mind."

Psychologically, this is called projection, wherein we take what we believe to be in the mind and put it outside, hurling the mind's contents away from us in the magical belief they will be safely outside us. Therefore, when we project a thought of separation—individuality, sin, guilt, and fear of death—the result is a physical world of separation—individuality, sin, guilt, and fear of death. This is the world of linear time that is the Course's version of the Big Bang, which many scientists posit as the beginning of the universe.

Projection not only gives rise to a separated world, but a fragmented one as well. When the ego's thought system was projected from the mind of God's separated Son, it shattered into an almost infinite number of pieces, much as what happens to a pane of glass when it breaks into countless fragments. Each fragment is unique, at the same time retaining the chemical characteristics of glass. Regarding the Sonship, the fragmentation yielded a quasi-infinite number of Sons, each one encased in form, delineating the individual expression of the split mind's single content of separation. Although these forms embrace the totality of the physical universe—animate and inanimate—we shall confine our discussion almost exclusively to the particular form we know as homo sapiens, the Son's self encased in the human body. This leads us into Level Two—the two ways of looking at the body and its world.

LEVEL TWO: THE EGO'S WRONG-MINDED THOUGHT SYSTEM OF GUILT AND ATTACK

Once in the world as a body—a shadowy fragment of the original thought of separation—the ego thought system becomes expressed in specific, individualized ways. Each of these, in its own manner, expresses the fundamental ego wish for all its fragments: to keep the separation it stole from God, but to project its responsibility onto something or someone else. In other words, we all get to have our ego's cake of separation, and enjoy its "sweetness" by eating it at the expense of others, who are judged responsible for our separated state. To say it another way, we are born into this world with the specific wish to be unfairly treated, seeing in others the sin we do not want to see in ourselves. Thus are we able to keep our individual identities but divorce the sin

that the ego had wedded to it, thereby becoming the face of innocence that hides the underlying face of the murderer.

In more general terms, the ego makes up one problem after another to be solved—the different forms of avoiding pain and pursuing pleasure—and each is deemed capable of disturbing or even destroying our peace. The world, like the mind that is its source, becomes a battleground from which there is no escape, a prison of sin and guilt that the mind will never leave, as it is seemingly trapped within the body.

And so we walk the world in "savage search for sin" (T-19.IV-A.12:7)—the cause of our distress—to be perceived in others and there to be attacked and judged. In so doing, we reinforce our identification with the mindless state of physical existence and maintain our lack of responsibility for what befalls us. All this can be summarized by the twin ego cycles of *guilt-attack* and *attack-defense*, which together constitute the double shield of oblivion discussed in Lesson 136.

We are born into this world with a fully-developed ego thought system (as well as a fully-developed Holy Spirit thought system, which we shall discuss presently), the purpose of this birth as bodies being to conceal the mind's guilt so it can never be undone. This guilt, as we have seen, is part of the ego's strategy to keep the Son's decision maker from choosing the Atonement thought of love that is also in the mind. Thus guilt is the ego's first shield of oblivion. Yet needing a second line of defense—the second shield—the ego convinces the Son to abandon his mind and enter the mindless state of physicality. This is the body that acts as a smoke screen, concealing the mind—the true source of the problem—behind the distracting hiding place of the world of problems and concerns. Once in the body, the Son has the perfect opportunity—over and over, from birth to death—of projecting his unconscious guilt onto others, thereby attacking them for the sin he placed on their guilty heads—the *guilt-attack* cycle. These attacks have two basic forms that are the heart of the ego's thought system of separation: special hate and special love relationships. Although these terms are never used in the workbook, they are referred to by implication throughout, and so deserve some explanation here.

The special relationship begins after the ego's separation leaves off, and the Son emerges as a creature of lack or scarcity, for something is indeed missing. Needless to say, the ego never reveals that what is missing is the memory of God's Love that has disappeared from awareness. Instead, it says that what is lacking is the innocence that was taken by another, and thus the experience of scarcity has given way to the experience of deprivation—someone has deprived me of what is rightfully mine. I am thus justified in taking back what was taken from me (the ego's fourth and fifth laws of chaos [T-23.II.9-12]).

My attempt to retrieve this lost innocence takes two basic forms: *Special hate* is where I directly attack another, thereby accusing them of the sin of theft and murder of which I secretly accuse myself. While it makes our attempts at projection easier to have someone actually attack us (or others with whom we identify), in the end it makes no difference. Whether your attack on me is real or imagined, I will blame you regardless. *Special love*, on the other hand, is more subtle. While our preference would be to attack another outright, society does not usually condone direct assault, and so more often than not we attempt to reclaim our innocence and fill our sense of lack by establishing dependent relationships with those special people who have the special something we require to meet our special needs. We thus seek to acquire the love, attention, respect, and approval we demand by bargaining with others to get what we want, and giving them what they need in return. Needless to say, the ego plans to give as little as possible and get as much as it can—the height of self-interest.

Either way we choose to proceed—special love or special hate—the outcome of guilt is the same. We have attacked others, and know on some level we have attacked falsely since, regardless of their actions, others are not responsible for our happiness or unhappiness—only the mind's guilt can lay claim to being the *cause* of the *effect* of peace or conflict. Thus we must believe that the objects of our projected attack will attack us in return:

> …those who project are vigilant for their own safety. They are afraid that their projections will return and hurt them. Believing they have blotted their projections from their own minds, they also believe their projections are trying to creep back in. Since the projections have not left their minds, they are forced to engage in constant activity in order not to recognize this (T-7.VIII.3:9-12).

This "constant activity" is our system of defenses, designed to protect us from the attack the projection of guilt demands. Thus we all walk the world encased in defensive shields. Lesson 153 describes this *attack-defense* cycle:

> Attack, defense; defense, attack, become the circles of the hours and the days that bind the mind in heavy bands of steel with iron overlaid, returning but to start again. There seems to be no break nor ending in the ever-tightening grip of the imprisonment upon the mind (W-pI.153.3:2-3).

Indeed, there appears to be no hope for breaking the grip these deadly cycles have on our minds, for the ego's strategy of preserving its identity has become a triumphant success, making itself virtually fool-proof. Yet Jesus reassures us that the ego plan is not God-proof (T-5.VI.10:6), for there remains a Voice of sanity within our right minds, which continually calls us to choose again.

LEVEL TWO: THE HOLY SPIRIT'S RIGHT-MINDED THOUGHT SYSTEM OF FORGIVENESS

All the while the ego's machinations are continuing, the loving Presence of the Holy Spirit, the Memory of who we are as Christ, remains in our minds. That Memory is our teacher. As the pain of our guilt becomes too great, we exclaim that there must be another way, another Teacher to help us instead of the ego (T-2.III.3:5-6). This is the moment the Holy Spirit has been waiting for, and His answer is to help us to shift our perceptions. Coming to Him, He offers us a different way of looking at the world of our special relationships, teaching that the world is an "outside picture of an inward condition" (T-21.in.1:5). Retracing with us the insane ladder of separation the ego led us down (T-28.III.1:2), the Holy Spirit gently undoes the ego's double-tiered strategy of guilt and projection by reversing our perceptions. We are thus taught that these come from the projection of our guilt, and it is important to recognize that in *A Course in Miracles* perception is interpretation, not what our sensory organs report. In other words, our right-minded focus is on how we interpret what our bodies tell us, not their sensory input. For example, if I see you attacking me physically or verbally, I have a choice whether or not to give your actions the power to take God's peace from me. I may or may not have power over your behavior, but I always have power over my mind, which nothing in this world can affect.

This recognition is the purpose of forgiveness or the miracle: returning awareness to my mind—"the inward condition"—from the world of bodies. Since the mind is hidden from awareness by the body, we have no way of returning to it except by our perceptions being redirected to their source, where they can be changed. Once the problem is returned to the decision-making part of the mind that had chosen guilt over Atonement, we can meaningfully choose again. Thus our healed minds extend the Holy Spirit's perception of shared interests—the reflection of Heaven's Oneness—and we look out on a world in which every Son of God contains the same wrong-minded thought system of guilt and hate, the same right-minded thought system of forgiveness and love, and the same power to choose between them. Therefore, despite the obvious differences among the Sonship on the level of form, the Holy Spirit's true perception has us see the unity underlying the ego's diversity, the sameness beyond the world of differences. Filled now with Christ's vision, we walk the earth teaching what we have learned, demonstrating to our brothers that they can make the same choice for the Holy Spirit's forgiveness that we made.

A Course in Miracles explains the healing power of forgiveness through the principle of cause and effect, which rests on two premises. First, every effect must have a cause, and without effects there can be no cause:

> Without a cause there can be no effects, and yet without effects there is no cause. The cause a cause is *made* by its effects.... Effects do not create their cause, but they establish its causation (T-28.II.1:1-3).

Secondly, if anything exists, it must be a cause (T-9.IV.5:5-6). Therefore, if you attack me and I do not react as if it were a sin, my defenselessness—an attitude, not necessarily behavior—demonstrates that your sin had no effect and thus is not a cause. If your sinful attack is not a cause, it cannot exist. Thus are sins forgiven.

What, then, is the right-minded perception of attack? If attack is the ego's defense against fear of the mind's guilt, which is itself a defense against the mind's power to choose love, then attack expresses fear, which in turn is a call for the love that has been denied (T-12.I.8:12-13; T-14.X.7:1-2). Therefore, if I am upset, the cause is not what your body has done (or not done)—the *form*—but my mind that has chosen to be upset—the *content*. I no longer focus on changing your behavior, but only on changing my mind's interpretation of your behavior—from the ego's purpose for the relationship to the Holy Spirit's. This highlights the contrast between magic and the miracle. The former addresses the body and its problems, seeking solution there, while the latter redirects our attention to the mind—the source of the problem *and* the solution.

Reacting defenselessly to an attack that never was is a specific expression of God's response to our tiny, mad idea—the prototype for forgiveness: our attacking thought of separation had no effect on the Oneness of His Love. Indeed God did not even see it because it never happened. In this world, our eyes may see the attack but the healed mind sees only the call for love, thus not making our brother's error real, showing him, again, that his sin had no effect.

This, then, is the meaning of asking the Holy Spirit or Jesus for help. Incidentally, from the point of view of having an internal Teacher—the Voice that speaks for the Atonement—the roles of the Holy Spirit and Jesus are identical, and thus will be used interchangeably throughout this book, as indeed they are throughout *A Course in Miracles*. We call upon Their help to shift the purpose of our experiences in the world from that of being a prison, from which we continually seek to escape at other people's expense, to that of a classroom, wherein

our new Teacher uses the curriculum of our special relationships to teach us to return to the mind where the original special relationship had its source—our joining with the ego in the illusion of separation.

When our forgiveness is complete and we have accepted the Atonement for ourselves—our one responsibility (T-2.V.5:1)—we enter *the real world*, the Course's term for the state of the healed mind that is outside the ego's dream of separation. There we wait but an instant longer for God to take the last step, wherein He lifts us back unto Himself. Thus is the Son's original choice for the ego undone at last.

We conclude this Prelude and complete preparations for the journey through the workbook by restating its purpose of teaching us we have a split mind, and the power to choose between truth and illusion. The lessons help us recognize and admit—gladly and gratefully—that we had been wrong in the choice for the ego, a mistake we now happily correct by choosing the Holy Spirit as our Teacher. Now we are ready to embark on our journey of learning—the 365 lessons the pathway, and Jesus our loving guide.

Introduction to the Workbook

The Introduction contains probably the clearest statements in *A Course in Miracles* about the importance of generalizing what we learn. It does not help us long term in our Atonement process if we forgive one or two people, but not everyone. The central idea is to practice with specifics in order to learn what non-specificity means. A paradox throughout the Course, and especially apparent in the early workbook lessons, is that we have to deal with the specifics of our everyday life, but solely for the purpose of realizing that everything is ultimately non-specific. That is the principle underlying generalization. Thus, when we were children learning basic arithmetic, as I mentioned briefly in the Prelude, we practiced with different examples and combinations of numbers so that eventually we could take any number in the universe and add, subtract, multiply, or divide it. We practice with specifics so that we learn to generalize.

In the context of practicing these lessons, consequently, we want to reach the point of accepting that there is absolutely nothing in our lives that the Holy Spirit or Jesus cannot help us with. This does *not* refer to help on the level of specifics or form, but rather with undoing the cause of our perception of the problem. As Jesus told Helen Schucman, scribe of *A Course in Miracles*, in Chapter 2 of the text, this cause always entails "a willingness to be separate" (T-2.VI.4:4). Asking Jesus for help in looking at the situation differently, in and of itself heals the problem, since we are now joining (or rejoining) with the love from which we had separated; a separation, reminiscent of the original separation from God, that leads to guilt that is inevitably projected and *voila*, we have a perceived problem external to our minds. Bringing our *specific* concerns to Their *abstract* (or non-specific) presence is what solves the true problem. Thus, when we experience Them as not helping us, it is because *we* have withheld certain specifics from Them. We all have in our repertoire certain things marked with a red flag or stop sign that says: "Don't come near. This is a non-negotiable item." The early workbook lessons, as I will be pointing out soon, are designed to help us get past that particular problem, which is everyone's. There will always be certain people that we

will forgive and be tolerant of, and others whom we will wish to crucify; there will be certain situations in which we have no trouble asking Jesus for help, but, just as surely, there will be others in which we would not even think of asking.

In a line that closes the text, Jesus says of the journey's end that: "not one spot of darkness still remains to hide the face of Christ from anyone" (T-31.VIII.12:5). To state it again: the purpose of the workbook, and these early workbook lessons in particular, is to help us understand that principle— we cannot withhold any part of the ego thought system from Jesus, because if we do, we are withholding all of it.

Let us begin, then, with the Introduction. As we proceed, keep in mind that the purpose of these lectures is to give you a head start into the lessons themselves, so you will know what to look for as you read and study them, and hopefully apply them.

The relationship of the workbook to the text is addressed in the opening sentences, a passage I already quoted in the Preface to these volumes:

(1) A theoretical foundation such as the text provides is necessary as a framework to make the exercises in this workbook meaningful. Yet it is doing the exercises that will make the goal of the course possible. An untrained mind can accomplish nothing. It is the purpose of this workbook to train your mind to think along the lines the text sets forth.

One of the serious mistakes students of *A Course in Miracles* tend to make is not seeing the connection between the text and the workbook. Quite often people will think that they are doing "the Course" when they practice the exercises in the workbook. In fact, I recently received a letter from someone who was beginning the Course, a psychologist as I recall, and he eagerly talked about doing this "one-year course." He had not even started; but his idea was—probably from what he had been told—that the workbook is a one-year training program, and therefore this is a one-year course.

As you may know, Jesus says in the Epilogue at the end of the workbook that "this course is a beginning, not an end" (W-ep.1:1). The workbook's purpose is to train our minds to begin the process of returning home; and then we spend the rest of our lives asking Jesus or the Holy Spirit to help us learn the specific lessons that will speed us along our path. But the workbook itself, without the text, is essentially meaningless. What makes the exercises in the workbook meaningful is the theoretical foundation of the text. Nothing in the workbook, therefore, should be taken as a substitute for what the text teaches.

On the other hand, the text without the workbook leaves you only in your head, so to speak. The purpose of the workbook, again, is to begin the process of training our minds, a mind training with two components: 1) There are two teachers—*not one*—within us whom we can choose between; and 2) What it means to ask the right teacher, the Holy Spirit, for help as opposed to the wrong teacher, the ego; recognizing, in the words of Lesson 193, that "All things are lessons [in forgiveness] God [i.e., the Holy Spirit] would have me learn." *A Course in Miracles* is training us to see that everything that happens in the world is an opportunity to learn. That is the meaning of *generalizing our lessons*.

(2) The exercises are very simple. They do not require a great deal of time, and it does not matter where you do them. They need no preparation. The training period is one year. The exercises are numbered from 1 to 365. Do not undertake to do more than one set of exercises a day.

We can see at the beginning that Jesus is not concerned with rituals, with his students becoming slaves to *form*. While clearly, even in this brief statement, we recognize the structured nature of these workbook lessons, we can nonetheless discern that he is asking us *not* to make a big deal of them. Indeed, one can also see here that the only real rule he is providing for us is not to do more than one lesson a day. Gloria and I still recall the young woman many, many years ago who proudly announced to *A Course in Miracles* group to which we were speaking that she had devised a way to do the entire workbook in a single twenty-four-hour period and, horrors of horrors, had actually done so. This overly zealous and sincere student obviously was in such a rush to reach salvation that she did not have time to read line 2:6. Jesus is also setting out for us the boundaries of a one-year training program that is

meant to be the beginning companion to our study of the text. I remember Helen telling me how impressed she was with the fact that at the beginning Jesus told her (and all of us) what he was going to do, and then proceeded to do just that.

(3) The workbook is divided into two main sections, the first dealing with the undoing of the way you see now, and the second with the acquisition of true perception. With the exception of the review periods, each day's exercises are planned around one central idea, which is stated first. This is followed by a description of the specific procedures by which the idea for the day is to be applied.

Part I deals primarily with the undoing of the ego system—although not every single lesson exemplifies this. Part II contains relatively little teaching as such, but has wonderful prayers that reinforce the ideas we have already learned: Jesus or the Holy Spirit is our Teacher, and our loving Creator and Source is our goal. These prayers also reinforce what we would already have learned, hopefully, that this is not a journey we make by ourselves, but one on which we must bring everyone else. Therefore, whatever teaching exists in the workbook by and large exists in Part I, and not in Part II. That does not mean that there are no important statements in Part II. Rather, Part I reflects the undoing of the ego thought system, which makes room for the right-minded thinking reflected in Part II.

The early lessons, though, are designed specifically to help us realize how much we do not understand, how much we do not know, and how wrong we are about all our perceptions. Jesus thus begins the crucial process of helping us undo our beliefs about what we are seeing.

(4:1) The purpose of the workbook is to train your mind in a systematic way to a different perception of everyone and everything in the world.

Here we see the first statement of generalization. *A Course in Miracles* is offering us a different way of perceiving every single thing in the world. In fact, we find here in the Introduction and early lessons specific applications of the first principle of miracles as stated in Chapter 1 of the text: there is no order of difficulty among them (T-1.I.1:1). Miracles are the corrections that we choose in our minds, and there is no order of difficulty because each problem is exactly the same as every other one. That is the metaphysical premise on which the statements about generalization rest. As long as we believe some problems are more difficult than others to solve—some people are more evil, sinful, or guilty than others—there is no way we are going to learn what this course is teaching because we would have made some part of the error real. In other words, as long as we see gradations of importance, small and large, we are in the ego system.

We emphasize in our classes that the state of reality is a state of perfect oneness, and there is no differentiation in Heaven. Even the terms *God* and *Christ* that *A Course in Miracles* uses to denote the state of Heaven are metaphors, because in truth there are no specific or named personages. The concept of reality as the state of perfect oneness means there is no individuality or differentiation. Everything in Heaven is the same, because there is only *one* reality: the Love of God, or spirit.

This also means, on the other side, that there is only *one* error. In "The Substitute Reality" (T-18.I.3-4) that point is made very clearly. Jesus explains that it may not appear there is only one error, but that does not alter the fact that there is. Once the fragmentation occurred, it *seemed* that there were many different forms and shapes, and then, subsequently, many different issues with which we have to deal. We do not yet realize they all stem from one basic mistake.

That is why, to jump ahead, in Lessons 79 and 80 Jesus teaches that there is only one problem and one solution. The one problem is the belief that we could separate from God, and the solution, of course, is the Atonement, which says that the separation never happened. This is the metaphysical premise of these workbook lessons, as well as the way Jesus, again, begins his text: There is no order of difficulty in miracles. Those of you who have read my book, *Absence from Felicity: The Story of Helen Schucman and Her Scribing of A COURSE IN MIRACLES,** know that the way the dictation actually began was not the way it is in the published Course. It starts, rather, with Jesus saying to Helen: "This is a course in miracles. Please take notes." He then continued with the principle—the first thing to know about miracles is that there is no order of difficulty among them. That is the central

principle of *A Course in Miracles*, because all its teachings, both of the Holy Spirit and the ego, rest on it.

The purpose of the workbook, therefore, is to have us look very specifically at the way we perceive everyone and everything. In the early lessons we are not even looking at people, but perceiving tables, coat hangers, windows, and other objects. It does not make any difference, however. The reason nothing in the room means anything and why we do not understand the meaning of anything is that we think that there are differences. And we think these differences make a difference and constitute reality.

Generalization means that we learn through our specific perceptions and relationships that everyone is exactly the same, because each and every one serves the same purpose. Later on in the workbook we will come across the idea of *purpose*, a central theme not only in the workbook but in the text as well. Purpose is everything, and the purpose of everything in the physical universe is to prove that we are right and God is wrong—to prove that the ego's interpretation of the tiny, mad idea was the correct one, and the Holy Spirit's incorrect. To repeat:

(4) The purpose of the workbook is to train your mind in a systematic way [i.e., the 365 lessons with their exercises] **to a different perception of everyone and everything in the world. The exercises are planned to help you generalize the lessons, so that you will understand that each of them is equally applicable to everyone and everything you see.**

As we just said, this is the central theme, not only of this Introduction, but of the early workbook lessons as well. If you keep that in mind, you will recognize it in what Jesus says in the core of each lesson, and just as clearly in the instructions, all of which relate to this idea of generalization. We need a structured, mind-training program that will help us retrain how we think, because this is *not* how we think now. The very fact we believe we are bodies is telling us we believe in differentiation. Therefore, we need to practice earnestly, realizing that everything we perceive is coming from a faulty way of thinking; faulty because it comes from the ego, whose purpose is to keep our individuality intact.

---

* For further information see our Online Bookstore at *www.facim.org*.

Therefore, if we think there are different meanings and purposes in the things of this world, we are glorifying our own individuality and upholding the thought system of the ego instead of the thought system Jesus is teaching us.

(5) Transfer of training in true perception does not proceed as does transfer of the training of the world. If true perception has been achieved in connection with any person, situation or event, total transfer to everyone and everything is certain. On the other hand, one exception held apart from true perception makes its accomplishments anywhere impossible.

Jesus is telling us that the world's version of transfer of training is restricted and limited. Returning to the example I used earlier of learning arithmetic, the transfer of training was specific to numbers. When you learn how to drive a car, you are then able to drive practically every other kind of car. That does not mean it helps you undo your guilt, though, nor does it help you cook a meal better or write a letter more fluently. It just means that you have now mastered how to drive a car.

On the other hand, transfer of training as it occurs in the practice of *A Course in Miracles* is not restricted in form, in that it would extend absolutely to everything, *with no exception*, because everything in the world is the same. The last statement that "one exception held apart from true perception makes its accomplishments anywhere impossible" reflects the passage at the end of the text that I quoted earlier: "not one spot of darkness still remains to hide the face of Christ from anyone" (T-31.VIII.12:4). This absolute aspect of *A Course in Miracles* is what makes it so difficult. Thus, accomplishment of true perception, the ultimate goal of the Course—i.e., the vision of Christ, the attainment of the real world—is impossible as long as we see anything as more or less important than anything else, or anyone as more or less important than anyone else, more or less deserving of our love or attack. It makes no difference what form the exception takes. The goal of *A Course in Miracles* will not be achieved as long as any exemption is made and justified.

(6:1) The only general rules to be observed throughout, then, are: First, that the exercises be practiced with great specificity, as will be indicated.

This is the paradox inherent in this system, already commented on: we are supposed to practice with great specificity in order to learn how to be non-specific. We learn how to live within a world of time and space so we can learn there is no world of time and space. That is what makes this such a powerful form of spirituality. We are not asked to deny our experiences in the world at all—we are not asked to deny our bodies, feelings, or thoughts, anything that happens here. We are simply asked to give everything a different purpose.

To restate this important point, purpose is everything; and the ultimate purpose of everything in the world is to be a means of learning from Jesus that there is no world. But you cannot learn there is no world if you deny it. So you have to learn specifically how to get beyond all the specifics of the world. And the workbook provides a beautiful exposition of how that is done.

(6:2) This will help you to generalize the ideas involved to every situation in which you find yourself, and to everyone and everything in it.

If I can learn that I have given this chair or this table all the meaning that it has, I can begin to understand that I have done it with everything else as well. Later, Jesus uses the example of a cup: when I have a cup of coffee or tea in the morning, I come to realize that I am looking at this cup through the eyes of the past, because if I looked at it freshly, I would not know what to do with it. He is certainly not saying we should literally do this—we would never be able to get out of the house, let alone out of bed in the morning if we did not know what to do with the ordinary things in our environment. He is using these examples pedagogically to help us realize how everything we see is determined by the past.

The ego's world of time—the world of our experience of past, present, and future—is nothing more than the projection in form of the ego thought system of sin, guilt, and fear, as I explained in the Prelude. We begin with the thoughts of sin, guilt, and fear in our minds, and when we project them out and make up a world, sin becomes the past (I have sinned in the past), guilt the ego's version of the present (I feel miserable now), and fear the future (I am afraid of the punishment I believe I deserve).

Therefore, when we say, "I see only the past in this cup," we are really saying we believe in the reality of sin, because sin is equated with the past, the home of the separation. The idea, though, is not to have us feel guilty when we realize that in picking up a cup we have made sin real. But it does help us to understand that that is what we *ultimately* are doing. We must believe in the entirety of the ego thought system, otherwise we would not understand the cup's purpose.

(6:3) Second, be sure that you do not decide for yourself that there are some people, situations or things to which the ideas are inapplicable.

What prevents us from generalizing is believing that somehow this idea cannot be applied to a particular situation, relationship, or object. A powerful example of this need to exclude certain things from our practice was illustrated by a nun I knew who was studying *A Course in Miracles* and practicing the workbook lessons. She was cloistered, which meant she and the other sisters spent a considerable portion of their time in the chapel. As those of you who are Catholic know, in almost every Catholic church or chapel there is a tabernacle that contains the Blessed Sacrament, believed to be the actual body of Jesus in the wafer or bread. For Catholics, this is the most sacred object in the world, because this *is* Jesus. This nun would thus be by herself in the chapel early in the morning; and when she began practicing the first lessons in the workbook—saying "Nothing in this world means anything," or "Nothing in this room means anything"—she deliberately excluded the Blessed Sacrament. For how could she remain a nun and believe that that did not mean anything? Yet this is the very thing Jesus is teaching us *not* to do. It is a striking example, but everyone has specific things, situations, or persons they would seek to exclude from these principles, whether or not they do so consciously. Again, that is precisely what Jesus is saying *not* to do. We shall return later to this all-important theme of *form* and *content*.

(6:4-6) This will interfere with transfer of training. The very nature of true perception is that it has no limits. It is the opposite of the way you see now.

We can see, even here at the beginning, how Jesus says the same thing over and over again, just as he does in the text—he repeats his themes within the same chapter, section, even paragraph. The

reason is that because of our identification with the ego we shall not want to hear what he is saying. Therefore, to be sure we understand transfer of training or generalization, he repeats this important point.

(7:1) The overall aim of the exercises is to increase your ability to extend the ideas you will be practicing to include everything.

The same point still again. If your practicing does not include everything and everyone, then it is failing its purpose, and you are not doing what Jesus is asking. As you know, he is not saying that this is what you *have* to do. He is saying that this is what you have to *want* to do. If he believed all his students could do this right away, he would not need a workbook, and the text would not be in its current form. The idea is that you be aware of how you are excluding certain parts of your life from him; certain things for which you would ask his help, but other things for which you would not. Jesus is asking you to be honest with yourself, so you come to realize how you exclude certain areas from your practice of forgiveness, and then be aware of *why* you are doing so.

(7:2-3) This will require no effort on your part. The exercises themselves meet the conditions necessary for this kind of transfer.

This can be understood in two ways. First, Jesus is saying that the workbook does not require a lot of time and hard work. If it does, then you are not doing it correctly. When you struggle to learn or unlearn something, you obviously have made it real, which means you will never undo it. That is why, in the first rule for decision at the beginning of Chapter 30 in the text, he says: "*Do not fight yourself*" (T-30.I.1:7). Forgiveness should not be a struggle. You need to be aware of how much you will resist what Jesus is teaching here, and accept it without struggling against it. The idea is certainly not that you have to do these lessons perfectly.

On another level, the reason the exercises require no effort is that *we* are not the ones who undo or forgive. That is Jesus' role. Ours is simply to have the little willingness to ask his help in looking at the world differently. To say it another way, quoting the text: Our task is "to deny the denial of truth," (T-12.II.1:5; italics omitted), which is accomplished by looking with Jesus at the problem "as it is [in the mind], and not the way... [we] have set it up [projecting it out into the world]" (T-27.VII.2:2). That is why the process requires so little effort; our function is simply to *look*, not to *do*. We shall return to this important point in Lesson 23, and many, many times thereafter.

(8-9) Some of the ideas the workbook presents you will find hard to believe, and others may seem to be quite startling. This does not matter. You are merely asked to apply the ideas as you are directed to do. You are not asked to judge them at all. You are asked only to use them. It is their use that will give them meaning to you, and will show you that they are true.

Remember only this; you need not believe the ideas, you need not accept them, and you need not even welcome them. Some of them you may actively resist. None of this will matter, or decrease their efficacy. But do not allow yourself to make exceptions in applying the ideas the workbook contains, and whatever your reactions to the ideas may be, use them. Nothing more than that is required.

It is important to understand that Jesus makes these statements in the workbook, not in the text. His point is that it is not necessary to understand what he is teaching in the workbook, but only that you do what he says, essentially because you trust him. In the text he *does* want us to understand and study, and think carefully about his teachings. Since the text provides the theory of *A Course in Miracles*

and the workbook its mind training, Jesus does not have to insist on such study here. Thus, he tells us: "Do not get bogged down in arguments. You do not have to agree with what I am saying or believe it, let alone like it. But simply do what I am asking." Again, that is not a requirement but a helpful suggestion.

This is how Jesus sneaks in through the back door. He knows that once we do what he says we will realize he is right, ceasing to argue or debate. He says to us, in effect: "I assume that since you are a student of my course you want to learn its truth from me. If you do not like it you can go to something else. But as my student try not to make exceptions, for thus will you allow me to teach that these principles hold for absolutely everything in the world, without exception."

We are now ready to begin the lessons. What will be interesting as we go through them is noticing how Jesus repeatedly makes the same point, reflecting the principles of generalization. These first lessons are brilliant ways of introducing to us, in very specific, down-to-earth situations, how committed we are to the idea that we exist as separate individuals. The exercises help us realize how that thought permeates every aspect of our experience, even the most mundane and plebeian. Therefore, as you read and practice these lessons, think about their implications for how and why you live your life as you do. Think carefully how you perceive things, and realize the thought system of separation lies underneath your perceptions.

LESSON 1

Nothing I see in this room [on this street, from this window, in this place] means anything.

The idea is to look around—without judgment—at these very prosaic objects in our world: a table, chair, hand, foot, pen, door, body, lamp, sign, shadow. Notice how Jesus sneaks the body in; the point is to realize that you normally would think that your hand is more important than a pen, or your body is more important than a lamp. There isn't anyone who does not believe that. Therefore, you need realize how you are coming to *A Course in Miracles* with a set of premises that you are not even aware of, a hierarchy of values that you hold about the world. That is why Jesus instructs us in the text:

> To learn this course requires willingness to question every value that you hold. Not one can be kept hidden and obscure but it will jeopardize your learning. No belief is neutral. Every one has the power to dictate each decision you make. For a decision is a conclusion based on everything that you believe. It is the outcome of belief, and follows it as surely as does suffering follow guilt and freedom sinlessness (T-24.in.2:1-6).

This very first lesson, which seems so simple, if not simple-minded if you do not really understand it, contains the complete thought system of *A Course in Miracles*. There is no difference among any of the things in this world. They are all equally the same because they are all part of the illusion, reflecting the same thought system of separation, which itself is unreal. As you know from your study of the text, the first law of chaos, the foundation of the thought system of the ego and the world, is that there is a hierarchy of illusions (T-23.II.2:3). If I believe that my body or hand is more important than a lamp, I am clearly saying there is a hierarchy of illusions. Again, it would be hard, if possible at all, to find someone in this world who does not share the belief in that hierarchy, or who even thinks about that as an issue. Thus, if you give some serious thought to this, it will become clear to you that your whole life is based upon a lie—the first law of chaos that says there is a hierarchy of illusions.

Skip to paragraph 3:

(3:1-2) Notice that these statements are not arranged in any order, and make no allowance for differences in the kinds of things to which they are applied. That is the purpose of the exercise.

This is not to say that you should give up your investment in your body or in your hand. Rather, the purpose of these reflections is to help you become aware of how, even on this very basic level, you are reflecting the ego's thought system. These lessons are humbling if you think deeply about them, because they help you realize how much your life goes against everything that *A Course in Miracles* is teaching. This means there is a part of you that does not want to learn this course, because there is a part of you that does not want to give up your life. You do not want to walk around actually believing your hand is as meaningless as a pen, because you believe that there is a body that is real, and that you are truly here in the world. If you believe this, as we all do, you cannot believe in the reality of God. In other words, the first part of the workbook has as its purpose, as we were just told, to undo the way that we perceive and we think. This sets the tone for what will follow.

(3:2-4) That is the purpose of the exercise [to have us realize that there are no differences]. **The statement should merely be applied to anything you see. As you practice the idea for the day, use it totally indiscriminately.**

That is what *generalizing* means. Obviously Jesus does not expect us to practice this exercise with total indiscriminateness; if we could, we would not need these lessons. The idea is to be aware of how we *do not* practice this in our lives, even when we are specifically trying to. When you do this lesson, therefore, you should actually think about whether you are truly ready to say that "this hand is as meaningless as a pen." And if you believe that you think they are the same, take a pen and break it, and then your hand and break that. You will suddenly realize that you believe there is a real difference. This is certainly not meant to make you feel guilty, but to help you realize your investment in identifying with the thought system of separation.

(3:5-7) Do not attempt to apply it to everything you see, for these exercises should not become ritualistic. Only be sure that nothing you see is specifically excluded. One thing is like another as far as the application of the idea is concerned.

It would be very easy to go around to everything in the room and look at different parts of your body and say: "This does not mean anything." But then you are just doing it as a ritual. Basically, a ritual leaves you mindless, which is why people like them. A friend once said that she liked to say the rosary because she did not have to think. You just do it. Jesus is telling you *not* to do that with this workbook. Do not make it into a ritual. Rituals are designed to keep you *mindless*. This is a course whose purpose is to make you mind*ful*. We shall repeatedly return to this theme of the potential danger of rituals.

It is easy to miss here how Jesus is being "sneaky." He seems to be telling us that this idea is only for this lesson. What he is *not* telling us is that *A Course in Miracles* itself rests on this principle!

(4) Each of the first three lessons should not be done more than twice a day each, preferably morning and evening. Nor should they be attempted for more than a minute or so, unless that entails a sense of hurry. A comfortable sense of leisure is essential.

As you do these lessons you should sense Jesus telling you: "These should be done gently. Do not crucify yourself with them. Do not try to get them perfect. Do not feel guilty when you *believe* you fail. Do not make your practice into an obsessive ritual. You should feel comfortable with these exercises." His gentleness becomes one of the significant principles of the workbook, and integrating this gentle kindness into our own lives is one of the most important lessons we could ever wish to learn. Jesus supplies us with a wonderful model.

LESSON 2

I have given everything I see in this room [on this street, from this window, in this place] all the meaning that it has for me.

The first lesson—that nothing means anything—is now extended. The reason nothing means anything is that you have given meaning to everything, obscuring, as we shall see presently, its *true* meaning of forgiveness. You know you have done so because you think your hand is more important than a pen. Since this clearly cannot be the way the Holy Spirit thinks, it can only have come from the way *you* think. God has not given everything you see around you its meaning, nor has Jesus. *You* have.

People will say they value something because their parents valued it, and because they were brought up in a certain culture, religion, socioeconomic stratum, etc. But that is not an honest statement. If they truly thought about it they would realize they have not adopted *all* of their parents' values, nor the values of their social system, and so on. They have adopted only those values that resonate with what they *want* their values to be.

Even though it is not mentioned here, Jesus is asking for complete honesty with him; to accept that nothing in this room or world means anything because I am the one who has given the world meaning, and I—my ego—could never understand *true* meaning: forgiveness.

(1) The exercises with this idea are the same as those for the first one. Begin with the things that are near you, and apply the idea to whatever your glance rests on. Then increase the range outward. Turn your head so that you include whatever is on either side. If possible, turn around and apply the idea to what was behind you. Remain as indiscriminate as possible in selecting subjects for its application, do not concentrate on anything in particular, and do not attempt to include everything you see in a given area, or you will introduce strain.

Jesus is telling us not to discriminate by saying that one thing is important and another is not, or that this thing does not mean anything, but that one does. He is telling us to be indiscriminate in our practicing. Attempting to include everything will lead to strain, he tells us, and then a ritual will soon

develop as well. Rituals involve strain because there is always a sense of *having* to do something. I *have* to say the prayer a certain way. I *have* to do the lesson at the same time every day. I *have* to go to church or synagogue every day or every week, or whatever. If it is a ritual, then it is something that has to be done the same way all the time. And usually, if it is done in a religious context, it has to be done the same way all the time because that is what God wants, or the Bible says, or my religious teachers insist on.

Therefore, Jesus is saying not to do these exercises as you would a ritual, and not to do them with a sense of strain. If you begin to feel strain, he will say you should stop. This is also an indication you are doing them wrong; that you are doing them with your ego and not with him.

(2:1) Merely glance easily and fairly quickly around you, trying to avoid selection by size, brightness, color, material, or relative importance to you.

The very fact that Jesus says "Try to avoid doing this" is telling you that you are going to try to do this; i.e., to select according to what is important and not important to you. Even if you do not think you are doing it consciously, *un*consciously this would certainly have to be the case in light of the hierarchy of values we all share.

(2:2-5) Take the subjects simply as you see them. Try to apply the exercise with equal ease to a body or a button, a fly or a floor, an arm or an apple. The sole criterion for applying the idea to anything is merely that your eyes have lighted on it. Make no attempt to include anything particular, but be sure that nothing is specifically excluded.

We need to read these lessons thoughtfully, moving beyond the *form* of the words to their underlying *content* or meaning. In other words, we need to realize that Jesus is teaching us to generalize; that all things are equally meaningless because everything serves the same ego purpose of separation. We will find later that all things then become equally meaningful, because everything in our perceptual world can also serve the purpose of the Holy Spirit. It does not matter what it is; it could be something that we believe is meaningful, like a body, or something that we believe is meaningless, like an apple or button. As long as we see, hear, taste, or feel anything, we are saying that the material world is real; duality and perception are real. This ultimately is a way of saying *I* am real. In back of that, of course, is the statement that because the material world is real, God cannot be. This is the metaphysics underlying these early and wonderful lessons.

LESSON 3

I do not understand anything I see in this room
[on this street, from this window, in this place].

Nothing in this room means anything because I have given it all the meaning it has. Therefore, since I have given it its meaning, how could I, a self separated *from* meaning, possibly understand it? I can understand it from my ego's point of view because it serves the purpose of making the world and my experience of it real. But I cannot truly understand it, because the purpose of the world, as I discussed in the Prelude to these volumes, is to prevent me from understanding. *True* understanding would have me realize the purpose I have given to everything and everyone in my life. Again, these early lessons have as one of their important goals to humble us, so that we realize we do not understand anything. This is what underlies Jesus' important (if not outrageous!) statement in the text: "You are still convinced that your understanding is a powerful contribution to the truth, and makes it what it is" (T-18.IV.7:5).

The lesson begins with the emphasis on indiscriminateness we have already seen:

(1:1) Apply this idea in the same way as the previous ones, without making distinctions of any kind.

This means I do not understand anything. I think I understand what the pen or cup is for, yet do not understand that their *ultimate* purpose is to keep me rooted in the illusion and out of Heaven. My ego would tell me the pen is for writing, the cup for drinking, and clothes for covering the body, but I do not understand the ego's underlying purpose for these and all other aspects of the material world.

(1:2-5) Whatever you see becomes a proper subject for applying the idea. Be sure that you do not question the suitability of anything for application of the idea. These are not exercises in judgment. Anything is suitable if you see it.

Unconsciously, we certainly do question the suitability of some things. Again, no one believes that their arm is less important than an apple or a button. We believe there is an extremely important difference between them.

"Anything is suitable if you see it," because if I see it, it cannot be real. That is because we "see" with our eyes, and our eyes, as indeed all our sensory organs, were specifically made not to *see*. In other words, they were made by the ego to look *outside* the mind, while true vision is only *within* the mind. It is that fundamental unreality that unites everything in this world.

(1:6-7) Some of the things you see may have emotionally charged meaning for you. Try to lay such feelings aside, and merely use these things exactly as you would anything else.

What is helpful about these lessons—if you pay careful attention to them—is that they will bring to the surface all our unconscious and hidden values, similar to the projective tests used by psychologists to help understand the underlying dynamics of a person's psychological disorder. We shall see this theme reflected in the lessons to come.

(2) The point of the exercises is to help you clear your mind of all past associations, to see things exactly as they appear to you now, and to realize how little you really understand about them. It is therefore essential that you keep a perfectly open mind, unhampered by judgment, in selecting the things to which the idea for the day is to be applied. For this purpose one thing is like another; equally suitable and therefore equally useful.

This is the deepest statement made so far, and its meaning should be abundantly clear. Jesus is trying to help us let go of the past, for as long as it remains hidden from our awareness we cannot undo it. Left buried, therefore, the past continues to rear its guilt-ridden and judgment-laden head time and time again. The key to this undoing lies in the principle underlying these exercises: the inherent sameness of all illusions.

LESSON 4

These thoughts do not mean anything.
They are like the things I see in this room [on this street, from this window, in this place].

Jesus is helping us realize it is not only what we see that has no meaning, but our *thoughts* about what we see have no meaning as well. In later lessons he explains that our thoughts are no different from what we perceive. The inner and outer are one and the same.

(1) Unlike the preceding ones, these exercises do not begin with the idea for the day. In these practice periods, begin with noting the thoughts that are crossing your mind for about a minute. Then apply the idea to them. If you are already aware of unhappy thoughts, use them as subjects for the idea. Do not, however, select only the thoughts you think are "bad." You will find, if you train yourself to look at your thoughts, that they represent such a mixture that, in a sense, none of them can be called "good" or "bad." This is why they do not mean anything.

Both our perception and thinking are variable. What is variable is not unchanging, by definition, and if it is not unchanging, it cannot be of God. This statement reflects one of the core premises on which the logic of *A Course in Miracles* rests. Anything of God *must* share in His attributes. If it does not, it cannot be of Him and so must be unreal or illusory. Thus, if there is something that changes it cannot be of the Changeless, and therefore does not exist and must be inherently meaningless, having separated from what alone has meaning. As we pay attention to our thoughts, therefore, we shall see their randomness, variableness, and fleeting nature, all of which attest to their meaninglessness. As variable, therefore, they must be of the ego, which is always about change, owing its origin to the original change from the Changeless One.

These early lessons, with their deceptively simple exercises, point us gradually and gently to the recognition of their truth as we apply them to our everyday lives.

(2) In selecting the subjects for the application of today's idea, the usual specificity is required. Do not be afraid to use "good" thoughts as well as "bad." None of them represents your real thoughts, which are being covered up by them. The "good" ones are but shadows of what lies beyond, and shadows make sight difficult. The "bad" ones are blocks to sight, and make seeing impossible. You do not want either.

Our real thoughts are of love or oneness, which must be non-specific, *A Course in Miracles'* definition of the term *abstract*. These abstract thoughts are covered by the ego's world of specifics. What we want is the truth, not a shadow or block. Like good Platonists, we want the Good that lies beyond the *concept* of good. *Good* and *bad* are concepts, and as we are taught near the end of the text:

> Salvation can be seen as nothing more than the escape from concepts. It does not concern itself with content of the mind, but with the simple statement that it thinks (T-31.V.14:3-4).

At best, our right-minded thoughts (the "good") are the corrections for our wrong-minded ones (the "bad"), but in the end their specificity, too, must disappear into the abstract or non-specific Love of our Source.

(3) This is a major exercise, and will be repeated from time to time in somewhat different form. The aim here is to train you in the first steps toward the goal of separating the meaningless from the meaningful. It is a first attempt in the long-range purpose of learning to see the meaningless as outside you, and the meaningful within. It is also the beginning of training your mind to recognize what is the same and what is different.

This is a pregnant thought—the meaningless is outside, because what is outside is unreal. The "meaningful within" are the Holy Spirit's thoughts in our minds. Anything that we perceive outside and believe is real serves the purpose of the ego, which is to keep us thinking that what is meaningless is true. All of this then becomes a cover for the truly meaningful. The Holy Spirit, however, teaches us to see that what is out in the world serves the purpose of teaching us that there is no world. Therein lies its meaning. The objects are not meaningful in themselves, but the Holy Spirit's purpose supplies their meaning. Everything seen without Him is meaningless.

The ego has us value what is in the world so that we will believe in the reality of the thought system of separation the world reflects. The Holy Spirit has us perceive what is in the world so that we will ultimately realize there is no world. Thus, "what is the same" is everything within the ego's thought system, and everything within the Holy Spirit's thought system: Guilt is guilt, regardless of its form; love is love, regardless of its form. But these two systems differ from each other, because the ego's thought system roots us further in hell, while the Holy Spirit's brings us home. Thus we learn the inherent *sameness* of all thoughts within the two thought systems, and the intrinsic *difference* between these two.

(4) In using your thoughts for application of the idea for today, identify each thought by the central figure or event it contains; for example:

> ***This thought about ___ does not mean anything. It is like the things I see in this room [on this street, and so on].***

Note this early emphasis—to be repeated throughout—on the need to be specific in our application of the day's idea. Without such application the exercises are meaningless to us.

(5) You can also use the idea for a particular thought that you recognize as harmful. This practice is useful, but is not a substitute for the more random procedures to be followed for the exercises. Do not, however, examine your mind for more than a minute or so. You are too inexperienced as yet to avoid a tendency to become pointlessly preoccupied.

This is part of Jesus' purpose in making us feel humble. We do not yet know the difference between what is harmful and what is harmless. This is similar to his instruction to us in the text that we do not know the difference between pain and joy (T-7.X), and imprisonment and freedom (T-8.II). And so we pointlessly preoccupy ourselves with pursuing what will hurt us, rather than learning what alone will bring us peace and joy.

(6) Further, since these exercises are the first of their kind, you may find the suspension of judgment in connection with thoughts particularly difficult. Do not repeat these exercises more than three or four times during the day. We will return to them later.

Jesus does not want you to feel guilty because you cannot do the exercises, but he does want you to be aware that you are having trouble doing them. Implied in that is the following statement: "I am having trouble doing them because I do not want to give up my belief, not only that the objects in my life are meaningful, as are my thoughts, but that *I* am meaningful. I, as an individual, special being am meaningful." That is why these lessons are "particularly difficult."

LESSON 5

I am never upset for the reason I think.

This is one of the lessons I frequently quote, for it goes to the heart of our practice. We obviously think we are upset because of what is going on in the world and how it impinges on us. But the *only* reason we are upset, which is not explicitly taught here, although implied, is that we chose the ego as our teacher instead of Jesus.

(1) This idea, like the preceding one, can be used with any person, situation or event you think is causing you pain. Apply it specifically to whatever you believe is the cause of your upset, using the description of the feeling in whatever term seems accurate to you. The upset may seem to be fear, worry, depression, anxiety, anger, hatred, jealousy or any number of forms, all of which will be perceived as different. This is not true. However, until you learn that form does not matter, each form becomes a proper subject for the exercises for the day. Applying the same idea to each of them separately is the first step in ultimately recognizing they are all the same.

Expressed here, again, is the paradox that we are to keep practicing with specifics so that we learn that everything is the same and non-specific. Indeed, this is the central theme of the process given us in *A Course in Miracles* that will eventually awaken us from the dream. By practicing forgiveness *each and every* time we experience upset or dis-ease—the *form* of our discomfort—we shall become aware of the underlying *content* of guilt that *is* the source of discomfort. That is when we finally learn the inherent *sameness* of all illusions. At this point they will disappear, leaving only the *content* of love, our only comfort and the true source of peace. This lesson is extremely important because we all get upset, and are always sure about the cause. This helps us realize that we are not upset because of what is outside, but only because of the way we are *looking* at what is outside.

The lesson's *specific* assignment of identifying the *specific* form of upset, and the cause we ascribe to it follows:

(2) When using the idea for today for a specific perceived cause of an upset in any form, use both the name of the form in which you see the upset, and the cause which you ascribe to it. For example:

> *I am not angry at ___ for the reason I think.*
> *I am not afraid of ___ for the reason I think.*

Jesus now quickly moves us from the bodily world of feelings to the mind's world of our thoughts:

(3) But again, this should not be substituted for practice periods in which you first search your mind for "sources" of upset in which you believe, and forms of upset which you think result.

Jesus returns us to the *mind-searching* aspect of his training. We are to become accustomed to looking within, learning to pay attention to our heretofore repressed guilt, the ultimate source of what we think are our upsets.

(4) In these exercises, more than in the preceding ones, you may find it hard to be indiscriminate, and to avoid giving greater weight to some subjects than to others. It might help to precede the exercises with the statement:

> *There are no small upsets. They are all equally disturbing to my peace of mind.*

We would all tend to discriminate. When something minor upsets us we think we are only "mildly annoyed." Then later in the day something major happens and we become really angry. And we think there is a difference. This is the issue we have been addressing. The ego has us reaffirm the principle that there is a hierarchy of illusions, since this is one of its primary defenses against the Oneness of God: the specificity of the dualistic world belies the unified reality of Divine Abstraction, to use a term from the text (T-4.VII.5:4). This is the reality the ego never wants us to remember or reflect here, since that means the end of the ego.

Jesus continues his instructions to us in the same vein:

(5-6) Then examine your mind for whatever is distressing you, regardless of how much or how little you think it is doing so.

You may also find yourself less willing to apply today's idea to some perceived sources of upset than to others. If this occurs, think first of this:

> *I cannot keep this form of upset and let the others go. For the purposes of these exercises, then, I will regard them all as the same.*

This is what we are to say when tempted to make a hierarchy of what upsets us. And then Jesus reiterates the point in the next sentence:

(7:1) Then search your mind for no more than a minute or so, and try to identify a number of different forms of upset that are disturbing you, regardless of the relative importance you may give them.

We can see how many times in these early lessons Jesus reminds us how we continually try to make a hierarchy of our experiences, believing some things are important and others are not. He is training us to realize they are all the same. Once again, an illusion is an illusion is an illusion.

A deeper study of what is taught in *A Course in Miracles* yields a rather disturbing revelation: when we are upset, we *want* to be upset, for that proves we are the innocent victims of what the victimizer is doing to us. We shall return to this very important teaching of the Course later, but for now I can mention two very specific discussions of this: "The Picture of Crucifixion" (T-27.I) and "Self-Concept versus Self" (T-31.V).

The remainder of the paragraph repeats the earlier instruction, emphasizing the need to be both specific and gentle in our practice.

LESSON 6

I am upset because I see something that is not there.

This lesson is a bombshell. What is so intriguing about these first lessons is that Jesus does not become involved with weighty metaphysics. Yet that is exactly what grounds the idea that "I am upset because I see something that is not there." What is upsetting me is *within* me, not outside. *There is nothing outside me.* What I think I see is merely a projection of a thought in my mind, and this thought—of separation from God—is not there either! My perceptions are of illusions, the projections of thoughts that are themselves illusions. What else can an illusion breed but further illusions?

The first paragraph, as it itself states, is already familiar in its emphasis on specificity. Paragraph 2 should also be familiar:

(2) Today's idea is useful for application to anything that seems to upset you, and can profitably be used throughout the day for that purpose. However, the three or four practice periods which are required should be preceded by a minute or so of mind searching, as before, and the application of the idea to each upsetting thought uncovered in the search.

Mind searching is the focal point of Jesus' message and the means of applying his teachings to our daily experiences. He then returns to two ideas mentioned in Lesson 5:

(3) Again, if you resist applying the idea to some upsetting thoughts more than to others, remind yourself of the two cautions stated in the previous lesson:

There are no small upsets. They are all equally disturbing to my peace of mind.

And:

I cannot keep this form of upset and let the others go. For the purposes of these exercises, then, I will regard them all as the same.

It would be difficult to over-emphasize the importance of this idea of the inherent *sameness* of all things—both large and small upsets (as well as large and small pleasures). It occupies a central place in Jesus' teaching, as it is the means of our learning to tell the difference between illusion and truth or, in Plato's words, appearance and reality.

LESSON 7

I see only the past.

Lesson 7 is essentially a summary of the previous six lessons, as we see in the first paragraph where they are repeated almost verbatim.

In the second paragraph we find Jesus returning to an idea he mentioned briefly in the second paragraph of Lesson 3—the importance of clearing our minds of past thoughts. Now, he elaborates: The reason that nothing means anything, that we have given everything the meaning it has, etc., is that we are seeing only the past. Keeping in mind the equation of sin, guilt, and fear with past, present, and future will help you understand the motivation for seeing only the past. Sin is equated with separation, which proves that I am an individual, autonomous from God. Once I believe this lie, it will automatically be projected out and take the form of the past. Thus, I see the past in everything, because I want to maintain my individual identity. Here is how Jesus says it:

(2) Old ideas about time are very difficult to change, because everything you believe is rooted in time and depends on your not learning these new ideas about it. Yet that is precisely why you need new ideas about time. This first time idea is not really so strange as it may sound at first.

Whenever we are upset it is because we are equating something that just happened with something that happened in the past. I see a particular person and I know what I am supposed to do: This is an authority, and so my hate is justified; this is my rival, and so I have to hate this person; this one is of a certain skin color, which I must hate. Hate is always based on the past. Most of the time, though, it is more subtle than these examples, which is why we need practice to recognize and accept this "first time idea."

In sum, then, the purpose of seeing the past in everything is that it enables me to say that I exist. Thus, making the past real is the same as saying sin or separation is real, and therefore so am I. Incidentally, note the word play on the word "time" in 2:2-3.

We are now given a very specific, albeit a seemingly trivial example:

(3) Look at a cup, for example. Do you see a cup, or are you merely reviewing your past experiences of picking up a cup, being thirsty, drinking from a cup, feeling the rim of a cup against your lips, having breakfast and so on? Are not your aesthetic reactions to the cup, too, based on past experiences? How else would you know whether or not this kind of cup will break if you drop it? What do you know about this cup except what you learned in the past? You would have no idea what this cup is, except for your past learning. Do you, then, really see it?

But this is true of *everything*. We literally see *nothing*, because we are seeing the past, which is not there.

(4) Look about you. This is equally true of whatever you look at. Acknowledge this by applying the idea for today indiscriminately to whatever catches your eye. For example:

> *I see only the past in this pencil.*
> *I see only the past in this shoe.*
> *I see only the past in this hand.*
> *I see only the past in that body.*
> *I see only the past in that face.*

It is interesting to note Jesus' choice of objects to be perceived; they include inanimate as well as animate ones. We shall continue to return to this point, but for now let me underscore again the important teaching that since the world is "the outside picture of an inward condition" (T-21.in.1:5) and this inward condition is an illusion, the outside picture must be an illusion, too. Moreover, as there is no "hierarchy of illusions," there can be no intrinsic difference among all the objects of our perceptual world, inanimate or animate. They are *all* equally illusory, and thus they are the same. While it goes without saying that this flies in the face of our experience, we are also being taught that our experiences are false. In these lessons we are seeing Jesus' preliminary and subtle attempts at teaching us this truth as he gently leads us to their acceptance, and beyond them to God—*the* truth.

Finally, still another caution against the temptation to exclude what we feel is not important, which very often is a veil concealing what we secretly believe to be quite important, what the text refers to as our "secret sins and hidden hates" (T-31.VIII.9:2):

(5) Do not linger over any one thing in particular, but remember to omit nothing specifically. Glance briefly at each subject, and then move on to the next. Three or four practice periods, each to last a minute or so, will be enough.

Indiscriminateness in responding to the illusory world of perception remains the central focus of this early part of the workbook. It contains the means of undoing the ego's thought system of separation, the essence of miracles: there is no order of difficulty among them (T-1.I.1:1).

LESSON 8

My mind is preoccupied with past thoughts.

There is a discernible sequence to the lessons as one continues to read and practice them. Jesus begins with simple ideas and statements about the way we perceive the world. He then quickly moves to the way we perceive our thoughts and, beginning with Lesson 8, he develops much more clearly the specific cause and effect connection between our thoughts and the world. Here, for the first time in the workbook, he speaks about the world's unreality. He also introduces the idea of projection, a principle that was implied in the first seven lessons, but will be clearly identified in the lessons to follow. Jesus has been telling us up to this point that what we see is meaningless because what we see is coming from what we think. And what we think (in our ego minds) is meaningless because it denies true Meaning. This has not been clearly stated in the lessons to date, although we have discussed it, but it certainly has been implied and will be more explicitly stated in the lessons to come.

(1:1) This idea is, of course, the reason why you see only the past.

Lesson 7, "I see only the past," introduced the idea that everything we perceive is meaningless because it is based on our thoughts of the past. In Lesson 8, Jesus continues and extends his discussion of time and the past: *My mind is preoccupied with past thoughts.* It is not simply that we see only the past, which, again, was the theme of Lesson 7, but we see only the past because we *think* only the past. Jesus is here introducing the idea that what we see *outside* comes from what we think *inside*, a major theme of the text: "projection makes perception" (T-13.V.3:5; T-21.in.1:1). What we believe and have made real about ourselves within, whether as children of the ego or children of God, will be directly reflected in what we perceive outside, because the inner and outer are the same. This is a variation of the essential principle in *A Course in Miracles* that *ideas leave not their source.* We shall return later to this all-important theme. That *my mind is preoccupied with past thoughts* is, of course, why we see only the past (1:1). Although not clearly stated here, but clearly implied, is the principle that what we see comes from what we think. That is why:

(1:2) No one really sees anything.

This is another of those statements that, when you begin to read the text and do the lessons, your mind would tend to gloss over, because you really do not want to accept what Jesus is saying. He means this literally: "No one really sees anything."

(1:3) He sees only his thoughts projected outward.

In the text there are many passages—a couple in the workbook, too—where Jesus explains that the body's eyes do not see, just as the body does not think, feel, hear, or do anything. It simply does what the mind tells it to do (e.g., T-28.V.5:3-8; VI.2:1-9; M-8.3:3–4:3). The body can be thought of then as simply a puppet or robot that carries out the dictates of its master. That is why we do not see anything. All that we "see," and basically this *see* should be in quotes, is a projection of what we have been thinking. And, as we have seen, what we have been thinking in listening to the ego is quite simply nothing.

(1:4) The mind's preoccupation with the past is the cause of the misconception about time from which your seeing suffers.

In the Prelude, as well as in discussing the Introduction to the workbook, I mentioned that one way of understanding time as we know it, i.e., as linear —past, present, and future—is to see it as nothing more than a reflection or shadow of the ego's thought system of sin, guilt, and fear. When we choose our individuality over the Holy Spirit's oneness, and then seek to preserve this individual identity, the ego has us construct its thought system of sin, guilt, and fear. To restate this important dynamic: *sin* says we have sinned against God in the past; we experience *guilt* over what we have done in what the ego calls the present; and since guilt always demands punishment, we then become *afraid* of God's punishment, which we believe we deserve. That fear of punishment, of course, points to the future. If you keep in mind this "unholy trinity" of sin (past), guilt ("present"), and fear (future) as you read this first paragraph, it will make much more sense. When we look outside we see a world ruled by time. It is, of course, also a world of space. Space and time, as the text describes them, are opposite sides of the same mistake (T-26.VIII.1:3-5).

Thus, everything we see outside we see in terms of the past, because we see it through the lens of our individual identity. This identity is rooted in sin, the belief that we have separated from God and now exist as separate entities. Since we believe we are at war with God, a theme to be developed later, we must then also believe we are at war with everyone else. As a result, every perception in our world is geared toward dealing with the issue of specialness: who is the special person who will win, and who the special person who will lose. When this is expressed directly, it is special hate; when concealed, it is special love. Moreover, specialness is rooted in the ego's notion of time, which, once again, comes from the belief in sin, guilt, and fear. Thus specialness cannot *not* be rooted in the past.

The "misconception about time" is that it is real —there *is* a past, present, and future—and that the present and future are directly caused by the past. Thus what we are today is because of our past. The future, likewise, will be merely an extension of the ego's present.

(1:5) Your mind cannot grasp the present, which is the only time there is.

The ego's present is not this "present," what *A Course in Miracles* refers to as the "holy instant." As this experience is not rooted in time, it is also not rooted in sin, guilt, and fear. It is rooted in the right-minded presence of the Holy Spirit, in which vision—not based on the past, and certainly not on specialness—becomes the means for love to guide us from within.

(1:6) It [your mind] therefore cannot understand time, and cannot, in fact, understand anything.

This is because everything we think we understand is rooted in the seeming reality of the spatial and temporal world. As long as we identify ourselves as individuals, separate and autonomous, we must believe in the entirety of the ego system. Everything we perceive, therefore, will be a shadow of its illusory thought of separation, which means we will not understand anything.

(2:1) The one wholly true thought one can hold about the past is that it is not here.

This is another of those lines that, if you pay careful attention to it, should have you jumping out the window. If you are a creature of the past and there is no past, then it must mean there is no *you*. In "The Present Memory" that opens Chapter 28 in the text comes the sentence: "This world was over long ago" (T-28.I.1:6). If this is true, it means *you* were over long ago, too. This forces us to ask: Who is the *you* that you think is reading those words? Or, in Jesus' words in the text: "Who is the 'you' who are living in this world?" (T-4.II.11:8) In other words, our existence is literally made up, and if you paid close attention to that thought you would be terrified. If you are not, it is because you are *not* paying close attention to it. That statement is literally saying, as is this statement in Lesson 8, that you do not exist.

This would explain, as we had mentioned earlier, why doing this workbook carefully and with diligence should make you extremely anxious, even if you are not quite sure where the anxiety is coming from. There is a part of you that recognizes what this is saying, even though, again, the language is simple and does not appear to have the same metaphysical weight found in the text. That is why you forget the lessons, do not want to do them, and tend to gloss over them and focus only on their more superficial aspects.

(2:2) To think about it at all is therefore to think about illusions.

To think about the past is to think about illusions. Stop for a moment as you do this lesson and consider how almost every single thought you have throughout the day is based on the past, whether it is something as commonplace as picking up a coffee cup, or something that would seem far more important. Thoughts about a situation, relationship, your body, or anything else—are all predicated on the past. And they must be, because the past is nothing more than sin's shadow, and sin is separation. As long as you believe you are a separate entity, you must believe in the reality of sin and therefore of time.

(2:3-4) Very few have realized what is actually entailed in picturing the past or in anticipating the future. The mind is actually blank when it

does this, because it is not really thinking about anything.

This statement is the basis of another statement we frequently say in workshops and classes: "The thoughts we think we think are not our real thoughts." If they are not our real thoughts, they do not exist. It follows then that since we have identified with our thoughts, *we* do not exist either. "The mind is actually blank when it does this, because it is not really thinking about anything." Not only is our existence an illusion; indeed, *all* existence is an illusion, for it contrasts with the reality of *being*. A discussion of this distinction can be found in T-4.VII.4-5.

(3:1) The purpose of the exercises for today is to begin to train your mind to recognize when it is not really thinking at all.

It is clear from statements like this, as well as many others, that Jesus' purpose in these lessons is to train our minds. Here, specifically, the focus is the idea of thinking—to have us realize that we are really not thinking at all. We will become aware of this by recognizing how much our thoughts are rooted in the past, or, although this is not the point of this lesson, how much they are rooted in fear of the future. We become preoccupied with what is going to happen—whether we are talking about the next five minutes or the next five years—because these concerned thoughts of the future are rooted in our concerned thoughts of the past.

(3:2) While thoughtless ideas preoccupy your mind, the truth is blocked.

This idea will be developed as we proceed—the purpose of thoughtless ideas and holding onto the past is to block the truth. *Purpose* remains one of the central themes of *A Course in Miracles*, and Jesus repeatedly emphasizes it as the means for understanding the ego's thought system, as seen, for example, in his introduction to the laws of chaos (T-23.II.1:1-5). This then, is another pregnant statement our minds could slide past, because it reveals the motivation for holding onto thoughtless ideas, be they concerns of the past, fears of the future, or present feelings of guilt. They are all purposive attempts to keep hidden the truth of our Identity as Christ.

(3:3) Recognizing that your mind has been

merely blank, rather than believing that it is filled with real ideas, is the first step to opening the way to vision.

As is the case throughout the three books of *A Course in Miracles*, Jesus' focus is on having us remove "the blocks to the awareness of love's presence" (T-in.1:7). These blocks are the problem. We do not have to be concerned about what Jesus or truth are doing, but we have to be vigilant about what the *ego* is doing. It is very helpful, therefore, to understand that in holding thoughtless ideas our minds are blank, because these ideas are about the past. That begins the process of opening up the door to true perception, the vision of true forgiveness that leads us to the truth.

(4:1-3) The exercises for today should be done with eyes closed. This is because you actually cannot see anything, and it is easier to recognize that no matter how vividly you may picture a thought, you are not seeing anything. With as little investment as possible, search your mind for the usual minute or so, merely noting the thoughts you find there.

Some of the earlier exercises call for our eyes to be open. The point here, and later on as well, is that there is no difference between what we see or what we think. They are the same. Here Jesus is not talking about what we are perceiving externally, but focusing on what we are thinking. We see again the important emphasis placed on not making any of our thoughts special, or more or less important than any other.

The lesson moves now to our specific thoughts:

(4:4–5:3) Name each one [thought] by the central figure or theme it contains, and pass on to the next. Introduce the practice period by saying:

I seem to be thinking about ___.

Then name each of your thoughts specifically, for example:

I seem to be thinking about [name of a person], about [name of an object], about [name of an emotion],

and so on, concluding at the end of the mind-searching period with:

But my mind is preoccupied with past thoughts.

Thus we are asked to practice the central aspect

of the process of forgiveness: bringing the specifics of our illusions to the non-specific truth of the Holy Spirit, expressed here in the statement: "But my mind is preoccupied with past thoughts."

(6) This can be done four or five times during the day, unless you find it irritates you. If you find it trying, three or four times is sufficient. You might find it helpful, however, to include your irritation, or any emotion that the idea for today may induce, in the mind searching itself.

Here is another wonderful example of how Jesus, at the same time he inspires us with his gentleness and patience, uses our resistance as part of our healing. As he states in the text, in the context of specialness:

> Such is the Holy Spirit's kind perception of specialness; His use of what you made, to heal instead of harm (T-25.VI.4:1).

Even our irritation can serve the Holy Spirit's purpose of forgiveness, if we let Him help us.

LESSON 9

I see nothing as it is now.

Lesson 9 logically follows from Lessons 7 and 8. If my thoughts are meaningless because they are preoccupied with a past that does not exist, and the past does not exist because it is rooted in sin and separation, which never happened, then it must logically follow that "I see nothing as it is now."

(1:1-2) This idea obviously follows from the two preceding ones. But while you may be able to accept it intellectually, it is unlikely that it will mean anything to you as yet.

This is a mild understatement. The idea will not mean anything to us because we are terrified of what it really means. In the holy instant, which is the meaning of "now," there is nothing to see. Chapter 18 in the text says: "At no single instant does the body exist at all" (T-18.VII.3:1), which means that in the holy instant there is no body. Why? Because there is no thought of separation; no sin, guilt, and fear, and therefore no body is needed to defend against those thoughts. These are the blocks to truth that Jesus referred to in the previous lesson. Thus, everything I "see" is a defense against the holy instant.

(1:3-7) However, understanding is not necessary at this point. In fact, the recognition that you do not understand is a prerequisite for undoing your false ideas. These exercises are concerned with practice, not with understanding. You do not need to practice what you already understand. It would indeed be circular to aim at understanding, and assume that you have it already.

This is the same idea I underscored in the previous lesson: the importance of recognizing that your mind is blank when it is thinking. We think we understand what we are thinking. But in truth we do not understand anything, because our so-called thinking is a block to real understanding, which in *A Course in Miracles* is equated with truth or vision.

I quoted earlier from "The Little Willingness" where Jesus says "you are still convinced that your understanding is a powerful contribution to the truth, and makes it what it is" (T-18.IV.7:5). In other words, our understanding is not necessary. What is necessary, however, is that we be willing to accept that we understand nothing. If we can accept that fact we are opening the way for our real Teacher to instruct us. But if we keep insisting that we understand and are right, there is no way Jesus can teach us. In our insane arrogance we believe there is nothing we need to learn. In a lesson to come later, we read:

> You will not question what you have already defined. And the purpose of these exercises is to ask questions and receive the answers (W-pI.28.4:1-2).

Thus, it is our willingness to *practice* and *apply* the lessons, each and every moment that we can, that will enable us ultimately to understand.

(2:1) It is difficult for the untrained mind to believe that what it seems to picture is not there.

It is extremely hard for us to believe that what we are seeing is not there. We think we see a room full of people and chairs, a clock, a frozen lake [this class was held during the winter in the New York Catskill Mountains], etc. In "reality," all we are seeing is an out-picturing of our thoughts of separation, the specific forms that are projections of our illusory thought system.

(2:2-3) This idea can be quite disturbing, and may meet with active resistance in any number of forms. Yet that does not preclude applying it.

Again, it is not necessary to understand or agree with the ideas in the workbook. Jesus is simply asking us to do them. The thought for today should be disturbing, and there is something wrong if it is not. As we have already discussed, if what you are seeing is not there, and you experience seeing yourself —your physical self and your thoughts—then *you* are not there. What could be more disturbing than that? It is not necessary to accept this idea as truth. Jesus is simply asking you to begin the process of training your mind to think the way he thinks.

(2:4-5) No more than that is required for these

or any other exercises. Each small step will clear a little of the darkness away, and understanding will finally come to lighten every corner of the mind that has been cleared of the debris that darkens it.

This is an extremely important theme, and one we shall restate again and again: undoing the interferences to remembering love. When you get the mind's darkening debris out of the way—i.e., the meaningless thoughts rooted in the ego's thought system—what is left is the vision of Christ, and that is understanding. This has nothing to do with what happens in the world, but with realizing that there is nothing here in the world to understand. I am reminded of a statement Michelangelo made about his sculpture. He explained that he first saw the image in the stone, and then took away what did not belong. The image of Christ, which is the light of our true Identity, is already in our minds through the Holy Spirit. Our responsibility is simply to bring to His truth the darkening debris of our illusions, which leads to an experience of the Love of God and the oneness of the Sonship.

The rest of the lesson provides instructions for the exercises. Note again that Jesus emphasizes indiscriminate application—*excluding nothing*. He is helping us to be specific without being ritualistic and obsessive, the ultimate purpose being to generalize from the specific to *all* aspects of the perceptual world—the trivial and important, both near and far. Jesus closes the lesson with still another reminder:

(5) It is emphasized again that while complete inclusion should not be attempted, specific exclusion must be avoided. Be sure you are honest with yourself in making this distinction. You may be tempted to obscure it.

As you progress through the workbook, you will see the significance of these instructions not to exclude, as well as to be honest in seeing the resistance to undoing the ego.

LESSON 10

My thoughts do not mean anything.

Lesson 4 stated: "These thoughts do not mean anything." As Jesus explains in the second paragraph, he now says "My" instead of "These," thus making the teaching much more personal for us.

(1) **This idea applies to all the thoughts of which you are aware, or become aware in the practice periods. The reason the idea is applicable to all of them is that they are not your real thoughts. We have made this distinction before, and will do so again. You have no basis for comparison as yet. When you do, you will have no doubt that what you once believed were your thoughts did not mean anything.**

Our "real thoughts" would be anything in our right minds, anything that comes from the Holy Spirit. In this sense, an *unreal* thought would be, for example, that someone is attacking me. The *real* thought would be that this is a call for love, and it is a call for love that is shared by me. However, as Jesus is teaching us here, we are still far too identified with *our* thoughts to be able seriously to entertain what he is saying to us about the thoughts that our thoughts are covering. But, we are only on Lesson 10!

(2) **This is the second time we have used this kind of idea. The form is only slightly different. This time the idea is introduced with "My thoughts" instead of "These thoughts," and no link is made overtly with the things around you. The emphasis is now on the lack of reality of what you think you think.**

Jesus is not talking about what we perceive outside; he is now talking about what we *think*. You can see in these lessons how he goes back and forth in his gentle attempts at convincing us that we are not who we think we are. It is a process that gradually leads us through the labyrinth of our ego's thought system—the seeming terror of the circle of fear he describes in the text (T-18.IX.3:7–4:1)—to the Love of God that happily awaits us just beyond.

Paragraph 3 is a nice statement of projection, although the term itself is not used:

(3) **This aspect of the correction process began with the idea that the thoughts of which you are aware are meaningless, outside rather than within; and then stressed their past rather than their present status. Now we are emphasizing that the presence of these "thoughts" means that you are not thinking. This is merely another way of repeating our earlier statement that your mind is really a blank. To recognize this is to recognize nothingness when you think you see it. As such, it is the prerequisite for vision.**

Jesus wants us to understand that our thoughts are nothing. However, we take these thoughts of nothingness and project them because we think they are real. Thus are they seen as real images in the outside world. Jesus wants us to understand that the thoughts that are now the projected source of our perceptions are not really there. Our minds, to repeat this important idea, are filled with thought-less thoughts, or thoughtless ideas, because they are based on the ego's illusory thought system of separation.

(4) **Close your eyes for these exercises, and introduce them by repeating the idea for today quite slowly to yourself. Then add:**

> *This idea will help to release me from all that I now believe.*

The exercises consist, as before, in searching your mind for all the thoughts that are available to you, without selection or judgment. Try to avoid classification of any kind. In fact, if you find it helpful to do so, you might imagine that you are watching an oddly assorted procession going by, which has little if any personal meaning to you. As each one crosses your mind, say:

> *My thought about ___ does not mean anything.*
> *My thought about ___ does not mean anything.*

This is an example of what it means to look with Jesus at your ego, the importance of which we continually emphasize. The *you* that looks, with no personal attachment to these thoughts, is the decision-making part of our minds, return to which is the Course's goal and the meaning of the miracle that gives *A Course in Miracles* its name. The process entails standing back with Jesus, watching your ego make a case against someone or yourself; seeing it take a fragment here and a piece from there, weaving together a seemingly complete picture in order to prove you are right about your perceptions of victimization in the world, and that everyone else is wrong, including the Holy Spirit. You simply watch your ego in action—"an oddly assorted procession going by"—its purpose being to confuse us about our identity, making us believe we are a *body* not a *mind*. While Jesus is not giving us his full teaching here, he is laying out its basic principles

Finally:

(5) Today's thought can obviously serve for any thought that distresses you at any time. In **addition, five practice periods are recommended, each involving no more than a minute or so of mind searching. It is not recommended that this time period be extended, and it should be reduced to half a minute or less if you experience discomfort. Remember, however, to repeat the idea slowly before applying it specifically, and also to add:**

> ***This idea will help to release me from all that I now believe.***

You can see, once again, the importance generalization holds for Jesus. We are asked to practice—with the same gentle kindness he exhibits toward us—with our specific misperceptions, in order to generalize the principles learned in these applications to *all* our experiences. This theme continues to recur throughout these early lessons.

LESSON 11

My meaningless thoughts are showing me a meaningless world.

Jesus now explicitly draws the connection between our thoughts and what we perceive, so that the reason nothing we see around us has any meaning (Lesson 1) is that what we are supposedly seeing comes from a thought that has no meaning. This lesson clearly expresses that cause-effect relationship.

(1:1-2) This is the first idea we have had that is related to a major phase of the correction process; the reversal of the thinking of the world. It seems as if the world determines what you perceive.

We could add: "what you feel, what you think, your emotions, your problems," etc. For example, I perceive two people having a fight because they are fighting. Or my body feels cold because the temperature is below freezing. That is how the world thinks, and how everyone experiences the world. However, if all this comes from our thoughts, part of the ego's dream of separation, it must be these thoughts that dreamt the freezing temperature and the bodies that react to it. Our sensory apparatus, therefore, proves to us there is a world that is independent of us, and that we are the innocent victims of events beyond our control. This surely does not mean we are to feel guilty if we are discomforted by a bitterly cold day. It simply means we should realize we are cold because we identify with the body, which in turn means we identify with the ego's thought system of separation, all of which is meaningless. Again:

(1:3-5) Today's idea introduces the concept that your thoughts determine the world you see. [They also determine the world that you experience.] **Be glad indeed to practice the idea in its initial form, for in this idea is your release made sure. The key to forgiveness lies in it.**

This is an extremely important statement. Jesus is telling us simply to listen to him and practice this idea in its initial form. He is implying that he is going to build this up over the course of the year of workbook lessons and through our systematic study of the text. That is how we learn forgiveness. I cannot forgive a world that is real. I cannot forgive

others for what they have actually done, regardless of the seeming effect it has had on me. I can forgive you only by realizing I am the one who put you in my dream, and it is *my* dream. That is the key to forgiveness, and to the important definition in *A Course in Miracles* that you forgive your brother for what he has *not* done to you (e.g., W-pII.1.1:1). It may very well be that the person has done a great deal to you or to others on the physical or psychological level. But on the level of your mind he has done nothing, because he is nothing but a thought in your mind. Just as you, the victim of the victimizer, are also a thought in your mind. Victim and victimizer are one and the same. It should be noted that the mind, which antedates the temporal and spatial world, is outside time and space. As I discussed earlier in this book, time and space are but the projection into form of the mind's content of separation, and sin, guilt, and fear.

All this is implied here, though not stated explicitly. Indeed, Jesus does not have to state it clearly here, because that is the purpose of the text. The workbook's purpose is to have us *begin* the process of applying these ideas, and to *begin* to understand that what we think we see is not what we are really seeing. We see but a projection of a thought within our minds; a purposive thought, as I mentioned briefly before, which ensures that our thought system wins out and Jesus' loses; we are right and he is wrong. The separated world of pain and suffering witnesses to the fact we are right. That is why we made it the way we did.

Now to the gentle instructions for the day's exercise:

(2) The practice periods for today's idea are to be undertaken somewhat differently from the previous ones. Begin with your eyes closed, and repeat the idea slowly to yourself. Then open your eyes and look about, near and far, up and down,—anywhere. During the minute or so to be spent in using the idea merely repeat it to yourself, being sure to do so without haste, and with no sense of urgency or effort.

We begin the exercise with our eyes closed, and

then we open them and look around. Jesus again underscores that there is no difference between what we see and what we think. They are one, for the inner and outer are the same. Note again Jesus' instructions in ease and effortlessness; pressure merely strengthens the very ego we are trying to undo.

Jesus' words in the next paragraph underscore the *process* of mind training he is leading us through:

(3) To do these exercises for maximum benefit, the eyes should move from one thing to another fairly rapidly, since they should not linger on anything in particular. The words, however, should be used in an unhurried, even leisurely fashion. The introduction to this idea, in particular, should be practiced as casually as possible. It contains the foundation for the peace, relaxation and freedom from worry that we are trying to achieve. On concluding the exercises, close your eyes and repeat the idea once more slowly to yourself.

As the tortoise taught us: Slow and easy wins the race. Jesus is setting the tone for our learning, undoing the ego's need to fight, struggle, and overcome—even itself. He asks us to practice, using terms such as "unhurried," "leisurely," "casually," "peace," "relaxation," "freedom from worry," and "slowly." Our mind training should be as free from tension and conflict as possible.

The final paragraph recounts the familiar instructions that gently urge us on:

(4) Three practice periods today will probably be sufficient. However, if there is little or no uneasiness and an inclination to do more, as many as five may be undertaken. More than this is not recommended.

More is not better, at least not in the thought system Jesus is imparting to us. If we can do five practice periods, fine. If not, then three will do. But—let us not strive for more, Jesus says. I am not in Heaven keeping score. In other words, it is the *content* he is interested in, not the *form*; quality, not quantity.

LESSON 12

I am upset because I see a meaningless world.

Lessons 5 and 6 stated that "I am never upset for the reason I think," and "I am upset because I see something that is not there." This lesson amplifies these ideas. Thus, "I am upset because I see a meaningless world." Jesus now explains why that statement is true:

(1) The importance of this idea lies in the fact that it contains a correction for a major perceptual distortion. You think that what upsets you is a frightening world, or a sad world, or a violent world, or an insane world. All these attributes are given it by you. The world is meaningless in itself.

We perceive violence, hostility, insanity, and a myriad of other conditions. Jesus is not denying that we perceive. He is simply saying that what we perceive is not real. He is not saying, however, that we should deny our experiences (see, e.g., T-2.IV.3:8-11). Rather, he is helping us realize where the experiences are coming from. If I am upset, it is not because of what someone or something in the world has done to me, as we are also taught later in Lesson 31: "I am not the victim of the world I see." This is a central theme throughout *A Course in Miracles*: the world itself is meaningless because it comes from a meaningless thought. The meaningless thought is that I can be separate from God; in fact, not only *can* I be separate, but I *am* separate. It is meaningless because the thought is a defense against what alone has meaning: God and His unified creation. Thus, when you believe you can separate from the only meaning, everything inevitably becomes meaningless.

(2:1-2) These exercises are done with eyes open. Look around you, this time quite slowly.

Jesus returns to having us focus on what we see, having already taught us there is no difference between what we see and what we think.

Note in the following the focus on all illusions being equal and thus equally illusory:

(2:3-7) Try to pace yourself so that the slow shifting of your glance from one thing to another involves a fairly constant time interval. Do not allow the time of the shift to become markedly longer or shorter, but try, instead, to keep a measured, even tempo throughout. What you see does not matter. You teach yourself this as you give whatever your glance rests on equal attention and equal time. This is a beginning step in learning to give them all equal value.

In introducing Lesson 1 I briefly discussed the ego's first law of chaos—there is a hierarchy of illusions, which means there are certain things and people that are more important than others. It will be difficult to break that strongly ingrained habit of making distinctions in practicing this idea that "I am upset because I see a meaningless world." Jesus wants us to understand that everything is equally meaningless, because it all comes from the same meaningless thought.

Everything we see in the universe of time and space, including ourselves, is nothing more or less than a fragment of the original thought we could be, and are, separate from God and on our own. Every fragment retains the characteristics of that original thought, a "tiny, mad idea, at which the Son of God remembered not to laugh" (T-27.VIII.6:2). Our need is to remember to laugh at it because of its meaninglessness, not because it is funny in the usual sense of the word. We laugh with a gentle smile that says it does not mean anything because it is an impossibility. To use a familiar image, it was as if a huge pane of glass fell, shattering into billions and billions of fragments. Each fragment retains the characteristics of the original pane; each has the chemical composition of glass, for example. Each of us, as well as everything in the world, is but one of those fragments—all meaningless because they come from a meaningless thought.

The reason I am upset, then, is that the world witnesses to the seeming fact that I am right about the world. Since I believe I exist in a world that is out there, this world reminds me of the original thought that gave rise to it, let alone to my individual existence: I destroyed Heaven and murdered God. This is extremely upsetting because I believe God will now return to punish me for what I did. This concept will be elaborated on in the next two lessons.

Again, Jesus does not ask you, as his student doing the workbook lessons, to understand the full implications of these statements. Such understanding comes from the study of the text. But he does want you to begin the practice of not taking your perceptions all that seriously.

In the next paragraph Jesus asks us to include terms in the exercise that are positive as well as negative:

(3:1-6) As you look about you, say to yourself:

I think I see a fearful world, a dangerous world, a hostile world, a sad world, a wicked world, a crazy world,

and so on, using whatever descriptive terms happen to occur to you. If terms which seem positive rather than negative occur to you, include them. For example, you might think of "a good world," or "a satisfying world." If such terms occur to you, use them along with the rest. You may not yet understand why these "nice" adjectives belong in these exercises but remember that a "good world" implies a "bad" one, and a "satisfying world" implies an "unsatisfying" one.

What is implied here without being specifically discussed is that contrasts and opposites root us solidly in the world of dualistic thinking. The text defines Heaven as "an awareness of perfect Oneness," in which there is no duality (T-18.VI.1:6). Thus, there is no good and evil in Heaven—only God. Learning to recognize this is an important part of our training.

(3:7-8) All terms which cross your mind are suitable subjects for today's exercises. Their seeming quality does not matter.

In other words, it does not matter whether or not the terms are important or holy; everything in the world comes from the one illusory thought; an illusion is an illusion is an illusion.

(4) Be sure that you do not alter the time intervals between applying today's idea to what you think is pleasant and what you think is unpleasant. For the purposes of these exercises, there is no difference between them. At the end of the practice period, add:

But I am upset because I see a meaningless world.

This important point about there being no real distinction between pleasant and unpleasant echoes the discussion in "The Obstacles to Peace," where Jesus states twice that pleasure and pain are the same (T-19.IV-A.17:10-12; IV-B.12). This distinction holds only if there *were* a hierarchy of illusions. Slowly and inevitably we are being taught there is *not*.

(5:1) What is meaningless is neither good nor bad.

When you say something is good or bad you obviously are assigning it a value. At the beginning of Chapter 24 Jesus says that "to learn this course requires willingness to question every value that you hold" (T-24.in.2:1). The same idea is stated here, although more simply. Having assigned a value to something, I am thereby saying it has meaning. If it has meaning, I must believe it comes from a meaningful thought, because what I perceive outside can only come from a thought that is within.

What, then, is the "meaningful" thought? It is that distinctions are valid, duality is real, and there is a value in esteeming one thing over another. The core of that thought is that I value my individual identity over the oneness of Christ; my life and my world over Heaven. If this is so, distinctions become all important because they establish me as a dualistic being in a dualistic world. That, then, is the world I perceive and stubbornly insist is real.

(5:2) Why, then, should a meaningless world upset you?

If you are affected by anything in the world, you obviously believe this is not a meaningless place. You would believe that because you think *you* are meaningful. To the ego, what is meaningful is what feeds our specialness; what is meaningless is anything irrelevant to it. Therefore, the ego tells us, we need to focus on what serves our special needs. The next lesson will explain why a meaningless world is upsetting.

(5:3) If you could accept the world as meaningless and let the truth be written upon it for you, it would make you indescribably happy.

If we accepted the world as meaningless we

would be saying: "My mind is a blank." That would allow the Holy Spirit's Atonement principle to shine through and have Jesus' love become our only reality. That is the truth, which would make us "indescribably happy." Since this is a self that is no longer identified with the thought system of separation and guilt, what makes us indescribably happy is finally realizing we were wrong and Jesus was right. However, as long as we identify with a separated and special self we will fear the truth that all this is a dream. Thus we are continually choosing *not* to be indescribably happy, because to cite the well-known line, we prefer to be right than happy (T-29.VII.1:9). To be sure, the thought of non-existence would not be very happy making, to say the very least. That is why Jesus continually urges us to take "little steps" (W-pI.193.13:7); otherwise our fear of being "abruptly lifted up and hurled into reality" (T-16.VI.8:1) would be too overwhelming. The happy and gentle dreams of forgiveness are the transition from our nightmare ego world to awakening in God (T-27.VII.13:4-5).

(5:4-6) But because it [the world] is meaningless, you are impelled to write upon it what you would have it be. It is this you see in it. It is this that is meaningless in truth.

Because the world is meaningless in itself I have to give it a meaning. Similarly, because the world is nothing and *I* am nothing, I have to pretend I am something. Indeed, we all think we are something—wonderful or wretched. The ego does not care how the specialness game is played, whether we are God's gift or Satan's gift, as long as we are a special gift. The one thing we do not want is to be nothing. Near the end of "The Anti-Christ" Jesus speaks of the ego as always wanting more of something—it does not matter whether it is more pleasure or more pain, it just wants *more* (T-29.VIII.8:6-12).

We are terrified of the possibility that we do not exist. This needs frequent repeating since it is the underlying assumption to these lessons, not to mention *A Course in Miracles* itself. This thought is the source of the resistance to the Course in general, and to the workbook specifically. I have to pretend I exist, and so quickly make up a thought system that I then project, thereby making up a world—cosmically (as we are all part of the one Son) as well as individually. The point is that we always seek to impose meaning, because otherwise we will be confronted by the inherent meaninglessness of our thinking, not to mention our separate self. This takes place on the metaphysical level of the mind, where it is a question of *existence* or *being*, as discussed earlier. However, on the level of our personal experience, as bodies living in the world, we fear losing our problems and grievances—all of which establish the self we believe ourselves to be, what the end of the text refers to as our face of innocence (T-31.V.1-3).

The real fear, as we shall see in the next lesson, is that if I do not put *my* meaning on the world, Jesus will put *his*. And so I have to beat him to the punch. This helps explain why being really quiet tends to make us anxious, and why we experience difficulty in meditating or praying: If we quiet our minds, Jesus will get there first—"The memory of God comes to the quiet mind" (T-23.I.1:1)—and if he does, our ego is out of business, as is our thought system of separation and specialness. This is why we end up, as we shall see in the next lesson, believing we are in competition with God, and also with Jesus and his course. As a result, before these ideas can penetrate our minds, giving us an opportunity to choose them, we quickly have to substitute our own. Finally, this is also why practically everyone attempts to change *A Course in Miracles* in some way—to write a better or simpler one, for example. We are terrified of what this course really says. Thus, before we would ever let its words and thoughts affect us, we will change them to suit our own special needs.

(5:7) Beneath your words is written the Word of God.

The "Word of God" in *A Course in Miracles* is almost always used as a synonym for the principle of the Atonement, or the Holy Spirit. It can also be understood as forgiveness, the correction for the ego's word of separation, which we chose to keep God's Word hidden.

(5:8-9) The truth upsets you now, but when your words have been erased, you will see His. That is the ultimate purpose of these exercises.

Now you know why you do not want to do these exercises: if your words are erased, then the thought system—the source of your words—is erased as well. Jesus will expand on this in Lesson 14.

The lesson closes with the now familiar expression of Jesus' gentle understanding of our resistance to his teachings:

(6) Three or four times is enough for practicing the idea for today. Nor should the practice periods exceed a minute. You may find even this too long. Terminate the exercises whenever you experience a sense of strain.

No imposition, no bullying, no guilt-inducing demands to be disciplined, let alone spiritual. Who would not have wished for teachers like this when we were growing up?

LESSON 13

A meaningless world engenders fear.

(1) Today's idea is really another form of the preceding one, except that it is more specific as to the emotion aroused. [It is not just that it upsets you, it makes you fearful.] Actually, a meaningless world is impossible. Nothing without meaning exists. However, it does not follow that you will not think you perceive something that has no meaning. On the contrary, you will be particularly likely to think you do perceive it.

This is because you do not want to realize that what you perceive has no meaning. Once again, if what I see out there in the world has no meaning, the thought within me that gave rise to it has no meaning either. Since I *am* my thoughts, it follows that *I* do not have any meaning, which means *I* do not exist. Therefore, rather than realize everything is meaningless, within and without, I will substitute my own meaning. Obviously, if I perceive something I think is out there, which affects me, I have already pronounced it real. And I want to keep the underlying thought real so *I* can continue to be real.

(2:1) Recognition of meaninglessness arouses intense anxiety in all the separated ones.

The anxiety arises because at some level I realize that the meaningless extends to *my* existence. This idea will be returned to very shortly.

(2:2) It represents a situation in which God and the ego "challenge" each other as to whose meaning is to be written in the empty space that meaninglessness provides.

The ego challenges, but God does not; that is why the word is in quotes. To the ego, then, competition is the nature of its relationship with God. An "empty space" exists because the ego is nothing. Yet it believes it must get to the emptiness before God, to claim the Son's identity as its own; thus the perceived competition with the Creator. If my existence as an ego is predicated on the belief in *one or the other*—I exist at God's expense; I killed Him so I can live—I will project that thought and believe He is doing the same thing back to me. This deeply rooted belief is the source of our perception that

people are out to get us, to hurt, abandon, and sabotage us, because we accused ourselves of doing the same to others, and ultimately to God. As Jesus states near the end of the text:

> You never hate your brother for his sins, but only for your own. Whatever form his sins appear to take, it but obscures the fact that you believe them to be yours, and therefore meriting a "just" attack (T-31.III.1:5-6).

(2:3-4) The ego rushes in frantically to establish its own ideas there, fearful that the void may otherwise be used to demonstrate its own impotence and unreality. And on this alone it is correct.

Namely, that it is nothing. The ego knows, as I have explained before, that its power rests in the decision maker, because the ego in and of itself is impotent. To ensure that we never recognize its inherent nothingness and meaninglessness, it seeks to make itself important and powerful through sin, guilt, and fear. If I have sinned against God and destroyed Him, I am certainly important and powerful. This also makes me fearful, but at least I have become something that God notices, which also makes me important.

The most frightening thing of all is to realize God does not even know about us, because then we are literally nothing—impotent and unreal. Thus we want God to pay attention to us, either because we are His most devoted follower or the most wretched sinner. It makes no difference to the ego, as long as God takes notice. Our real fear, of course, is that He knows nothing about us. Somewhere deep inside we know that to be true. But rather than accept its truth, we cover it over with the ego's lies; first with the thoughts of separation—sin, guilt, and fear—and next with a world that reflects those thoughts.

(3:1) It is essential, therefore, that you learn to recognize the meaningless, and accept it without fear.

This acceptance comes from developing a relationship with Jesus or the Holy Spirit that allows you to look at your ego without fear, helping you realize its meaninglessness. If you are fearful or guilty about your ego, or if you embrace it, you obviously believe it is real. Once again, however, if you step back and watch this "oddly assorted procession" go by, you realize it is nothing, understanding its meaning lies in trying to protect you from what *is* meaningful. Finally, since we want that meaningfulness more than anything else—it is our identity as God's Son—we would then realize everything else makes no sense and choose against it.

(3:2) If you are fearful, it is certain that you will endow the world with attributes that it does not possess, and crowd it with images that do not exist.

In this sense we talk about the world as powerful, hostile, threatening, wonderful, peaceful, blissful, holy, etc. These are its attributes; and the "images that do not exist" are everything we see in the world, which are of course the projections of thoughts that do not exist.

(3:3) To the ego illusions are safety devices, as they must also be to you who equate yourself with the ego.

Safety devices are defenses. Sin, guilt, fear, and the world that arises from them are illusions, the purpose of which is to preserve the fundamental illusion that I exist as a separate individual.

And now we go to the blockbuster line in the next paragraph:

(4) The exercises for today, which should be done about three or four times for not more than a minute or so at most each time, are to be practiced in a somewhat different way from the preceding ones. With eyes closed, repeat today's idea to yourself. Then open your eyes, and look about you slowly, saying:

I am looking at a meaningless world.

Repeat this statement to yourself as you look about. Then close your eyes, and conclude with:

A meaningless world engenders fear because I think I am in competition with God.

We thus go from our mind's thoughts to our bodies' perceptions, and then back within. To state it once again, the world is fundamentally meaningless.

Yet we strive to give it meaning, since that ultimately gives meaning to our separated self. Listening to the ego we make up a thought system of *sin, guilt,* and *fear*: Our *sin* of separation leads to the experience of *guilt,* which culminates in the *fearful* belief that we deserve to be punished by a vengeful God, who now is in mortal competition with us for existence; either He survives, or we do, or, as the manual states: *kill or be killed* (M-17.7:11). But the inherent meaninglessness of this constellation of insanity does not preclude its having tremendous power, for we have invested our belief in it. Such investment means we must strive to give it meaning so we can defend against the ego's meaningless thought system, which is the basis for our meaningless identity.

To summarize this important point: When I realize the world is nothing, since it is simply a defense against my mind's thoughts, I am thrown back to these thoughts. If the world is meaningless and I am meaningless, I do not exist, which means God has won. But rather than lose the battle, I strive to give meaning to myself and to the world around me.

Jesus is helping us realize how we project everything onto the world. If we pay careful attention to our perceptions and what we value here, we would realize none of them comes from anything inherent in the world, because there is no world. They are but the result of a need within ourselves to justify and reinforce the spurious fact that we exist.

(5:1-2) You may find it difficult to avoid resistance, in one form or another, to this concluding statement. Whatever form such resistance may take, remind yourself that you are really afraid of such a thought because of the "vengeance" of the "enemy."

The fear is that this is a competition we cannot win—God will be victorious. The terror engendered by such insanity is beyond what we can tolerate. We defend against it by constructing a thought system and then a world, behind which we can hide. Having become identified with this defense that culminates in the body, we *resist* having it taken from us, which exposing its foundation to the truth of the Atonement would surely do. And so we do not think about the wrath of God. That thought, as horrifying as it is, nonetheless protects the individual identity, which in turn defends against our acceptance of the Atonement.

(5:3-4) You are not expected to believe the statement at this point, and will probably dismiss it as preposterous. Note carefully, however, any signs of overt or covert fear which it may arouse.

Obviously, if you are relatively new to *A Course in Miracles*, this statement will make no sense. But Jesus is asking for your vigilance, that you pay careful attention to any anxiety or fear that is within you.

(6) This is our first attempt at stating an explicit cause and effect relationship of a kind which you are very inexperienced in recognizing. Do not dwell on the concluding statement, and try not even to think of it except during the practice periods. That will suffice at present.

The cause and effect connection is between our thoughts—the ego's thought system of sin, guilt, and fear—and the way we perceive the world. In other words, I am fearful *not* because of what is outside me, but because of my thought system, which tells me that survival is between God and me. Note, too, how Jesus does not confront or attack our resistance. He simply and gently reminds us of the truth. This allows us to accept it when *we* are ready, without any pressure or guilt inflicted on us. A wonderful example for all Course students!

LESSON 14

God did not create a meaningless world.

(1) The idea for today is, of course, the reason why a meaningless world is impossible. What God did not create does not exist. And everything that does exist exists as He created it. The world you see has nothing to do with reality. It is of your own making, and it does not exist.

Lines like these are frequently used by students of *A Course in Miracles* as a way to dilute the metaphysics and claim that the Course does *not* say that God did not create the world. Rather they claim that the Course teaches only that God did not create the world *we see*. It is true that the words of some statements say just that, but only because Jesus is teaching us to pay careful attention to what we perceive. He makes it abundantly clear both in the workbook, as well as many, many other places in the rest of the material that God could not have created the world because it is His opposite. (See, for example, T-4.I.11; T-29.VI.2:7-10; W-pI.132.4-6; W-pI.152.5-7; C-4.1.) Everything in the world of specifics and form changes and dies. Such a world is outside God, and therefore could not exist.

The very fact that we *perceive* the world means it is unreal, and also that we are unreal. Again, this does not mean just the world we see. Students sometimes mistakenly think this means, for example, that God did not create the cancer I am perceiving. The very fact that I see a world at all is saying there is a reality outside God; if I perceive a world, there must be a perceiver and a perceived, subject and object, observer and observed, which means we are rooted in duality. God can create only like Himself, which means a Being or Spirit of perfect Oneness and Love, changeless and eternal. In other words, what God did not create does not exist, and everything that does exist, exists as He created it—the state of Heaven.

(2) The exercises for today are to be practiced with eyes closed throughout. The mind-searching period should be short, a minute at most. Do not have more than three practice periods with today's idea unless you find them comfortable. If you do, it will be because you really understand what they are for.

Again, Jesus exerts no pressure on us. The fourth sentence is an interesting one, because our comfort can also be due to our *not* understanding, as we are so afraid of this very purpose of retraining our minds, which these periods of mind searching will bring about. In this instance our "comfort" would be a spurious one, which is not Jesus' point here.

(3:1) The idea for today is another step in learning to let go the thoughts that you have written on the world, and see the Word of God in their place.

Jesus is helping us understand there is a specific motivation involved in holding onto our thoughts. They do not come and go as if by magic, a phrase used later (W-pI.158.4:1); they do not just appear. For example, when I am trying to be quiet in order to meditate and pray, and all of a sudden extraneous, distracting thoughts arise, they do not come out of nowhere. They come because I am afraid of the love and peace that arise in my mind if I am quiet. I therefore quickly have to substitute *my* thoughts instead of Jesus' thoughts, my experience of specialness rather than the experience of his love.

What is important and clearly implied here is that there is a specific motivation for the way I perceive the world and the thoughts that give rise to it. If I can release those thoughts, which occurs when I ask Jesus for help in looking at them, they will disappear. What is left is the Word of God, which, as defined earlier, is the principle of the Atonement that says that the separation never happened.

(3:2-3) The early steps in this exchange, which can truly be called salvation, can be quite difficult and even quite painful. Some of them will lead you directly into fear.

This is the first time Jesus makes such a statement in the lessons. More will follow, and they are found throughout the text and manual as well—forgiveness is a difficult process, and cannot but arouse tremendous fear (e.g., T-27.VII.13:3-5; W-pI.196.10; M-4.I-A.3-5,7). There is almost certainly something wrong if you do not struggle with this issue; if you do not fight against forgiveness, become terrified or bored with it, or even want to throw the book away. If you never experience anything like this discomfort, it almost always means you are not paying careful attention to what is being said.

A Course in Miracles says frightened people can be vicious (T-3.I.4:2). These lessons have to arouse anxiety because they challenge not only the way you perceive something outside you, but challenge your basic identity. That is what is referred to in Lesson 13 when Jesus says: "Recognition of meaninglessness arouses intense anxiety in all the separated ones." Anyone who believes he is a separated and autonomous being will experience anxiety with these thoughts. Jesus is thus telling you it is all right if you find this difficult, fear-inducing, and are therefore resistant.

These statements are extremely important, because probably the biggest mistake people make with *A Course in Miracles* is to deny the ego and the difficulty inherent in looking at it, thereby letting it go. Everyone wants to smooth over the process and "make nice," because no one really wants to deal with the full implications of these thoughts. These are, again, that you literally do not exist. Recall the line I quoted earlier (T-28.I.1:6)—if the world were over long ago and you are part of the world, *you* were over long ago. Who, then, is the *you* that is thinking and feeling, and doing these exercises? The answer to this question leads "directly into fear."

(3:4-6) You will not be left there. You will go far beyond it. Our direction is toward perfect safety and perfect peace.

Jesus wants you to understand that the anxiety, terror, resistance, and difficulty are part of a longer process, and there is Someone with you Who will lead you through it. As we have seen, he talks about the Holy Spirit being there to lead you through seeming terror. He will lead you through the circle of fear to the Love of God that is on the other side (T-18.IX.3). That is why it is essential to cultivate a relationship with Jesus or the Holy Spirit: Someone within you, some non-ego thought that can lead you through the process. If you try to look at your ego without Him, you will either be thrown into terror or denial, believing that everything is really wonderful. Jesus is telling you, "Yes, there will be

difficulty and resistance and fear, but I will lead you through it."

Paragraphs 4 and 5 caution against being compulsive about the exercises, at the same time urging us *not* to exclude anything from our perceptual field. Needless to say, this is easier said than done, which is why Jesus makes non-exclusivity in our practice a central theme in this first part of his mind-training program for us:

(4-5) With eyes closed, think of all the horrors in the world that cross your mind. Name each one as it occurs to you, and then deny its reality. God did not create it, and so it is not real. Say, for example:

> *God did not create that war, and so it is not real.*
> *God did not create that airplane crash, and so it is not real.*
> *God did not create that disaster [specify], and so it is not real.*

Suitable subjects for the application of today's idea also include anything you are afraid might happen to you, or to anyone about whom you are concerned. In each case, name the "disaster" quite specifically. Do not use general terms. For example, do not say, "God did not create illness," but, "God did not create cancer," or heart attacks, or whatever may arouse fear in you.

Jesus wants us to be sure to include both personal and collective horrors, reflecting the importance of recognizing there is no hierarchy of illusions.

Now to paragraph 6:

(6:1) This is your personal repertory of horrors at which you are looking.

Jesus is focusing on the negative. He could just as easily have focused on positive things, too. Thus, God not only did not create cancer, He did not create a healthy body either; He did not create an airplane crash; but he also did not create a rocket ship that lands safely on the moon.

(6:2-8) These things are part of the world you see. Some of them are shared illusions, and others are part of your personal hell. It does not matter. What God did not create can only be in your own mind apart from His. Therefore, it has no meaning. In recognition of this fact, conclude the practice periods by repeating today's idea:

God did not create a meaningless world.

Anything you think that has to do with duality, separation, individuality, or specialness is not in God's Mind, because His is only perfect Oneness and Love, in which there is no separation at all. Therefore, if it is not in His Mind, it can have no meaning and certainly does not exist. Note the term "shared illusions." As part of the one Sonship—the one mind—we agree on certain things that are perceived in the physical world: size, shape, color, etc. Yet the fact they are shared does not make them real. These are *shared illusions*: "Nothing so blinding as perception of form" (T-22.III.6:7), the text states, an important statement to which we shall frequently return. Only God's knowledge is true, in contrast with the ego's illusory world of perception.

(7) The idea for today can, of course, be applied to anything that disturbs you during the day, aside from the practice periods. Be very specific in applying it. Say:

> ***God did not create a meaningless world. He did not create [specify the situation which is disturbing you], and so it is not real.***

You can see how Jesus is repeatedly asking us in these lessons to apply his teachings *very specifically* to our everyday lives. Not doing so ensures they will never truly be learned, which of course is always the temptation of our egos. Gently, he guides us in learning the process of bringing the illusions of our specific world of *form* to the *content* of his non-specific truth of forgiveness.

****

In these last seven lessons, following upon the first group of seven, we can observe Jesus building one lesson or idea upon another. He leads us from understanding that the meaninglessness of the world we perceive is coming from the meaninglessness of the world we made real in our minds, to understanding that at the core of these meaningless thoughts is the most terrible thought of all: God is in competition with us and will most certainly destroy us. It is important to understand, even though it is not stated here, that that thought, too, is a defense. It says I exist, am important, and have the power to

make God angry, making Him think as insanely as I, as the text explains in this telling passage from "The Laws of Chaos":

> Think what this seems to do to the relationship between the Father and the Son. Now it appears that They can never be One again. For One must always be condemned, and by the Other. Now are They different, and enemies. And Their relationship is one of opposition, just as the separate aspects of the Son meet only to conflict but not to join. One becomes weak, the other strong by his defeat. And fear of God and of each other now appears as sensible, made real by what the Son of God has done both to himself and his Creator.... Here is a principle that would define what the Creator of reality must be; what He must think and what He must believe; and how He must respond, believing it. It is not seen as even necessary that He be asked about the truth of what has been established for His belief. His Son can tell Him this, and He has but the choice whether to take his word for it or be mistaken.... For if God cannot be mistaken, He must accept His Son's belief in what he is, and hate him for it (T-23.II.5; 6:2-4,6).

God now reacts as psychotically as I, mirroring my vicious and sinful vengeance in His Own:

> If this were so [the reality of sin], would Heaven be opposed by its own opposite, as real as it. Then would God's Will be split in two, and all creation be subjected to the laws of two opposing powers, until God becomes impatient, splits the world apart, and relegates attack unto Himself. Thus has He lost His Mind, proclaiming sin has taken His reality from Him and brought His Love at last to vengeance's heels (T-26.VII.7:3-5).

Imagine the power this gives me! Moreover, if I am powerful enough to force God to react to me, I must exist. Recognizing the ultimate meaninglessness of that thought engenders my anxiety.

Thus, the anxiety over the anticipated vengeance from God is a defense against the real anxiety, which is that I do not exist at all. I can live very well with the thought that God wants to kill me. It may not make me happy, but I know how to deal with that—I can establish a religion: make bargains with God, perform rituals to appease His wrath, and project responsibility onto non-believers in justified judgment for their heresies. I do not, however, know how to deal with the thought I do not exist, except to deny it and quickly make up something to take its place.

LESSON 15

My thoughts are images that I have made.

(1:1) It is because the thoughts you think you think appear as images that you do not recognize them as nothing.

The "images" are what we perceive in the world outside us. The ego takes our thoughts of separation—sin, guilt, and fear—and projects them so that we "see" them in the world, rather than accepting their presence within. Thus, we perceive these thoughts as images of a person, room, coat hanger, clock, and everything else. We can have an image of a vengeful or benevolent God, a happy or miserable world, but all images of specific forms are projections of our separation thoughts. Because we believe we see something outside, we believe that what we see is real.

This process, then, becomes the ego's ultimate line of defense. Since we believe that the world outside is real, we never think about the fact that the images we perceive outside are coming from our inner thoughts, and if we do not know they are coming from our thoughts, there is no way we can realize that the thoughts themselves are really nothing. The entire thought system of the ego, and all the specific thoughts associated with it, are *nothing*—a defense against the reality of Who we are, our true Identity as Christ.

The phrase "the thoughts you think you think" is extremely important. We actually think we are thinking, as we discussed in the earlier lessons. In fact, we could say that the fundamental ego problem is that we *think*—not *what* we think so much as the fact that we think we *can* think (cf., again, T-31.V.14:3-4). We believe our thoughts *are* our thoughts. In other words, we believe they belong to *us,* and we do not realize that the only true Thought is the Thought of our Identity as Christ, which is one with God's Thought.

Thus, the fact that we believe we can think presupposes that we have an autonomous mind or self that is outside and independent of God. Once again you can see how, even though the language of these early lessons is simple, it is a deceptive simplicity in that it covertly reveals the Course's metaphysical foundation.

(1:2-6) You think you think them [your thoughts], **and so you think you see them. This is how your "seeing" was made. This is the function you have given your body's eyes. It is not seeing. It is image making.**

Jesus puts "seeing" in quotes because this is really not seeing. Since we literally see nothing, how could we see anything? The ego has us substitute for the magnitude of our Identity as Christ the littleness of our autonomous individuality, which is what we cherish above all else. In order to have us keep this individuality intact, the ego then has us identify it with the sin of separating from God. This leads to guilt, which means we believe we deserve to be punished. This is the competition with God discussed in Lesson 13.

This constellation of separation and sin is so terrifying that we deny and project it out in order to forget it, which itself protects the thought of individuality. We are then left with the images we have made, but with no recollection of how we made them. At that point there is absolutely no hope for correction. Again, by "image making" Jesus means that we literally make up an image of our own thoughts. Since our thoughts are nothing, the images that come from them must also be nothing.

(1:7) It takes the place of seeing, replacing vision with illusions.

Rather than sharing Christ's or the Holy Spirit's vision, based on the Atonement thought that says the separation never happened, the ego replaces that vision or thought with its own. Thus we first make these ego thoughts real in our minds, and then project them out and "see" them as real things outside us. Jesus teaches us in this lesson that the images we perceive outside ourselves are but the reflections or shadows of the thoughts we have made real within.

He, of course, is not really talking about images of a clock, waste paper basket, or pencil. His ultimate purpose is to have us realize that the most frightening aspect of this process is the image we have made of ourselves—separated, autonomous beings, in control of our lives. This image of ourselves comes from a thought, too—wanting to be separate—and that is why, as I have been saying, if you really pay attention to these lessons they should strike terror in your heart, for they literally say you do not exist. You thus want to explore more and more how frightening these thoughts are, trying to identify how you defend against them. This is extremely important—watch how you defend against what these lessons are teaching you.

(2:1) This introductory idea to the process of image making that you call seeing will not have much meaning for you.

Jesus is once again making a mild understatement. The idea will not have much meaning for us because we do not want to accept what it is saying. One of the more important lines of defense that the ego uses is to prevent our understanding what Jesus is really saying here. That is why he says, again, this will probably not have much meaning for you. He does not even say "probably." He says it *will not* have much meaning for you, and that is because we are defending against that very meaning as a means of defending our individual identity.

(2:2-4) You will begin to understand it when you have seen little edges of light around the same familiar objects which you see now. That is the beginning of real vision. You can be certain that real vision will come quickly when this has occurred.

In my earlier audio set, "The Workbook of *A Course in Miracles*: Its Place in the Curriculum— Theory and Practice," I went into this passage in depth.* Rather than repeat that here, let me say briefly that Jesus is not talking about *literally* seeing edges of light around objects. This was originally meant for a friend of Helen and Bill's. You will do much better to understand this statement in terms of the *content*. When Jesus says you will see "little edges of light" around objects, he is really talking about the light of understanding or vision that is coming to you. In other words, you will understand that the objects are images you made as projections of the thoughts of separation you do not want to look at in your mind. If you try to take this literally you will guiltily feel yourself to be a failure when you do not see "little edges of light" around objects, not to mention glorifying those who claim they do.

(3:1-4) As we go along, you may have many "light episodes." They may take many different forms, some of them quite unexpected. Do not be afraid of them. They are signs that you are opening your eyes at last.

If you do have perceptions of light, all well and good, but Jesus is saying that what would really instill fear in you is your sudden recognition that this thing you are looking at is not there at all. When suddenly a "light" goes on in your mind and you realize: "My God! This is what Jesus is talking about," and you realize that if this waste paper basket is not really there, being a projection of a thought, what about those who believe they are perceiving the waste paper basket? Again, that recognition is the source of fear. No one really cares if a waste paper basket is there or not, but you *do* care whether *you* are there or not.

(3:5-7) They will not persist, because they merely symbolize true perception, and they are not related to knowledge. These exercises will not reveal knowledge to you. But they will prepare the way to it.

In many places, especially in the text, Jesus makes it clear that the goal of *A Course in Miracles* is not Heaven, knowledge, or love (T-in.1:6-7; T-8.in.1:1-2), but the correction of the ego's false perception, which would be true perception or vision, the peace that forgiveness or the miracle brings about.

Jesus also makes the same point in the text that he does here in 3:5: "...visions, however holy, do not last" (T-3.III.4:6). That is because all forms, however holy their content, are still part of the illusion of separation. Therefore they but *reflect* truth, and are not the truth itself.

The remaining two paragraphs reiterate the need to be non-selective yet not compulsive, as well as emphasizing the crucial idea of *specific* application whenever we find ourselves tempted to be upset. These emphases are the *content* behind the exercises' *form*:

(4-5) In practicing the idea for today, repeat it first to yourself, and then apply it to whatever

---

* An edited transcript of this workshop is presented in the Appendix in Volume One.

you see around you, using its name and letting your eyes rest on it as you say:

This ___ is an image that I have made.
That ___ is an image that I have made.

It is not necessary to include a large number of specific subjects for the application of today's idea. It is necessary, however, to continue to look at each subject while you repeat the idea to yourself. The idea should be repeated quite slowly each time.

Although you will obviously not be able to apply the idea to very many things during the minute or so of practice that is recommended, try to make the selection as random as possible. Less than a minute will do for the practice periods, if you begin to feel uneasy. Do not have more than three application periods for today's idea unless you feel completely comfortable with it, and do not exceed four. However, the idea can be applied as needed throughout the day.

Being faithful to the specifics of the daily exercises allows us to generalize the lesson of the inherent sameness of all things to each and every experience of our lives. Such generalization is the heart of forgiveness, and the key to achieving the peace that is Jesus' goal for us.

LESSON 16

I have no neutral thoughts.

This idea is an attempt to correct the mistaken belief that our thoughts have no power. On one level it is true they have no power, because they cannot change Heaven nor can they destroy God. Within the dream, however, which is what Jesus is speaking about here, our thoughts have tremendous power. Just imagine what our thoughts are capable of doing: literally make up a physical universe, and a physical and psychological self that dwells within it; this self then actually believes it exists in the universe. That is Jesus' point in the first section of Chapter 31, "The Simplicity of Salvation," when he urges us not to underestimate the power of our learning skill. Although that was a message originally meant for Helen Schucman, in response to her constant complaints, Jesus is saying to each of us: "Do not tell me you cannot learn this course. Do not tell me your mind and its thoughts have no power. Look at what your learning *is* capable of doing." Here are *his* very clear words:

> What you have taught yourself is such a giant learning feat it is indeed incredible. But you accomplished it because you wanted to, and did not pause in diligence to judge it hard to learn or too complex to grasp.
>
> No one who understands what you have learned, how carefully you learned it, and the pains to which you went to practice and repeat the lessons endlessly, in every form you could conceive of them, could ever doubt the power of your learning skill. There is no greater power in the world. The world was made by it, and even now depends on nothing else. The lessons you have taught yourself have been so overlearned and fixed they rise like heavy curtains to obscure the simple and the obvious. Say not you cannot learn them. For your power to learn is strong enough to teach you that your will is not your own, your thoughts do not belong to you, and even you are someone else.
>
> Who could maintain that lessons such as these are easy? Yet you have learned more than this. You have continued, taking every step, however difficult, without complaint, until a world was built that suited you. And

every lesson that makes up the world arises from the first accomplishment of learning; an enormity so great the Holy Spirit's Voice seems small and still before its magnitude. The world began with one strange lesson, powerful enough to render God forgotten, and His Son an alien to himself, in exile from the home where God Himself established him. You who have taught yourself the Son of God is guilty, say not that you cannot learn the simple things salvation teaches you! (T-31.I.2:7–4:6)

These are strong words, but upon their truth rests *A Course in Miracles*. Throughout the text, as well as at the heart of these lessons, is Jesus' overriding emphasis on the power of our minds to choose against God, which fact alone contains the promise of salvation. The mind that housed the separation thought is the *only* power in the universe that can save itself. And yet it has been this power that the ego has seemingly and successfully stifled and silenced by its plan to make a world and body, rendering the Son of God mindless. Jesus' purpose in *A Course in Miracles* is simple: restore to our awareness the power of our minds, that we may finally recognize our mistake, where it was made, and *choose again*.

Thus, this lesson reminds us that our thoughts are tremendously powerful. Indeed, that is the problem. We believe—within the dream—that these thoughts have destroyed God, Heaven, and the Holy Spirit as well. We gave this belief such power—the power of guilt—that we had to deny the thoughts, project them out and make up a world, all as a defense against what the ego told us: the tremendous power of our minds destroyed Heaven. That is why guilt is such a central concept in *A Course in Miracles*, for it tells us we have committed the unmentionable sin: destroying God and His Love. Before we can understand these thoughts are literally nothing and have had no effects, we first must get in touch with the power these thoughts are having in our dreams. That is the purpose of this lesson.

(1:1-2) The idea for today is a beginning step in

dispelling the belief that your thoughts have no effect. Everything you see is the result of your thoughts.

You should underline in multi-colors "Everything you see is the result of your thoughts"! This important sentence needs to be understood on two levels, as it means everything you see in terms of *form*, but also in terms of *interpretation.* Both are the "result of your thoughts." Hence, on one level, since we believe we separated from God, we see all kinds of separate things: people, chairs, pencils, clocks, walls, etc. We see them as separate objects because they are the direct result, or the shadow, of our thoughts of separation.

On another level and even more importantly, for the purposes of *A Course in Miracles* and the workbook lessons specifically, we understand that it is not only *what* we see, but *how* we see it. Jesus makes it very clear in the text and manual that perception is interpretation (e.g., T-3.III.2:3; T-11.VI.2:5-6; T-21.in.1-2; M-8.1-4; M-17.4:1-2). We cannot separate our perception of "objective reality" from our interpretation of it, because they are one and the same. Again, it is not only *what* we see, but *how* we see it.

As Jesus explains in many other places, especially in the text, if you begin with guilty thoughts—and guilt is rooted in our belief we betrayed Heaven and sabotaged God's plan of creation, and thus demands punishment—those are the thoughts with which we will look out, the lens through which we look on everything. We will therefore see not only a separated world, but a separated world that will punish and betray us; a world in which there is no hope but only the despair of certain death. Thus we read, for example:

> The certain outcome of the lesson that God's Son is guilty is the world you see. It is a world of terror and despair. Nor is there hope of happiness in it. There is no plan for safety you can make that ever will succeed. There is no joy that you can seek for here and hope to find (T-31.I.7:4-8).

Further, as we monitor our perceptions and find ourselves becoming angry, anxious, or depressed, the cause will always be an interpretation of something we believe is external to us. The interpretation will directly follow from our secret thoughts, and if we accuse ourselves of betraying God, which is

everyone's secret sin, we must and will see betrayal all around us.

(1:3-7) There is no exception to this fact. Thoughts are not big or little; powerful or weak. They are merely true or false. Those that are true create their own likeness. Those that are false make theirs.

The true thoughts that "create their own likeness" are the Thoughts of God—truth, love, spirit, etc.—which constitute Heaven. The ego's false thoughts are of separation—guilt, betrayal, murder, death, suffering, etc.—and they will make their own likenesses as well. If these are our thoughts, we will then perceive a world in which all these things happen—*to us.*

As we proceed through these early lessons it will become increasingly clear that Jesus is trying to establish for us the causal connection between our thoughts and what we perceive: Our thoughts determine the world we see; ultimately, then, our minds are the *cause* and the world the *effect.*

(2:1) There is no more self-contradictory concept than that of "idle thoughts."

Our thoughts cannot be "idle," as in the popular expression, because they have the power either to create reality, our function in Heaven, or to make illusions, at least in our dreams. Inherent in the power to make illusions is the power to forget that we made them—the power of denial. When we forget we made them, we believe what we perceive outside is fact. That is why we shall never countenance anyone telling us that what we perceive is *not* what we perceive. We are so sure we are right about what we perceive in the world because we are so sure we exist. Since the world comes from that thought of separate existence, we have the equal certainty that the world exists the way we made it up and the way that we see it. Consequently, we would not at all be inclined to question our perceptions of ourselves and the world.

(2:2-4) What gives rise to the perception of a whole world can hardly be called idle. Every thought you have contributes to truth or to illusion; either it extends the truth or it multiplies illusions. You can indeed multiply nothing, but you will not extend it by doing so.

What is interesting here is that Jesus specifically says *perception* of a world. He is making the distinction that thoughts do not give rise to a world, but to a *perception* of a world. He does not always make such distinctions, but he does here. He is essentially saying there is no world out there.

We are free within our dream to see whatever it is we want to see, as many times over as we want to see it. But that does not make it real. *Extension* is a term in *A Course in Miracles* that is almost always associated with the Holy Spirit, and the Holy Spirit cannot extend nothing. In our insanity, however, we believe we can, and multiply illusions as well. Yet in truth they are all nothing. One times zero is the same as a thousand times zero.

(3:1-2) Besides your recognizing that thoughts are never idle, salvation requires that you also recognize that every thought you have brings either peace or war; either love or fear. A neutral result is impossible because a neutral thought is impossible.

In the next lesson Jesus will develop this even further by saying that what we see outside is not neutral because what we think inside is not neutral either. Jesus is thus telling us that what is important for salvation is recognizing the power of our thoughts—only within our dream, of course—and that there are only two thoughts in the split mind: the ego's, which leads to war or fear, and the Holy Spirit's, which leads to peace or love.

Therefore Jesus tells us first that our thoughts are not idle and are not neutral. Then he says there are only two thoughts. That makes it very simple, because our perceptions and interpretations can become quite complicated. For instance, we believe, as we shall see presently, that there are gradations of anger, such as "a slight twinge of annoyance" or "intense fury" (W-pI.21.2:5). In truth they are the same, because they come from one thought of separation. This is what makes everything so simple; not easy, but simple because everything is recognized as the same.

(3:3-4) There is such a temptation to dismiss fear thoughts as unimportant, trivial and not worth bothering about that it is essential you recognize them all as equally destructive, but equally unreal. We will practice this idea in many forms before you really understand it.

This is aimed at the "blissninnies" who say that God and love are truth, and everything else trivial and unimportant, not worth bothering about because it is an illusion. From the point of view of Heaven this is indeed the case, but in this world it is *not* so, and that is why Jesus says it is "a temptation to dismiss fear thoughts as unimportant." We try to treat them as unimportant, telling ourselves that since *A Course in Miracles* teaches these thoughts are not real we do not have to pay attention to them. We then cover them with a blissninny smile and see only love and calls for love, wherein all will reach home as one happy chorus that sings a hymn of joy, and on and on and on, *ad nauseam*. However, we are not aware that we have dismissed the thought that we have destroyed Heaven. Within our deluded minds that is hardly trivial and unimportant, and so it cannot be denied if we are truly to let it go.

That is why Jesus says "it is essential that you recognize them all as equally destructive, but equally unreal." Before you can see them as equally unreal, you first have to realize their destructive nature. In the text Jesus says that "what is not love is murder" (T-23.IV.1:10), and that love without ambivalence is impossible in this world (T-4.III.4:6). If you add two and two, you get four: If love is not possible in this world, and what is not love is murder, then all thoughts in this world are murderous and equally destructive, whether a thought is a mild twinge of annoyance or a thought of outright fury that says: "I want to destroy you." We clearly are talking only about what goes on in the wrong mind, but within that wrong mind all our thoughts are "equally destructive"—there is no hierarchy of illusions, as we have already observed.

This one paragraph is extremely important. You should read it very carefully and see how, even though you may not think of yourself as a blissninny, it is tempting to fall into the trap of dismissing your ego thoughts. Jesus certainly is not telling us to obsess about the ego or make its thoughts into a big deal; after all, they *are* inherently unreal. But it cannot be said often enough that before you can dismiss these thoughts as unreal, you must first look at what they are. This point is strongly and often emphasized in the text where, for example, Jesus says:

> No one can escape from illusions unless he looks at them, for not looking is the way they

are protected. There is no need to shrink from illusions, for they cannot be dangerous. We are ready to look more closely at the ego's thought system because together we have the lamp that will dispel it.... We must look first at this to see beyond it, since you have made it real. We will undo this error quietly together, and then look beyond it to truth (T-11.V.1:1-3,5-6).

The next paragraph is about mind searching, a central theme throughout *A Course in Miracles*. This term occurs in Jesus' instructions to us in almost all these early lessons, where he accentuates the importance of looking within our minds at our thoughts. Again, if we are not aware of what is there, how can we bring them to him for help and for correction?

(4) In applying the idea for today, search your mind for a minute or so with eyes closed, and actively seek not to overlook any "little" thought that may tend to elude the search. This is quite difficult until you get used to it. You will find that it is still hard for you not to make artificial distinctions. Every thought that occurs to you, regardless of the qualities that you assign to it, is a suitable subject for applying today's idea.

This is yet another example of Jesus teaching us there is no order of difficulty in miracles. A miracle undoes problems regardless of their form, because they are all the same. We must realize that even our seemingly unimportant thoughts conceal the enormity of the ego thought system, as do the so-called major thoughts. "Artificial distinctions" would be deciding, for example, that one thing is important, another is not; or that this little annoyance is not important, but the grievance I hold against this person really is.

The last two paragraphs of this lesson repeat the same gentle instructions we have been seeing in the lessons so far, indicating once more the need for us to apply the idea for the day to each instance of discomfort we experience:

(5-6) In the practice periods, first repeat the idea to yourself, and then as each one crosses your mind hold it in awareness while you tell yourself:

> *This thought about ___ is not a neutral thought.*
> *That thought about ___ is not a neutral thought.*

As usual, use today's idea whenever you are aware of a particular thought that arouses uneasiness. The following form is suggested for this purpose:

> *This thought about ___ is not a neutral thought, because I have no neutral thoughts.*

Four or five practice periods are recommended, if you find them relatively effortless. If strain is experienced, three will be enough. The length of the exercise period should also be reduced if there is discomfort.

We are thus gently and kindly trained in the healing process of looking at our thoughts, especially learning to become aware of those that produce uneasiness. We most likely had not allowed ourselves to feel discomfort, let alone recognize its source of guilt in our minds.

LESSON 17

I see no neutral things.

This follows directly from "I have no neutral thoughts." We find here the same pattern seen in the earlier lessons, where Jesus goes back and forth between our thoughts and what we perceive, trying to help us understand they are the same. His purpose is to cultivate in us a vigilance in watching how we think, realizing that nothing we think, perceive, or interpret as the truth is correct. This takes great humility. The ego's arrogance seeks to cover the fear of realizing we are wrong about absolutely everything, which ultimately includes ourselves.

Any time you see an enemy "out there," or believe someone has the power to victimize, betray, or hurt you, you are saying you are right and Jesus is wrong; you are right because you can see and feel the attack, and have the evidence to prove it. However, you are not aware that *you* planted the evidence so you could find it. What you see is what you *want* to see, and so you put the evidence there and say: "See! My thoughts are *not* the problem. In fact, my thoughts are nothing. The problem is out there. That is the problem." And almost always there is some special person that is the focus of your problem.

These lessons attempt to train your mind to think this way all the time, so that you automatically translate what you perceive outside into an inner thought. It does not matter so much with coat hangers or waste paper baskets, but it does matter with the important relationships in your life. It also matters with the *un*important ones, but there are always special people that take center stage. Remember, you see outside what you put there because you *want* to see it in the *body,* not the *mind,* thereby saying: "My thoughts are unimportant because what I see is the fact." Thus you must first realize the *fact* is what you think. When you can look at that thought with Jesus, you will finally realize it is not a fact at all. As the text says, God is the only Fact (T-3.I.8:2).

(1:1) This idea ["I see no neutral things"] **is another step in the direction of identifying cause and effect as it really operates in the world.**

The thoughts in our minds are the *cause,* and our perceptions are the *effect.* This is another way of expressing the important principle we cited in the first paragraph of commentary in Lesson 8 above: "Projection makes perception." I first choose my teacher, the ego or Holy Spirit, and that choice determines the thought system with which I identify: separation or forgiveness. I have made it real, because that is what I perceive within me (the *cause*) and, once projected, I perceive its manifestations all around me (the *effects*).

(1:2-3) You see no neutral things because you have no neutral thoughts. It is always the thought that comes first, despite the temptation to believe that it is the other way around.

We can most likely attest to the fact, even though we have read these lines both here and in the text, and on some level believe they are true, that our daily lives do not reflect this understanding at all. We react to what is external, forgetting that what we are really reacting to is our having pushed Jesus away again, and then identifying with the ego's thought system of guilt. We quickly forget this "fact," project the guilt from our minds and see it in people, events, and things—all threatening to hurt us and take away our peace.

The purpose of these lessons and exercises is to practice seeing how we do *not* live this way; how we react to what is outside us. Remember, what is outside not only includes other people's bodies, but our own as well, for *outside* refers to what is outside our *minds,* not bodies. The point again is that we are not reacting to the world, but to our minds' decision. Moreover, it is important to remember that the decision for the ego is made up, for we react to the ego's illusory thought system that tells us how worthless, sinful, and wretched we are—"the home of evil, darkness and sin" as Lesson 93 states (1:1). This is the insanity we have made real and never challenge. Thus we are learning that not only is the world a defense, but so is our thought system of separation. The reality *beyond* both the world and the thoughts that made it is the Love of God—the only truth.

(1:4) This is not the way the world thinks, but you must learn that it is the way you think.

Jesus is making it unmistakably clear that this causal connection between mind and body is something we have to learn, as he also makes clear in the other lessons, and that it takes tremendous vigilance and practice because our way of life is set up in the opposite way. We have been programmed to think that it is the world that impinges on us, and that the bad guys are out there in the world. Yet Jesus is saying to us here: "This is something you are not going to understand right away, for it requires much practice. I am introducing it to you now for the first time, but we will go over it again and again." Jesus is therefore emphasizing that we are the student and he our teacher, and whenever we have difficulty with the text, workbook, or manual, it is simply because we have become afraid of what he is teaching us.

(1:5) If it were not so, perception would have no cause, and would itself be the cause of reality.

If it were correct that the world determines what we think, then perception would be a reality and a *cause*; namely, the objects of our perception would cause us to think and feel in certain ways. The truth, however, is that perception is the *effect*, caused by our thoughts. Always keep in mind that *projection makes perception.* If perception has no cause but is a reality independent of our thoughts, then it simply exists and there is nothing we can do about it. This, of course, describes the condition of practically everyone in the world. That is why there is no hope once we have bought into the ego thought system: we cannot change what is. If our perceptions are not effects caused by our thoughts, then they must be real. Thus do death, evil, war, and suffering become reality, and there is nothing we can do except get through our lives as best we can. Jesus, therefore, teaches that what is out there—the world and body, suffering and death—is an *effect*, and the *cause* rests within our minds. Once we identify the cause we can do something about it. Otherwise, again, it is a hopeless situation.

And then this final comment about perception:

(1:6) In view of its highly variable nature, this is hardly likely.

Perception, obviously, is highly variable. We can see that even within ourselves. A perception we had of someone one day, when we could forgive, the next day becomes quite different. Depending on our inner state—choosing the ego or the Holy Spirit as our teacher—we either perceive the world through the eyes of judgment and hate, or through forgiveness.

The exercise follows, continuing the training of our minds to understand the relationship between our thoughts and our perceptions:

(2) In applying today's idea, say to yourself, with eyes open:

I see no neutral things because I have no neutral thoughts.

Then look about you, resting your glance on each thing you note long enough to say:

I do not see a neutral ___ , because my thoughts about ___ are not neutral.

For example, you might say:

I do not see a neutral wall, because my thoughts about walls are not neutral.
I do not see a neutral body, because my thoughts about bodies are not neutral.

Jesus' instructions for the exercises now focus on his ongoing refutation of the ego's first law of chaos: the hierarchy of illusions:

(3) As usual, it is essential to make no distinctions between what you believe to be animate or inanimate; pleasant or unpleasant. Regardless of what you may believe, you do not see anything that is really alive or really joyous. That is because you are unaware as yet of any thought that is really true, and therefore really happy.

There is no animate or inanimate, because nothing here is alive. As we recall, one of the basic categories we are taught from grade school on up is that there are living things that can be categorized as animate, part of "the great chain of being," and non-living things that can be categorized as inanimate, like wood, metal, etc. Yet both categories are illusory, as we see in "The Laws of Chaos" section, which categorically states "there is no life outside of Heaven" (T-23.II.19:1). Jesus means that quite literally.

Real life and real joy are found only by taking Jesus' hand and identifying with his thought system of forgiveness. It is joyful because it returns us to our real life as part of God, the only joy. However, we yet must learn how to attain this life and joy, and these exercises, along with the gentle instruction we find in this next paragraph, are among the means Jesus employs to fulfil his pedagogical purpose:

(4) Three or four specific practice periods are recommended, and no less than three are required for maximum benefit, even if you experience resistance. However, if you do, the length of the practice period may be reduced to less than the minute or so that is otherwise recommended.

Mention of our resistance is Jesus' helpful way of reminding us not to feel guilty. He would not bring it up as frequently as he does if he were not expecting us to be fearful of his teaching, and thus seek to resist it. Learning to accept this resistance is an essential step toward letting it go.

LESSON 18

I am not alone in experiencing the effects of my seeing.

I noted in my Prelude that in the workbook, as well as in the text, Jesus often develops a specific theme, sets it down, introduces a related theme, sets that one down and returns to the previous one. We see here the introduction of the idea that minds are joined, a theme central to *A Course in Miracles*—the oneness of God's Son and, specifically here, the oneness of God's Son in his separated state.

(1) The idea for today is another step in learning that the thoughts which give rise to what you see are never neutral or unimportant. It also emphasizes the idea that minds are joined, which will be given increasing stress later on.

Just as things in the world are different projections of the one thought of separation, so are the seemingly different people but part of the one separated Son. This means that all split minds are joined, because they come from one thought.

Before the fragmentation occurred, a topic discussed at the beginning of Chapter 18 in the text, there was only one error or thought, just as in Heaven there is only one Son. Minds are joined as one, because there is only the Mind of Christ, which is One, and at one with the Mind of God. Much more importantly for our purposes, however, is the principle that all *split minds* are joined, too. We are but fragmented perceptions and images that we—our decision-making minds, outside time and space—made so we would believe that separation is reality. In truth, all the seemingly separated fragments of God's Son, which we usually think of as homo sapiens, but actually include everything we perceive—animate and inanimate—are simply split-off parts of the one thought that says: "I have achieved the impossible. I am separate, autonomous, independent, free, and in control of my life." Here is that important passage from Chapter 18, which presents the concept of the *one* thought that made the world:

> You who believe that God is fear made but one substitution. It has taken many forms, because it was the substitution of illusion for truth; of fragmentation for wholeness. It has become so splintered and subdivided and divided again, over and over, that it is now almost impossible to perceive it once was one, and still is what it was. That one error, which brought truth to illusion, infinity to time, and life to death, was all you ever made. Your whole world rests upon it. Everything you see reflects it, and every special relationship that you have ever made is part of it.

> You may be surprised to hear how very different is reality from what you see. You do not realize the magnitude of that one error. It was so vast and so completely incredible that from it a world of total unreality *had* to emerge. What else could come of it? Its fragmented aspects are fearful enough, as you begin to look at them. But nothing you have seen begins to show you the enormity of the original error, which seemed to cast you out of Heaven, to shatter knowledge into meaningless bits of disunited perceptions, and to force you to make further substitutions (T-18.I.4-5).

(2) Today's idea does not refer to what you see as much as to how you see it. Therefore, the exercises for today emphasize this aspect of your perception. The three or four practice periods which are recommended should be done as follows:

This is the point I mentioned earlier—perception is not only *what* we see, but *how* we see it, There is no distinction between the two. We make a distinction for teaching purposes, but it is arbitrary because the *interpretation* is what gives rise to what we see. The ego's interpretation is that I *want* to see a separated, hostile, vengeful world so I do not have to see these attributes in myself. In other words, the fact that my need to see a certain way determines what I see is why we can say that what we see and how we see it are one and the same.

The instructions in the remainder of the lesson are certainly familiar to us by now:

(3) Look about you, selecting subjects for the application of the idea for today as randomly as possible, and keeping your eyes on each one long enough to say:

I am not alone in experiencing the effects of how I see ___ .

Conclude each practice period by repeating the more general statement:

I am not alone in experiencing the effects of my seeing.

A minute or so, or even less, will be sufficient for each practice period.

We thus move from our specific perceptions to the generalization that teaches us that *all* our perceptions are the same, for they emanate from the same split mind that unites the Sonship as one.

LESSON 19

I am not alone in experiencing the effects of my thoughts.

(1) The idea for today is obviously the reason why your seeing does not affect you alone. You will notice that at times the ideas related to thinking precede those related to perceiving, while at other times the order is reversed. The reason is that the order does not matter. Thinking and its results are really simultaneous, for cause and effect are never separate.

Jesus extends the idea of one split mind, saying that not only are our minds joined, but our minds and the world are joined as well; the world being nothing but the projection of the mind's thought of separation. This is another way of saying *ideas leave not their source*, a principle that is central to the teaching of *A Course in Miracles*. It is emphasized in the text (e.g., T-26.VII.4), and Jesus brings it up later in the workbook (e.g., W-pI.132.5; W-pI.156.1)—*ideas do not leave their source*; effects do not leave their cause; the world does not remain separated from the mind.

We are so sure, however, that we are right—the world exists *outside* us—because we actually see ourselves here as well as see a separated world outside. Even further, by minimizing, if not negating the power of our thoughts, we are proven right by our perceptions of ourselves as victims of what the world does to us. We think our thoughts have no effect, and therefore we split them off and hide them behind a physical shield, so that we are aware only of our bodies; how they and other bodies react. This has come about because we think the world is separate from our minds; that the *effect*, which is the world, is separate from the *cause*, which is the mind. But remember, again—*ideas leave not their source*.

As an analogy, whatever you see on a movie screen is nothing but a film in the projector that is projected out. Yet what is on the screen never left its source, the film running through the projector. To expand on that analogy, what is on the film is what the script writer, director, producer, actors, and actresses *wanted* to be on the film. Therefore, once it is there it will be projected and seen on the screen *as if it were* on the screen.

Shifting to our lives, we, as the decision maker, are the writer, director, producer, not to mention the people starring in it. The film is exactly what we have chosen, precisely so we *could* and *would* see it on the screen. People would not go through the trouble of making a movie if they did not want others to see it. And if we did not react to movies as though they were real we would not go to see them. Thus, we attend movies for excitement, enlightenment, and distraction because we like to believe there is something out there that can affect us, positively or negatively. That is the goal, and everything leading up to it is purposive.

This is exactly what we do with the world. There is a very specific purpose in making up our dream. We want people to react to it, including ourselves, *as if it were real*. Thus I see everything out there in the world, totally forgetting it is my movie. Not only did I make it up, but I made it up to see sin all around me; to see victimizers in everyone except in me.

Once we see that cause and effect are never separated, we understand what we are seeing outside, to repeat, is simply an image that came from a thought. The key point to keep in mind is that there is a specific motivation—which we will get to in the next lesson—to learn that the ego's lessons are true but we are not responsible for them. The ego teaches that we have separated from God, victimized and murdered Him, and thus acquired our individual existence. We believe this to be true, except we are not responsible for it; *someone else is*.

Thus we have all gone to great trouble, with a very high budget indeed—it has cost us *Everything*—to make this grandiose movie of our lives. We invest tremendous energy in this movie in order to fulfill the ego's ultimate purpose: proving the separation is real, but *we are not responsible for it*. We forget we are actors with specific names and roles in the movie, as well as being script writers, directors, and producers.

If we were to realize we made the whole thing up, that we, as directors, *are* in control of our movie by virtue of excluding another Director, we would suddenly recognize that our greatest efforts were nothing because everything we had done was a defense against the truth. In a passage with which we will become increasingly familiar, we read:

> What if you recognized this world is an hallucination? What if you really understood you made it up? What if you realized that those who seem to walk about in it, to sin and die, attack and murder and destroy themselves, are wholly unreal? Could you have faith in what you see, if you accepted this? And would you see it? (T-20.VIII.7:3-7)

In other words, the defensive purpose of the world is sustained by keeping cause and effect separate, not remembering that our minds are the cause of the world.

One other point about this lesson: the way I see does not affect me alone. The great illusion of the world is that I can have my private, hateful thoughts without affecting anyone. Yet if the Sonship is one, there must be an effect, because thoughts are unified and minds are joined. These effects are not usually observable, which is part of the reason for making the movie, yet they are there. That is why our guilt is so great—deep down we know the effect of our anger, for example. Whether or not we express it—whether it be physical, verbal, or in our conscious thoughts—anger's effect is continually telling God and Jesus They are wrong and we are right: the separation is alive and well, and we have the power to destroy Heaven. Again, this is the source of our guilt, and why Jesus is telling us to look at our expressions of anger, and even more importantly, at their underlying thoughts. If they do not change, nothing will change.

We return to the idea of oneness:

(2:1-3) Today we are again emphasizing the fact that minds are joined. This is rarely a wholly welcome idea at first, since it seems to carry with it an enormous sense of responsibility, and may even be regarded as an "invasion of privacy." Yet it is a fact that there are no private thoughts.

Within the dream there certainly are private thoughts. We all have the illusion we have them. We think, for example: "Thank God I didn't say that, so my friend doesn't know what I *really* think." On a conscious level that person may not know, but remember, we are all part of the one mind, and on that level another's fear and guilt are reinforced by our thoughts, just as we are. Therefore, the effects of our thoughts may not show up right away on an individual level within the dream, but in the larger mind, of which all of us are an effect, thoughts have tremendous power as they reinforce the ego's thought system. They are reminders to everyone that the ego is alive and well, and Jesus does not know what he is talking about.

(2:4-5) Despite your initial resistance to this idea, you will yet understand that it must be true if salvation is possible at all. And salvation must be possible because it is the Will of God.

What is important here is that salvation is possible only if there is *one* problem. The key to salvation within *A Course in Miracles* is its first principle: *there is no order of difficulty among miracles*. This tells us that each problem is like every other problem, and so the solution—the miracle—is the same for all. The problem is unreal; but we will not know its unreality until we realize that every problem is the same. The seemingly external form of each problem is but a shadow of the inner problem: the single thought that says: "I am separated and am on my own." If we *could* be separate and have private thoughts, that would mean the separation is real. Salvation can occur only when we realize the separation is illusory, which means we can have no private thoughts.

The concluding three paragraphs present the daily exercise to be performed:

(3) The minute or so of mind searching which today's exercises require is to be undertaken with eyes closed. The idea for today is to be repeated first, and then the mind should be carefully searched for the thoughts it contains at that time. As you consider each one, name it in terms of the central person or theme it contains, and holding it in your mind as you do so, say:

> *I am not alone in experiencing the effects of this thought about ___ .*

Here Jesus is having us focus solely on our thoughts, as reflecting their unity with the Sonship.

(4-5) The requirement of as much indiscriminateness as possible in selecting subjects for the practice periods should be quite familiar to you by now, and will no longer be repeated each

day, although it will occasionally be included as a reminder. **Do not forget, however, that random selection of subjects for all practice periods remains essential throughout. Lack of order in this connection will ultimately make the recognition of lack of order in miracles meaningful to you.**

Apart from the "as needed" application of today's idea, at least three practice periods are required, shortening the length of time involved, if necessary. Do not attempt more than four.

In a sense, Jesus is revealing his process to us, explaining the purpose of the first nineteen lessons. Over and over, he insists that we not discriminate in the choice of objects we perceive outside, or in our choice of thoughts as we search our minds. Jesus wants us to realize that *everything* we perceive and think is the same. By learning to practice this idea with specific objects in the room and specific thoughts within our minds, we will come to realize that everything is the same, and therefore our problems have one solution—the miracle.

Thus we find a clear statement of Jesus' underlying method, and why the workbook lessons appear to be as simple as they are. He wants us to practice on a level that is comfortable—coat hanger, waste basket, lamp, telephone, cup, etc.—until we get the idea they are all the same, serving the purpose of proving the reality of the separation and the absence of our responsibility for it. This helps us ultimately to realize there is no hierarchy of illusions; the correction for the first law of chaos, which seeks to establish this hierarchy.

LESSON 20

I am determined to see.

There are relatively few lessons like this in the workbook; Lesson 95 is especially similar. Their importance lies not so much in the specific theme, as much as it lies in Jesus explaining what he is doing in these exercises: how to do them, and how not to do them. He begins by discussing the practice periods.

(1:1-2) We have been quite casual about our practice periods thus far. There has been virtually no attempt to direct the time for undertaking them, minimal effort has been required, and not even active cooperation and interest have been asked.

In other words, Jesus is being very gentle. He says: "Take a minute or two, and if that is too much, take less. Do it two or three times a day. If that is too much, do it less." He explains:

(1:3-6) This approach has been intentional, and very carefully planned. We have not lost sight of the crucial importance of the reversal of your thinking. The salvation of the world depends on it. Yet you will not see if you regard yourself as being coerced, and if you give in to resentment and opposition.

Thus Jesus tells us: "I am not trying to convince you that I am right and you are wrong, nor am I trying to compel you to believe these concepts. I am being as gentle as I can, asking only that you go along with me, whether you believe in this or not." This is not an argument. Since Jesus is not trying to prove that you are wrong and he is right, you should not be trying to prove yourself right and him wrong. Our *only* reason for reversing our thinking should *not* be because of *him*, but because of *us*: we would feel better if we did. Becoming happy is the motivation Jesus is trying to instill in us, as we shall see presently. It is important to proceed as you would with a new pair of shoes: Try them on and walk around for a while. If they feel comfortable, keep them; if not, discard them. And so, pardon the pun, we are ready for the next step as Jesus says: "I have not been giving you a lot of structure, *until now*":

(2:1-5) This is our first attempt to introduce structure. Do not misconstrue it as an effort to exert force or pressure. You want salvation. You want to be happy. You want peace.

Motivation now is the focus. The ego's motivation is the exact opposite of happiness. Everyone would *say* they want salvation, happiness and peace, but it is always acquired at someone else's expense, an inevitability of the ego thought system. If I am happy, I have to get something from someone else; if I have to get something, someone will have less of it. This is the essence of the special relationship, a term, incidentally, that does not appear at all in the workbook, although clearly its hateful dynamics are reflected throughout. Jesus is thus trying to tell us we really *want* salvation, which means we really *want* to be free of our guilt. We really *want* to be happy and peaceful.

(2:6) You do not have them now, because your mind is totally undisciplined...

If you have any questions about this, just think how difficult it is for you to go around realizing that everything you see or react to is literally not there. That provides some idea of the undisciplined nature of your mind. You can be attentive right now and understand everything that is being said. Yet, it is almost guaranteed that within minutes, if not seconds, you will return to your old way of being: holding grievances, becoming upset about something, and actually believing there is no connection between your thoughts and the images you perceive. That is what Jesus means by being "undisciplined." He is not rebuking us, but simply saying: "You must recognize that this is true. Otherwise you will not let me help you."

(2:6-8) ...and you cannot distinguish between joy and sorrow, pleasure and pain, love and fear. You are now learning how to tell them apart. And great indeed will be your reward.

This is a major theme in *A Course in Miracles*, both here and in the text (e.g., T-7.X; T-8.II; T-19.IV-B.12-15). It has not been the first time we have made this observation, nor will it be the last. It goes to the heart of Jesus' attempt at motivating us to learn his course so that we would be truly happy and joyful. Normally, what brings us joy and pleasure is getting what we want. We think love is specialness—having our needs met—and we are not aware that this is part of the ego system, and thus will only bring us guilt and pain.

(3:1) Your decision to see is all that vision requires.

The problem is that we do not want to see, and so Jesus first has to help us realize how much we do not want to, a wish that comes from the recognition that if we see through his eyes we can no longer blame anyone. Seeing through his eyes means that reality is not what we perceive outside, but his love for us, the reflection of the reality of God's Love.

Thus we need to be aware of how much we do not want to give up the certainty that we are right about our perceptions, because we certainly do not want to give up our certainty about what we perceive inside—our sinful and guilty self. As painful as that self-image may be, it is still *my* selfishness, which establishes *my* existence. I am reminded of one of Helen's favorite poetic lines—which she would misquote, by the way—from Yeats' poem, "Aedh wishes for the Cloths of Heaven*": "Tread lightly on my dreams. They are dreams. Yet they are *my* dreams."*

(3:2-8) What you want is yours. Do not mistake the little effort that is asked of you for an indication that our goal is of little worth. Can the salvation of the world be a trivial purpose? And can the world be saved if you are not? God has one Son, and he is the resurrection and the life. His will is done because all power is given him in Heaven and on earth. In your determination to see is vision given you.

The language in these passages is clearly biblical: New Testament terms and descriptions of Jesus. He is God's Son, and "the resurrection and the life," and "all power is given him in Heaven and on earth." But Jesus is telling us here: "Yes, this is true of me, but it is also true of you. Moreover, the world cannot be saved if you are not." It is obvious by now that this world is not external, for Jesus' focus is always on the internal—what we *think*. Again, we need to be motivated to *think* differently, and thus to *see* differently.

(4) The exercises for today consist in reminding yourself throughout the day that you want to see. Today's idea also tacitly implies the recognition that you do not see now. Therefore, as you repeat the idea, you are stating that you are determined to change your present state for a better one, and one you really want.

This is how Jesus begins the process of changing our motivation—from guilt to happiness. We do not want to see now because we believe vision will bring pain. Only when we learn that it brings happiness will we *want* to change from the ego's form of seeing.

(5:1-2) Repeat today's idea slowly and positively at least twice an hour today, attempting to do so every half hour. Do not be distressed if you forget to do so, but make a real effort to remember.

Jesus is slowly and gently introducing us to the all-important concept of sin vs. error. To forget today's idea is not a sin, but merely an error or mistake that we wish to correct *so that we shall feel better*. It is Jesus' gentle teaching that undoes the ego's harshness, and provides us with a model of kindness for *all* our interactions.

And finally:

(5:3-6) The extra repetitions should be applied to any situation, person or event that upsets you. You can see them differently, and you will. What you desire you will see. Such is the real law of cause and effect as it operates in the world.

If we see separation, vengeance, betrayal, or suffering, it is because we *want* to see them. This desire is the cause, and what we see is the effect. Jesus is trying to convince us that we really want to see differently. We obviously are not as yet convinced.

---

* The original reads: "But I, being poor, have only my dreams; / I have spread my dreams under your feet; / Tread softly because you tread on my dreams."

LESSON 21

I am determined to see things differently.

This lesson directly follows from the preceding one. It is interesting to note that Jesus talks specifically about anger in this lesson, even though it is not reflected in the title at all. He illustrates the idea that there is no hierarchy of illusions by having us realize that anger consists of a wide range of thoughts. We begin with the specific instructions, which usually come at the end of the lesson:

(1:1–2:2) The idea for today is obviously a continuation and extension of the preceding one. This time, however, specific mind-searching periods are necessary, in addition to applying the idea to particular situations as they may arise. Five practice periods are urged, allowing a full minute for each.

In the practice periods, begin by repeating the idea to yourself. Then close your eyes and search your mind carefully for situations past, present or anticipated that arouse anger in you.

This is the mind searching we had discussed earlier, and now Jesus wants us to focus specifically on our anger. The problem is that we cannot be determined to see things differently at the same time we are angry, because our anger says: "I am determined to see things the way *I* have always seen them. *My* perception is right, Jesus' is wrong, and I will go to my death to prove it." Jesus is now helping us realize that before we can say "I am determined to see differently," we have to understand our thoughts, which is why he asks us to get in touch with them. In other words, vision can come *only* by undoing our thoughts of anger, or correcting our mistaken decision for the ego. Saying *no* to the ego is the way of learning to see.

(2:3-5) The anger may take the form of any reaction ranging from mild irritation to rage. The degree of the emotion you experience does not matter. You will become increasingly aware that a slight twinge of annoyance is nothing but a veil drawn over intense fury.

This last line is the one I mentioned earlier in Lesson 16, one of the more famous lines in *A Course in Miracles*. It is so important, in fact, that

Jesus virtually repeats it in the manual for teachers (M-17.4:5). Everything is the same. Forms vary, but their content remains the same, as this lesson clearly explains. Statements such as these illustrate just how radical this course is. For all intents and purposes it invalidates *all* our experiences and beliefs.

(3:1-2) Try, therefore, not to let the "little" thoughts of anger escape you in the practice periods. Remember that you do not really recognize what arouses anger in you, and nothing that you believe in this connection means anything.

We think that what arouses anger in us is what people do or fail to do, but what truly arouses our anger is the need to project responsibility for the separation:

> Anger always involves projection of separation, which must ultimately be accepted as one's own responsibility, rather than being blamed on others (T-6.in.1:2).

That fact is what we do not want to acknowledge. We need to proclaim: "I am not guilty of the sin of murdering God and betraying His Love. Someone else is." When I see it out there—because I put it there—I believe I am justified in getting angry; a neat trick, at which we all are pretty expert. It matters not whether I am enraged or only mildly annoyed. Either way I am saying that my well being depends on something or someone external. In the absence of that special object I will be upset, and it will not be my fault.

(3:3-5) You will probably be tempted to dwell more on some situations or persons than on others, on the fallacious grounds that they are more "obvious." This is not so. It is merely an example of the belief that some forms of attack are more justified than others.

For the first time we see a specific example of the principle that there is no hierarchy of illusions. Jesus uses anger as the example because it is so central to the ego's thought system. Everyone walks around angry, because everyone walks around guilty over the separation and not wanting to accept responsibility for it. Thus again, before we can be determined to see things differently, we have to recognize and understand the *interference* to seeing things differently: there is something out there—whether in our own body or another's—that causes us pain that is not of our doing. In other words, our thoughts have no power, and thus cannot cause us distress. Someone else has brought this upset about, or some disease or circumstance. We are innocent, the helpless victim of forces beyond our control.

The rest of the lesson repeats instructions we have seen before.

(4-5) As you search your mind for all the forms in which attack thoughts present themselves, hold each one in mind while you tell yourself:

I am determined to see ___ [name of person] differently.

I am determined to see ___ [specify the situation] differently.

Try to be as specific as possible. You may, for example, focus your anger on a particular attribute of a particular person, believing that the anger is limited to this aspect. If your perception is suffering from this form of distortion, say:

I am determined to see ___ [specify the attribute] in ___ [name of person] differently.

"Try to be as specific as possible" is the key here. Our temptation will often be to gloss over the specific forms of upset of our life, unconsciously trying to deny them as the means of denying their source. Thus our ego would get us twice: first by teaching us to deny our guilt, and then to deny its specific defense of anger. This is the double shield of oblivion Jesus describes in Lesson 136.

LESSON 22

What I see is a form of vengeance.

This continues Lesson 21, which discussed anger and attack; specifically that there are no differences among their many forms—from annoyance to rage—for they all conceal the thought of separation and victimization. This lesson takes those principles one step further.

It is extremely important as we proceed to keep in mind the impossibility of being in this world without attack thoughts. If the world is made as an attack on God, as Jesus says much later in the workbook (W-pII.3.2:1)—to prove we are right and He is wrong—and if we identify with this world and the body, we are an inherent part of that thought system of attack. Therefore, the very concept of individual existence entails attack, if not murder, because in order for there to be existence God had to be destroyed. Consequently, it is impossible to identify with the body—physically and psychologically—without sharing the entirety of the ego thought system. Of the many words that encapsulate the ego, *attack* is certainly high on the list.

(1:1-2) Today's idea accurately describes the way anyone who holds attack thoughts in his mind must see the world. Having projected his anger onto the world, he sees vengeance about to strike at him.

As long as there are attack thoughts in our minds, we must see the world about to take vengeance on us. The second sentence, which is a classic description of projection, provides us with the reason. We all harbor attack thoughts, because, again, our individual identity is based on it. Given its origin—if I am to exist, then God must be destroyed—it rests on the principle of *one or the other* or *kill or be killed*. We all believe we are sinful because we believe we attacked God. This sense of sinfulness, along with the guilt that inevitably follows from it, is so overwhelming it cannot be tolerated. The ego therefore tells us to push sin and guilt into our unconscious and then project them out. Furthermore, since the expectation of punishment is inherent in the very idea of guilt, the world arises as the ego's means to prove we deserve to be punished, unfairly treated, and victimized.

The beginning of our physical lives—conception and birth—is then seen as proof that we are the innocent victims of what other people have done to us. We are not here as a result of our own choices, but of a biological accident. This reflects the almost universal belief that we had nothing to do with our birth. Everything that happens to us from the time we are conceived is seen in the context of our being innocent victims of powers and forces beyond our control. The ego will always interpret these powers and forces as some form of attack on us, which the ego convinces us we deserve because of our original attack on God.

This is the central idea of the lesson. In fact, without understanding this unconscious dynamic one will not be able to understand *A Course in Miracles* —either the thought system of the ego, or its undoing through the Holy Spirit. As long as we believe we are separated, we believe we have attack thoughts, and these attack thoughts *must* be projected out. We will further believe, therefore, that others are doing, are about to do, or have already done to us what we believe we originally did to God and to His Son.

We can certainly assume that Jesus' ongoing assignment to us as his students is understanding these dynamics in the context of the lessons and exercises in the workbook. He then asks us to apply the principles of their undoing—forgiveness—to our personal lives by recognizing how we manifest these ego thoughts in our everyday behavior.

(1:3) His own attack is thus perceived as self defense.

We forget we had the original attack thought, for we have projected it and now see everyone and every aspect of the world poised to attack *us*. We therefore feel justified in attacking in self-defense. This is the "face of innocence" I mentioned earlier, a concept described in greater detail in many places in the text (e.g., T-27.I; T-31.V). In Lesson 170 we shall see this concept of self-defense elaborated on in more depth as well.

(1:4-6) This becomes an increasingly vicious

circle until he is willing to change how he sees. Otherwise, thoughts of attack and counter-attack will preoccupy him and people his entire world. What peace of mind is possible to him then?

Jesus says this *vicious circle* of attack and defense—defense is always counterattack—cannot change until we change how we see. This means changing how we think, because perception and thinking are one: *Ideas leave not their source.** What we perceive outside is simply a shadow of what we first perceived and made real in our minds. Whenever we feel at the mercy of forces beyond our control—forces within our own bodies, the bodies of others, the laws of the world or of nature—we affirm the truth of the ego's thought system, which means that the reality of God and the Love of God are untrue.

Again, once we begin with the premise that we exist as separate, individual selves, it is impossible not to be trapped in this vicious circle of attack and counterattack. There is no way out unless we change the premise of our thinking, a process which is explained in more depth in Lesson 23.

(2:1-2) It is from this savage fantasy that you want to escape. Is it not joyous news to hear that it is not real?

It is most definitely *not* joyous news if you still believe you exist and are important, not to mention special. As long as you cling to your individual identity, it is not joyous news to be told that you could escape from this. This explains everyone's resistance to these lessons, both in understanding them and certainly in applying them, not to mention resistance to what the text teaches. It would be extremely helpful as you go along to identify how much you cling to your self and the conviction you are right.

(2:3-5) Is it not a happy discovery to find that you can escape? You made what you would destroy; everything that you hate and would attack and kill. All that you fear does not exist.

What we would destroy is other people, as well as any other objects of our anger. We made the world that we seek to destroy, and that we believe

seeks to destroy us. Everything we hate, would attack, and kill is part of our "savage fantasy," the purpose of which is to prove our existence, but that someone else is responsible for it. Once again, we perceive ourselves to be the innocent victims of what has been done to us.

As you do this lesson, try to identify the fear and anxiety that arise as you begin to think about what Jesus is saying. The next paragraph provides a good opportunity for practicing this:

(3:1-6) Look at the world about you at least five times today, for at least a minute each time. As your eyes move slowly from one object to another, from one body to another, say to yourself:

> *I see only the perishable.*
> *I see nothing that will last.*
> *What I see is not real.*
> *What I see is a form of vengeance.*

Do this exercise in front of a mirror and see how much you believe what you say. As you gaze at a reflection of your separated self, say: "I see only the perishable"; "I see nothing that will last." If you do this properly and thoughtfully, there is bound to be anxiety. If not, search your mind for your defenses against it. As long as you think you exist, and are special, unique, and important—whether positively or negatively—you will find these lessons difficult and anxiety-inducing, and will need to identify the resistance in yourself. Thus you will be better able to honestly address the final three sentences:

(3:7-9) At the end of each practice period, ask yourself:

> *Is this the world I really want to see?*

The answer is surely obvious.

While the answer may be quite obvious to the right mind, to our egos this perishable self is nonetheless *our* self, and so the unfortunate, yet honest answer is: "Yes, I do want to see this." But again, we are still, to quote *Psychotherapy: Purpose, Process and Practice*: "at the very start of the beginning stage of the first journey" (P-3.II.8:5). There is much for us to learn.

---

* This central principle is stated in different ways in the Course. See, for example, T-26.VII.4:7; W-pI.132.5:3; W-pI.167.3:6. See also p. 1102 in the *Concordance of A Course in Miracles* for a complete listing.

LESSON 23

I can escape from the world I see by giving up attack thoughts.

This is among the most important lessons in the workbook, providing us with clear statements about the nature of the world, and what salvation is *and* what it is not. Another valuable aspect of this lesson is its simple language, which makes it even more difficult to mistake its message. This certainly does not mean, of course, that people will not try valiantly to overlook it.

The title itself is a blockbuster. The world we see is a world of death: vengeance, violence, pain, and suffering. It might also be described as a world of pleasure and happiness, but no pleasure and happiness in this world lasts. As they begin to fade, our anxiety and anger grow, our specialness feels unfulfilled, and we inevitably experience pain. Jesus is teaching us now that the way to escape from this pain is not by doing anything to the world, but by changing how we *look* on the world.

(1:1-3) The idea for today contains the only way out of fear that will ever succeed. Nothing else will work; everything else is meaningless. But this way cannot fail.

You do not deal with fear by overcoming it directly, or by changing anything of the world or the body. You can escape from fear only by changing its *cause*, which is the decision to be separate. Many of the world's methods will work, but not all the time. In other words, the gains you may receive from following the world's guidelines will not last—no matter how noble and ideal they might seem—because the *cause* of the distress is overlooked. This was Jesus' pointed response to Helen, to which we shall return periodically, when early in the dictation she asked him to remove her fear:

> The correction of fear *is* your responsibility. When you ask for release from fear, you are implying that it is not. You should ask, instead, for help in the conditions that have brought the fear about. These conditions always entail a willingness to be separate.... You may still complain about fear, but you nevertheless persist in making yourself fearful.... If I intervened between your thoughts [*cause*] and their results [*effect*], I

would be tampering with a basic law of cause and effect; the most fundamental law there is. I would hardly help you if I depreciated the power of your own thinking. This would be in direct opposition to the purpose of this course. It is much more helpful to remind you that you do not guard your thoughts carefully enough (T-2.VI.4:1-4; VII.1:1,4-7).

Jesus was thus appealing to the power of Helen's mind to *choose* to be afraid, directing her attention to the *cause* of her distress, away from its *effect*.

(1:4-5) Every thought you have makes up some segment of the world you see. It is with your thoughts, then, that we must work, if your perception of the world is to be changed.

This is another clear statement of cause and effect, and one that is meant literally. The *cause* of everything in the world is our thoughts, and the *effect* is everything we experience in the world. This principle, however, must be understood from the point of view of the mind, otherwise we would be tempted to believe that a particular thought of ours could have a harmful effect on something external. For instance, if you as an individual have an angry thought about someone, and then something unfortunate occurs, you could mistakenly think this lesson means you are responsible for what happened to that person. The intention here is not to induce guilt because something happens to someone with whom you are angry. Jesus is talking about a thought in the mind, which means that if the person falls off a ladder, it is to be viewed as a choice that that person made, perhaps along with you if you react to it—but not the *you* that you think you are.

It is essential to remember that thoughts are of the mind, not the brain. What we usually identify as our thoughts belong to the brain, which, we are told time and time again, does not truly think. Jesus is speaking to us exclusively about the mind. Remember, the mind is outside time and space, and the world of time and space emanates from the one thought of separation. Once we believe we are here, everything appears to be real and governed by laws we have established. These will always be some expression of cause and effect. For instance, I drink poison and my body experiences the effect: I become ill and may even die. Both the seeming cause—my drinking poison—and the seeming effect—my body's illness or death—are effects of a larger cause, which is the thought that says: "I am going to prove I am right and God is wrong. I am going to prove separation is real, the body real, and that sin most definitely has an effect: my death."

This lesson, as is obvious, does not truly discuss these principles; that is the function of the text. But its underlying teachings are certainly *reflected* here. Jesus is not expecting students at this point to have a thorough understanding of the text's theoretical principles. He simply asks us to begin practicing the exercises. Consistent practice will eventually lead to an understanding of the deeper metaphysics of *A Course in Miracles'* thought system. Recall that the *world* was made as a defense against getting in touch with the thoughts in our *minds*.

"It is with your thoughts, then, that we must work" is an extremely important statement. This is a course in mind training, a course in changing your mind and how you perceive. In practice, changing how you think really means changing the teacher from whom you will learn. The bottom line of *A Course in Miracles* is always: Do I choose my ego to teach me how I should perceive the world, or do I let Jesus or the Holy Spirit be my Teacher? My thoughts—guilt, anger, and suffering; or thoughts of peace and forgiveness—automatically follow from the teacher I have chosen. That is why it is important to understand that an integral part of the Course's curriculum is developing a personal relationship with Jesus or the Holy Spirit. From that relationship our right-minded thoughts, and therefore our right-minded perceptions and behavior will inevitably follow.

(2) If the cause of the world you see is attack thoughts, you must learn that it is these thoughts which you do not want. There is no point in lamenting the world. There is no point in trying to change the world. It is incapable of change because it is merely an effect. But there is indeed a point in changing your thoughts about the world. Here you are changing the cause. The effect will change automatically.

It is necessary first to accept the premise that the cause of the world is attack thoughts. This is true both on the larger level—that the cause of the entire physical universe is an attack thought—as well as on the personal level—that the individual world of our physical and psychological self is caused by an attack thought, which is the belief that we are separate.

Jesus is telling us that—to express it in a specific example—if you do not like a shadow on a wall, you do not approach it and try to change the shadow, ignoring the object that is casting the shadow. If you do not like what you see on the wall, change the object! To try to peel off the shadow, or modify it in some way is silly. The physical universe can be likened to a shadow, reminiscent of Plato's Allegory of the Cave, which is why Jesus says in an oft-quoted line: "Trust not your good intentions. They are not enough" (T-18.IV.2:1-2). It is the well-intentioned people in the world who want to change, fix, or make it better. They may succeed up to a point, but they will ultimately fail if they ignore the world's underlying cause of separation.

Statements such as the ones expressed here—i.e., "There is no point in trying to change the world"—have frequently been taken out of context by students of *A Course in Miracles* and wrongly interpreted to mean that we literally are to do nothing. They erroneously think this means that we should let rapists go free, Hitlers invade countries, the environment go to hell, pay no attention to what we put into our stomachs, etc.—because the world and body are illusory and all we need do is change our minds. This, however, is exactly the opposite of what Jesus is teaching us. Ultimately it is true that the universe is illusory and nothing here matters; but as long as we believe we are here, our bodies are symbols, and before we can let them go, we first have to change what they symbolize—from separation to joining, attack to forgiveness.

We thus return to the central point—changing our teacher. If we have chosen Jesus, he will have us act in a loving way, in forms understood by the world. Lesson 184 makes that explicit point. These passages, therefore, should not be used as an excuse for doing nothing about the world, or our or other people's bodies. Rather, whatever we do about the world or ourselves should be done with Jesus' guidance instead of the ego's. As he says later on in the context of perceiving specifics to learn abstraction: "We need to see a little, that we learn a lot"

(W-pI.161.4:8). Thus we practice on the "little" things of the body, so that we may come to learn about the magnitude of spirit.

It is highly unlikely Jesus would tell you: "Do not do anything because I will bring everything to you, and the world is an illusion." He will not teach you that because you are still too terrified of understanding and accepting it. As long as you identify with your body (and that includes everyone who studies this course), its *meaning* for you has to be changed. You do not give up the body; you do not go from the nightmare of the ego to the truth of eternity. Rather, you go from the nightmare dreams of the ego to the happy dreams of the Holy Spirit:

> Nothing more fearful than an idle dream has terrified God's Son, and made him think that he has lost his innocence, denied his Father, and made war upon himself. So fearful is the dream, so seeming real, he could not waken to reality without the sweat of terror and a scream of mortal fear, unless a gentler dream preceded his awaking, and allowed his calmer mind to welcome, not to fear, the Voice that calls with love to waken him; a gentler dream, in which his suffering was healed and where his brother was his friend. God willed he waken gently and with joy, and gave him means to waken without fear (T-27.VII.13:3-5).

This means that the body comes to serve another purpose and has a different meaning: the means for undoing all guilt and hatred of others. With this new purpose in mind, you are free to use your body lovingly, treating yourself and others more kindly. The forms do not matter; the *teacher* you choose does. Everyone, however, is tempted to skip steps, because the fear of looking at what it truly means to live in the ego's world is too painful. As a result, *A Course in Miracles* all too often becomes a way of *escaping* the pain of our everyday lives, rather than the means of *undoing* it.

When Jesus talks about changing your thoughts, understand him to mean changing the *teacher* of your thoughts. Again, if you choose him as your teacher, all your thoughts, perceptions, and behavior will be loving. But be wary of the ego ploy that would have you believe you are choosing Jesus, when you are really choosing the ego itself. You can tell you have chosen the ego when you are caught in a way of thinking that causes you to look different from others, separating yourself in some

way—behavior that makes you special. Anything that causes you to deny your body or to live in a way that calls attention to yourself you can bet 99.99 percent of the time is of your ego and not Jesus. The real *cause* you want to change is your need to prove that you are right and Jesus is wrong, which you do by establishing your personal identity. Remember, this identity is one of specialness, which is a red flag signalling you have chosen the ego as your teacher.

Another expression of the ego's hidden agenda of specialness is the *special* focus students of *A Course in Miracles* place on the *effect* of the mind's change. Indeed, very often the physical world will change as our thoughts change, but this means nothing if the world is nothing. The *effect* that *always* changes is the inevitable result of our attack thoughts: guilt, anxiety, fear, depression, disease, etc. Peace will always result when these attack thoughts are given up. To place emphasis on the *form* of the effect is merely to allow the ego thoughts back into our minds. We must always "*be vigilant only for God and His Kingdom*" (T-6.V-C).

(3:1) The world you see is a vengeful world, and everything in it is a symbol of vengeance.

These are very strong statements, and as uncompromising as any you will come across in the text. *Everything* in this world is a symbol of vengeance. Why? Because if you believe there is a world, you are saying God no longer exists. If God no longer exists, it is because you killed Him and perforce believe He is justified in taking vengeance on you. You block out that horrendous thought and conflict, project it, and then believe it is the world that will seek its vengeance on you. There is of course another meaning we can give to the symbol of the world—the Holy Spirit's purpose of forgiveness—but here the focus is on the ego.

(3:2) Each of your perceptions of "external reality" is a pictorial representation of your own attack thoughts.

"External reality" is in quotes because there is no reality outside. This is similar to the idea Jesus presents early in the text: "All thinking produces form at some level" (T-2.VI.9:14), which appears in the first paragraph of this lesson: "Every thought you have makes up some segment of the world you see." By "pictorial representation" Jesus means *projection*, as we have already seen in this statement that cannot be quoted too often:

> It [the world] is the witness to your state of mind, the outside picture of an inward condition (T-21.in.1:5).

Once again, Jesus refers to the thinking occurring within the ego system, which always reflects some aspect of attack.

(3:3-4) One can well ask if this can be called seeing. Is not fantasy a better word for such a process, and hallucination a more appropriate term for the result?

Fantasy is a psychological term for thoughts that are not real, usually pertaining to bringing you something you want. This means calling upon the ego's trusted ally: specialness. If you want to defend against your guilt, you invoke fantasies of killing someone or attaining vengeance on another; or if you feel you are in a state of lack, you indulge fantasies of pleasure, of getting what you want. Everything in this world—special hate or special love—comes from a fantasy thought. Thus the world gives me what I want: a haven in which I can hide from God. And since the world is the effect of a thought of fantasy, it exists in the realm of hallucination—the perceptual counterpart of the mind's delusional thought system of fantasy.

(4:1) You see the world that you have made, but you do not see yourself as the image maker.

This is denial, discussed in detail later in Lesson 136, "Sickness is a defense against the truth," which instructs us that we make up a sickness, and then forget we did so. It is another way of saying we are the dreamer of the dream, but have forgotten the dream's source and instead believe the dream is dreaming us. This is a major theme in the text, to which we shall return. For now, note these representative statements that can serve as prelude to the more extensive discussions to come:

> This is how all illusions came about. The one who makes them does not see himself as making them, and their reality does not depend on him. Whatever cause they have is something quite apart from him, and what he sees is separate from his mind. He cannot doubt his dreams' reality, because he does not see the part he plays in making them and making them

seem real.... *You* are the dreamer of the world of dreams. No other cause it has, nor ever will (T-27.VII.7:6-9; 13:1-2).

> Let us return the dream he gave away unto the dreamer, who perceives the dream as separate from himself and done to him (T-27.VIII.6:1).

> The miracle does not awaken you, but merely shows you who the dreamer is.... He [the dreamer] did not see that he was author of the dream, and not a figure in the dream (T-28.II.4:2; 7:4).

(4:2-3) You cannot be saved from the world, but you can escape from its cause. This is what salvation means, for where is the world you see when its cause is gone?

Ultimately you cannot be saved from the world because there is no world. You are saved from your belief system that tells you there is a world. This belief system, as I have been saying, rests on the self-accusation we have killed God so we could exist in His place.

In the real world you are literally outside the dream and totally identified with the Holy Spirit's Love. You no longer identify with the *cause* of the world, which is the belief in separation from God. You may appear to be in the world, as Jesus did, but your reality remains outside it, and so for you the world has disappeared.

(4:4-5) Vision already holds a replacement for everything you think you see now. Loveliness can light your images, and so transform them that you will love them, even though they were made of hate.

Vision is the Course's term for right-minded or true perception, identifying with the Holy Spirit's thought system of Atonement.

This refers back to Lesson 15, "My thoughts are images I have made," which talked about the sparks of light that creep up around objects. I explained then that the references to light were originally meant for a friend of Helen's and Bill's, and not to be taken literally. They are best understood in terms of *content*, which means we learn to see things differently. This new way of seeing is represented by light: "Loveliness can light your images." Everything in the world now becomes lovely in our light-filled perception, because its purpose has been changed. We shall return to the important concept of purpose.

Even though our images were made of hate—a stronger word than "attack"—their purpose is now changed. We look at them in love, despite their origin. As the text says of specialness in an important statement we have already quoted: "Such is the Holy Spirit's kind perception of specialness; His use of what you made, to heal instead of harm" (T-25.VI.4:1). The purpose of our making the world was to protect our individuality and sinful thoughts through projection. With its purpose changed, the world becomes a classroom in which we learn there is no world by reversing the projection, bringing it back to the mind that was its source. This lovely thought frees us, as its loveliness lights up our vision and everything we see.

(4:6) For you will not be making them alone.

This is another expression of the principle that minds are joined. Jesus is not speaking of bodily joining of any kind. We "will not be making them alone" because when we choose to identify with Jesus we are making a distinct choice against separation and for unity. That is the meaning of being with Jesus. If he is the Christ because he is God's one Son, and I join with him in a holy instant, I am the Christ, too, along with everyone else.

When I choose the *un*holy instant, since everyone is one with me within the ego thought system as well, I am sending out the message that we are right and God is wrong. We are right in our belief that we are separated; you are right in feeling unfairly treated, and I am right in feeling angry at you. We are thus not alone in experiencing the effects of our wrong-minded or right-minded thoughts, the effects of what we see or Christ's vision: the mind of God's Son is one.

This principle has nothing to do with this world or with our experience here, but only with our minds' thoughts, of which there are two, both perfectly unified: the ego's thought of separation that we share as one Son, and the Atonement correction for that thought, which we also share.

In the text Jesus says that vision or judgment are our choice, but not both of them (T-20.V.4:7). Vision sees us all as one, reflected in this world through sharing a common purpose. Judgment sees guilt over the sin of murdering God so we could exist; and because of this guilt we try continually to

kill another, fulfilling the ego's principle of *one or the other*. We thus have the power to reinforce our decision for the ego, or to remind each other there is another choice to be made.

Paragraph 5 is the principal source for the three steps of forgiveness I have taught for so many years:

(5:1-2) The idea for today introduces the thought that you are not trapped in the world you see, because its cause can be changed. This change requires, first, that the cause be identified and then let go, so that it can be replaced.

Identifying the cause is to recognize the problem is not what is in the world; my upset is not caused by what my or someone else's body does or does not do to me. The cause rests in a decision made in my mind. That is *the first step* in forgiveness.

Letting go—*the second step*—means asking Jesus for help to look at my guilt and attack thoughts differently. I realize that as my attack on you was a made-up projection, so was my attack on myself made up, too—I remain as God created me; who I am as God's Son has not changed. Letting go thus entails looking at my guilt with the love of Jesus beside me. And then *the third step*:

In the instant in which I ask Jesus for help in looking at my guilt, his shining and forgiving light causes the guilt to disappear. My responsibility is only to bring the guilt to him, the meaning of accepting the Atonement for myself (T-2.V.5:1).

To briefly summarize these steps: 1) I bring back within my mind the guilt I have projected onto you; 2) By looking with Jesus, I bring my mind's guilt to him; in which instant, 3) the guilt is gone, for I have accepted the love and light that was already present but had been concealed beneath the darkness of my guilt, protected by my attack thoughts.

(5:3-6) The first two steps in this process require your cooperation. The final one does not. Your images have already been replaced. By taking the first two steps, you will see that this is so.

Our job, again, is simply—the reflection of the "little willingness"—to bring to Jesus our ego thoughts; those we projected out, wherein we made the world, and those we made up about ourselves.

Everything we believe in has already gone, as the passage I quoted earlier states: "This world was over long ago" (T-28.I.1:6). We just *believe* the world is here, which is why Jesus uses the term *hallucination* to describe it (T-20.VIII.7-8). We come to realize the truth of the Atonement principle by changing our minds about what we were so sure was right: there is an external world that victimizes us and others. Moreover, we unconsciously believe this hostile world is a defense against an inner world of guilt that is even more painful. We were wrong about the world outside and the world inside.

(6:1-2) Besides using it throughout the day as the need arises, five practice periods are required in applying today's idea. As you look about you, repeat the idea slowly to yourself first, and then close your eyes and devote about a minute to searching your mind for as many attack thoughts as occur to you.

As I have already discussed, "searching your mind" is a prominent theme in *A Course in Miracles* because our attack thoughts are hidden. Part of the training we undergo as students of the workbook and of the Course itself is to allow ourselves to see the heretofore concealed attack thoughts in our minds.

(6:3-5) As each one crosses your mind say:

> *I can escape from the world I see by giving up attack thoughts about ___.*

Hold each attack thought in mind as you say this, and then dismiss that thought and go on to the next.

These instructions highlight the important process of bringing the darkness of our illusions to the light of truth. These lessons are not meant to be affirmations that simply state this truth. Rather, they are meant to represent the truth, *to which* we bring our thoughts of attack. Bringing light to illusion merely strengthens the illusion. On the other hand, bringing illusions to the light is what shines them away.

(7) In the practice periods, be sure to include both your thoughts of attacking and of being attacked. Their effects are exactly the same because they are exactly the same. You do not recognize this as yet, and you are asked at this time only to treat them as the same in today's practice periods. We are still at the stage of identifying the cause of the world you see. When you finally learn that thoughts of attack and of being attacked are not different, you will be ready to let the cause go.

There is no difference between being a victim or a victimizer. Attack is attack is attack. Jesus reiterates that he does not expect us to understand this, let alone identify with, or even believe in it, but he *is* asking us to practice it, and he tells us precisely how to do so.

As we learn there is no difference between self-attack (guilt) and attack, we realize that being a victim is the most vicious form of attack possible. If we see ourselves as victims, it is clear that someone else will pay the price of punishment for *our* sin. It is this victimized suffering that points the accusing finger at another (see, e.g., T-27.I.1-4). Giving up our investment in seeing ourselves as victims is the hardest illusion of all to lose; our very existence is based on the idea that *we* are the victims: We did not choose to come into this world—it was our parents who brought us here; we did not choose to have our bodies, personalities, or problems—it was our genes or environment that were the determining factors. So we believe.

It is very difficult to accept that seeing yourself at the mercy of forces beyond your control is an attack. Yet this is the point of the lesson. Again, Jesus is not asking us to accept it just yet, but he is asking that we hear his words and try to understand them, and thus include thoughts of victimization in our practice periods. Needless to say, we are still in the early stages of our mind training.

LESSON 24

I do not perceive my own best interests.

This lesson introduces the theme of humility. We are so sure we know what is best for us, let alone what is best for others. In one sense, as this lesson makes clear, it is understandable we would think that way. In one way or another we have been taught that if we do not take care of ourselves, who will? We learn we cannot trust the world; it is not set up to meet our needs instantaneously—physically or emotionally. We cannot completely trust our parents either, for even the best of them, as judged by the world, are never there for us *all* the time. A part of us thus learns we must take care of ourselves: we cannot fully trust anyone. The context of this lesson, therefore, is the correction of the conviction that we know our best interests.

(1) In no situation that arises do you realize the outcome that would make you happy. Therefore, you have no guide to appropriate action, and no way of judging the result. What you do is determined by your perception of the situation, and that perception is wrong. It is inevitable, then, that you will not serve your own best interests. Yet they are your only goal in any situation which is correctly perceived. Otherwise, you will not recognize what they are.

No ego is going to read these lines without being highly insulted! Jesus is saying we have no guide because we have chosen ourselves as the guide, reminiscent of the lines from the text I frequently quote: "Resign now as your own teacher.... for you were badly taught" (T-12.V.8:3; T-28.I.7:1). This, then, is a subtle plug for choosing him as our guide.

The reasoning behind this teaching is obvious, once we think of it. To know what is in our best interests presupposes that we truly know our needs, problems, and desires. Only then, it goes without saying, could we know how to meet our needs, solve our problems, and fulfill our desires. And yet, as we have already seen and have been clearly taught in the text, the world and body were *literally* made to keep the real problem of separation—*in our minds*—hidden from us. Therefore, our experience of our needs and problems is but a smoke screen, the purpose of which is to root our attention

to our *bodies*—physical and psychological—thus distracting us from the *mind*, wherein is found both the problem and the answer.

Moreover, an inevitable result of our initial arrogance compounds it still further by asking Jesus or the Holy Spirit to help us with a problem that *we* have determined needs to be solved. Thus we expect Them to share our insane need to protect our separation from ever being undone. We shall return to this important theme below.

(2) If you realized that you do not perceive your own best interests, you could be taught what they are. But in the presence of your conviction that you do know what they are, you cannot learn. The idea for today is a step toward opening your mind so that learning can begin.

The humility required is the admission that you do not know what is best for you, and that there is Someone within you who does, and Whom you will ask for help. The next step is to realize how much you do not want His help, and when you do ask for it, how often it is for help on your own terms—in which case you are not giving up your investment in believing you know what the problem *and* the answer are.

Moreover, why are you going to learn something when you already believe you have the answer? How can he help you, then, if you already believe you know the answer to your question, the solution to your problem. That is why in *A Course in Miracles* Jesus needs you to understand that *you do not know*. Thus he teaches you that real learning is *un*learning: you cannot be taught the truth until you first understand you do not know it. That is why Jesus always impresses on his students the *undoing* aspects of his correction (see, e.g., T-1.I.26:2-3; T-28.I.1:1-4; W-pII.2.3:1-3; M-4.X.3:6-7).

Jesus is asking here that you trust him enough to suspend all your beliefs, and then say with sincerity: "I do not perceive my own best interests." His is a plea for total humility, and implied in that plea is that we choose him as our teacher instead of the ego. The beginning of the next paragraph echoes Jesus' plea:

(3) The exercises for today require much more honesty than you are accustomed to using. A few subjects, honestly and carefully considered in each of the five practice periods which should be undertaken today, will be more helpful than a more cursory examination of a large number. Two minutes are suggested for each of the mind-searching periods which the exercises involve.

In expressing himself this way, Jesus is telling us we have not been all that honest up to now. This is why there is repeated emphasis on searching our minds. Part of the problem inherent in our mind searching is that we think we are searching our brains. At this point we really do not understand the distinction in *A Course in Miracles* between the brain and the mind, an understandable mistake when we consider our almost complete identification with the body. Thus we forget our brain is a defense. If the world were made as an attack on God, then certainly the body was made as an attack on God as well, and the brain is the principal organ of the body: governing what it thinks, perceives, says, and does.

Jesus is asking us to be able to come to him and say: "I do not understand anything. Please teach me." We need to get in touch with how difficult that is. There is a part of us that truly believes we know what is best for ourselves.

(4) The practice periods should begin with repeating today's idea, followed by searching the mind, with closed eyes, for unresolved situations about which you are currently concerned. The emphasis should be on uncovering the outcome you want. You will quickly realize that you have a number of goals in mind as part of the desired outcome, and also that these goals are on different levels and often conflict.

Note the use of the word *uncovering* in sentence 2, echoing our discussion of the centrality of *undoing* to the practice of forgiveness. It is also clear from Jesus' instructions how we do not *really* know what is in our best interests. How could we? In case we had any doubts about this, the following exercise makes it crystal clear to us:

(5) In applying the idea for today, name each situation that occurs to you, and then enumerate carefully as many goals as possible that you would like to be met in its resolution. The form of each application should be roughly as follows:

> *In the situation involving ___ , I would like ___ to happen, and ___ to happen,*

and so on. Try to cover as many different kinds of outcomes as may honestly occur to you, even if some of them do not appear to be directly related to the situation, or even to be inherent in it at all.

This sets the stage for the next paragraph, which contains the lesson's central point:

(6) If these exercises are done properly, you will quickly recognize that you are making a large number of demands of the situation which have nothing to do with it. You will also recognize that many of your goals are contradictory, that you have no unified outcome in mind, and that you must experience disappointment in connection with some of your goals, however the situation turns out.

The message of this lesson, therefore, is that if we are truly honest we would recognize the contradictory nature of much of our desires and goals. This is inevitable when you consider the impossibility of having non-conflicted goals when we do not recognize our own best interest. To our egos, this interest is self-preservation, but since this conflicted self is filled with guilt and fear, how could satisfaction of our goals be anything but conflicted and fraught with the same guilt and fear that led to them?

The lesson's final paragraph emphasizes one more time the essential point to be learned if we are successfully to complete *A Course in Miracles'* curriculum:

(7) After covering the list of as many hoped-for goals as possible, for each unresolved situation that crosses your mind say to yourself:

> *I do not perceive my own best interests in this situation,*

and go on to the next one.

Jesus wants us to generalize this lesson to all situations in our lives. To be certain we did not miss the point, nor forget it, he continues this teaching in Lesson 25.

LESSON 25

I do not know what anything is for.

This lesson directly discusses the theme of *purpose*, so crucial in *A Course in Miracles*. Indeed, one could say that purpose alone helps us understand the ego's thought system, the world's role within it, and how through shifting the world's purpose the Holy Spirit uses the ego's plan to undo it.

(1) Purpose is meaning. Today's idea explains why nothing you see means anything. You do not know what it is for. Therefore, it is meaningless to you. Everything is for your own best interests. That is what it is for; that is its purpose; that is what it means. It is in recognizing this that your goals become unified. It is in recognizing this that what you see is given meaning.

Jesus is picking up from the early lessons, including the preceding one, by helping us realize why nothing here means anything. Something has meaning for us only because we do not understand what it is for, which comes from not knowing our own best interests. We think these have to do with satisfying our specialness needs, whether physical or emotional, while what is truly in our interest is learning to forgive. That is why everything in this world is for our own best interests, if we choose the right Teacher. Every situation or relationship can become a classroom in which we are helped to understand that the world we made comes from our attack thoughts, and everything we see, given to the Holy Spirit to reinterpret for us, can be a reminder that we can choose to look at the world differently. This process, as we have already seen, and shall see many times still, involves shifting our perception of the problem, and therefore our understanding of our best interests, from the *body* to the *mind*. To accomplish such a perceptual shift is the main goal of these lessons, not to mention *A Course in Miracles* itself.

The ego sees the meaning and purpose of everything in the world as an opportunity to satisfy its specialness needs. Jesus, on the other hand, sees opportunities, after our first making the ego mistake, to turn to him for help and be taught there is another way of looking at everything. This other way of looking, summarized in the three steps of forgiveness in Lesson 23, is realizing that what we

see outside is a projection of what we have first seen within. Once again, Jesus is teaching us to shift our attention from the body to the mind.

We learn that our perceptions, and the way we organize our personal world and relate to others, are based on the premise that we have an ego that has to be treated a certain way; that we have definite needs based on our separated existence that dictate how we must see our world, especially the people in it. Now that we have a teacher who shows us what we perceive outside is a projection of an inner thought, we can change this thought by having changed teachers. The world now has great meaning for us, for its new purpose has become our classroom, in which we learn from our new teacher his lessons of forgiveness.

When Jesus says purpose is everything, he means there are two: the ego's purpose of rooting us in this world so that our individuality—located in the mind—is safe; and the Holy Spirit's purpose of our realizing there is no world, for there is nothing in us that needs defense. Thus it is the world's new purpose to help us learn that happy fact, which is our salvation from our belief in guilt. "Perception and Choice" in the text summarizes the dual purpose of our split mind:

> But this world has two who made it, and they do not see it as the same. To each it has a different purpose, and to each it is a perfect means to serve the goal for which it is perceived.... There is another purpose in the world that error made, because it has another Maker Who can reconcile its goal with His Creator's purpose. In His perception of the world, nothing is seen but justifies forgiveness and the sight of perfect sinlessness (T-25.III.3:3-4; 5:1-2).

Thus is the real world of forgiveness made by the Holy Spirit as correction and substitute for the ego's error-filled world of guilt and hate.

(2:1) You perceive the world and everything in it as meaningful in terms of ego goals.

This idea could not have been stated more clearly. The "ego goals," as we have seen, are some expression of the need to preserve your own identity, individuality, and specialness. Through the mind-searching exercises you need to realize how true that is. Watch the way you think about things throughout the day—not necessarily your whole life, just your day; how everything is organized around what will meet your needs, what will make you feel good physically and emotionally. Then see how those needs distort how you perceive the world. In fact, it is those very specialness needs that cause you to believe you are perceiving the world at all!

(2:2-4) These goals have nothing to do with your own best interests, because the ego is not you. This false identification makes you incapable of understanding what anything is for. As a result, you are bound to misuse it.

This is an extremely important statement. The *you* of which Jesus speaks is not the ego—the physical or psychological self; it is what we have referred to as the decision maker. Jesus makes the same point in the text, as we have already seen, when he asks rhetorically: "Who is the 'you' who are living in this world?" (T-4.II.11:8). This early lesson is the beginning stage in having us dis-identify or disassociate from this ego self and realize that the *you* Jesus is addressing is in the mind.

By virtue of our having chosen the wrong teacher we have made the wrong identification. Consequently, we shall misunderstand, misinterpret, and distort everything that goes on around us because our perceptions will be geared toward fulfilling the purpose of preserving that identification. The guilt associated with our special relationships is thus reinforced, because we are misusing everyone and everything. This guilt seems so enormous that we can never let ourselves look at what we are doing. That is why it is so important to change teachers and allow Jesus to look at our guilt with us. Let him look with us at our misperceptions, misuse, distortions, and attacks, and he will help us realize they come from one mistake. In our joining with him is that mistake of separating from love undone.

(2:5) When you believe this, you will try to withdraw the goals you have assigned to the world, instead of attempting to reinforce them.

When we realize what we are doing, we will inevitably change the goal. In the text Jesus reflects this change as the shift from the unholy to the holy relationship; a relationship whose purpose was guilt or illusion becoming one whose purpose is forgiveness or truth—the letting go of guilt:

> And as the unholy relationship is a continuing hymn of hate in praise of its maker, so is the holy relationship a happy song of praise to the Redeemer of relationships.
> The holy relationship.... is the old, unholy relationship, transformed and seen anew (T-17.V.1:7–2:2).

(3) Another way of describing the goals you now perceive is to say that they are all concerned with "personal" interests. Since you have no personal interests, your goals are really concerned with nothing. In cherishing them, therefore, you have no goals at all. And thus you do not know what anything is for.

"Personal" is in quotes because there is no "personal." Within the dream, having personal interests means I have interests that are separate from yours. This can be true only if the separation were real. However, if minds are joined, there can be no personal interests; only the single interest we share as one Son to awaken from this dream and return home.

A careful and thoughtful reading of these lines is bound to engender tremendous anxiety—and that is certainly a mild understatement. Jesus is saying you have no personal interests, and where does that leave you but nowhere? In essence this means you do not even exist. Incidentally, *personal* in this context has the same meaning as *special*.

Again, Jesus is not asking you to accept his words and live as if they were true; he is asking you only to begin to understand the insanity of your thinking and distorted perceptions because you are literally believing and seeing what is not there. If you do not question these beliefs and perceptions, if only intellectually, you will never be open to receive the answer that is waiting for you. Thus, you need to observe your everyday thoughts, moment to moment, and realize how they come from everything Jesus is speaking about. They are all based on preserving an ego goal, which is your own identity. This means that you do not care about anyone or anything else, but only having your needs met and goals fulfilled.

(4) Before you can make any sense out of the exercises for today, one more thought is necessary. At the most superficial levels, you do recognize purpose. Yet purpose cannot be understood at these levels. For example, you do understand that a telephone is for the purpose of talking to someone who is not physically in your immediate vicinity. What you do not understand is what you want to reach him for. And it is this that makes your contact with him meaningful or not.

We all are aware of superficial purposes, but we are not aware of the true purposes underlying them. Using the example of the telephone, the *real* purpose of the call is to provide an opportunity for us to reconsider the ego's goal of separate interests in favor of the Holy Spirit's goal of shared or common interests. Therefore, what makes *A Course in Miracles* so simple is that it teaches us there are only two purposes we ever need consider, as we have already discussed: the ego's purpose, which is to retain individuality and separation, make the world real, and prove Jesus wrong; and Jesus' purpose, which is to *un*learn everything we had learned before, and finally accept with humility that he was right and we were wrong—the separation from God was a dream that never happened in reality.

(5:1) It is crucial to your learning to be willing to give up the goals you have established for everything.

Remember, because the goal you have established for everything is the preservation of your individuality, Jesus is asking that you abandon this purpose. That is why these lessons are so difficult, and must be perceived by our egos as extremely threatening.

The rest of the lesson underscores a point we have already seen: illusions remain illusions, regardless of the attributes we project onto them. From the ego's point of view, all illusions—*good* or *bad*, *important* or *unimportant*, *human* or *non-human*—serve the single purpose of convincing us that they *are* what they are *not*. That is why we do not know what they are for. These ostensibly simple sentences continue Jesus' training of our minds *not* to make distinctions among illusions, learning instead to make the *only* distinction that is valid—between the purposes of the ego and the Holy Spirit:

(5:2–6:8) The recognition that they [our goals] are meaningless, rather than "good" or "bad," is the only way to accomplish this. The idea for today is a step in this direction.

Six practice periods, each of two-minutes duration, are required. Each practice period should begin with a slow repetition of the idea for today, followed by looking about you and letting your glance rest on whatever happens to catch your eye, near or far, "important" or "unimportant," "human" or "non-human." With your eyes resting on each subject you so select, say, for example:

I do not know what this chair is for.
I do not know what this pencil is for.
I do not know what this hand is for.

Say this quite slowly, without shifting your eyes from the subject until you have completed the statement about it. Then move on to the next subject, and apply today's idea as before.

A more sophisticated statement of this teaching of the illusory nature of everything is found in the following passage from the text, which describes the shared insanity of our special relationships—our "little, senseless substitutions":

> Your little, senseless substitutions, touched with insanity and swirling lightly off on a mad course like feathers dancing insanely in the wind, have no substance. They fuse and merge and separate, in shifting and totally meaningless patterns that need not be judged at all. To judge them individually is pointless. Their tiny differences in form are no real differences at all. None of them matters. *That* they have in common and nothing else. Yet what else is necessary to make them all the same? (T-18.I.7:6-12)

Recognizing the inherent meaninglessness of everything allows us to accept the Holy Spirit's purpose of making room for His truth as replacement for the ego's illusions.

We are ready now to move to the next segment of our training: understanding the relationship between our attack thoughts and our perceptions of attack.

LESSON 26

My attack thoughts are attacking my invulnerability.

This is another crucial lesson and, as I just indicated, takes our learning (and practice) one step further. If I have attack thoughts, I must believe I am vulnerable. If I believe I am vulnerable, I cannot be Christ because He is invulnerable. If, as Jesus will repeatedly remind me, "I am as God created me,"* and if my reality is spirit, I must be one with everything and everyone. Therefore, there is literally nothing and no one "out there" who could hurt me. However, as long as I believe I can be hurt—whether in my own body or through someone else's—I am attesting to my vulnerability. Moreover, in saying I am vulnerable I am also saying that I am right in my self-evaluation and the Holy Spirit is wrong.

(1:1-3) It is surely obvious that if you can be attacked you are not invulnerable. You see attack as a real threat. That is because you believe that you can really attack.

The very fact that I am here is proving to me that I can really attack, because I could only have gotten here by attacking God first. And I "know" I have attacked first because I perceive attack all around me. The dynamic of *projection* helps me to understand how this phenomenon of perception of attack occurs: *projection makes perception*—what I perceive outside is the projection of what I have made real inside, a point we shall pick up again:

(1:4-6) And what would have effects through you must also have effects on you. It is this law that will ultimately save you, but you are misusing it now. You must therefore learn how it can be used for your own best interests, rather than against them.

As we have seen several times in these early lessons, the inner and outer are one and the same. The thought of attacking and the thought of being attacked come from the same thought system. We project out our ego thoughts, and then believe they are going to hurt us in return. As Jesus teaches in the

text, in the context of our needing to project ("get rid of") conflict ("what we do not want"):

> …the idea that you can get rid of something you do not want by giving it away. Giving it is how you *keep* it. The belief that by seeing it outside you have excluded it from within is a complete distortion of the power of extension. That is why those who project are vigilant for their own safety. They are afraid that their projections will return and hurt them. Believing they have blotted their projections from their own minds, they also believe their projections are trying to creep back in (T-7.VIII.3:6-11).

It is also true, as we have seen, that the Love of God we allow to come through us in forgiveness will come back to us as well—it is that Love we shall perceive all around us; either expressions of it or calls for it.

The laws of projection and extension operate similarly, but with different contents. That is why, early in the text, Jesus speaks of *projection* as the "inappropriate use of extension" (T-2.I.1:7)—it was the same law of the mind, simply "misused," leading to miscreation instead of creation. This law will ultimately save us in another sense as well, because it reflects that everything is an illusion. What seems to be outside is an illusion because what seems to be inside—the ego thought system—is an illusion. Recognizing this is the ego's undoing.

(2:1-2) Because your attack thoughts will be projected, you will fear attack. And if you fear attack, you must believe that you are not invulnerable.

This is what proves that you are right and Jesus is wrong. Jesus asks: "Why are you so upset? All of this is a dream." And we say to him: "What do you mean all of this is a dream? Look at how I have been attacked! Look at how I suffer and all the pain I am feeling! Look at what other people are feeling—*we are all vulnerable*! Please do not tell me this is a dream." That is how we prove our perceptions are

---

* There are more than 140 occurrences of this concept throughout *A Course in Miracles*. They have been compiled in Appendix C of the *Concordance of A Course in Miracles*, pp. 1101-1102.

correct. Our pain—whether in others or in ourselves—is final proof that God is dead and we exist in His stead.

(2:3-5) Attack thoughts therefore make you vulnerable in your own mind, which is where the attack thoughts are. Attack thoughts and invulnerability cannot be accepted together. They contradict each other.

If I perceive attack thoughts in you, it is only because I have first made them real for myself, which I have done out of the wish to make my separation from God—the original attack—real as well. It is only *after* that decision to establish attack as real that my ego's plan calls for me to project them out, thereby rendering me vulnerable to my perceived attack from others. It is clear that these attack thoughts—again, reflective of the separation from God and hence from everyone else—"cannot be accepted together" with our invulnerability as God created us. This is yet another way of saying that God and the ego are mutually exclusive. The dynamic of *dissociation* is what enables us to maintain these contradictory beliefs in our minds, as the text explains in these two passages:

> The ego and the spirit do not know each other. The separated mind cannot maintain the separation except by dissociating (T-4.VI.4:1-2).

> Dissociation is a distorted process of thinking whereby two systems of belief which cannot coexist are both maintained. If they are brought together, their joint acceptance becomes impossible. But if one is kept in darkness from the other, their separation seems to keep them both alive and equal in their reality. Their joining thus becomes the source of fear, for if they meet, acceptance must be withdrawn from one of them. You cannot have them both, for each denies the other. Apart, this fact is lost from sight, for each in a separate place can be endowed with firm belief (T-14.VII.4:3-8).

(3:1) The idea for today introduces the thought that you always attack yourself first.

To repeat, if I perceive you attacking me and then react as if that were true, it is only because I attacked first. This has nothing to do with behavior, for the attack exists only in my mind. Today's idea is reflected well in an incisive passage in the text: "If he speaks not of Christ to you, you spoke not of Christ to him" (T-11.V.18:6). Projection is the ruling principle governing the activity of the mind, since it determines how we *perceive* the world around us. Remember, perception is *interpretation*: *how* we see, not *what* we see.

It cannot be said too often that in order to properly understand passages such as these, the student must realize that Jesus is never talking about what people are doing behaviorally, but only about our *perception* of what others are doing. When you feel you have been attacked by another, you have *interpreted* their behavior. This does not mean you do not see attack thoughts in other people—Jesus sees attack thoughts in all his students. It is in our judgments that the attack thoughts are made real. Thus we read in the manual for teachers:

> Perhaps it will be helpful to remember that no one can be angry at a fact. It is always an interpretation that gives rise to negative emotions, regardless of their seeming justification by what *appears* as facts (M-17.4:1-2).

(3:2-5) If attack thoughts must entail the belief that you are vulnerable, their effect is to weaken you in your own eyes. Thus they have attacked your perception of yourself. And because you believe in them, you can no longer believe in yourself. A false image of yourself has come to take the place of what you are.

Having weakened ourselves in our own eyes (our vulnerability), we have once again proven we are right and the Holy Spirit is wrong; we are sons of the ego instead of Sons of God. We no longer believe we are the Christ, of which the Holy Spirit in our right minds is the reminder. We have replaced the truth of who we are with a false image—a special, unique, and individualized self. Again, it is our use of *dissociation* that allows us to maintain two contradictory images of ourselves: the truth of knowledge we have chosen to forget, and the illusion of attack we choose to remember. These passages cogently describe this dynamic and its undoing through the Holy Spirit:

> Unless you first know something you cannot dissociate it. Knowledge must precede dissociation, so that dissociation is nothing more than a decision to forget.... Offer the Holy Spirit only your willingness to remember, for He retains the knowledge of God and of yourself for you, waiting for your acceptance....

His Voice will tell you that you are part of Him when you are willing to remember Him and know your own reality again.... To remember is merely to restore to your mind *what is already there*. You do not make what you remember; you merely accept again what is already there, but was rejected....

When you attack, you are denying yourself.... Your denial of reality precludes the acceptance of God's gift, because you have accepted something else in its place.... This is always an attack on truth, and truth is God.... All attack is Self attack.... [and] is thus the way in which your identification is lost, because when you attack, you must have forgotten what you are. And if your reality is God's, when you attack you are not remembering Him (T-10.II.1:1-2; 2:3,5; 3:1-2; 4:1,3-4; 5:1,4-5).

(4) Practice with today's idea will help you to understand that vulnerability or invulnerability is the result of your own thoughts. Nothing except your thoughts can attack you. Nothing except your thoughts can make you think you are vulnerable. And nothing except your thoughts can prove to you this is not so.

The focus of our exercises is solely on our thoughts, the source of the problem and its solution. Indeed, everything is thought, acceptance of which is the aim of the workbook's mind training. These thoughts are not of a physical organ, the brain, but of the mind, coming from identifying either with the ego or Jesus. From these two thoughts or thought systems—guilt or innocence—arise a world and our perception of the world. If you feel yourself attacked, you have chosen the ego as your teacher and therefore believe you are vulnerable and deserve attack. This has nothing to do with behavior; it has to do only with the way you perceive the behavior. On the other hand, if we remember our invulnerability as God's perfect creation, our perception of the world changes accordingly. A passage near the end of the text succinctly expresses the principle that *projection makes perception*:

> The lessons to be learned are only two. Each has its outcome in a different world. And each world follows surely from its source. The certain outcome of the lesson that God's Son is guilty is the world you see. It is a world of terror and despair. Nor is there hope of happiness

in it.... Yet this is not the only outcome which your learning can produce.... The outcome of the lesson that God's Son is guiltless is a world in which there is no fear, and everything is lit with hope and sparkles with a gentle friendliness. Nothing but calls to you in soft appeal to be your friend, and let it join with you (T-31.I.7:1-6,9; 8:1-2).

The rest of the lesson presents an exercise and instructions with which we are quite familiar by now. The focus, as always, is on our thoughts and feelings that seem to upset us, looking at them as dispassionately as possible, and with more than cursory attention. It is this thoughtful non-evaluation that allows us to understand that these upsets *all* share the same underlying purpose of keeping us from the Thought of Love, which our thoughts attempt to conceal. In other words, all forms of upset reflect the hidden *content* of attacking ourselves by denying Who we are as God's one Son.

(5-7) Six practice periods are required in applying today's idea. A full two minutes should be attempted for each of them, although the time may be reduced to a minute if the discomfort is too great. Do not reduce it further.

The practice period should begin with repeating the idea for today, then closing your eyes and reviewing the unresolved questions whose outcomes are causing you concern. The concern may take the form of depression, worry, anger, a sense of imposition, fear, foreboding or preoccupation. Any problem as yet unsettled that tends to recur in your thoughts during the day is a suitable subject. You will not be able to use very many for any one practice period, because a longer time than usual should be spent with each one. Today's idea should be applied as follows:
First, name the situation:

> *I am concerned about ___.*

Then go over every possible outcome that has occurred to you in that connection and which has caused you concern, referring to each one quite specifically, saying:

> *I am afraid ___ will happen.*

This exercise reflects the ego's axiomatic principle: guilt demands punishment, an outcome we justifiably fear. Our concerns of what will happen —"the unresolved questions whose outcome are causing you concern"—inevitably lead to fear of what will happen. We thus have no choice but to erect defenses against these objects of our fear, predicted by our guilt. We shall return later on to this important theme of defense.

(8-9) If you are doing the exercises properly, you should have some five or six distressing possibilities available for each situation you use, and quite possibly more. It is much more helpful to cover a few situations thoroughly than to touch on a larger number. As the list of anticipated outcomes for each situation continues, you will probably find some of them, especially those that occur to you toward the end, less acceptable to you. Try, however, to treat them all alike to whatever extent you can.

After you have named each outcome of which you are afraid, tell yourself:

> ***That thought is an attack upon myself.***

Conclude each practice period by repeating today's idea to yourself once more.

This, of course, is the point. We bring the darkness of our illusions to the light of Jesus' truth. The problem is *not* with the outcome we expect, but with the underlying decision to attack ourselves by denying God. After these first twenty-five lessons, you can see how—step by step, lesson by lesson—Jesus is slowly and gently guiding us to the *specific* experience of the more *abstract* teachings in the text.

LESSON 27

Above all else I want to see.

This lesson and the next form a pair—"Above all else I want to see" and "Above all else I want to see things differently"—and move us still further along in our learning, returning to the theme of motivation. Teachers recognize that the most important trait they wish to see in their students is the *desire* to learn. Without that motivation, *nothing* will go on in the classroom. Likewise, therapists cannot be of help to their patients unless they are motivated to change. Thus, we have to *want* to learn what *A Course in Miracles* is teaching us, otherwise even the world's greatest teacher will fail. We want to learn Jesus' course because it will make us happy. To do this, Jesus first has to convince us that we are not happy now. His need is nicely expressed in the opening to "The Happy Learner" in the text:

> The Holy Spirit needs a happy learner, in whom His mission can be happily accomplished. You who are steadfastly devoted to misery must first recognize that you are miserable and not happy. The Holy Spirit cannot teach without this contrast, for you believe that misery *is* happiness. This has so confused you that you have undertaken to learn to do what you can never do, believing that unless you learn it you will not be happy (T-14.II.1:1-4).

Now to the lesson itself:

(1:1-4) Today's idea expresses something stronger than mere determination. It gives vision priority among your desires. You may feel hesitant about using the idea, on the grounds that you are not sure you really mean it. This does not matter.

Jesus is not expecting anyone to really mean these words. If we give up judgment and choose vision, it is because we have chosen to let go of our investment in specialness, which to the ego means we are leaving ourselves wide open for attack. Without specialness to defend against our inner emptiness and lack, so the ego counsels us, we become vulnerable to the hostile world around us, hell-bent on our destruction.

(1:5) The purpose of today's exercises is to bring the time when the idea will be wholly true a little nearer.

Jesus is making it clear, as he does throughout *A Course in Miracles*, that this is a process. Thus he does not expect us suddenly to drop the ego's hand and take his. But he does want us to understand what the choices entail, so we know what we are growing into.

(2:1) There may be a great temptation to believe that some sort of sacrifice is being asked of you when you say you want to see above all else.

The theme of sacrifice will appear later in the lessons. To the ego, seeing through Christ's vision is to sacrifice our personal identity, which is based on separation and judgment, fear and hate. From the ego's point of view sacrifice is definitely involved if we are to survive: either we sacrifice our happiness and pleasure to atone for past sins, or others need be sacrificed for us to be happy and peaceful. Either way, someone must lose so that another wins—the ego's principle of *one or the other*. The next lines provide the Holy Spirit's answer to this principle of sacrifice:

(2:2-5) If you become uneasy about the lack of reservation involved, add:

> *Vision has no cost to anyone.*

If fear of loss still persists, add further:

> *It can only bless.*

Jesus is urging us to reflect our deeper motivation to learn by attempting to remember the lesson as often as possible throughout the day. It should be noted here, to be repeated again and again, that it is not sinful when we forget. Indeed, such forgetting provides us with very helpful information about ourselves. If we are truly to learn this course, we first have to understand how *resistant* we are to learning it. Unless we can undo this resistance—ultimately born of our fear of losing our self—we shall forever be obstructing our progress. The first step in this process of undoing is becoming aware of the problem. Only then can it be truly addressed and gone beyond.

(3) The idea for today needs many repetitions for maximum benefit. It should be used at least every half hour, and more if possible. You might try for every fifteen or twenty minutes. It is recommended that you set a definite time interval for using the idea when you wake or shortly afterwards, and attempt to adhere to it throughout the day. It will not be difficult to do this, even if you are engaged in conversation, or otherwise occupied at the time. You can still repeat one short sentence to yourself without disturbing anything.

But Jesus knows his audience, and so he gently speaks to us. On the one hand he calls upon our motivation to learn, expressed in the recommended increase of practice; and on the other hand he reminds us *not* to feel guilty when we are resistant, as we now read:

(4:1-5) The real question is, how often will you remember [the lesson for the day]**? How much do you want today's idea to be true? Answer one of these questions, and you have answered the other. You will probably miss several applications, and perhaps quite a number. Do not be disturbed by this, but do try to keep on your schedule from then on.**

Thus, Jesus is telling us not to feel guilty when we forget. He expects us to forget. But he is telling us that when we remember that we forgot, at least we should try to understand *why* we did so: we are not so sure we really want to learn this course. Part of us does, obviously; otherwise we would not be doing it. However, there is another part that has serious reservations about continuing on this path. Our identification with the ego and its thought system of separation and judgment is still quite strong.

(4:6) If only once during the day you feel that you were perfectly sincere while you were repeating today's idea, you can be sure that you have saved yourself many years of effort.

In the text, Jesus refers to saving thousands of years (e.g., T-1.II.6:7). Even if you can only be sincere once during the day, that has already accomplished a great deal. It is helpful to recall that linear time is an illusion, and since our very existence is predicated on the reality of time and space, it is impossible for us to understand the truth of this last statement. Fortunately, our understanding is not necessary, only our little willingness (T-18.IV.7:5-6).

In the next lesson Jesus expands on these ideas.

LESSON 28

Above all else I want to see things differently.

(1) Today we are really giving specific application to the idea for yesterday. In these practice periods, you will be making a series of definite commitments. The question of whether you will keep them in the future is not our concern here. If you are willing at least to make them now, you have started on the way to keeping them. And we are still at the beginning.

The fundamental commitment is to prove that our whole identity rests on a lie—or to state it in a less threatening way, the commitment is to realize we are wrong and Jesus is right: there is another way of looking at the world. Once again Jesus is applying no time pressure on us; he is quite aware of our resistance to (or fear of) making this commitment. Incidentally, his last sentence is reminiscent of his comment to psychotherapists:

> Most professional therapists are still at the very start of the beginning stage of the first journey. Even those who have begun to understand what they must do may still oppose the setting-out (P-3.II.8:5-6).

Clearly, Jesus sees us *all* as beginners, resistant to change and growth.

(2:1-5) You may wonder why it is important to say, for example, "Above all else I want to see this table differently." In itself it is not important at all. Yet what is by itself? And what does "in itself" mean? You see a lot of separate things about you, which really means you are not seeing at all.

Lesson 183 focuses more directly on this idea of giving different names to the "separate things" in the world, a process that reflects the ego's need to make separation and individuality into reality. Jesus is asking us to understand the underlying premise of his course, which is that everything is the same because everything shares the same purpose. In terms of *form*, the things of the world are clearly different and have a different purpose from each other. On the level of *content*, however, we share the one purpose of having our minds healed. In that sense everything is the same, because all things can be utilized to accomplish that purpose. *A Course in Miracles*, we need to remember, is about *content*, not *form*.

(2:6-8) You either see or not. When you have seen one thing differently, you will see all things differently. The light you will see in any one of them is the same light you will see in them all.

What changes is not what is outside, but our choice of teacher. When our inner Teacher has been changed, we shall see everything through His eyes instead of the ego's.

Once again, Jesus is not talking about a physical light. The light we shall see is the light of Christ's vision, the light of understanding that recognizes a shared or common purpose in everyone and everything.

(3) When you say, "Above all else I want to see this table differently," you are making a commitment to withdraw your preconceived ideas about the table, and open your mind to what it is, and what it is for. You are not defining it in past terms. You are asking what it is, rather than telling it what it is. You are not binding its meaning to your tiny experience of tables, nor are you limiting its purpose to your little personal thoughts.

This is the humility that says: "I do not know." A table is not important since we typically do not project onto it, but it serves here as an example to make the point. What is more important is our humbly admitting that we do not know the meaning and purpose of a relationship or situation. If we think we know, we shall never be open to receive the answer and learn the truth. Holding on to the past is what reflects this arrogant belief that we know, the defense against the vision that comes from choosing the holy instant.

(4:1-2) You will not question what you have already defined. And the purpose of these exercises is to ask questions and receive the answers.

Again, our humility is called upon. If you think you understand *A Course in Miracles* you will not be open to what it is teaching you. If you think you understand the purpose of any particular workbook lesson, you will not be open to receiving the answer that Jesus has for you. If you think you understand, a wall suddenly drops before your mind and you will not be taught anything. You will *think* you are being taught, but what you will be "learning" is simply what your ego wanted you to learn in the first place. We have already considered this subtle ego ploy, wherein we consciously believe we are asking for help, but all we are really doing is telling Jesus what we want him to tell us by defining our problem or framing our question. This inevitably dictates the answer we shall receive, thereby limiting him. He reminds us of this in the text as well:

> You have been as selective in your questioning as in your perception. An open mind is more honest than this (T-13.IV.3:7-8).

All this of course is reminiscent of our ontological limiting of God by defining the nature of our self. Jesus is thus helping us undo or unlearn everything we believe about everything—acquiring an *open mind*—including what we believe about this course. As he states in the text:

> To learn this course requires willingness to question every value that you hold. Not one can be kept hidden and obscure but it will jeopardize your learning (T-24.in.2:1-2).

(4:3-5) In saying, "Above all else I want to see this table differently," you are committing yourself to seeing. It is not an exclusive commitment. It is a commitment that applies to the table just as much as to anything else, neither more nor less.

We again see Jesus' attempts to motivate us to learn what he is teaching us, and to generalize this vision to all things. Indeed, if it cannot be generalized, it is not true vision.

(5) You could, in fact, gain vision from just that table, if you would withdraw all your own ideas from it, and look upon it with a completely open mind. It has something to show you; something beautiful and clean and of infinite value, full of happiness and hope. Hidden under all your ideas about it is its real purpose, the purpose it shares with all the universe.

The purpose shared with all the universe is forgiveness—"beautiful and clean and of infinite

value"—the source of true happiness and genuine hope. None of these comes from the table itself, the experience, or a person. Rather, our happiness and hope come from the *purpose*, the beauty of which is found in the beauty of the Teacher you have chosen. That is why purpose is the bottom line. To say it again, purpose is not inherent in the object, but in the decision made by the mind to learn from the Holy Spirit how to see the world truly.

(6) In using the table as a subject for applying the idea for today, you are therefore really asking to see the purpose of the universe. You will be making this same request of each subject that you use in the practice periods. And you are making a commitment to each of them to let its purpose be revealed to you, instead of placing your own judgment upon it.

Your judgment comes from a thought that says you are right and Jesus is wrong. *You* are going to teach *him* what his course ought to be teaching you, rather than being open to having him be the teacher. However, when we are open, we can be taught the inherent *sameness* of all things in the universe. They are the *same* because they share the *same* purpose. Purpose, to make this point one more time, is everything.

Remember, too, that you need to work at thinking about the ideas in these exercises in light of the thoughts you are having at the moment you are doing them. It is the specific application, made as often as possible, that will facilitate your learning.

The final paragraphs reiterate the non-obsessional, yet thoughtful application of the day's exercises. We try to remember that we *want* to learn what Jesus is teaching us—to see the world differently:

(7-8) We will have six two-minute practice periods today, in which the idea for the day is stated first, and then applied to whatever you see about you. Not only should the subjects be chosen randomly, but each one should be accorded equal sincerity as today's idea is applied to it, in an attempt to acknowledge the equal value of them all in their contribution to your seeing.

As usual, the applications should include the name of the subject your eyes happen to light

on, and you should rest your eyes on it while saying:

> *Above all else I want to see this ___ differently.*

Each application should be made quite slowly, and as thoughtfully as possible. There is no hurry.

"Quite slowly," "as thoughtfully as possible," "no hurry." These should be the shibboleths of our days. As our new teacher, Jesus is asking us to adopt a new perspective—one that avoids the tension and pressure of undoing our egos, but seeks instead the gentle and patient approach he is providing us in these exercises. Since we are being taught that our daily lessons are the same, their form is immaterial. Thus, important and unimportant, major and minor, become irrelevant designations of events and relationships. Uniting them all as one leaves us with the only choice to make: the ego or the Holy Spirit. Choosing God's Voice to guide us, our lives slow to the quiet pace of those who know the outcome is sure. Thus we proceed in confidence that our Teacher will teach us all we need to know, and that, in time, we shall learn His lessons.

LESSON 29

God is in everything I see.

When people seek to criticize *A Course in Miracles* on grounds of pantheism—a major heresy for Catholics that teaches that God is literally found in the materiality that is His manifestation—this lesson in particular, as well as the one following, are selected as prime examples. Many years ago I was speaking to a Jesuit priest, who was reminiscent of an old-time heresy hunter. A very conservative Catholic, his major function in life seemed to be to find every heretical teaching in contemporary Christianity. After he heard about me and *A Course in Miracles*, he took it upon himself to save the nuns and priests with whom I had been working from falling into the depths of perdition with this course. I spent an hour with him one evening, during which time he proceeded to enumerate the Course's heresies. He actually had examined only the workbook, and had spent considerable time on this particular lesson as proof of *A Course in Miracles*' pantheism. It is true, in fact, when this initial statement, "God is in everything I see," is taken at face value, it does seem to be pantheistic: God is in the table, God is in the chair, God is in the body, God is in the plants, etc. It becomes clear as you study this lesson carefully, however, that that is precisely *not* what Jesus is talking about. The theme of these two lessons—Lessons 29 and 30—is that the *purpose* of God—i.e., the purpose of forgiveness—is in everything I see. This is so because purpose is in the mind, which will be explained as we proceed.

The reader may recall my discussion in this book's Preface of how the language in the workbook, not to mention in *A Course in Miracles* itself, can be misleading. For example, as I mentioned before, in the workbook especially, Jesus will say *God* when, technically speaking, he is referring to *the Holy Spirit*. An explicit example, to cite it again, is found in Lesson 193, "All things are lessons God would have me learn," where in the lesson itself Jesus clearly states that God does not teach, for that is the Holy Spirit's role. In this lesson, too, in saying the purpose of God is in everything I see, Jesus is really speaking of the Holy Spirit's teaching purpose.

(1) The idea for today explains why you can see all purpose in everything. It explains why nothing is separate, by itself or in itself. And it explains why nothing you see means anything. In fact, it explains every idea we have used thus far, and all subsequent ones as well. Today's idea is the whole basis for vision.

As we shall see in the next lesson as well, vision has absolutely nothing to do with the body's eyes, but with a state of mind or attitude. More specifically, vision refers to our having chosen Jesus as our teacher so his are now the "eyes" through which we see. We are taught that *the inner and outer are the same.* Therefore what we perceive outside is nothing more than a shadow of what we have first perceived within. When Jesus says "God is in everything I see," he means that God is in everything I *think*, because seeing and thinking are the same: perception comes from thoughts, and remains one with them. The basis for vision then is seeing the *purpose* of God. I see forgiveness in everything I see because I have fired the ego as my teacher, and hired Jesus. To again cite these two statements, taken together: "Resign now as your own teacher.... for you were badly taught" (T-12.V.8:3; T-28.I.7:1). At that point, everything I perceive, think, and feel is the opposite of what it had been prior to taking Jesus as my new teacher.

(2:1-3) You will probably find this idea very difficult to grasp at this point. You may find it silly, irreverent, senseless, funny and even objectionable. Certainly God is not in a table, for example, as you see it.

We find it difficult because we think there actually is a table that is separate from our bodies, and that our eyes actually perceive it—the world's illusory version of seeing. In that sense God cannot be in the table because there is no table. Again, the point to notice is that Jesus is shifting the emphasis from what we perceive *outside* to what we see *inside*. It is the *way* in which we see that is the focus of his teaching—our thoughts—which have to do only with the purpose or teacher we are choosing.

Incidentally, if it has not already occurred to a student doing these lessons for the first time how radically different Jesus' teaching is here, these two lessons should make that abundantly clear. *A Course in Miracles* is nothing like what is usually taught in other spiritual disciplines. This radicalness is based on the underlying metaphysics that teaches that the phenomenal world is an illusion. Therefore, what we perceive and think here is not real at all. It must be, then, that the true activity is not what happens in our bodies or the world, but in our minds. This is more clearly enunciated in these lessons than heretofore.

(2:4) Yet we emphasized yesterday that a table shares the purpose of the universe.

That purpose, to repeat, is to be an object that appears to be outside us, onto which we project our minds' ego thoughts. With Jesus as our teacher, we now look at what we perceived and see it differently. Forgiveness entails realizing that what we perceive outside mirrors what we have first made real inside. That is why—to state the Course's unique definition—we forgive our brothers for what they did *not* do; they have not done anything in the sense of having the power to take away our peace. What needs to be forgiven, therefore, are *our* thoughts of guilt, born of the belief that we have separated from peace; it is this guilt we have projected onto others.

(2:5) And what shares the purpose of the universe shares the purpose of its Creator.

Here Jesus uses the words *universe* and *Creator* loosely—another example of the "looseness" of the Course's language—because clearly he is talking about the physical universe. But God cannot be the creator of the physical, as is unmistakably clear throughout *A Course in Miracles*. If you take these lines literally, you will end up pulling your hair out because they will seem to say the exact opposite of what Jesus is teaching elsewhere. You want to grasp the *content* of what he is teaching, rather than analyzing it to death and arguing with the *form*. I shall return frequently to this important point.

(3:1) Try then, today, to begin to learn how to look on all things with love, appreciation and open-mindedness.

If you choose Jesus as your teacher you will

identify with his love. Thus what you see outside will be an expression of love or the call for it. You will look with appreciation on the world, especially your special relationships, because these will have become the opportunities to learn you are forgiven and your ego can be undone. "Open-mindedness" means your mind is no longer closed to the truth of the Holy Spirit. When we choose the ego as our teacher and dismiss the Holy Spirit, our minds become closed to His truth. "Open-mindedness" here, as in the tenth characteristic of the teacher of God discussed in the manual for teachers (M-4.X), means our minds are open to the love of Jesus. There is then no distortion in our thinking, which in turn means there is no distortion in our perception. What we hear and see will come from love, rather than from our having superimposed ego thoughts on these objects of our perception.

(3:2-4) You do not see them now [i.e., you do not see things as they really are]. **Would you know what is in them? Nothing is as it appears to you.**

This is another of those sentences which, if you stopped and meditated on it, should make you extremely anxious. If you see nothing as it is— "nothing is as it appears to you"—and everything you perceive is wrong, then the way you perceive *yourself* must be wrong as well. *All* your thoughts about everything are wrong.

(3:5-6) Its holy purpose stands beyond your little range. When vision has shown you the holiness that lights up the world, you will understand today's idea perfectly.

This is a reference back to Lesson 15, the idea of seeing edges of light around objects. Jesus makes it very clear here, as well as in the lessons we have already studied, that he is not talking about auras or any form of external light. He is referring to a different way of seeing; a vision based on the light of truth, the new understanding that comes when we choose him instead of the ego's narrow band of distortion ("your little range").

(3:7) And you will not understand how you could ever have found it difficult.

Everyone has had this experience at one time or another: When even for an instant our minds are clear—when guilt and judgmental thoughts are gone and we feel Jesus' love within us—everything in *A Course in Miracles* becomes crystal clear. When the fear arises from our having realized the implications of what it means to be wrong and have Jesus be right, our minds close again and vision and perception become distorted.

The last two paragraphs repeat the usual instructions:

(4) Our six two-minute practice periods for today should follow a now familiar pattern: Begin with repeating the idea to yourself, and then apply it to randomly chosen subjects about you, naming each one specifically. Try to avoid the tendency toward self-directed selection, which may be particularly tempting in connection with today's idea because of its wholly alien nature. Remember that any order you impose is equally alien to reality.

This simple directive reflects a much deeper point. Our fear of leaving the ego's dream of illusion for the truth is so great that we are all sorely tempted to bring the truth to the illusion. One form of this temptation is thinking we understand what we are being taught, and why these exercises take the form they do. Thus, we seek to impose our own familiar

thought system on the "wholly alien nature" of Jesus', thereby unconsciously, but with great ingenuity, negating the teachings and goal of *A Course in Miracles*. The last paragraph provides examples of our freedom from "self-directed selection":

(5:1) Your list of subjects should therefore be as free of self-selection as possible.

Suggested subjects include the "important" and "unimportant": finger, body, coat hanger, magazine, lamp, door, and waste basket (5:3-9). Jesus next gives us a hint of the wondrous effects of our learning, the peace that lies beyond our own fear:

(5:10-11) In addition to the assigned practice periods, repeat the idea for today at least once an hour, looking slowly about you as you say the words unhurriedly to yourself. At least once or twice, you should experience a sense of restfulness as you do this.

It is the desire for this "sense of restfulness"— what in the text Jesus refers to as finding the "quiet center" within our minds (T-18.VII.8)—that supplies our motivation for practicing these exercises and learning *A Course in Miracles'* message.

LESSON 30

God is in everything I see because God is in my mind.

This lesson also is extremely important, explaining *why* God is in everything I see: He is in my mind. The context, again, is not what we perceive outside, but what is in our minds. Therefore, "think" can be substituted for "see," because our eyes report to us nothing more than the reflection of what we have been thinking: *Projection makes perception.* Indeed, this lesson advances our understanding and experience of projection, the ego's defense *par excellence* for retaining our guilt under the guise of getting rid of it.

(1) The idea for today is the springboard for vision. From this idea will the world open up before you, and you will look upon it and see in it what you have never seen before. Nor will what you saw before be even faintly visible to you.

This is a theme that is repeated many times throughout *A Course in Miracles*: when our minds are awakened and we see with Jesus' love, everything we saw before will disappear. Our judgments against others and against ourselves, our strange ways of understanding events—all will disappear. As we reinforce this new way of thinking and seeing, those judgments, which are defenses against the truth of our and our brothers' reality, will gradually fade until they disappear entirely. This is what Jesus is saying to us here. It is easy to see why these ideas can frighten us. It is not just our judgments, distorted perceptions, and thinking that will disappear; *we*, as we have always known ourselves to be, will disappear as well. This is the real meaning of defenselessness: being *without* defenses. The ego would attempt to convince us that we need defenses to protect us from our pain, either inflicted from within or without. It never lets us in on its secret: its entire defensive structure is aimed at protecting us from *God*.

Psychology—the study of the ego—helps us understand how everyone's life—certainly by adulthood—is built up as a defense against the pain and hurt of childhood. We came into this world so that we would feel victimized as children; that is the point of being born into this world, as I discussed in the Prelude. Our entire lives, from the

ego's point of view, are made up of defenses to protect us from what we have come to accept as undeniable truths about the world, and especially our personal worlds: I cannot trust my mother, I cannot trust my father, I cannot trust women, I cannot trust men, I cannot trust my body, I cannot trust authorities, and on and on and on. In everyone's life these conclusions are perfectly justified, because our scripts, as we have already seen, were specifically written to justify our feelings of unfair treatment. Once our victimization is accepted as truth, we build up wall upon wall of defenses to protect us against these imagined hurts, slights, and pains of our childhood and youth. They are *imagined* because they are not there anymore. In fact, they were never truly there, being but part of our dream. However, we never want to look at this truth through Jesus' vision, because we would then realize it was all made up.

There is actually no justification for us to build walls of defenses, since our problems are inherently non-existent. That is the truth we fear. The meaning our lives have taken on is surviving the onslaughts of this hard, cruel, unfeeling, insensitive, and vicious world—Hamlet's "slings and arrows of outrageous fortune." There is no question the world *is* cruel, insensitive, and vicious. *That is why it was made*, and what is meant by the statement, "the world was made as an attack on God" (W-pII.3.2:1).

Our existence is predicated on the truth of what we are so sure is reality. We do not want to be told there is another way of looking, because it is obvious Jesus is not talking about another way of looking at a table. That is just an exercise to help us realize there is another way of looking at *ourselves*. Once again, as you practice these lessons, thinking about them and meditating, try to get in touch with the fear that comes from understanding what they are saying. It is helpful to look back and see how your life has been built as a defense against what you believe is the problem: how to survive as an innocent victim in a harsh world. Jesus teaches us there is another way of looking at absolutely everything, but this vision comes at a price: replacing our victimized self—buttressed by a lifetime's accumulation of defenses—with a self that can be truly defenseless, "protected" by the innocence that is the reflection of Heaven's sinlessness.

(2:1-2) Today we are trying to use a new kind of "projection." We are not attempting to get rid of what we do not like by seeing it outside.

While the word is not used here, Jesus is clearly speaking of *extension*; half of the dynamic of looking within, and having that affect what we see outside. With projection we see our sinfulness and guilt, judge against it, and project it onto others. We get rid of what we do not like within us. That literally is how the world was made. In a line which we shall read in Lesson 161, Jesus says: "Thus were specifics made"—we made a world of specifics so that we could have someone and something onto whom we project the guilt we do not want.

Jesus is teaching us now about "a new kind of 'projection'" (extension), in which we take the love we first looked at within—the Love of Christ we are, the love of Jesus to which we can relate—and have it extend so we see it all around us. Importantly, we do not see love as separate from us as we do when we project our guilt, wherein we *must* see the guilt in someone other than ourselves—intrinsic to the purpose of projection. Christ's Love, which is first seen within, is now experienced in everyone else, regardless of the veils of fear and hate unconsciously used to conceal it. Again, we experience this love in everyone because we have first experienced it in ourselves. The shift Jesus is discussing is the shift to our right minds—from the ego's projection of guilt to the Holy Spirit's extension of forgiveness—and is key to the practice of *A Course in Miracles*.

(2:3) Instead, we are trying to see in the world what is in our minds, and what we want to recognize is there.

The key thought is "what we want to recognize is there." As the text states:

> Perception seems to teach you what you see. Yet it but witnesses to what you taught. It is the outward picture of a wish; an image that you wanted to be true (T-24.VII.8:8-10).

Our secret wish is to keep the separation, but to see the responsibility for it in another. The "image that you wanted to be true" is our brother's guilt. Thus

the ego says guilt is real and we do *not* want to recognize it. By convincing us not to recognize the mind's guilt, the ego hopes we will never look at the love that is already in our minds. In the text, Jesus says we have but two emotions: love and fear—one we made and one was given us (T-13.V.10:1). The emotion of fear, which is really the same as guilt, is what we made to cover the love that God gave us. We need to recognize the guilt so we can look beyond it to identify with the love that is there. This, of course, is totally different from the ego's way of proceeding, which makes guilt real and then makes us promise never to look at it. It tells us not to recognize it in ourselves, but rather to get rid of the guilt by seeing it in everyone else. However, the ego never tells us that its plan does not work, for the guilt remains within our minds, despite our fevered attempts to disown it. All this is described quite clearly in the text:

> The ultimate purpose of projection is always to get rid of guilt.... Yet consider how strange a solution the ego's arrangement is. You project guilt to get rid of it, but you are actually merely concealing it. You do experience the guilt, but you have no idea why (T-13.II.1:1; 2:1-3).

> In any union with a brother in which you seek to lay your guilt upon him, or share it with him or perceive his own, *you* will feel guilty.... You will see guilt in that relationship because you put it there. It is inevitable that those who suffer guilt will attempt to displace it, because they do believe in it. Yet though they suffer, they will not look within and let it go.... Their main concern is to perceive the source of guilt outside themselves, beyond their own control (T-13.X.3:1,3-5,7).

Following the ego's guidance, then, we draw upon our background of decades of experience and confidently declare that the guilt is in all these others. Moreover, we have all the proof needed to justify the way we feel about them. We expound on how they have abused and mistreated us, or have abused and mistreated others with whom we identify as victims. We are so absolutely certain we are right about our conclusions. That is why *A Course in Miracles* is so difficult and frightening. Over and over, Jesus tells us we are wrong, that "God thinks otherwise" (T-23.I.2:7). But we are positive that He is wrong and we are correct!

(2:4-5) Thus, we are trying to join with what we see, rather than keeping it apart from us. That is the fundamental difference between vision and the way you see.

The way we see, again, is to see problems or objects of pleasure outside us. We always want to keep separate from us what is outside. Even when we seem to want to join with others, we are really trying to have the illusion of joining so we can protect our specialness. In vision, however, we no longer see ourselves as separate from anyone. Early in the manual Jesus makes an important statement I have already cited: the qualifications of a teacher of God consist solely in his not seeing his interests as apart from anyone else's (M-1.1:2). That vision could begin only by not seeing our interests as separate from those of the Holy Spirit or Jesus. At the beginning, our interests are quite separate, because if we join with Them our ego's individuality and specialness are gone. Thus we *must* keep Them split off from us, just as we have done with God. Based upon this dynamic of splitting, we split off our guilt, projecting it onto others whom we now see as separate from us. Vision is exactly the opposite, seeing all people as the same, reflecting our inherent oneness as Christ.

The radicalness of *A Course in Miracles'* thought system is that Jesus is not talking about the brain or the body, but only the mind, which cannot be seen or touched because it is beyond our senses or anything physical or quantifiable.

(3) Today's idea should be applied as often as possible throughout the day. Whenever you have a moment or so, repeat it to yourself slowly, looking about you, and trying to realize that the idea applies to everything you do see now, or could see now if it were within the range of your sight.

Jesus is once again reminding us about generalizing; not to exclude anything in our application of the lessons. Remember, once you believe there is a hierarchy of illusions and a range of what you perceive, you are saying that separation and differences are reality and truth. The only reality is the one thought of the Atonement, the only reality within our minds. Because that thought is one, it is seen as one. Everything in this world is the same as everything else, because all things share the one purpose of forgiveness.

(4) Real vision is not limited to concepts such as "near" and "far." To help you begin to get used to this idea, try to think of things beyond your present range as well as those you can actually see, as you apply today's idea.

Here we can see Jesus subtly getting across his point that this idea works not only for what our eyes physically see, but for what we think about, too—what we see in our minds as well as what we "actually" see. Again, real vision has nothing to do with anything physical. It does not apply to what we physically perceive (see, hear, feel, touch, or whatever), but to what we *think*. Recall that there is no difference between what we think and what we see. It is only in accepting this truth that one can begin to have the understanding that will hopefully lead to the experience of our inherent oneness, a unity that can exist only in the mind, since bodies separate. As Jesus reminds us in the text: "Minds are joined; bodies are not" (T-18.VI.3:1).

(5:1-2) Real vision is not only unlimited by space and distance, but it does not depend on the body's eyes at all. The mind is its only source.

We could not ask for a clearer statement than this. Jesus is not talking about anything that we perceive, because we are always seeing some form of separation, which means what we see comes from a thought of separation in our minds, a thought that is intrinsically mistaken. As Jesus states in a line we shall quote frequently: "Nothing so blinding as perception of form" (T-22.III.6:7).

Even though it is not yet specifically mentioned in these lessons, though I discussed it in the Prelude, the idea of going to Jesus or the Holy Spirit for help is central to our practice of *A Course in Miracles*. By separating ourselves from Them we are separating ourselves from God, which means we are regarding separation as reality. Everything we think, see, or believe from that point on will be wrong. That is why there is so much fear associated with doing this course. It slowly begins to dawn on us that we are mistaken about everything we think, perceive, and judge—about ourselves and everyone else.

(5:3-4) To aid in helping you to become more accustomed to this idea as well, devote several practice periods to applying today's idea with your eyes closed, using whatever subjects come to mind, and looking within rather than without. Today's idea applies equally to both.

The answer to why today's idea applies equally to what is within and without is that there is nothing out there. What appears outside is simply a projection of our thoughts. Whether we are looking at our thoughts outside or our thoughts within our minds does not make any difference. They are still our thoughts. These two lessons are quite explicit that everything begins in our minds. This is directly related to the principle described in the text and that we have already seen in these lessons: *Ideas leave not their source*—the idea of a separated world, relationship, and body, has never left its source in the mind. Everything we perceive are our projected thoughts. The only thing that is important, then, is getting in touch with the source of these thoughts—the ego or the Holy Spirit. This is the ultimate purpose of these exercises and of *A Course in Miracles* itself.

LESSON 31

I am not the victim of the world I see.

This is many people's favorite lesson, or else their most *un*favorite one. As I said in the preceding lesson, everyone's life has developed as a defense against the pain of childhood victimization, which our society holds sacrosanct. Therefore, to take this lesson seriously undermines everyone's physical and psychological existence. If you are not the victim of the world you see, then you do not need any defenses. Imagine your life without defenses! In traditional psychology, if you are without defenses you are thought to be psychotic, which is true from the world's point of view. To be identified with the Love of God is indeed a form of psychosis as the world sees it, because it goes against everything judged to be reality, beginning with the other-worldly selflessness that *is* our Self. Thus, if the statement "I am not the victim of the world I see" is true, your life is a lie—meaningless and purposeless, which has been the major theme of these early lessons. You can therefore understand why *A Course in Miracles* must engender anxiety, and why you would always have to attack it in one way or another, or attack those who represent it to you. These teachings undermine everything you believe about yourself, beliefs which have given your life its meaning.

(1:1-3) Today's idea is the introduction to your declaration of release. Again, the idea should be applied to both the world you see without and the world you see within. In applying the idea, we will use a form of practice which will be used more and more, with changes as indicated.

Obviously, this is not release as the world sees it. This is a declaration of release from your ego, from the prison of your life of guilt and projection.

The next few lines describe a new form of exercise, encompassing both a more sustained meditation on the day's idea as well as the frequent applications throughout the day that will come to characterize our daily experience with the workbook. Without these "frequent applications," one's work could easily lapse into mere intellectual practice. Jesus is asking us to cultivate the discipline of becoming increasingly vigilant for our ego's temptation of illusory thoughts of attack, so we may bring them to the truth-filled presence of the Holy Spirit in our minds, the process we are coming to recognize as forgiveness:

(1:4) Generally speaking, the form includes two aspects, one in which you apply the idea on a more sustained basis, and the other consisting of frequent applications of the idea throughout the day.

When we read Lesson 95 we shall see a discussion of the need to forgive ourselves for forgetting the exercises throughout the day. It is important to recognize our resistance; otherwise it is impossible to let it go and move beyond the defense to the truth of God's Love.

(2) Two longer periods of practice with the idea for today are needed, one in the morning and one at night. Three to five minutes for each of these are recommended. During that time, look about you slowly while repeating the idea two or three times. Then close your eyes, and apply the same idea to your inner world. You will escape from both together, for the inner is the cause of the outer.

Here, again, Jesus is making it clear that the inner and the outer are one and the same. The exercises, then, have to do with applying the idea both to what you perceive outside you as well as to what you think within your own mind. We continue to be reminded that the inner is the *cause* of the outer. This cause-effect theme acquires more and more significance as the teaching proceeds and our understanding deepens.

If, contrary to what Jesus has been saying, we believe that the way we feel is a result of the way people have treated us, we are saying the cause is outside us—the outer is the cause of the inner. This approach makes us absolutely helpless in this world, because even though we may have the illusion of being able to control some things, there is very little we can do to control everything in the world that affects us. After all, our bodies were made to be fragile and vulnerable, and indeed they are.

If, on the other hand, we invert this and see that the cause is inside, it does not matter what happens outside, because now we are in control of what we feel: our *reactions* to external happenings. We have learned that what we feel and experience comes from a choice we have made. Much later in the workbook Jesus says we are in control of the universe (e.g., Lesson 253). As we have already discussed, if we choose the ego as our teacher, we perceive and experience the world in one way. If we take Jesus as our teacher, we perceive and experience it in another. *We*, therefore, are the determiners of our experiences. That is the importance of this lesson, an importance not to be underestimated, since it contains the core of Jesus' teachings in *A Course in Miracles*.

(3) As you survey your inner world, merely let whatever thoughts cross your mind come into your awareness, each to be considered for a moment, and then replaced by the next. Try not to establish any kind of hierarchy among them. Watch them come and go as dispassionately as possible. Do not dwell on any one in particular, but try to let the stream move on evenly and calmly, without any special investment on your part. As you sit and quietly watch your thoughts, repeat today's idea to yourself as often as you care to, but with no sense of hurry.

This is similar to many Buddhist mind-training exercises. The idea is merely to watch the thoughts in your mind. If you are watching them, who is the *you* who are watching? That is the key. You will end up realizing that the *you* who are watching the thoughts in your mind, as well as watching your perceptions outside, is the *decision maker*, the part of your mind that chooses between the ego and the Holy Spirit, illusions and the truth. It is not the *you* that you normally think of, because some of the thoughts you will be watching will be thoughts about yourself. Jesus is thus beginning the process of training us to dissociate, in the positive sense of the word, from the ego identification that we have made real. If I watch my thoughts—and what I am watching is my ego in action, whether in a positive or a negative form—the *I* that watches is not the *I* that I think I am. It is, again, the *decision maker*.

(4) In addition, repeat the idea for today as often as possible during the day. Remind yourself that you are making a declaration of independence in the name of your own freedom. And in your freedom lies the freedom of the world.

We see here again the instruction about frequent repetitions, hopefully leading to frequent applications of the lesson's wisdom in helping us bring our foolish illusions to the wise truth held for us in our minds by the Holy Spirit. In my freedom "lies the freedom of the world" because the world is part of me. I made up this world, which is a product of my thoughts. If these change, my world has to change. Jesus is not speaking of liberating the world, or freeing it from its suffering; nor does he mean doing anything with the world that is outside. He is speaking only of our *perception* of the world; the only world there truly is.

The language of *A Course in Miracles*, especially in the workbook, would strongly suggest that Jesus is actually talking about saving an external world. Christians have always spoken like this. First it was Jesus who was going to be the world's savior, and now we, as his disciples, are going to save it, too. In the Course Jesus uses the same terms that have been used in traditional Christianity, but has given them a totally different meaning. These lessons explain this difference in meaning. For example, Lesson 186 is entitled "Salvation of the world depends on me"; it is *my* world alone that has to be saved. As I change my mind and free myself from the ego's tyranny, the world I perceive and experience will be saved as well. Once again, Jesus is not talking about anything external. It should be noted here, though we shall return to this important point later, that this is not to be taken as an excuse not to do anything in the world. Rather, we are asked to be *passive* to the ego, but quite *active* to the Holy Spirit, Whose Love automatically guides our thoughts, words, and actions.

That is why these passages must be read very carefully and kept in the context of what Jesus has been teaching. If there is no outer world, how could there be a world out there that has to be saved? It is when students of *A Course in Miracles* want to make their egos real that they take sentences out of context without understanding their metaphysical background, and then make the Course seem to say the exact opposite of what it actually is saying.

The next lesson makes this point even clearer, but before we proceed to it, the final paragraph of this lesson encourages us to begin making the "frequent applications" that Jesus mentioned near the beginning of the lesson. Once again, without these applications the workbook will not have succeeded in its purpose.

One more thing before moving to the end of the lesson—note the explicit reference above to the American Declaration of Independence. Students may recall a similar reference in the text (T-4.III.1:12–2:2), the message of which is echoed in this final paragraph:

(5) The idea for today is also a particularly useful one to use as a response to any form of temptation that may arise. It is a declaration that you will not yield to it, and put yourself in bondage.

At the end of the text Jesus describes temptation as believing we are a body, victimized by forces beyond our control:

> Temptation has one lesson it would teach, in all its forms, wherever it occurs. It would persuade the holy Son of God he is a body, born in what must die, unable to escape its frailty, and bound by what it orders him to feel (T-31.VIII.1:1-2).

Choosing the Holy Spirit and His thought system shifts our identification from the body to the mind, which is the cause of everything the body does and feels. Thus are we freed at last from the ego's bondage.

LESSON 32

I have invented the world I see.

(1:1-2) Today we are continuing to develop the theme of cause and effect. You are not the victim of the world you see because you invented it.

I am not a victim of the world I see because I am the victim of my thoughts, which made up this world. Looked at from a metaphysical point of view, my entire life—from birth to death—is my dream; the script of victimization I wrote to accomplish the ego's purpose. As we have already seen, this purpose is to keep my individual existence, but split off my belief in sin by projecting it onto others. If my life is my dream, my play, my script, then I am obviously its author. Thus am I a victim of my own script-writing. In truth, the decision maker identified with the ego—the part of my split mind that identifies with separation—wrote this script to teach that the world is a prison and everyone in it is my jailor. When I invite Him in, the Holy Spirit joins me there to teach me this world can now become a classroom in which I learn I made it up. He teaches me further *why* I did so: to protect my individuality and specialness. Therefore, because I made it up, because I invented the world I see, I can change it.

Again, "I have invented the world I see" refers back to the idea that my life is an invention, based on the unreal premise I have been unfairly treated as a little child and therefore in need of defenses. Thus I, as a healthy ego, literally invent the world that will always prove I am right and everyone else is wrong, and so my attack thoughts and behavior are justified.

(1:3-5) You can give it up as easily as you made it up. You will see it or not see it, as you wish. While you want it you will see it; when you no longer want it, it will not be there for you to see.

Jesus once again is talking about motivation: it is my *wish* to see a victimizing world, even if that wish is out of awareness, as most our wishes are. The world of victimization I see is there because I *want* it to be there. While it is not explained in this lesson, the reason I want a world of victimization is to be able to say the sin of separation is yours and not

mine. A telling passage near the end of Chapter 27 in the text makes this dynamic—here implicit—quite clear:

> The world you see depicts exactly what you thought you did. Except that now you think that what you did is being done to you. The guilt for what you thought is being placed outside yourself, and on a guilty world that dreams your dreams and thinks your thoughts instead of you. It brings its vengeance, not your own…. The world but demonstrates an ancient truth; you will believe that others do to you exactly what you think you did to them. But once deluded into blaming them you will not see the cause of what they do, because you *want* the guilt to rest on them (T-27.VIII.7:2-5; 8:1-2).

The reigning principle of the ego's thought system, to make this important statement again, is the preservation of separation and individuality, but without their concomitant sin. Therefore, in the world of specifics I project my sin onto you and declare you to be the sinning victimizer, not me. In this way I have my ego's cake and eat it too. I have my individuality and specialness—my self—*but I am not responsible for them*: someone else has made me what I am.

To repeat, I can give the world up as easily as I made it when I took the ego as my teacher instead of Jesus. I merely change my decision by dropping the ego's hand and taking his instead. It is very simple. What makes it difficult to do is its implication: if I do this, I will disappear as I know myself, and then who will I be? That is the fear. Our task is to allow ourselves to get in touch with that fear, and then watch the insane defenses we choose to protect ourselves against something *that is not there anyway*.

Jesus is appealing here to our motivation, as he does consistently throughout *A Course in Miracles*. If we really want to be happy we need to follow what he says, because that alone will make us happy. But that means that we have to be able to say that he was right and we were wrong. That is the most difficult thing for anyone in this world to admit.

(2:1) The idea for today, like the preceding ones, applies to your inner and outer worlds, which are actually the same.

You can see how often in these early lessons Jesus makes this point. He is not speaking metaphorically or figuratively; he is speaking quite literally. You want to think deeply about what this really means—the full implications of saying the inner and outer worlds are the same. It is these implications that are so frightening and unsettling.

(2:2-3) However, since you see them as different, the practice periods for today will again include two phases, one involving the world you see outside you, and the other the world you see in your mind. In today's exercises, try to introduce the thought that both are in your own imagination.

A passage like this is crucial because Jesus is explaining why he uses the language of duality. Most of the time he speaks to us as if there were a world out there; people who have to be forgiven; a world of time and space in which all this occurs; a Holy Spirit and Jesus that run around in our minds trying to help us. Moreover, Jesus speaks of God as if He, too, were a person with different body parts: arms, hands, feet, voice, lips, etc. Thus he tells us here that he uses the terms of duality because *we* see the inner and the outer as different; and therefore he will construct practice periods to reflect that duality—not because the inner and the outer are truly different, but because that is our experience, and he will meet us in the condition in which we think we are (T-25.I.7:4).

Students of *A Course in Miracles* repeatedly get trapped in duality when they miss lines like this and take its words literally, when Jesus is stating it is not like that at all. Thus he says that he will treat the outer world as if it were separate from the inner; indeed, as if there were even an outer world. A passage in the text provides perhaps the best explanation of this dualistic style of *A Course in Miracles* in presenting Jesus' teaching message. Its importance is such that it will be repeated often throughout these volumes, helping to forestall students mistaking the Course's form for its content:

> Since you believe that you are separate,
> Heaven presents itself to you as separate, too.
> Not that it is in truth, but that the link that has
> been given you to join the truth may reach to

you through what you understand…. All this takes note of time and place as if they were discrete, for while you think that part of you is separate, the concept of a Oneness joined as One is meaningless…. Yet must It use the language that this mind can understand, in the condition in which it thinks it is (T-25.I.5:1-2; 7:1,4).

The final sentence of this lesson's second paragraph is also extremely important. Both the world we see outside and the world we see within our minds exist only in our imagination. We made it all up: the thought of separation; an inner world of sin, guilt, and fear, which the belief in separation spawns; and the projected world that is *nothing but* the shadow of the ego's imaginary inner world. All we are really talking about, therefore, is a make-believe world that appears outside, but is really within our minds. Very slowly in these early lessons Jesus is training us to understand it is our thoughts alone that are important, not the world outside.

This teaching is continued:

(3) Again we will begin the practice periods for the morning and evening by repeating the idea for today two or three times while looking around at the world you see as outside yourself. Then close your eyes and look around your inner world. Try to treat them both as equally as possible. Repeat the idea for today unhurriedly as often as you wish, as you watch the images your imagination presents to your awareness.

Jesus is reinforcing what he has been teaching us: these thoughts are made up—thoughts of anger, specialness, self-hatred, anxiety, and terror exist only in our imagination; whether they come in thoughts of pleasure or thoughts of pain. Because we are talking about imaginary thoughts, we are also talking about imaginary worlds. There is no difference.

(4) For the two longer practice periods three to five minutes are recommended, with not less than three required. More than five can be utilized, if you find the exercise restful. To facilitate this, select a time when few distractions are anticipated, and when you yourself feel reasonably ready.

Here we see Jesus urging us to find a peaceful, restful time (and implicitly space as well) in which to meditate. From his comments in other parts of the Course, it is understood that Jesus does not want us to make our spiritual life ritualistic. However, since we are still early in our training and not very disciplined as yet in our vigilance for the ego, this kind of structure is helpful (see, e.g., the discussion in M-16.2-5).

The lesson's concluding paragraphs underscore our *new* kind of practicing: using the day's idea "as often as possible," and especially when we are tempted to perceive the cause of our distress as being outside us:

(5-6) These exercises are also to be continued during the day, as often as possible. The shorter applications consist of repeating the idea slowly, as you survey either your inner or outer world. It does not matter which you choose.

The idea for today should also be applied immediately to any situation that may distress you. Apply the idea by telling yourself:

I have invented this situation as I see it.

You can see how radically different this is from the world's view, from how we normally perceive things. We think choosing either our inner or outer world does make a difference. This would be apparent, for example, when we conclude that what we think does not matter as long as we do not say or act on it. Jesus, though, is explaining that it makes no difference whether we express our thoughts or silently think them. Our judgments have as much effect on us and the mind of the Sonship as do our acting them out. It is fine not to act them out—he once told Helen that he was not against a certain amount of discipline—but if we do not change the underlying thinking, these thoughts simply remain in our minds, awaiting their inevitable fate of projection. The consequences are that we shall always be fighting the losing battle of trying to curtail our aggression: the mind's hostility and specialness. Therefore, we need to go to the source of the problem—our thoughts—which was having turned to Jesus, saying: "You are wrong and I am right." Undoing that source is telling him: "Thank God you were right and I was wrong. There *is* another way of looking at the world."

In these lessons Jesus has been helping us realize we have two ways of looking at the world, which come from two thought systems or selves— a wrong and right mind—and two teachers: the ego and Jesus. This realization will grow as the lessons continue. Up to now, most of the emphasis has been on the ego's way of looking at the world. That is why the early lessons told us we do not truly see anything, for we see what is not there. Therefore, everything we perceive is meaningless. It is also why the lessons have emphasized our attack thoughts, perceiving a world of vengeance, etc. From here through Lesson 50, however, Jesus teaches us there is another available choice, another way of looking at the world. It is that thought he introduces in the next lesson.

LESSON 33

There is another way of looking at the world.

(1:1) Today's idea is an attempt to recognize that you can shift your perception of the world in both its outer and inner aspects.

We can shift the perception because there is something within our minds to which we can go for meaningful change. This "something" is the *decision maker*; the only aspect of our dream in which we find true choice. It is not our outer perceptions that need to be changed, but the inner perception of ourselves: are we children of God, or of the ego; is our reality the changeless Oneness of Christ, or the changing individuality of separation; is our teacher the Holy Spirit or the ego? In other words, this *other* way of looking at the world begins in our minds, with our choice through which eyes we choose to see: vision or judgment.

(1:2–2:2) A full five minutes should be devoted to the morning and evening applications. In these practice periods, the idea should be repeated as often as you find comfortable, though unhurried applications are essential. Alternate between surveying your outer and inner perceptions, but without an abrupt sense of shifting.

Merely glance casually around the world you perceive as outside yourself, then close your eyes and survey your inner thoughts with equal casualness. Try to remain equally uninvolved in both, and to maintain this detachment as you repeat the idea throughout the day.

Jesus does here what we have seen before. He takes a blockbuster of a theme but does not discuss it much in the actual lesson because he is going to pick it up again later. Thus, "I am not the victim of the world I see" is a heavy thought, but is treated briefly in that lesson. "I am never upset for the reason I think" was also not discussed much in the lesson itself, but the idea returns later as well. And again here, Jesus simply introduces the thought that there is another way of looking at the world, and then focuses on the sameness of our inner thoughts and the world we perceive outside. This truth is the foundation for the *other way of looking at the world.*

Let me call your attention to another significant theme that is brought up in the following paragraphs, and appears over and over again in these lessons—applying the thought for the day *throughout* the day, whenever we become aware of distress:

(3-4) The shorter exercise periods should be as frequent as possible. Specific applications of today's idea should also be made immediately, when any situation arises which tempts you to become disturbed. For these applications, say:

There is another way of looking at this.

Remember to apply today's idea the instant you are aware of distress. It may be necessary to take a minute or so to sit quietly and repeat the idea to yourself several times. Closing your eyes will probably help in this form of application.

These exercises are intended to be practical and helpful. Jesus is not simply presenting us with a set of metaphysical principles to master intellectually. He is training us to become increasingly vigilant as we go through our day. As soon as we become aware of feeling distressed, upset, angry, frightened, or guilty, we would quickly go to him and say: "Help!" Even if we can say nothing else, we can at least acknowledge there is another thought in our minds, another teacher we could choose. Even if we do not choose that teacher at the moment, we at least know he is there.

The point is that you become more accustomed to recognizing that if you feel separated from someone or something, you would know that feeling is coming from your ego. You do not have to go any further. The ego loves to indulge thoughts of victimization: justifying and reinforcing them, finding allies who will agree with its misperceptions. As soon as a feeling of victimization comes, try to think of the lesson, whatever the lesson is for you that day; it really does not matter which one, as their content is the same. If you happen to be working with today's lesson, as quickly as possible after catching yourself feeling separate or victimized, say: "I can look at this differently." If you can do nothing else, you are at least keeping the door open, reminding yourself there is another thought system or teacher you could choose, but because you are so fearful, you would much rather be right and miserable than wrong and happy (T-29.VII.1:9). However, you are being honest about what is going on; an immensely helpful part of learning to forgive. The next lesson continues this line of thinking.

LESSON 34

I could see peace instead of this.

(1:1-3) The idea for today begins to describe the conditions that prevail in the other way of seeing. Peace of mind is clearly an internal matter. It must begin with your own thoughts, and then extend outward.

Peace of mind is an "internal matter." The problem is that most of the time we think it results from the outer world meeting our needs. However, Jesus teaches that peace has nothing to do with the external. The implications of this fact, once again, *must* evoke anxiety, because he is informing us that nothing outside can either hurt us or give us peace—the outer world does not threaten, victimize, or please us—*there is nothing outside us!* The challenge lies in allowing ourselves to become increasingly aware of this *without* lapsing into denial. What helps *not* to fall into this ego trap is recognizing that the practical implications of this thought are that even though we may experience anxiety we attribute to external causes, we can still go within to the Teacher of truth, Who gently reminds us that peace is a choice *we* can make (and therefore experience), independent of outer circumstances. I remember when I first did this lesson I substituted *Jesus* for *peace*. In other words, when tempted to make some aspect of the error real, I could always choose Jesus as my teacher and remember to smile at the silliness of believing there could ever be anything in my mind but his love.

(1:4) It is from your peace of mind that a peaceful perception of the world arises.

This is all that is important, and all *A Course in Miracles* addresses: that we perceive the world peacefully. Jesus is not pleading for peace in the world, because there is no objective world outside our minds. To ask for external peace is to have first made conflict real—*out there*. Again, there is no world apart from the way we perceive it. What matters to me as a student of this course is correcting how I perceive, which I do by correcting how I think. This is accomplished by correcting my mistaken choice of teachers—always the bottom line. In this lesson, therefore, instead of saying "I could see

peace instead of this," you could say, as I said above, "I could see Jesus instead of this." That would highlight even more the personal nature of his teaching.

(2) Three longer practice periods are required for today's exercises. One in the morning and one in the evening are advised, with an additional one to be undertaken at any time in between that seems most conducive to readiness. All applications should be done with your eyes closed. It is your inner world to which the applications of today's idea should be made.

We are thus urged to practice with our eyes closed, as Jesus focuses attention on our thoughts—the *internal matter* of being at peace. This is the prerequisite for what follows: emphasizing the process of searching your mind, a theme, as we have said, that is central to *A Course in Miracles*. As you process this material, the fear level can get so high you would be tempted to cover your ego thoughts and think you do not have to deal with them because you believe that to do so would be to make the illusion real, inappropriately citing some of the Course's metaphysical ideas such as, you are holy and loved by God, moreover, nothing has happened and you are not even here. Just as in many other places, Jesus urges us here to search our minds for ego thoughts. If you think you do not have any, *A Course in Miracles* is perfect for you as it teaches that you *do* have these thoughts. Indeed, you could not be here if you did not have them. The idea is to get in touch with your attack thoughts, either those directed against yourself or others, as we now see:

(3:1-2) Some five minutes of mind searching are required for each of the longer practice periods. Search your mind for fear thoughts, anxiety-provoking situations, "offending" personalities or events, or anything else about which you are harboring unloving thoughts.

You do not have to scratch too far beneath the surface before confronting one of these thoughts. It is essential to search them out when you do these lessons. If you are not aware of them, the idea of "seeing peace instead of this" has no meaning. I could see peace instead of *what*? If my mind is filled only with loving thoughts, I certainly do not need this lesson. Therefore, the lesson has particular meaning when you allow yourself to get in touch with the *unloving* thoughts, which come from your *unloving* teacher. At this point it does make sense to say "I could see peace [or Jesus] instead of this." We see reflected here Jesus' overriding emphasis in his course of looking at the darkness and bringing it to the light. To cite just one representative passage, the first of many such citations in this series:

> Your task is not to seek for love, but merely to seek and find all of the barriers within yourself that you have built against it. It is not necessary to seek for what is true, but it *is* necessary to seek for what is false (T-16.IV.6:1-2).

(3:3) Note them all casually, repeating the idea for today slowly as you watch them arise in your mind, and let each one go, to be replaced by the next.

To restate this point, you cannot let a thought go if you are not aware that you have it. Moreover, you cannot let it go unless you have actually chosen Jesus or the Holy Spirit as your Teacher. If you have not, you are not letting the thoughts go. Choosing *against* Them means choosing *for* the ego, which means choosing separation, not to mention the guilt, fear, and anxiety that is inevitable once you have chosen wrongly. To "note them all casually" means not to make a big deal about them, which is the meaning of looking at your ego with Jesus. *Not* looking reflects already having made them into a big deal, since if we had not taken them so seriously we would not have invested these thoughts with the guilt that prevents us from looking.

Jesus' kind gentleness is apparent in this next paragraph, even as he urges us to continue our practice in the face of anxiety and resistance:

(4) If you begin to experience difficulty in thinking of specific subjects, continue to repeat the idea to yourself in an unhurried manner, without applying it to anything in particular. Be sure, however, not to make any specific exclusions.

Slow, steady, and gentle wins this race.

In paragraphs 5 and 6, Jesus again makes the point of applying the lesson whenever we are distressed, emphasizing the need to allow ourselves to be in touch with these thoughts:

(5-6) The shorter applications are to be frequent, and made whenever you feel your peace of mind is threatened in any way. The purpose is to protect yourself from temptation throughout the day. If a specific form of temptation arises in your awareness, the exercise should take this form:

> *I could see peace in this situation instead of what I now see in it.*

If the inroads on your peace of mind take the form of more generalized adverse emotions, such as depression, anxiety or worry, use the idea in its original form. If you find you need more than one application of today's idea to help you change your mind in any specific context, try to take several minutes and devote them to repeating the idea until you feel some sense of relief. It will help you if you tell yourself specifically:

> *I can replace my feelings of depression, anxiety or worry [or my thoughts about this situation, personality or event] with peace.*

Therefore, to make this essential point again, this lesson—indeed, *all* lessons—will have no meaning to you, and will be of no help unless you first admit to yourself these thoughts and feelings of depression, anxiety, worry, attack, etc. It is not that they are bad to have; you are here because you *do* have them. Thus, Jesus says to us in the text, in the context of our willingness to choose the holy instant:

> Concentrate only on this [your willingness], and be not disturbed that shadows surround it. That is why you came, if you could come without them you would not need the holy instant (T-18.IV.2:4-6).

What is "bad," therefore, is pretending that you do not have them, because then Jesus *will* be of no help to you and *can* be of no help to you. You must bring the thoughts to him. That is *our* function, as he reminds us in the text:

> You may wonder why it is so crucial that you look upon your hatred and realize its full extent. You may also think that it would be easy enough for the Holy Spirit to show it to

you, and to dispel it without the need for you to raise it to awareness yourself (T-13.III.1:1-2).

Because of this need to raise our awareness of these hate-filled thoughts, we require the "frequent applications" Jesus recommends. Discipline and vigilance are necessary if we are to catch these dark thoughts and bring them to his healing and forgiving light.

These next lessons begin to show us the wondrous things that lie *beyond* our ego thoughts: the *other* side when we ask for help in choosing "another way of looking at the world." You may recall my stating that one of the purposes of the workbook was to help us recognize we have a split mind: the *wrong-minded* state of the ego and the *right-minded* home of the Holy Spirit. Only through such recognition can we meaningfully use the *decision-making* part of our minds to make the right choice.

LESSON 35

My mind is part of God's. I am very holy.

As noted at the end of the last lesson, Jesus continues his shift to a right-minded emphasis. He begins instructing us on what is found in the *other* part of our minds. Everyone should have trouble believing this, as Jesus himself says in the lesson. If you really knew you were a part of God, and therefore your mind was holy, you would have no thoughts of separation and specialness. In fact, you would know you were not here at all. Thus, that you are here—or better: that you *believe* you are here—says your mind is not part of God's, and therefore you could not be holy.

In this lesson, and increasingly so for the next fifteen, Jesus helps us realize there is another part of us—what is known in the early part of the text as the *right mind*. This part, through the Holy Spirit, is still connected with the holiness of God that has never changed, despite our unholy dreams of guilt and judgment.

(1:1-3) Today's idea does not describe the way you see yourself now. It does, however, describe what vision will show you. It is difficult for anyone who thinks he is in this world to believe this of himself.

Jesus is letting us know that he knows this is not how we see ourselves, and he does not expect us to believe what he says about us. His purpose is to *begin* the process of teaching us there is a true alternative in our minds. He does not want this used as a mantra that we repeat over and over throughout the day to shout down our unloving thoughts. Rather, in keeping with our training, he wants us to bring our unloving thoughts to this loving thought. These unloving thoughts involve some expression of our belief that we are unholy or sinful. Thus would we rise to our new way of understanding, which is that there is another way of not only *looking* at ourselves, but another way of *thinking* about ourselves. When we bring the darkness of our unholy, illusory thoughts to the light of the holy and true thought, the light dispels the darkness.

(1:4) Yet the reason he thinks he is in this world is because he does not believe it.

This is the point I was just making. Because we do not believe we are a part of God, we must believe we are in this world. Living here as a separated being—physically and psychologically—among other separated beings is the shadow of the thought that says: I am on my own, separate from God. Again, the very fact that we believe we are here as bodies attests to the underlying belief that we are separated, and therefore do not believe our minds are part of God's and are holy. This lesson, then, reflects the principle of the Atonement—the belief that although we *think* we have left God, in truth the separation never happened. Therefore, I truly am a part of God, and thus very holy.

(2:1-2) You will believe that you are part of where you think you are. That is because you surround yourself with the environment you want.

We believe we are in this world, and part of it as a separate body, living among other separate bodies. On the ontological level, as one separated Son we made an environment that maintains separation, and then forgot we had done so, following the ego's plan for *its* salvation. As a result, we now believe the world is real, and we are real as part of it. On an individual level, if, as discussed previously, we want to feel unfairly treated, what better way to accomplish that than always to be around those who treat us unfairly? Whether they do or do not, we shall perceive them that way. As Jesus reminds us in this paraphrased statement from the text, a wonderful line we have already quoted: If we experience our brother as not speaking of Christ to us, it is *only* because we have first accused ourselves of having not spoken of Christ to him (T-11.V.18:6). We thus wind up thoroughly convinced our perceptions of victimization are valid.

(2:3) And you want it [the environment of a separated world] to protect the image of yourself that you have made.

Again, this is an unmistakable causal statement. We have made up a physical world of separation to protect the image of ourselves as separate beings.

This is why it should be clear that Jesus is never talking about changing or saving the world—*there is no world*. He speaks only of saving ourselves from the self-image we made: the sinful, guilty, fragmented, image of fear we harbor within. It is our *wish* to be separate that is the cause of the separated world. Therefore, it is that wish we must change if true peace is to come to us.

(2:4-7) The image is part of this environment. What you see while you believe you are in it is seen through the eyes of the image. This is not vision. Images cannot see.

What is the image? I am limited, fragmented, separated, independent, and autonomous. The world's nature, and *all* that it is, is the projection of that image. Everyone in this world is alone, which is why specialness is such a powerful defense. One of our needs is to have people be with us so we do not experience the pain and loneliness that inevitably comes with being part of this world, living in a place outside Heaven, our true Home.

This paragraph is quite significant and should be carefully studied. The thought system of *A Course in Miracles*—its metaphysics, the thought system of the ego and its undoing through forgiveness—all can be recognized in these passages.

(3:1-2) The idea for today presents a very different view of yourself. By establishing your Source it establishes your Identity, and it describes you as you must really be in truth.

In other words, I am a part of God and am very holy. That is why *Source* and *Identity* are capitalized: Jesus is talking about God and the Christ that is our true Self.

Jesus turns now to the perceiver, rather than to what he perceives. Indeed, at this point Jesus is not interested in what we perceive outside, but only in what we *think*:

(3:3) We will use a somewhat different kind of application for today's idea because the emphasis for today is on the perceiver, rather than on what he perceives.

We can better understand the overriding emphasis in these early lessons on searching our minds, since it is our minds—the true *perceiver*—that need correction. Thus we read:

(4) For each of the three five-minute practice periods today, begin by repeating today's idea to yourself, and then close your eyes and search your mind for the various kinds of descriptive terms in which you see yourself. Include all the ego-based attributes which you ascribe to yourself, positive or negative, desirable or undesirable, grandiose or debased. All of them are equally unreal, because you do not look upon yourself through the eyes of holiness.

What we find within our minds are the multitudinous forms of the *one* error, the *one* illusory thought of separation. In other words, as I said earlier, once you identify with the ego's separated self, everything you think, believe, feel, perceive, and experience will be wrong. Whether it is noble, beautiful, holy, and good, or simply terrible, it will be wrong because it will have been based on specialness and separation.

(5) In the earlier part of the mind-searching period, you will probably emphasize what you consider to be the more negative aspects of your perception of yourself. Toward the latter part of the exercise period, however, more self-inflating descriptive terms may well cross your mind. Try to recognize that the direction of your fantasies about yourself does not matter. Illusions have no direction in reality. They are merely not true.

Jesus is cautioning us not to take too seriously the fact that we shall most likely only be recognizing the negative thoughts within, even though *both* positive and negative thoughts are illusory. He obviously cannot emphasize enough that it does not matter whether these thoughts are one or the other. As long as you believe you have a self that is positive or negative, that can relate positively or negatively to other people, you will be wrong about yourself and whatever you think is going on. Separate selves are not holy. The one Self united with God *is* holy, and beyond all our self-concepts (T-31.V). In subsequent lessons Jesus talks more and more about our true Self. Remember again, we cannot get to the true Self without first looking at the false one. That is why the early workbook lessons focused on our *mis*thoughts and *mis*perceptions. The correction for these mistakes is realizing there is another way of looking at the world; another way of looking at ourselves.

The next paragraph provides a suggested list for us to follow. Of the nine traits listed, three are positive—*victorious, charitable,* and *virtuous*—while six are negative—*imposed on, depressed, failing, endangered, helpless,* and *losing out.* Again, for the purposes of this exercise the category makes no difference.

Paragraph 7 urges us to be *specific* as the steppingstone to achieving the mind state of the *non-specific—the* trait of our real Self:

(7) You should not think of these terms in an abstract way. They will occur to you as various situations, personalities and events in which you figure cross your mind. Pick up any specific situation that occurs to you, identify the descriptive term or terms you feel are applicable to your reactions to that situation, and use them in applying today's idea. After you have named each one, add:

> **But my mind is part of God's. I am very holy.**

Focusing on the specific, once again, is the prerequisite for achieving the non-specific. It is also an essential part of our training in not denying our thoughts, feelings, and perceptions. The darkness of guilt cannot be brought to light and undone unless we first look at its specific manifestations, the doorway through which we return to our thoughts.

The next paragraph sees Jesus returning to his gentle urgings that we be gentle with ourselves in these exercises. It is a useful guideline to remember that whenever we experience a sense of urgency or intimation of force coming from "the other side," we should recognize immediately that this is the ego guiding us. Jesus and the Holy Spirit are *only* gentle and patient, knowing that time is illusory. Only an impatient ego, uncertain of the outcome, would apply pressure. We experience Jesus' gentle teaching about gentleness in this passage from the text:

> The Voice of the Holy Spirit does not command, because It is incapable of arrogance. It does not demand, because It does not seek control. It does not overcome, because It does not attack. It merely reminds. It is compelling

only because of what It reminds you *of.* It brings to your mind the other way, remaining quiet even in the midst of the turmoil you may make. The Voice for God is always quiet, because It speaks of peace. Peace is stronger than war because it heals (T-5.II.7:1-8).

Here, then, is the gentle eighth paragraph:

(8) During the longer exercise periods, there will probably be intervals in which nothing specific occurs to you. Do not strain to think up specific things to fill the interval, but merely relax and repeat today's idea slowly until something occurs to you. Although nothing that does occur should be omitted from the exercises, nothing should be "dug out" with effort. Neither force nor discrimination should be used.

Gentleness always wins against force, since it reflects the inner strength of Christ. Force, on the other hand, is the shadowy expression of the ego's inherent weakness. Thus we read about this fourth characteristic of God's advanced teachers:

> …God's teachers are wholly gentle. They need the strength of gentleness, for it is in this that the function of salvation becomes easy…. Who would choose the weakness that must come from harm in place of the unfailing, all-encompassing and limitless strength of gentleness? The might of God's teachers lies in their gentleness… (M-4.IV.2:1-2,7-8).

In the lesson's close, we once again see Jesus asking us to be quite specific throughout the day—"as often as possible"—about applying the day's lesson. Only in that way, to repeat this important idea, can the teachings of *A Course in Miracles* become our experience:

(9) As often as possible during the day, pick up a specific attribute or attributes you are ascribing to yourself at the time and apply the idea for today to them, adding the idea in the form stated above to each of them. If nothing particular occurs to you, merely repeat the idea to yourself, with closed eyes.

To repeat an earlier point, make every effort to be vigilant throughout the day for ego thoughts, but also be mindful of the need to forgive yourself when you remember you have forgotten.

LESSON 36

My holiness envelops everything I see.

This lesson along with the next few are extremely important, as they explore the theme of our holiness. In so doing, they provide the obvious correction of the ego's wrong-minded thinking, which we have been discussing a great deal. They also clarify what Jesus means and does not mean by *holiness*. Another significant but unfortunate aspect of these lessons is that many students of *A Course in Miracles* have taken their inspiring message and run the wrong way with them, totally misunderstanding Jesus' teaching. I shall therefore explore that idea, among other important themes as we go along.

(1:1) Today's idea extends the idea for yesterday from the perceiver to the perceived.

In the preceding lesson—"My mind is part of God's. I am very holy"—we had discussed the relationship between our inner world and what we perceive to be outside. The lesson now shifts the focus from the perceiver, namely our thoughts, to what we perceive outside. This is not really a shift, because the inner and outer are one and the same. What we see within, which really means what we *think* about ourselves, is exactly what we believe we are seeing outside. As we have discussed already, our *perception* does not mean simply *what* we see (or hear, etc.), but our *interpretation* of what we perceive. As always, the focus is on the *content*—what is in the mind—and never the *form*—part of the physical world.

(1:2-3) You are holy because your mind is part of God's. And because you are holy, your sight must be holy as well.

The implication of this statement is that if we are holy within, what we perceive must be holy as well. If what we perceive is not holy—i.e., if we perceive anything other than an expression of love or a call for love—we did not first perceive ourselves as holy. We can thus tell whether we have chosen to identify with the ego or the Holy Spirit by paying attention to our perceptions; what we perceive will always be a direct mirror of what we have made real

inside ourselves. An important passage in the text explains this:

> Damnation is your judgment on yourself, and this you will project upon the world. See it as damned, and all you see is what you did to hurt the Son of God. If you behold disaster and catastrophe, you tried to crucify him. If you see holiness and hope, you joined the Will of God to set him free. There is no choice that lies between these two decisions. And you will see the witness to the choice you made, and learn from this to recognize which one you chose (T-21.in.2:1-6).

That is why it is so important we be vigilant about our thoughts. If we are aware of our thoughts about people *outside* us, they will reveal to us the thoughts with which we have identified *within*; our special relationships are thus at the core of healing our minds through forgiveness. If you want to know what is in the camera after you have used it, develop the film and look at the photos. That will tell you whether or not you took a good picture. The purpose of *A Course in Miracles* can therefore be seen, in this context, as having us recognize that our perceptions directly mirror what we have chosen within. Only then, can we choose again.

(1:4-6) "Sinless" means without sin. You cannot be without sin a little. You are sinless or not.

This is another example of what we have referred to as a Level One statement, meaning that something either is wholly true or wholly false; there is absolutely no compromise between non-duality and duality. Statements such as these form the bedrock for the thought system of *A Course in Miracles*: its uncompromising metaphysics. We either sinned against God by separating from Him; or we did not, thus remaining as God created us—at one with Him Who is our Source.

(1:7) If your mind is part of God's you must be sinless, or a part of His Mind would be sinful.

The logic here is compelling, and if you accept the basic premise that God is perfect holiness, and anything that comes from Him—i.e., is a part of

Him—must share in that holiness, it must follow that anything appearing to be sinful or unholy cannot be part of God, and therefore cannot exist. That is why, from the point of view of *A Course in Miracles*, there can be no evil. There can be perceptions, beliefs, and dreams about evil; but no objective evil. If there were, it would mean a part of God must be evil as well. This is another example of the Course's radical metaphysical stance.

(1:8) Your sight is related to His Holiness, not to your ego, and therefore not to your body.

We have briefly explored this theme of our having a split mind, and it will come up again and again. There is the ego part of our minds, but there is the other part that is holy. The implication to be drawn from the last part of this statement is that our body comes from the wrong mind, not the right mind. I have often said that no one in his or her right mind would be born into this world. It is only someone in the wrong mind, fleeing from the perceived wrath of God, who would come here. This does not mean the body cannot be used to serve a different purpose, as we have already seen and shall discuss again; but ontologically, the body is an expression of separation, sin, and attack. Its purpose of protecting the separation defines it. Likewise, the dynamic of *protection* can serve a different purpose, as we see in the next paragraph where the phrase "protect your protection" is noteworthy:

(2:1-2) Four three-to-five minute practice periods are required for today. Try to distribute them fairly evenly, and make the shorter applications frequently, to protect your protection throughout the day.

The "protection" is the thought for the day: "My holiness envelops everything I see." In a larger sense, of course, our protection is the Presence of the Holy Spirit or Jesus. We have seen the parallel between this and what Jesus refers to in the text as the third lesson of the Holy Spirit: "*Be vigilant only for God and His Kingdom*" (T-6.V-C). This means to be vigilant *against* our decision to choose the ego thought system. To "protect the protection" requires that we be vigilant to what we are thinking, which we do by being vigilant to what we are perceiving. If I want to know what I think about myself and God, all I need do is devote one moment to what I think about *you*. This is because my thoughts about you—whoever the object of my specialness is at any given moment—will directly reflect how I think about God and myself. That is the meaning of "protecting the protection," carried out under the guidance of the Holy Spirit.

The last two paragraphs deal with specific instructions for the practice periods, and emphasize the sequence of first going within—*closing one's eyes*—and then looking—*quite slowly, as effortlessly and unhurriedly as possible*—at the specifics in the world around us. The idea, of course, is to have us first identify the holiness within—the Holy Spirit's Presence in our right minds—and then have it extend through us to embrace our perceptions of what appear to be external to us. The full metaphysical implications of this lesson are perhaps still far from our experience, but these early exercises are the steppingstones—the aforementioned "little steps" described in Lesson 193 (13:7)—that will bring us there. The instructions begin with the last sentence of the second paragraph:

(2:3–3:2) The longer practice periods should take this form:
First, close your eyes and repeat the idea for today several times, slowly. Then open your eyes and look quite slowly about you, applying the idea specifically to whatever you note in your casual survey.

Suggestions for objects we envelop in our holiness include, once again, the important and unimportant; to wit: *fingers, body, rug, wall, chair,* and *pen.*

(3:10–4:2) Several times during these practice periods, close your eyes and repeat the idea to yourself. Then open your eyes, and continue as before.
For the shorter exercise periods, close your eyes and repeat the idea; look about you as you repeat it again; and conclude with one more repetition with your eyes closed. All applications should, of course, be made quite slowly, as effortlessly and unhurriedly as possible.

Slowly and gently—"effortlessly and unhurriedly" —we are being led along salvation's path that takes us from the world without to the world within, there to rediscover our holiness, which our need for specialness sought to deny.

LESSON 37

My holiness blesses the world.

This is another lesson that is extremely important in terms of what Jesus is teaching us, as well as correcting common mistakes made by students of *A Course in Miracles*. Jesus obviously is not telling us that we should bless the world that is outside us. This would directly contradict everything he has been teaching us so far. Remember, Jesus is teaching us the world is nothing more than a mirror of our thoughts. Therefore, the lesson's *content* is not that we should bless a chair, stick, clock, or another person. Rather, he is saying that if we choose his blessing—within our minds—and see ourselves as holy because we have joined with him, that blessing will automatically extend through us and envelop everything we see. The principle *projection makes perception* must never be too far away from our thinking. This will become increasingly manifest as we look at this lesson.

(1:1-2) This idea contains the first glimmerings of your true function in the world, or why you are here. Your purpose is to see the world through your own holiness.

This is another way of saying our purpose or function is forgiveness. *Forgiveness* has not really made an appearance yet in these lessons, but the process of seeing the world through our own holiness is a wonderfully succinct description of it. The problem is that we see the world through our own *un*holiness, as separated egos and bodies whose mission in life is to protect and preserve our specialness. Thus, a lesson such as this presents the right-minded thought that undoes the ego's dictum that "my *un*holiness envelops and condemns the world I see." The focus of this lesson, therefore, is not really on the world at all; it is on our *thoughts*. If our thoughts are rooted in the holiness of Christ that we are, everything we perceive must automatically be its extension. The importance of this idea cannot be overemphasized.

(1:3) Thus are you and the world blessed together.

The world is only a reflection of my thought, which is one of holiness and blessing because I am a child of blessing. The world "out there" must share in that holiness, because it comes from that holiness. In other words, the world I perceive is rooted in who I am. Another principle that should never be far from our thoughts is *ideas leave not their source*. In this instance, if my holiness is the source, the idea of the world must be perceived as holy as well. Indeed, these two principles—*projection makes perception* and *ideas leave not their source*—are essentially the same: Projection (or its right-minded form of extension) is the reason ideas leave not their source. The *ideas* that comprise our *perceptual* world are merely the *projected* self-image that has its *source* in our minds, and what is projected out always remains within. Thus *source* and *idea* remain one.

(1:4-6) No one loses; nothing is taken away from anyone; everyone gains through your holy vision. It signifies the end of sacrifice because it offers everyone his full due. And he is entitled to everything because it is his birthright as a Son of God.

This is the first time in the lessons that Jesus discusses sacrifice, another of the key themes in the text, for it is at the heart of the ego's thought system. The root of sacrifice lies in the principle of *one or the other*, more graphically stated in the manual, as we have already seen, as *kill or be killed* (M-17.7:11). The ego—the thought of individuality—begins with the idea that it is God or my self. If God is to exist, I cannot exist as a separate being because there is no separation, individuality, or differentiation in Heaven. Therefore, if I am to exist as an individual—the foundation of everyone's thought system—God can no longer exist, at least as He truly is. He would have to be changed, and if God ceases to be perfect Oneness He ceases to be. Perfect oneness and individuality cannot coexist. That is the origin of the thought of sacrifice: someone must lose if another is to win.

Since the sacrifice of God is the foundation of the split mind, when that mind further splits into billions and billions of fragments, the thought of sacrifice remains, in accord with the principle *ideas leave not their source.* The *idea* of a separated, individual world filled with bodies has never left its *source*, which is the mind's thought that I exist on my own—at God's expense.

A direct corollary of the thought that I have killed God so I could exist is the ego's teaching that God is somehow going to rise from the dead and come after me. Therefore, in order to appease His wrath I have to call again upon the principle that gave me my existence: *one or the other*, the idea of sacrifice. This is the same principle, by the way, that has led most world religions to entertain the strange notion that God demands sacrifice: If I am to exist, I have to pay God back for what I stole from Him. That concept becomes the foundation stone of special relationships: If I am to get what I want from you, I must pay you for it. Thus does the principle of *one or the other*, beginning with the ontological premise if I am to exist God must die, filter through the fragmentation process and end up being the foundation of *everyone*'s thought system.

What we find in this early workbook lesson, then, is the first attempt to counteract that fundamental line of thinking. If I see the world as nothing more than a part of me, everything that happens to me happens to the world. If I am blessed, the world and everyone in it must be blessed, too. In "The Rock of Salvation," Jesus states that the rock on which salvation rests is that no one loses and everyone wins (T-25.VII.12), which is the same idea he is presenting here. Hence I no longer presume that my happiness depends on beating you up, putting you down, cannibalizing, or stealing from you. I can learn to generalize this lesson, recognizing that you are part of me; not my individual physical or psychological self, but the part of me who is the Son of God. If I seek to exclude you by seeing you as separate from me—an enemy or object of my special love—I am saying the Son of God is fragmented. In truth he cannot be, so by attacking you I am really attacking my own Identity. However, if I begin with the premise that my mind is part of God's and I am holy (Lesson 35), I shall see that *you* must share in that holiness, if indeed holiness is true. This step marks the end of sacrifice—the principle of *one or the other*.

There is a series of statements in the text that reflect this correction:

Salvation is a collaborative venture (T-4.VI.8:2).

Together or not at all (T-19.IV-D.12:8).

The ark of peace is entered two by two (T-20.IV.6:5).

No one can enter Heaven by himself (W-pI.134.17:7).

None of this means that you literally have to be in a relationship with someone on a physical level. It does mean, however, that in your *mind* you do not see that your peace, salvation, or happiness comes at someone else's expense.

The key point of this lesson, therefore, is that "my holiness blesses the world" because the world is an extension of me. As long as I believe there is someone "out there," I must believe there is someone "in here" who perceives someone "out there," which means I am into separation, specialness, and individuality. I then automatically believe in sacrifice; some expression of *one or the other*.

(2:1) There is no other way in which the idea of sacrifice can be removed from the world's thinking.

In other words, the only way sacrifice can be removed from the world's thinking is to shift from the ego's thought system of separation, judgment, and hate to the Holy Spirit's thought system of unity, forgiveness, and healing. This does *not* mean denying our bodies or other people's bodies, but rather denying the seeming truth of the *one or the other* principle. That is what this lesson is all about, reflecting the central teaching of *A Course in Miracles*.

Again, we do not deny there are bodies, or that there is a body we identify with. Rather, we look at the *one or the other* principle operating in our minds and choose to deny its seeming validity. That is the only way the idea of sacrifice can be undone. I realize you and I are making the same journey home. It began as a path of insanity away from home, and in my mind I realize that the way back —the way of sanity—is to take your hand. It does not matter whether you even know who I am or whether you died thirty years ago. We are not talking about something that happens externally in the world, because all relationships exist *only* in the mind. We are talking about a relationship I am still holding onto in my thoughts. If my ego is in charge, the relationship will reflect *one or the other,* and that is sacrifice. If I put Jesus in charge as my teacher, however, I shall see my special relationship as an opportunity to look at my *one or the other* thinking, and then ask his help to change it.

(2:2-3) Any other way of seeing will inevitably demand payment of someone or something. As a result, the perceiver will lose.

I must believe I will lose, because in my mind my existence comes from having stolen from God, not to mention murdering Him. I will therefore believe, through the dynamic of projection, that He, along with everyone in my dream are going to do to me what I believe I did to them, and am still doing. In the end, my guilt tells me you are going to steal back from me what I stole from you. The "reasoning" in the ego thought system is once again as follows: Individual existence is identified with sin, which means I reached where I am by stealing from you and killing you off, the horrifying *final solution* brought about by the *one or the other* principle. Thus, if everything I see outside mirrors what is inside, I must believe everyone out there, whom literally I put there, would do exactly what I believe I have done; i.e., steal and kill. Remember that we are speaking of the *content* of killing, not its *form,* as reflected in the statement from Lesson 21 that "a slight twinge of annoyance is nothing but a veil drawn over intense fury" (2:5). The *thought* of murder is the same as the *thought* of mild annoyance. That is also what is behind the seemingly outrageous statement in the text, which I cited earlier: "What is not love is murder" (T-23.IV.1:10). Guilt ultimately rests on our belief that we separated from God, and so any thought of separation—be it "a slight twinge of annoyance" or murder—recalls to mind this sin of betraying the love that is *only* perfect oneness.

In light of this, we can understand why death is the central phenomenon in the physical universe. Death to the ego is God's punishment. That is why, on one level, the entire Bible rests on the third chapter of Genesis, which tells the story of Adam and Eve's sin and the punishment from God, Who created death, and later, the plan of atonement through suffering and sacrifice. Death, then, is the final proof that in the end my sin will be punished. Thus it is that every seemingly separated fragment

of the Sonship *must* die, as justified punishment for *being* separate, which life in the body clearly embodies. This is the foundation of the statement: "As a result, the perceiver will lose."

(2:4) Nor will he have any idea why he is losing.

I will think I am losing because of what you did to me, or are planning to do to me. I will not realize that the real reason I am losing is that I am the dreamer of my own dream; a dream of loss, *one or the other*, and winners and losers. We see again the efficacy of the ego's strategy of keeping us in a state of mindlessness. As long as we perceive ourselves to be in a body (and therefore not in our minds), we *must* believe other bodies are doing to us what is, in fact, the shadow of what our mind's guilt is bringing about. Thus the following passage from the text, which cogently describes this dynamic of projection:

> Of one thing you were sure: Of all the many causes you perceived as bringing pain and suffering to you, your guilt was not among them. Nor did you in any way request them for yourself. This is how all illusions came about. The one who makes them does not see himself as making them, and their reality does not depend on him. Whatever cause they have is something quite apart from him, and what he sees is separate from his mind. He cannot doubt his dreams' reality, because he does not see the part he plays in making them and making them seem real (T-27.VII.7:4-9).

(2:5) Yet is his wholeness restored to his awareness through your vision.

I not only heal my own mind when I ask Jesus for help and identify with his holiness, but I serve as a reminder to you. Thus, if we are in a relationship and I can change my mind, no longer holding *one or the other* as my reigning principle but rather seeing the relationship as a classroom in which I can learn the exact opposite, I give you the same message. In other words, verbally or non-verbally, I tell you that the lesson I have learned, the teacher I have chosen, is also available inside you. That is what is meant at the end of the text when Jesus says that Christ is within us, saying "my brother choose again" (T-31.VIII.3:2). When we are able to choose again, we become that same expression of Christ's vision of forgiveness, reflecting His words to our brother.

The manual for teachers offers a wonderful description of how our brother's "wholeness is restored to [the] awareness" of those who are sick:

> To them God's teachers come, to represent another choice which they had forgotten. The simple presence of a teacher of God is a reminder. His thoughts ask for the right to question what the patient has accepted as true. As God's messengers, His teachers are the symbols of salvation. They ask the patient for forgiveness for God's Son in his own Name. They stand for the Alternative. With God's Word in their minds they come in benediction, not to heal the sick but to remind them of the remedy God has already given them. It is not their hands that heal. It is not their voice that speaks the Word of God. They merely give what has been given them. Very gently they call to their brothers to turn away from death: "Behold, you Son of God, what life can offer you. Would you choose sickness in place of this?" (M-5.III.2).

(2:6-7) Your holiness blesses him by asking nothing of him. Those who see themselves as whole make no demands.

If you look honestly at your relationships, even as you go through this very day, you will realize how you are demanding something from everyone. Sometimes it is quite obvious, other times it is subtle. This dynamic must be there, though, as long as you believe you are an individual, which we all clearly do. If you believe you are an individual, you also believe in the concept of lack, which can be traced to our very origin: I had to steal from God at the beginning because something was missing in me. And therefore I have to steal from everyone all the time because something is still missing in me. How could it not? As long as the underlying belief in scarcity (another word for *lack*) remains uncorrected, this inner perception will generate the continual need to fill up what is missing—to "supply a lack"—in the words of the early miracle principle (T-1.I.8:1). Consequently, a major aspect of specialness is that I always have to take from someone else to fill the lack that I perceive in myself.

That is what Jesus is talking about in these passages. When you identify with holiness, you ask nothing of anyone because you *are* everything and *have* everything. You are everything, because *having* and *being* are the same (e.g., T-6.V-B.3:4; V-C.5).

Vigilance is essential to the process of your learning so that you become aware that you are making a demand of someone. If you are making demands and believe in the reality of the attack, that tells you that you do not believe you are whole. You are unhappy, therefore, not because you did not receive what you believe you should have gotten from someone, but *solely* because you have chosen the wrong teacher.

(3:1) Your holiness is the salvation of the world.

Here again, Jesus is not talking about the external world. As discussed earlier, Jesus uses the language of Christianity throughout *A Course in Miracles*. In Christianity, especially in the Easter season, there is great emphasis on the thought of Jesus saving the world. Yet he would have us realize in the Course that there is no world out there to be saved. Saving the world really means saving ourselves from the *belief* there is a world. Since all minds are joined in the holiness of Christ, if my mind is healed in any given instant, the Sonship's mind is healed as well.

None of this is understandable from the world's perspective, as I have said. None of this will make sense within our experience here, and can be understood only when we lift ourselves above the battleground and be with Jesus in what he refers to as the holy instant. From there we look back on the world and see it differently, realizing what has to be saved are our *thoughts* about the world. These thoughts, again, result from our thoughts about ourselves. The outer and the inner are one and the same: *Ideas leave not their source.*

(3:2) It lets you teach the world that it is one with you, not by preaching to it, not by telling it anything, but merely by your quiet recognition that in your holiness are all things blessed along with you.

These lines are significant. We change and save the world not by preaching *A Course in Miracles*, not by teaching *A Course in Miracles* (i.e., in form), not by doing anything with *A Course in Miracles* except learning it ourselves. In order for my world to be saved, there is nothing that I have to do or say but to accept what the lessons are teaching me, which is the meaning of accepting the Atonement for oneself. These are hardly insignificant lines, for they go to the heart of the Course's metaphysics, which is the foundation for understanding Jesus' teachings and their application. If there is no world, how can it be saved? Again, what needs saving, or correcting, is our *minds* that believe there is a world. Once our minds are healed, we remember that the separation never happened, and thus a world that arose from that thought of separation could not have happened either. Moreover, if there were no separation, God's Son remains perfectly united as *one* Son. Our minds reflect the blessing of our Creator, and following the oft-repeated principle *ideas leave not their source*, it must be the case that "all things [are] blessed along with [us]." It is from this inner blessing that our holiness inevitably extends through us, as we see in these three parallel passages from the text. All of them highlight the process of our doing nothing except *un*do the belief in the ego, reflecting the little willingness that does indeed save the world—*from our belief in it*:

> Concern yourself not with the extension of holiness, for the nature of miracles you do not understand. Nor do you do them. It is their extension, far beyond the limits you perceive, that demonstrates you do not do them. Why should you worry how the miracle extends to all the Sonship when you do not understand the miracle itself? (T-16.II.1:3-6)

> Extension of forgiveness is the Holy Spirit's function. Leave this to Him. Let your concern be only that you give to Him that which can be extended. Save no dark secrets that He cannot use, but offer Him the tiny gifts He can extend forever. He will take each one and make of it a potent force for peace (T-22.VI.9:2-6).

> The miracle extends without your help, but you are needed that it can begin. Accept the miracle of healing, and it will go forth because of what it is. It is its nature to extend itself the instant it is born. And it is born the instant it is offered and received.... Leave, then, the transfer of your learning to the One Who really understands its laws.... Your part is merely to apply what He has taught you to yourself, and He will do the rest (T-27.V.1:2-5; 10:1-2).

What makes all this possible of course is our having chosen the right teacher. Thus, the crucial point to which we constantly return: "Do I have a relationship with Jesus or do I not?" If not, it is because I have excluded him by excluding *myself*, and do not want to acknowledge my "sin." That is always the bottom line.

The next two paragraphs emphasize the lack of difference between our perceptions and our thoughts, being one and the same:

(4) Today's four longer exercise periods, each to involve three to five minutes of practice, begin with the repetition of the idea for today, followed by a minute or so of looking about you as you apply the idea to whatever you see:

> *My holiness blesses this chair.*
> *My holiness blesses that window.*
> *My holiness blesses this body.*

Then close your eyes and apply the idea to any person who occurs to you, using his name and saying:

> *My holiness blesses you, [name].*

Note how Jesus has us begin with the "unimportant"—a chair, window, and the relatively neutral body—and then asks us to apply our blessing to a specific person. Thus he gently eases us into *A Course in Miracles*' central focus: forgiveness of our special relationships—those from whom we would seek to withhold our blessing.

Jesus' instructions continue, inviting us to practice with eyes open and eyes closed, as we see fit:

(5) You may continue the practice period with your eyes closed; you may open your eyes again and apply the idea for today to your outer world if you so desire; you may alternate between applying the idea to what you see around you and to those who are in your thoughts; or you may use any combination of these two phases of application that you prefer. The practice period should conclude with a repetition of the idea with your eyes closed, and another, following immediately, with your eyes open.

Even though this practice of eyes open and closed has been an important emphasis in Jesus' training, he always remains gentle in his approach, as seen in his use of words such as "you may," "if you so desire," and "that you prefer." Good teachers never coerce their students, and Jesus wants us to *want* to learn his lessons; otherwise our learning will be weak.

(6:1-2) The shorter exercises consist of repeating the idea as often as you can. It is particularly helpful to apply it silently to anyone you meet, using his name as you do so.

In other words, Jesus is asking us to be vigilant in watching our egos in action, especially in relationship to others. He fully expects us to make the wrong choices, as we shall see in the lessons that follow. A lesson like this, therefore, is the correction for the mistakes we shall inevitably make. Again, Jesus is *expecting* us to misperceive and have attack thoughts, and once aware we have done so, to ask him for help as we try to remember the lesson for the day.

(6:3-4) It is essential to use the idea if anyone seems to cause an adverse reaction in you. Offer him the blessing of your holiness immediately, that you may learn to keep it in your own awareness.

I think 99.9 percent of students who do lessons like this do so almost by rote. They think all they need do is say to someone with whom they are angry, "I bless you," and all is healed. That is *not* what Jesus is talking about; he is talking about recognizing that our perception of another is coming from our *mis*perception of ourselves. Simply saying words like "My holiness blesses you" is going to accomplish nothing. Actually, that is not entirely true; saying those words will accomplish a great deal: *It will push your ego thoughts down even further*! The idea is to bring the ego thought to the truth, the darkness to the light. When you do a lesson like this, therefore, you should do exactly what Jesus says, but realize also *what he is saying*. Pay attention to your need to keep this other person separate from you. Above all, be aware of the need to keep guilt secure in your mind. Only then can Jesus and these exercises help you to let it go.

LESSON 38

There is nothing my holiness cannot do.

Jesus does not mean that your holiness will enable you to walk on water or heal people's physical symptoms. His focus, as we have already observed many times, is not on behavior, even though the language may sometimes suggest it is. The concern of *A Course in Miracles* is always on the thinking in your mind. The reason there is nothing your holiness cannot do is that everything you do, think, say, or feel will come directly from your right-minded decision to identify with the holiness of Christ. That means there will be no interference or distortion: with guilt and judgment gone, all that remains is the love that transcends all problems and concerns.

(1:1-2) Your holiness reverses all the laws of the world. It is beyond every restriction of time, space, distance and limits of any kind.

This is because your holiness resides in your right mind, accessed by choosing the holy instant in which you are joined with Jesus or the Holy Spirit. This means there is no separation, and so there can be no sin, guilt, or fear. If there is no *sin*, there is no *past*; if there is no *guilt*, there is no *present*; and if there is no *fear*, there is no *future*. In other words, there is no time in the holy instant. Moreover, if there is no thought of separation from God, there is no body. To cite a previously cited statement from the text: "At no single instant [i.e., the holy instant] does the body exist at all" (T-18.VII.3:1). Thus holiness is completely outside time and space. When you identify with your holiness you know the world of time and space is a dream, and you can literally watch your dream figure—the dream figure with the name you think you are—come and go, realizing at last that is *not* who you are. There is nothing your holiness cannot do because there is nothing you have to do: "I need do nothing," as the text says (T-18.VII).

(1:3) Your holiness is totally unlimited in its power because it establishes you as a Son of God, at one with the Mind of his Creator.

That is what joining with the Holy Spirit or Jesus effects. In that instant, once again, everything changes, and all your problems are solved.

Lessons 79 and 80 tell us our problems are solved because there is only one problem: the belief we are separated. Therefore there is only one solution: accepting the Atonement, which denies the reality of guilt because it denies the reality of the separation. At that point the memory of our Identity as God's one Son dawns on our unclouded minds.

(2:1-3) Through your holiness the power of God is made manifest. Through your holiness the power of God is made available. And there is nothing the power of God cannot do.

Jesus is not talking about anything external, as I have already said a number of times. For two thousand years the miracle stories in the gospels have been regarded as testimony of the power of God: Jesus can heal the sick, raise the dead, turn water into wine, and resurrect in the flesh. This represents a total misunderstanding of what Jesus taught. It is interesting to observe students of *A Course in Miracles* who are trying to get away from their Christian upbringing making the same mistake of confusing *form* and *content*, *body* and *mind*: the confusion of levels that early in the text Jesus discusses as the cause of all sickness (T-2.IV.2).

Jesus is therefore not talking about what your body will do, because when you identify with the power of God and your holiness, you realize that the body is simply a figment in your imagination, a figure in your dream. We are all figures in a dream in which the body literally does nothing, and we can liken it to a puppet that is nothing more than a lifeless piece of wood. Thus do we live as puppets, in a make-believe world that has no more reality than that enjoyed by little children in a theater. This, too, is an idea to which we shall return again and again.

(2:4-6) Your holiness, then, can remove all pain, can end all sorrow, and can solve all problems. It can do so in connection with yourself and with anyone else. It is equal in its power to help anyone because it is equal in its power to save anyone.

The source of all our pain, sorrow, and problems is our decision to push Jesus away. If we invite him back there can be no distress. Remember that we are speaking only on the level of the mind, since that is the source of all pain. It is possible that perceived negative external circumstances, totally beyond our human control, will continue, as might physical symptoms. However, without guilt, they will no longer be experienced as problems or sources of pain or distress. In the manual for teachers, Jesus explains how a healed mind perceives:

> The body's eyes will continue to see differ-ences. But the mind that has let itself be healed will no longer acknowledge them. There will be those who seem to be "sicker" than others, and the body's eyes will report their changed appearances as before. But the healed mind will put them all in one category; they are un-real. This is the gift of its Teacher; the under-standing that only two categories are meaningful in sorting out the messages the mind receives from what appears to be the out-side world. And of these two, but one is real. Just as reality is wholly real, apart from size and shape and time and place—for differences cannot exist within it—so too are illusions without distinctions. The one answer to sick-ness of any kind is healing. The one answer to all illusions is truth (M-8.6).

It cannot be emphasized too often that *A Course in Miracles* is concerned only with the *cause* of the world—the *mind*—and not the *effect*—the *world*. That is why Jesus makes this important statement in the text: "This is a course in cause and not effect" (T-21.VII.7:8). Thus when we ask Jesus to help end our physical or emotional pain, or to solve an external problem, we are bringing his truth into our illusion. Sometimes the problem is resolved and sometimes it is not, but involving Jesus in our ex-ternal problems only glorifies specialness, the exact opposite of what he is teaching us to correct.

This certainly does not mean that one should *not* ask him for this kind of help. However, to remain at that level of relationship with him is to ensure that we never grow beyond it. Indeed, the pamphlet *The Song of Prayer* was written specifically to help stu-dents of *A Course in Miracles* move beyond what is described there as the bottom rung of the ladder of prayer—asking for specifics—to the higher rungs that reflect our shift in focus from the world

to the mind, a shift that helps us to see that there is, again, only *one* problem and therefore only *one* solution. Such insight of course is what the very first principle of miracles teaches us:

> There is no order of difficulty in miracles. One is not "harder" or "bigger" than another. They are all the same (T-1.I.1:1-3).

To make this important point one more time: Our holiness is "equal in its power to help anyone" because there is one problem. There is also only one Son. If my mind is healed because I have chosen the holiness of Christ as my identity instead of the ego's sinfulness, in that instant I realize I am that one Son, and everyone is part of that Sonship with me. Therefore, in my experience all pain is gone. This has nothing to do with other people's choices still to remain asleep, for in the holy instant I am beyond their dream, as was Jesus.

(3:1-3) If you are holy, so is everything God cre-ated. You are holy because all things He created are holy. And all things He created are holy be-cause you are.

If I am holy, so is everything God created, be-cause what God created is One. When you read lovely and inspiring sentences like these, you have to penetrate beyond the words to the meaning, be-yond the *form* to the *content*. If you truly believe what Jesus is saying, then throughout your day you must attempt to generalize his meaning to every-thing, *without exception*. In doing so you need real-ize how you do *not* believe the Son of God is holy because you do not believe the Son of God is one. You need realize that you choose to believe some people are holy and some are not. Remember, your judgment of anyone directly reflects your judgment of yourself. Vigilance, once again, means paying careful attention to what you perceive outside you, realizing this is a mirror of what you have made real inside.

(3:4-5) In today's exercises, we will apply the power of your holiness to all problems, difficul-ties or suffering in any form that you happen to think of, in yourself or in someone else. We will make no distinctions because there are no distinctions.

We can see once again why Jesus begins *A Course in Miracles* with "There is no order of difficulty in miracles" (T-1.I.1:1). That is his alpha and omega. The ego's version is that there *is* a hierarchy of illusions (T-23.II.2:3), which is why in these lessons Jesus repeatedly instructs us not to make any distinctions in what we perceive or think. Either everything is of the ego or the Holy Spirit, and there is no in between. As Jesus said a moment ago, either you are sinless or sinful. It is one or the other, the right-minded use of that ego principle.

Paragraphs 4 and 5 instruct us in the day's exercise, focusing on the role of choosing our right-minded thought of holiness in solving *all* our problems. It is important to note that Jesus asks us to make no distinction between perceived problems in ourselves or in others:

(4) In the four longer practice periods, each preferably to last a full five minutes, repeat the idea for today, close your eyes, and then search your mind for any sense of loss or unhappiness of any kind as you see it. Try to make as little distinction as possible between a situation that is difficult for you, and one that is difficult for someone else. Identify the situation specifically, and also the name of the person concerned. Use this form in applying the idea for today:

> *In the situation involving ___ in which I see myself, there is nothing that my holiness cannot do.*
> *In the situation involving ___ in which ___ sees himself, there is nothing my holiness cannot do.*

Since their source remains the same—the unholiness (guilt) in our minds—it matters not where the projection is perceived. There *is* no hierarchy of illusions—the illusory *idea* of separation has never left its illusory *source* in the mind. That is why distinctions among illusions—e.g., separate bodies—are ultimately irrelevant. This is the *content* behind the *form* of Jesus' instruction to us "to make as little distinction as possible between a situation that is difficult for you, and one that is difficult for someone else."

(5) From time to time you may want to vary this procedure, and add some relevant thoughts of your own. You might like, for example, to include thoughts such as:

> *There is nothing my holiness cannot do because the power of God lies in it.*

Introduce whatever variations appeal to you, but keep the exercises focused on the theme, "There is nothing my holiness cannot do." The purpose of today's exercises is to begin to instill in you a sense that you have dominion over all things because of what you are.

Jesus is asking us to continue our practice of generalizing his lesson to as many thoughts and situations as possible. The final sentence is a reference to the Adam and Eve story in Genesis, where God gives Adam dominion over all things (Genesis, 1:28), symbolized in the myth by Adam giving everything a name. Naming something is a symbol of having power over it, a thought we shall return to in Lesson 184. Jesus uses the same idea here, although obviously he is not speaking of power as the world regards it, but as the power of God's Love—His total Oneness. I thus have dominion over all things because all things are me. Remember, everything I perceive outside is not out there at all, but is a projection or extension of what I have first made real in my mind. I have dominion over all things because of what I am—the holiness of Christ. Therefore, everything I perceive as separate from me must also be holy; not because its form is inherently holy, but because it is a projection of the mind that contains holiness. This important concept is expressed in the following prayer of Jesus from the text, said on our behalf:

> I thank You, Father, knowing You will come to close each little gap that lies between the broken pieces of Your holy Son. Your Holiness, complete and perfect, lies in every one of them. And they are joined because what is in one is in them all. How holy is the smallest grain of sand, when it is recognized as being part of the completed picture of God's Son! The forms the broken pieces seem to take mean nothing. For the whole is in each one. And every aspect of the Son of God is just the same as every other part (T-28.IV.9).

If I am tempted not to see you as holy, but as an entity separate from me—having something I want, or having power over me—this misperception represents a *prior* choice to keep my holiness separate from *me*. I would have made this choice out of fear that in my holiness all individuality and specialness disappear. In other words, power is in our minds because there is nothing outside them. That power rests in our decision maker's ability to choose the

Love of God or attack it. There *is* no other power in the world.

The lesson concludes with Jesus again asking us to apply the day's thought to any *specific* form of upset:

(6) In the frequent shorter applications, apply the idea in its original form unless a specific problem concerning you or someone else arises, or comes to mind. In that event, use the more specific form in applying the idea to it.

As we have remarked, and will continue to remark, these exercises have no value if we do not learn to generalize their principles to *all* situations in which we find ourselves—minor or major, pleasurable or painful. We must learn that all problems are the same since they share the common source of separation or unholiness. When brought to the Atonement—the thought of holiness in our minds—they cannot but disappear.

LESSON 39

My holiness is my salvation.

(1:1) If guilt is hell, what is its opposite?

There are two ways of answering this question. On one level, and the most obvious, the answer is the lesson title: the opposite of guilt is holiness, and the opposite of hell is salvation. As we shall see in the second paragraph, however, another opposite of *guilt is hell* is that *guilt is heaven*.

(1:2) Like the text for which this workbook was written, the ideas used for the exercises are very simple, very clear and totally unambiguous.

This is not what most students of *A Course in Miracles* believe about the text. The problem is that once you understand what the Course is saying, which means you have set aside your guilt, specialness, and investment in being an individual, what is left is the simple truth. You then read *A Course in Miracles* in that state of mind and it is ever so "simple...clear and...unambiguous." What makes it difficult to understand is not the language, the blank verse, or any other aspect of its form, but your unwillingness to understand it. This is not intended as an attack or condemnation, but simply as a means to help you understand why you find this so difficult to comprehend, let alone practice. As long as you have an investment in keeping your mind hidden, in keeping your body real and individuality paramount, you will find what this course is saying to be terribly threatening. Inevitably, then, the natural defense against the perceived threat would be to obscure what it is saying.

You cannot understand *A Course in Miracles* without first letting it inside. Once you do, however, you find that when you read something that a week, month or a year ago made no sense, the words suddenly leap off the page and are "totally unambiguous." Thus, when Jesus says here—as he says in many other places—that his course is simple and clear, he is not being facetious, nor mocking you. He is simply saying that if it is not clear to you it is because you are defending against it, a statement made in the text that was originally meant for Helen:

This course is perfectly clear. If you do not

see it clearly, it is because you are interpreting against it, and therefore do not believe it. And since belief determines perception [a reference to *projection makes perception*], you do not perceive what it means and therefore do not accept it (T-11.VI.3:1-3).

(1:3-4) We are not concerned with intellectual feats nor logical toys. We are dealing only in the very obvious, which has been overlooked in the clouds of complexity in which you think you think.

So much for our holy and brilliant thoughts we think we are thinking. But we have already learned we are not thinking at all. Rather, these "profound" thoughts are but shadows of the mind's thought of fear. The underlying dynamic here is our fear of the clarity of *A Course in Miracles*, which gives rise to the defense of complexity. This renders its simple truths temporarily inaccessible to us.

The Course's teachings shine in our minds like the sun, and we become so frightened of the light that we quickly produce clouds, more clouds, and more clouds still. These defenses, which elsewhere are described as symbols of guilt (T-13.IX) or "screens of smoke" (W-pI.133.12:3), "protect" us from the light of the "sun's" truth. In the context of this passage, then, the clouds represent our intellectual ruminations, all designed, under the rationalization of seeking understanding, to defend against the simplicity of the teachings. In the end, truth's simplicity can only be experienced, not understood through the brain. As Jesus explains in the text about complexity:

> Complexity is of the ego, and is nothing more than the ego's attempt to obscure the obvious (T-15.IV.6:2).

> Complexity is not of God. How could it be, when all He knows is one? He knows of one creation, one reality, one truth and but one Son. Nothing conflicts with oneness. How, then, could there be complexity in Him? (T-26.III.1:1-5)

(2:1-4) If guilt is hell, what is its opposite? This is not difficult, surely. The hesitation you may

feel in answering is not due to the ambiguity of the question. But do you believe that guilt is hell?

That is the problem. We believe guilt is *heaven*, but are not aware that we do. There is a subsection of "The Obstacles to Peace" called "The Attraction of Guilt" (T-19.IV-A.i) in which Jesus specifically talks about our attraction to seeing guilt in other people. It is obvious, though, that if I see it in others it is because I want to keep it real in myself. That is the problem. We believe that guilt is heaven and holiness is damnation. In the text Jesus says our real fear is not of crucifixion but of redemption (or holiness) (T-13.III.1:10-11). In the presence of this holiness—the principle of the Atonement that *is* our redemption—our self-concept of individuality disappears: our ego is gone, as are our problems and their false solutions. Nothing remains but the light of truth, which truly frightens us. That is the problem.

Guilt preserves individuality because it tells us never to look within our minds; our guilt and self-hatred are so overpowering that if we go anywhere near them we will be destroyed. Thus, following the ego's strategy, which we outlined in the Prelude, we make a world and body to conceal the "awful truth" about ourselves. This dynamic, which reveals the true purpose of the body, is most clearly articulated in the following passage from the text. We shall occasionally return to parts of it, but here is the passage in its entirety. I have supplied the appropriate nouns, where the pronouns might be confusing:

> The circle of fear lies just below the level the body sees, and seems to be the whole foundation on which the world is based. Here [the world] are all the illusions, all the twisted thoughts, all the insane attacks, the fury, the vengeance and betrayal that were made to keep the guilt in place, so that the world could rise from it [guilt] and keep it [guilt] hidden. Its [guilt's] shadow rises to the surface, enough to hold its [guilt's] most external manifestations in darkness, and to bring despair and loneliness to it [the world] and keep it [the world] joyless. Yet its [guilt's] intensity is veiled by its [guilt's] heavy coverings, and kept apart from what [the world] was made to keep it [guilt] hidden. The body cannot see this [guilt], for the body arose from this [guilt] for

its [guilt's] protection, which depends on keeping it [guilt] not seen. The body's eyes will never look on it [guilt]. Yet they will see what it [guilt] dictates.

> The body will remain guilt's messenger, and will act as it [guilt] directs as long as you believe that guilt is real. For the reality of guilt is the illusion that seems to make it [guilt] heavy and opaque, impenetrable, and a real foundation for the ego's thought system. Its [guilt's] thinness and transparency are not apparent until you see the light behind it [guilt]. And then you see it [guilt] as a fragile veil before the light (T-18.IX.4-5).

Thus we are not aware that guilt is the choice to preserve our individuality by making up imaginary thoughts that equate it with sin and guilt, which deserve punishment. All this is protected by the world and body, which keeps the horror of our guilt hidden. When Jesus asks, then, "Do you believe that guilt is hell?" we emphatically answer "No." The proof we have answered thus is that we believe we are here as bodies and personalities. Jesus knows this to be a fact in the perceptual universe, which is evident in what he says next:

(2:5-6) If you did [believe that guilt is hell], **you would see at once how direct and simple the text is, and you would not need a workbook at all. No one needs practice to gain what is already his.**

This is Jesus' reply when you say you cannot understand his course; that it is too complicated, difficult, or convoluted. He is telling you that is *not* the problem. In saying, a line we have already quoted, "And God thinks otherwise" (T-23.I.2:7), Jesus tells you: "*I* think otherwise." The problem is that you believe guilt is heaven, and do not believe guilt is hell and your holiness is your salvation. Clearly, Jesus is not attacking or judging anyone here. Rather, he tells you: "You will not be able to learn this course as long as you do not listen to what I am telling you, which is that you do not want to learn this course. Bring to me your fear of learning so I can teach you that *A Course in Miracles* will help and not hurt you. Love will not abandon, betray, or crucify you, but will simply accept you for the Christ you are. It is that love you fear."

This passage is also an appeal to our humility. Jesus is gently informing us that we are still spiritual children, babes in the ego's woods that need a wise older brother to extend his gentle hand and lead us through. As long as we identify with our physical and psychological self, we need *A Course in Miracles* as the means whereby Jesus leads us through the darkened thickets of the ego's thought system to the light of truth that shines just beyond them. It is only the ego's arrogance that would have us believe we are beyond the need for such help.

(3:1-3) We have already said that your holiness is the salvation of the world. What about your own salvation? You cannot give what you do not have.

The world is nothing more than a mirror of what you believe you are; and therefore the salvation of the world and yourself are identical.

Having and *giving*, *giving* and *receiving*, *having* and *being*—all are equated in the Course (see e.g., T-6.V), and thus are the same. If the reality of love, which is the *only* reality, is perfect undifferentiated unity and nothing else, then what I *have* is what I *am*, and what I *give* is what I *receive*: again—they are the same. The four are synonymous with the dynamic that says that love is, and there is nothing else. In this world, of course, *having*, *being*, *giving* and *receiving* are separate. If I give you something, I do not have it. These sentences, moreover, emphasize the need for us to accept the Atonement for ourselves, not for anyone else. I cannot be of help to others if I remain *an unhealed healer* (T-9.V). The next lines make this clear:

(3:4-5) A savior must be saved. How else can he teach salvation?

Nothing in *A Course in Miracles* will make sense to you—intellectually or experientially—unless you realize that everything is one—within the ego's dream and in Heaven. The guilt in your wrong mind is the same guilt in everyone. Likewise in your right mind: If you forgive one person you forgive everyone, because everyone is the same. Forgiveness must begin and end where it is needed—in our minds, where the original choice for guilt was made. We have already seen that as we accept salvation for ourselves, it automatically extends through us to embrace the Sonship as one.

(3:6) Today's exercises will apply to you, recognizing that your salvation is crucial to the salvation of the world.

I do not have to worry about saving the world or ameliorating a terrible condition, whether it is global or personal. I need only "worry" about saving myself, which means asking Jesus to help me look at my mistaken decisions and thoughts another way.

(3:7) As you apply the exercises to your world, the whole world stands to benefit.

This of course makes no sense from the world's point of view. Thus, when students approach this lesson, still thinking they are real persons, living in a world they can save, they misinterpret Jesus' teaching that there is no world, which is given detailed attention later in the workbook (e.g., Lesson 132). Here he is teaching that if I save myself and take him as my teacher instead of the ego, the whole world is saved as well. The oneness of the world reflects the oneness of our minds, a oneness that remains at one with itself, since *ideas leave not their source.*

(4:1-2) Your holiness is the answer to every question that was ever asked, is being asked now, or will be asked in the future. Your holiness means the end of guilt, and therefore the end of hell.

That is what we are afraid of, and therefore why we choose to be unholy. Whenever we attack another, whether in our thoughts, words, or actions, we seek to prove we are unholy and undeserving of love. It is very simple. There is but one specific motivation: to keep yourself guilty. If you are guilty, you are right and Jesus is wrong, for he tells you that you are holy. This, then, becomes our ego's response to his "attack": "I will show you! Look at what I am doing or what I am thinking. Look at what I am not doing or what I am not thinking." You need to get in touch with the underlying motivation that wants to prove guilt is not hell but heaven. Once caught in the maelstrom of guilt, your thought system quickly evolves to wanting the guilt to rest on another, not yourself. Such projection is the ego's heaven, since it protects the unforgiveness of ourselves (W-pII.1.2), and therefore our individual and guilt-ridden identities. Preserving that identity is the ultimate motivation for our thoughts of judgment and attack.

(4:3) Your holiness is the salvation of the world, and your own.

Why? Because they are exactly the same: *ideas leave not their source.*

(4:4-6) How could you to whom your holiness belongs be excluded from it? God does not know unholiness. Can it be He does not know His Son?

Having firmly established this in the text (e.g., T-4.I.2:6,11-12; II.8:6-7), Jesus is clearly implying here that God does not know about this world. This is an unholy world coming from an unholy thought, and God does not know his Son in an unholy state. If He did, the unholy state would be real and duality would be the truth of the Kingdom. Even though the ego is outraged to be told God does not know about it, in truth that is the most comforting thought of all. If God does not know about you, then you—the separated Son of God—do not exist. But what God *does* know about does exist: the Self you *truly* are.

(5) A full five minutes are urged for the four longer practice periods for today, and longer and more frequent practice sessions are encouraged. If you want to exceed the minimum requirements, more rather than longer sessions are recommended, although both are suggested.

Again, we see Jesus gently encouraging and leading us forward in our practicing. He clearly wants us to think of him and his message as often as possible throughout the day, yet he does not wish us to feel coerced, for coercion merely reinforces fear.

(6) Begin the practice periods as usual, by repeating today's idea to yourself. Then, with closed eyes, search out your unloving thoughts in whatever form they appear; uneasiness, depression, anger, fear, worry, attack, insecurity and so on. Whatever form they take, they are unloving and therefore fearful. And so it is from them that you need to be saved.

This is a striking and unequivocal statement that you need be saved only from your thoughts. The problem is that we do not know them because we think our thoughts have taken flight and exist outside us. That is why I have been emphasizing how Jesus emphasizes our need to search our minds. Indeed, one of the most important themes of these lessons is mind searching for unloving thoughts. Occasionally Jesus says to search for loving ones, as will be coming up shortly, but by and large his focus is on the unloving thoughts, because they are the problem. It is they we need to bring to the light of truth. Once their darkness is dispelled, the loving thoughts simply *are.*

(7) Specific situations, events or personalities you associate with unloving thoughts of any kind are suitable subjects for today's exercises. It is imperative for your salvation that you see them differently. And it is your blessing on them that will save you and give you vision.

That is a very strong statement: "It is imperative for your salvation that you see them differently." How can you see them differently if you do not see them at all? That is why you have to search your mind for the unloving thoughts. Jesus has already told you he understands that you do not understand what he is talking about. Moreover, you certainly do not accept his teachings because you do not believe that guilt is hell. The idea here, therefore, is that you *not* pretend you are a wonderful student and believe everything in these lessons. What makes you a wonderful student of *A Course in Miracles* is to forgive yourself for *not* believing everything that is here. Remember, the idea is to bring your unloving thoughts to his love so he may reinterpret them for us. That is why our recognition and acceptance of their presence—in our minds—is so essential to our healing and salvation.

(8) Slowly, without conscious selection and without undue emphasis on any one in particular, search your mind for every thought that stands between you and your salvation. Apply the idea for today to each of them in this way:

> *My unloving thoughts about ___ are keeping me in hell. My holiness is my salvation.*

That is what Jesus means in the text when he says, to quote this important statement again:

> Your task is not to seek for love, but merely to seek and find all of the barriers within yourself that you have built against it (T-16.IV.6:1).

This aspect of our forgiveness process is so essential it could almost be repeated for each lesson. We need to be continually vigilant for our unloving thoughts, in order to bring them to the Presence of Love in our minds, which gently shines them away. Our task, again, is merely to seek and find; removal belongs to the Holy Spirit.

The remainder of the lesson contains further guidance and instructions for the day's practice. Note especially these gentle reminders that we are, after all, just beginners on the journey:

(9) You may find these practice periods easier if you intersperse them with several short periods during which you merely repeat today's idea to yourself slowly a few times. You may also find it helpful to include a few short intervals in which you just relax and do not seem to be thinking of anything. Sustained concentration is very difficult at first. It will become much easier as your mind becomes more disciplined and less distractible.

"Sustained concentration" becomes one of the characteristics of our more advanced state of learning, when we are consistently able to think of Jesus and his message of forgiveness. The attainment of the real world, the ultimate goal of *A Course in Miracles*, comes when our sustained concentration becomes permanent—the right-minded correction having undone the wrong-minded problem, leaving only the memory of God to dawn on our healed and holy minds.

(10) Meanwhile, you should feel free to introduce variety into the exercise periods in whatever form appeals to you. Do not, however, change the idea itself as you vary the method of applying it. However you elect to use it, the idea should be stated so that its meaning is the fact that your holiness is your salvation. End each practice period by repeating the idea in its original form once more, and adding:

If guilt is hell, what is its opposite?

Jesus introduces the idea we can be flexible in our practicing, an obvious attempt to help us begin the process of generalizing the specific lessons to *all* situations and circumstances. By instructing us *not* to change the idea, he is also gently introducing us to the important theme of *form* and *content*; we may vary the *form* in which we express forgiveness or love, as long as the *content* remains the same.

The final paragraph encourages us to become increasingly mindful throughout the day, as well as to apply the day's idea to temptations to listen to the ego's doctrine of guilt:

(11) In the shorter applications, which should be made some three or four times an hour and more if possible, you may ask yourself this question [If guilt is hell, what is its opposite?], repeat today's idea, and preferably both. If temptations arise, a particularly helpful form of the idea is:

My holiness is my salvation from this.

To the extent we can respond quickly to our ego's temptations to feel guilt and anger, to that extent we shall progress to the goal of knowing that our holiness is our salvation, and that we *are* holy.

LESSON 40

I am blessed as a Son of God.

(1:1) Today we will begin to assert some of the happy things to which you are entitled, being what you are.

In these early lessons, as we have previously discussed, Jesus makes it clear that our minds are split, part of which worships guilt and attack thoughts, while the other contains the memory of Who we truly are. Beginning with this lesson and continuing for the next ten, Jesus gives our egos a respite as he speaks almost exclusively about the other side—"the happy things to which you are entitled"—our right minds.

(1:2-6) No long practice periods are required today, but very frequent short ones are necessary. Once every ten minutes would be highly desirable, and you are urged to attempt this schedule and to adhere to it whenever possible. If you forget, try again. If there are long interruptions, try again. Whenever you remember, try again.

The exercises for today thus represent a departure from the previous ones because of the absence of a long exercise period. In addition, Jesus continues his strong yet gentle urgings that we keep trying to remember—as often as possible each hour—without making our forgetting into a sin. Quite obviously he knows we will.

The next paragraph is extremely important because it helps us recognize that these exercises must be applied *all* the time, whether we are meditating in a quiet room, or being about our busyness. *We do not have to close our eyes in order to remember God and His Son*:

(2) You need not close your eyes for the exercise periods, although you will probably find it more helpful if you do. However, you may be in a number of situations during the day when closing your eyes would not be feasible. Do not miss a practice period because of this. You can practice quite well under any circumstances, if you really want to.

Thus, no matter where you are during the day—driving your car, eating with a friend, quietly alone, busy at work—you can remember today's lesson.

(3) Today's exercises take little time and no effort. Repeat the idea for today, and then add several of the attributes you associate with being a Son of God, applying them to yourself. One practice period might, for example, consist of the following:

> *I am blessed as a Son of God.*
> *I am happy, peaceful, loving and contented.*

Another might take this form:

> *I am blessed as a Son of God.*
> *I am calm, quiet, assured and confident.*

If only a brief period is available, merely telling yourself that you are blessed as a Son of God will do.

Jesus is asking us to take the general statement of our Identity and make it more specific, thereby making it more personal to us. The lesson's final line reiterates how we do not need a quiet place or set time to remember.

Underlying Jesus' teaching here is that we need time and place—i.e., rituals—as long as we identify with our bodies. But since Jesus' ultimate teaching is that we are minds, weaning us of our dependency on externals is an important step toward our eventual identification with the mind: the source of our blessedness, as well as the birthplace of our resistance to accepting Who we truly are.

LESSON 41

God goes with me wherever I go.

This is obviously a happy thought, and just as obviously Jesus is not talking about a literal physical God Who walks with us, reminiscent of the song in the movie version of *The Student Prince*, "I walk with God." Jesus is telling us here that the memory of God is in our minds—the home of the Holy Spirit—and thus is always with us. In that sense, God is indeed with us wherever we go. This will become more evident as we go through the lesson.

(1) Today's idea will eventually overcome completely the sense of loneliness and abandonment all the separated ones experience. Depression is an inevitable consequence of separation. So are anxiety, worry, a deep sense of helplessness, misery, suffering and intense fear of loss.

What reappears here is the important theme of *cause and effect*. Although the words are not specifically used, Jesus' teaching can nonetheless be seen as a reflection of that theme. Our problems are all the same and come from one *cause*: believing we are separated from God. The *effects* of this mistake are worry, depression, misery, suffering, and fear of loss. We have discussed before how the world exists to provide causes of our distress, which merely disguise the true cause. Our egos are incredibly skillful in concealing the truth, leading us to be certain we know the sources of our unhappiness—everything but the mind's decision for guilt.

Thus, if I know that "God goes with me wherever I go" because He is in my mind, that means I have not abandoned Him and He has not abandoned me. Further, it means I have not killed Him, nor am separated from Him. If I accept this truth of the Atonement, I cannot be depressed, lonely, anxious, or fearful, as these come from guilt, which, without the belief in separation, cannot exist. The way I will know about my belief in separation is to become aware of my feelings of anxiety, worry, and unhappiness. That is why it is essential not to cover over negative experiences. If we do, there is literally no hope, which lies in first recognizing our discomfort and despair, then realizing these are simply the effects of the thought that God does *not* go wherever we go because we killed Him off. That sinful

thought represents a decision that can now happily be changed.

You need to learn you were wrong, and that you now want to be a happy learner who is happy to be wrong, not happy because you have proven yourself to be right (T-29.VII.1:9). This is an idea that cannot be cited often enough. If you have an investment in being right, you will never be happy. Perhaps you are right today, but the "rightness" (or innocence) that you stole from someone else will be stolen back by the one from whom you took it in anger. The only way you can be truly right is to know that God is with you wherever you go, which means that everything the ego has taught you is a lie. You *did* not separate from God because you *could* not.

(2:1-2) The separated ones have invented many "cures" for what they believe to be the "ills of the world." But the one thing they do not do is to question the reality of the problem.

"Ills of the world" is in quotes because there are no "ills of the world." Since there is no world, how could it have ills? There is only an ill thought. "Cures" is in quotes as well because you cannot cure a problem that does not exist. The true problem is separation, and if we do not recognize that thought as the cause of our problems, how can we question it, let alone change it? The ego has convinced us that separation is real, and is such a horrid thought we can never look at it again, lest we be destroyed. As Jesus explains in the text:

> Loudly the ego tells you not to look inward,
> for if you do your eyes will light on sin, and
> God will strike you blind. This you believe,
> and so you do not look (T-21.IV.2:3-4).

The ego thus counsels us to run away from the mind, the home of the separation thought, and erect one defense after another, put up wall upon wall upon wall, all of which serve the purpose of rooting our attention in the world of the body. Thus we are protected from questioning the seeming reality of the statement: "I separated from God." As long as we remain in the state of *mindlessness*, we can never truly "question the reality of the problem," which remains always in its source: the *mind*.

(2:3) Yet its effects cannot be cured because the problem is not real.

Our attempts to cure a problem in the world, whether in our personal worlds or the world at large, will never meet with success. Perhaps the symptom will disappear temporarily, but we will still believe the problem—the *cause*—is real. As long as we do, the cause of guilt will continue to generate symptoms—Freud's *symptom substitution*—that plague us. Despite their pain demanding constant attention, however, the underlying cause of the symptoms remains unnoticed, and the ego continues to reign triumphant until we can exclaim: "There must be another way!" Our Teacher helps us finally get beyond the effect to the cause, so that it can be changed.

(2:4-5) The idea for today has the power to end all this foolishness forever. And foolishness it is, despite the serious and tragic forms it may take.

Importantly, Jesus does not use the word *sinful*; he simply says it is *foolish*. What he expresses here is identical to what he teaches in "The 'Hero' of the Dream," where he says that the problem is our having forgotten to laugh at the tiny, mad idea, and that the Holy Spirit looks at our concerns and laughs at them, not derisively, but with the gentleness that knows that upsets are not real. This theme recurs throughout *A Course in Miracles*, but the following passage from the end of Chapter 27 is representative:

> In gentle laughter does the Holy Spirit perceive the cause, and looks not to effects. How else could He correct your error, who have overlooked the cause entirely? He bids you bring each terrible effect to Him that you may look together on its foolish cause and laugh with Him a while. *You* judge effects, but *He* has judged their cause. And by His judgment are effects removed. Perhaps you come in tears. But hear Him say, "My brother, holy Son of God, behold your idle dream, in which this could occur." And you will leave the holy instant with your laughter and your brother's joined with His (T-27.VIII.9).

Later in the workbook we shall examine the use of the metaphor of *toys* to depict the seeming

gargantuan nature of sin, which but serves to conceal its innate foolishness.

(3) Deep within you is everything that is perfect, ready to radiate through you and out into the world. It will cure all sorrow and pain and fear and loss because it will heal the mind that thought these things were real, and suffered out of its allegiance to them.

If I know that God goes with me, that through the Holy Spirit His Love is always with me, I realize everything I had believed and perceived is not true. Again, that is the fear—if my beliefs and perceptions are not true, then *I* am not true either. Thus, I unconsciously hold on to the belief that guilt is heaven, for it proves that I exist, the *I* that I think myself to be.

(4) You can never be deprived of your perfect holiness because its Source goes with you wherever you go. You can never suffer because the Source of all joy goes with you wherever you go. You can never be alone because the Source of all life goes with you wherever you go. Nothing can destroy your peace of mind because God goes with you wherever you go.

Jesus would like you to see how steadfastly and stubbornly you try to prove these statements wrong and your beliefs right. You do this by proving the world is hostile, threatening, and sinful, or that *you* are hostile, threatening, and sinful. It does not matter which. It is extremely helpful to look at how you defend against this truth by continually asserting you are right and seek to prove it. It is also crucial that you recognize that you do not believe Jesus' words, as he will tell you in the next sentence.

One more point before we move on: If we were to accept as true the beautiful statements in the above paragraph, our guilt would have nowhere to go except to remain within our minds, where the ego told us waits our certain death at the hands of a vengeful god, hell-bent on our destruction. Our projected suffering and unhappiness *without* protects this terrible thought *within*. It is this need to protect ourselves that provides the resistance to acceptance of Jesus' comforting words.

(5:1-2) We understand that you do not believe all this. How could you, when the truth is hidden deep within, under a heavy cloud of insane

thoughts, dense and obscuring, yet representing all you see?

How could you possibly understand this when you still believe there is a *you* reading these words? How could you possibly understand when you remain preoccupied with your specialness, individuality, and problems? Once again, we see the *purposive* nature of our insane thoughts leading to our insane perceptions: they keep hidden the truth that would indeed make us free of the ego's thought system of fear, hate, and suffering.

(5:3) Today we will make our first real attempt to get past this dark and heavy cloud, and to go through it to the light beyond.

Jesus will use this form again in Lesson 70, the thought being that Jesus is the one who leads you through the cloud. He asks you not to deny the presence of this cloud of guilt, individuality, and specialness, but to pay close attention to it. We can never get to the light without going through the cloud, "dark and heavy" only to the ego. In truth, however, it is but a "fragile veil before the light," as we read in this wonderful extended passage from the text:

> For the reality of guilt is the illusion that seems to make it heavy and opaque, impenetrable, and a real foundation for the ego's thought system. Its thinness and transparency are not apparent until you see the light behind it. And then you see it as a fragile veil before the light.
>
> This heavy-seeming barrier, this artificial floor that looks like rock, is like a bank of low dark clouds that seem to be a solid wall before the sun. Its impenetrable appearance is wholly an illusion. It gives way softly to the mountain tops that rise above it, and has no power at all to hold back anyone willing to climb above it and see the sun. It is not strong enough to stop a button's fall, nor hold a feather. Nothing can rest upon it, for it is but an illusion of a foundation. Try but to touch it and it disappears; attempt to grasp it and your hands hold nothing. … So should it be with the dark clouds of guilt, no more impenetrable and no more substantial. You will not bruise yourself against them in traveling through. Let your Guide teach you their unsubstantial nature as He leads you past them, for beneath them is a world of light whereon they cast no shadows (T-18.IX.5:2-4; 6; 8:1-3).

Indeed, this teaching about guilt's "unsubstantial nature" is the heart and soul of *A Course in Miracles*; the essence of the Atonement. It teaches there is no need to defend against the thought of guilt, which has no effect and therefore is not there. Again, we can note how the profundity of the text's teachings is found "hidden" in these "simple" workbook lessons.

We continue now with the instructions for the day, which have us return to a long practice period. This time Jesus urges us more directly to go within, making clear the distinction between the brain's activity of thinking and that of the mind, the true source of our thoughts:

(6:1–7:2) There will be only one long practice period today. In the morning, as soon as you get up if possible, sit quietly for some three to five minutes, with your eyes closed. At the beginning of the practice period, repeat today's idea very slowly. Then make no effort to think of anything. Try, instead, to get a sense of turning inward, past all the idle thoughts of the world. Try to enter very deeply into your own mind, keeping it clear of any thoughts that might divert your attention.

From time to time, you may repeat the idea if you find it helpful. But most of all, try to sink down and inward, away from the world and all the foolish thoughts of the world.

And everything here is foolish; or, better, it is foolish to believe that the things of the world can bring us pleasure or pain. Sinking past them means moving past our bodily identification—the *seeming* locus of our pleasure and pain—to the mind that is the only source of our feelings and thoughts. It is in the mind that we experience God's Presence through the Holy Spirit, and it is in the mind that the decision is made to substitute the ego's presence for His.

The next two sentences emphasize the crucial distinction, borrowed from Plato, between appearance and reality, awareness of which is the purpose of our going inward:

(7:3-4) You are trying to reach past all these things. You are trying to leave appearances and approach reality.

Jesus wants us first to look carefully at what appears to us as real: the world, replete with people hearing and seeing our bodies, and whose bodies we hear and see. The next step, then, following Jesus' gentle guidance, is recognizing the illusory nature of these appearances and moving beyond them to the thoughts of the ego; and then, finally, beyond the ego to the Holy Spirit's thought of the Atonement.

(8:1-4) It is quite possible to reach God. In fact it is very easy, because it is the most natural thing in the world. You might even say it is the only natural thing in the world. The way will open, if you believe that it is possible.

Jesus is not saying you have to believe this totally, you just have to believe that perhaps, just maybe, it is possible he is right and you are wrong. If the only natural thing in this world is to reach God, and everything in this world is a movement against Him, then nothing in this world is natural, including yourself, your body, personality, and individual existence. It is your *belief* that will lead you Home, once you place its power under the Atonement principle of the Holy Spirit, correcting the mistaken belief in the separation.

Jesus next underscores for us the importance of this lesson, trying to buttress our confidence in the workbook's process of retraining our minds. This is one among the many "pep talks" he gives us along the way:

(8:5–9:3) This exercise can bring very startling results even the first time it is attempted, and sooner or later it is always successful. We will go into more detail about this kind of practice as we go along. But it will never fail completely, and instant success is possible.

Throughout the day use today's idea often, repeating it very slowly, preferably with eyes closed. Think of what you are saying; what the words mean. Concentrate on the holiness that they imply about you; on the unfailing companionship that is yours; on the complete protection that surrounds you.

These last lines point to the truth that lies just beyond the illusion, a truth that is ours once we truly focus on the lessons and the practice of the exercises.

And then the last line of the lesson:

(10) You can indeed afford to laugh at fear thoughts, remembering that God goes with you wherever you go.

Jesus returns to the theme of laughing at the ego; i.e., not taking it seriously. This is only possible when we have brought our fear thoughts to the Love of God that is remembered for us by the Holy Spirit. Without this process of bringing the illusions to the truth, our laughter will be superficial at best, and derisive and judgmental at worst. The Holy Spirit's laughter is born of the gentle smile that knows the difference between appearance and reality, illusion and truth, separation and Atonement. In Lesson 187 Jesus makes the seemingly outrageous statement that you could look at the pain, suffering, and starvation in the world and laugh at it. You will laugh at suffering, not because you are making fun of people, but because, having joined with the Holy Spirit in your right mind, you will know it is not true—it has no power to take the peace and Love of God away from you.

LESSON 42

God is my strength. Vision is His gift.

(1:1-2) The idea for today combines two very powerful thoughts, both of major importance. It also sets forth a cause and effect relationship that explains why you cannot fail in your efforts to achieve the goal of the course.

The "cause and effect relationship" is that if I know God "walks with me" and He is my strength, I shall automatically perceive through the eyes of His Love and Holiness. Christ's vision comes from the thought I am holy and part of God. When I look out, which, as we have learned, has nothing to do with our physical eyes, all I shall see are figures in a dream either expressing love and trying to return home, or still too afraid of love and attempting to attack it. In other words, the *cause* is my remembering Who I am, and the *effect* is the vision that sees all people as part of the one Sonship, regardless of their disparate forms.

(1:3-5) You will see because it is the Will of God. It is His strength, not your own, that gives you power. And it is His gift, rather than your own, that offers vision to you.

Jesus is urging us to trust him that we cannot fail. Illusions of ego strength can have no power over the real Source of strength within us. Jesus now sets out the wonderful consequences of this happy fact:

(2:1-2) God is indeed your strength, and what He gives is truly given. This means that you can receive it any time and anywhere, wherever you are, and in whatever circumstances you find yourself.

Since the mind, the home of God's strength, is beyond time (and space), it is *always* available to us. It simply awaits our acceptance. That is why Jesus tells us in the text, already cited, that we need do nothing (T-18.VII). We need do nothing *except* to accept what is already there. Thus our need is to learn to *un*do what the ego has taught us, releasing God's strength to once again be our own. Since this is a process occurring in our *minds*, which are totally under our control, this joyful acceptance can

occur anywhere, any time, regardless of external circumstances.

The discussion next moves more specifically to the topic of time, which we shall examine much more carefully later on. For now I shall just make some brief comments:

(2:3-6) Your passage through time and space is not at random. You cannot but be in the right place at the right time. Such is the strength of God. Such are His gifts.

Jesus is saying that nothing is at random because it is all our dream. The ego chooses our scripts as a way to keep us further and further away from the truth. When we look at these scripts with Jesus, they then become classrooms. But nothing is at random. I—the mind that my current physical identity is but a fragment of—have chosen my life and what happens in it as a way of reinforcing my individuality and specialness. If I look at any aspect of this life with Jesus and ask his help, I see it as the means of learning forgiveness so I may return to an awareness of my true Identity. Thus I am "in the right place at the right time," for lessons of forgiveness can *always* be learned, regardless of the outer circumstance.

For the two longer practice periods today, Jesus encourages us to focus on having *quiet* time. Looking at the instructions for these lessons as a whole, we can see how Jesus has emphasized different aspects of our practice at different times; sometimes focusing on the *form (*the external), other times on the *content* (the internal). The point here, of course, is to help us at our own level of learning, so that we may come to understand that *cause* and *effect*, *content* and *form*, *inner* and *outer*, are never separated:

(3) We will have two three-to-five-minute practice periods today, one as soon as possible after you wake, and another as close as possible to the time you go to sleep. It is better, however, to wait until you can sit quietly by yourself, at a time when you feel ready, than it is to be concerned with the time as such.

Jesus' weaning us from reliance on the *form* of our practicing is part of his training us not to be slaves to ritual. We previously cited the discussion in the manual for teachers in this regard, and here is the relevant passage:

> There are some general rules which do apply, although each one must use them as best he can in his own way. Routines as such are dangerous, because they easily become gods in their own right, threatening the very goals for which they were set up.... This course is always practical.... Duration is not the major concern. One can easily sit still an hour with closed eyes and accomplish nothing. One can as easily give God only an instant, and in that instant join with Him completely (M-16.2:4-5; 4:1,4-6).

We shall return to this important theme of the *quality* of our time spent with the Holy Spirit, rather than its *quantity*.

The fourth paragraph discusses our personal thoughts "in relation to the idea for the day."

(4) Begin these practice periods by repeating the idea for today slowly, with your eyes open, looking about you. Then close your eyes and repeat the idea again, even slower than before. After this, try to think of nothing except thoughts that occur to you in relation to the idea for the day. You might think, for example:

> *Vision must be possible. God gives truly,*

or:

> *God's gifts to me must be mine, because He gave them to me.*

Once again we can observe the emphasis Jesus places on bringing *our* thoughts to *his*, and thereby practice bringing them into harmony with his vision of forgiveness and peace.

In the next paragraph Jesus plays down the active mind-searching exercises of before, asking us to be quiet, letting his thoughts come to us, rather than our coming to them:

(5) Any thought that is clearly related to the idea for today is suitable. You may, in fact, be astonished at the amount of course-related understanding some of your thoughts contain. Let them come without censoring unless you find your mind is merely wandering, and you

have let obviously irrelevant thoughts intrude. You may also reach a point where no thoughts at all seem to come to mind. If such interferences occur, open your eyes and repeat the thought once more while looking slowly about; close your eyes, repeat the idea once more, and then continue to look for related thoughts in your mind.

However, if nothing "comes," our gentle teacher instructs us in the next paragraph to become more active again and look for the thoughts. Yet, this looking is *not* the focus here, but rather the letting go of control, allowing his guidance to take over, reminiscent of this statement from the text:

> My control can take over everything that does not matter, while my guidance can direct everything that does, if you so choose.... This [your behavior] is controlled by me automatically as soon as you place what you think under my guidance (T-2.VI.1:3; 2:9).

(6:1) Remember, however, that active searching for relevant thoughts is not appropriate for today's exercises.

Jesus is thus saying you do not have to search for God. Once you have removed your negative thoughts, the work of earlier lessons, the resultant blank slate allows the thoughts of love to appear to you. Therefore:

(6:2-3) Try merely to step back and let the thoughts come. If you find this difficult, it is better to spend the practice period alternating between slow repetitions of the idea with eyes open, then with eyes closed, than it is to strain to find suitable thoughts.

I might add that in reality the thoughts do not come to us; *we come to them*. It was our mind's decision maker that chose to leave the thought of the Atonement for the thought of separation, and so it is this decision maker that now must make the choice to return to that thought, although our experience may well be that the Atonement and its reflected thoughts come to us. That experience is reflected in this lesson, as is Jesus' emphasis on the gentle and non-coercive nature of this learning.

(7) There is no limit on the number of short practice periods that would be beneficial today. The idea for the day is a beginning step in

bringing thoughts together, and teaching you that you are studying a unified thought system in which nothing is lacking that is needed, and nothing is included that is contradictory or irrelevant.

This is a point that Jesus makes in many other places as well. Everything you ever need is in this course; there is no need to seek elsewhere. Once you decide *A Course in Miracles* is your spiritual path, to do anything else will simply confuse you. As Jesus told Helen specifically, in words meant for *all* his students:

> You are not making use of the course if you insist on using means which have served others well, neglecting what was made for *you* (T-18.VII.6:5).

A Course in Miracles contains everything that will help you undo your ego, and therefore everything that will help remind you of who you are. Insisting on "using means which have served others well" will simply defend against accepting the Course's message of forgiveness as your own.

(8) The more often you repeat the idea during the day, the more often you will be reminding yourself that the goal of the course is important to you, and that you have not forgotten it.

You need to realize there is a part of you, despite your fear, that does want to learn what this course is teaching, and that its goal is truly important to you. Despite all attempts to cover it with clouds of guilt, there remains the right-minded self that remembers your goal: above all you want to return home. *A Course in Miracles*, with Jesus as your teacher, will be the means to help you ultimately reach that goal.

LESSON 43

God is my Source. I cannot see apart from Him.

Before discussing this lesson, I should like to review a chart I hope will help in our study of this and subsequent lessons. This is a modified version of the chart I usually use, because in these lessons the mind's structure is portrayed as going from the bottom up, instead of the other way around.

At the bottom is *God*, the *One Mind*, the place of truth in our minds and subsumed under the term *knowledge*. This is the realm of our real thoughts, which we have always thought with God. These do not have form, and can be understood as an expression of eternal life, love, the Will of God, and the oneness of creation.

```
                   P
                   E   │  WORLD – BODY
          ─ ─ ─ ─ ─R─ ─┼─ ─ ─ ─ ─ ─ ─ ─ ─ ─ ─ ─ ─ ─ ─ ─
                   C    │
                   E    │  EGO (WRONG MIND) – UNREAL THOUGHTS
   DECISION        P    │
    MAKER      ─ ─ ─ ─ ─┼─ ─ ─ ─ ─ ─ ─ ─ ─ ─ ─ ─ ─ ─ ─
      ●            T    │
                   I    │
                   O    │  HOLY SPIRIT (RIGHT MIND) – REAL THOUGHTS
                   N    │
          ──────────────┼─────────────────────────────
      KNOWLEDGE          │  GOD – REAL THOUGHTS
```

The split mind is represented by the layers above God, beginning with the *right mind*, the home of *the Holy Spirit*. In these lessons Jesus does not make a distinction between our *right-minded* real thoughts and our *One-minded* real thoughts. This is but another example, incidentally, of how *A Course in Miracles* cannot be approached as a scientific treatise in which each term is carefully analyzed. Jesus is relatively loose with words, probably more so in the workbook than in the text. It would thus be more accurate to say that our right-minded thoughts are the *reflection* of our real thoughts. For the purposes of these lessons, however, our real thoughts include both those that are held for us by the Holy Spirit in our right minds, as well as the Thoughts of God in the One Mind.

Above the Holy Spirit is the *wrong mind*, the domain of the *ego*, wherein reside our unreal thoughts. It is these that are projected out, thereby making the world in which our bodies live.

The *wrong* and *right minds* are the domain of perception. The ego's false perceptions are corrected in our right minds by what is referred to in the text as *true perception*. The entire realm of the split mind—the right and wrong minds, and the projections that make the world—comprises the world of *perception*. All of this, as will be evident in a moment, is contrasted with the realm of *knowledge*, the Home of Christ, our true Self.

We shall see in the lessons that follow how Jesus guides us in the process of sinking down into our minds, past our *external perceptions* and through the *ego's unreal thoughts* that gave rise to them, to the *real thoughts* of the Holy Spirit. These correction thoughts will then ultimately fade into the *Thoughts of God*.

Let us now look at Lesson 43:

(1) Perception is not an attribute of God. His is the realm of knowledge. Yet He has created the Holy Spirit as the Mediator between perception and knowledge. Without this link with God, perception would have replaced knowledge forever in your mind. With this link with God, perception will become so changed and purified that it will lead to knowledge. That is its function as the Holy Spirit sees it. Therefore, that is its function in truth.

Having been made as an attack on God (W-pII.3.2:1-5), perception cements our belief that separation and individuality are real. However, once arising in apparent opposition to knowledge, it can then be used to serve a different purpose. The section called "The Special Function" provides a clear description of this shift in function or purpose: What we made to harm, the Holy Spirit uses to heal (T-25.VI.4). Specialness is an aspect of perception, and although it was made to harm and keep us separated from each other, when brought to the Holy Spirit and looked at differently, it becomes an expression of forgiveness. Everything the ego has thought, done, and used to separate itself from God, and each of us from each other, can be turned around to become a vehicle for our forgiveness—if we ask Jesus' help. This shift in purpose is the cornerstone of forgiveness and the Holy Spirit's redirected purpose for our being in this world.

In this first paragraph we find a clear example of what I sometimes refer to as the two levels on which *A Course in Miracles* is written. Level One reflects the Course's metaphysical principle that *only God is true and real, and everything else is unreal, an illusion*. Or as the very opening of the text states:

Nothing real can be threatened.
Nothing unreal exists (T-in.2:2-3; bold italics omitted).

It is that distinction between what is true and untrue that comprises this highly important aspect of *A Course in Miracles*. The first two sentences of this paragraph express Level One: the world of perception—which is not just the world we see with our eyes, but the very fact that we *think* we see a world at all—is an illusion. The split mind, which includes our thoughts of separation, the world which expresses those thoughts, as well as the Holy Spirit's correction, is totally unreal. Since this separated mind cannot be part of totality, wholeness, and perfect Oneness—the very nature of God—it cannot be true in any way. Stated differently, if the contents of the split mind are not part of God, they must be outside Him. If they are outside God, they cannot exist. Only knowledge is true and therefore real.

Level Two deals *only* with illusion: the contrast between the ego's *wrong-minded* perceptions of separation and specialness, and the Holy Spirit's *right-minded* corrected perceptions of forgiveness and healing. This level can be thought of as the more practical one, insofar as this is the part of *A Course in Miracles* that deals with *the condition in which we think we are* (T-25.I.7:4): the world of the body. Thus is the world of illusion split into perceptual realms: the false perception of the ego and its correction, the true perception of the Holy Spirit.

Sentence 3 represents the transition from Level One to Level Two. The Holy Spirit can be understood as that part of our split minds that remembers truth. Thus He can be defined as the memory of God's Love we took with us into the dream when we fell asleep. Remember that all of this is metaphorical, since we never fell asleep in the first place. We, like Jesus in *A Course in Miracles*, are using symbols to denote the reality from which they are "twice removed" (M-21.1:9-10). The Holy Spirit, representing our right-minded thinking, is the expression of the Atonement principle that is the mediator or bridge between the *unreal* world we made and the *real* world of Heaven. The Holy Spirit's thoughts are reflected in any expression of forgiveness, and these are reflections of the real thought of love that is in our minds.

One final comment, it is the integration of these two levels—the uncompromising non-dualistic view of reality, along with the specific guidelines for living within the illusory world under the principle of forgiveness—that makes *A Course in Miracles* so unique as a spirituality, and so perfect for our age.

(2:1-2) In God you cannot see. Perception has no function in God, and does not exist.

Many times students will try to bend or twist statements in *A Course in Miracles* so that it seems to be saying that God *did* create the world and it is holy, but did not create the world that we *mis*perceive. That is *not* what Jesus is teaching, and sentences like this make it very clear. "In God you cannot see" because seeing presupposes duality: a perceiver and a perceived. The realm of perception, therefore, is outside God. This is reflected in statements like this: "Your life is not a part of anything you see" (W-pI.151.12:1). Again, the very fact we think we can *see*—i.e., something outside us—is proof the *seeing* self cannot be real. Duality and non-duality, perception and knowledge, are mutually exclusive states. True life is only of the spirit, which is beyond the subject-object or perceiver-perceived duality. That is why Jesus makes this Level One statement in the text:

There is no life outside of Heaven. Where God

created life, there life must be. In any state apart from Heaven life is illusion (T-23.II.19:1-3).

(2:3) Yet in salvation, which is the undoing of what never was, perception has a mighty purpose.

We have in this one sentence expressions of both Level One and Level Two: The "undoing of what never was" is a Level One statement: the separation never occurred. Yet as long as we believe we are here in this dream world, the Holy Spirit, the expression of God's Love within the dream, has a purpose and function. This function, which we know to be forgiveness, constitutes the Level Two aspect of *A Course in Miracles*.

(2:4-6) Made by the Son of God for an unholy purpose, it must become the means for the restoration of his holiness to his awareness. Perception has no meaning. Yet does the Holy Spirit give it a meaning very close to God's.

This echoes the early lessons in which Jesus teaches that nothing in the world has meaning because we have given everything all the meaning it has; the meaning of proving we are right and Jesus is wrong: the separation is real. Once we ask Jesus for help, however, perception does have a meaning; not in reality, but a meaning based upon reality. In other words, the right-minded meaning of perception is that it is a reflection of the truth; not the truth, but a reflection of the truth that we are one in God, and the separation a meaningless dream. Truth's reflection within the dream is that *we are one in sharing a common purpose and need*. This is because we share the same ego.

It is helpful to remember that the Sonship is one: in Heaven as Christ (the One Mind), and on earth as an ego (the split mind). Therefore, each seemingly separated fragment of the Sonship carries within it the totality of the ego's wrong-minded thought system of separation and judgment, *and* the totality of the Holy Spirit's right-minded thought system of unity and forgiveness. Thus we all share the insanity of the guilt-laden shadowy fragment of separation as well as the sanity of forgiveness, the light-filled reflection of Heaven's Oneness. Clearly, therefore, it could not be the ego that provides the meaning of our true perception. That is why it is essential to distinguish between these two voices within our split minds, one of the principal goals of the workbook.

(2:7) Healed perception becomes the means by which the Son of God forgives his brother, and thus forgives himself.

This is an extremely important teaching—not elaborated on here—a key theme in *A Course in Miracles*. We read, for example:

> To perceive the healing of your brother as the healing of yourself is thus the way to remember God. For you forgot your brothers with Him, and God's Answer to your forgetting is but the way to remember (T-12.II.2:9-10).

Future lessons will express this theme as well.

Forgiving our brother, thus forgiving ourselves, is the reflection of the Atonement principle that says the separation never happened. The oneness of God's Son has never been compromised, thus my forgiveness of you recognizes we share the same purpose. What we thought happened never happened at all, and we remain as God created us: one Son, united within himself and with his Source.

(3:1-2) You cannot see apart from God because you cannot be apart from God. Whatever you do you do in Him, because whatever you think, you think with His Mind.

Jesus is speaking only of right-minded seeing, doing, and thinking, because the ego's seeing, doing, and thinking are an attack on God, designed to keep us separate from Him. Therefore, in our right minds we cannot see apart from God. If we are going to see our brothers as sinless, it can be done only when we call upon Jesus or the Holy Spirit for help, a call that says: "I want to be proven wrong. If I am wrong, God is right." In truth He does not see, for there is no seeing in Heaven, but God's reality becomes the basis for vision—truth's reflection in the dream.

(3:3) If vision is real, and it is real to the extent to which it shares the Holy Spirit's purpose, then you cannot see apart from God.

Once again, Jesus clearly implies that vision is not real, except in the sense that it reflects the oneness of reality. This reflection is the Holy Spirit's purpose, which is to forgive. Once that purpose is fulfilled vision is unnecessary, and its inherently illusory nature causes it to disappear. This use of *real* in terms of *vision* is similar to Jesus' explanation of the *real world*:

> This is the journey's end. We have referred to it as the real world. And yet there is a contradiction here, in that the words imply a limited reality, a partial truth, a segment of the universe made true. This is because knowledge makes no attack upon perception (T-26.III.3:1-4).

The real world is *real* insofar as its state of mind *reflects* the reality of Heaven: the unity of the Son. However, still being a correction of an illusion—albeit the *final* one—it remains illusory as well.

The instructions that follow in paragraphs 4-6 reflect the earlier emphasis on the implicit *sameness* of what we see and our thoughts.

(4) Three five-minute practice periods are required today, one as early and one as late as possible in the day. The third may be undertaken at the most convenient and suitable time that circumstances and readiness permit. At the beginning of these practice periods, repeat the idea for today to yourself with eyes open. Then glance around you for a short time, applying the idea specifically to what you see. Four or five subjects for this phase of the practice period are sufficient. You might say, for example:

> *God is my Source. I cannot see this desk apart from Him.*
> *God is my Source. I cannot see that picture apart from Him.*

We again see Jesus asking us to apply the idea for the day to the specifics of our lives, even the mundane ones. That is how we learn there is no hierarchy of illusions—all problems are the same—and therefore no order of difficulty in miracles—all solutions are the same. As a later lesson teaches: "One problem, one solution" (W-pI.80.1:5).

(5) Although this part of the exercise period should be relatively short, be sure that you select the subjects for this phase of practice indiscriminately, without self-directed inclusion or exclusion. For the second and longer phase, close your eyes, repeat today's idea again, and then let whatever relevant thoughts occur to you add to the idea in your own personal way. Thoughts such as:

> *I see through the eyes of forgiveness.*
> *I see the world as blessed.*
> *The world can show me myself.*

I see my own thoughts, which are like God's.

Any thought related more or less directly to today's idea is suitable. The thoughts need not bear any obvious relationship to the idea, but they should not be in opposition to it.

Exercises like these remind us that we do indeed have a right mind, and therefore a right-minded way of looking. It is important that we recognize this in ourselves, for it affords us the necessary means of comparison when our thoughts turn to the ego's judgment. Comparing the two—bringing judgment to vision—allows us to make the correct choice and know we are truly blessed as God's Son.

(6) If you find your mind wandering; if you begin to be aware of thoughts which are clearly out of accord with today's idea, or if you seem to be unable to think of anything, open your eyes, repeat the first phase of the exercise period, and then attempt the second phase again. Do not allow any protracted period to occur in which you become preoccupied with irrelevant thoughts. Return to the first phase of the exercises as often as necessary to prevent this.

In a sentence we shall revisit often, Jesus says:

> You are much too tolerant of mind wandering, and are passively condoning your mind's miscreations [i.e., your projections] (T-2.VI.4:6).

As in the text, Jesus is asking us in this lesson to become increasingly vigilant for our ego thoughts. They do not come unbidden, but are defenses we choose to prevent our achieving the goal of these exercises. The last thing our egos want is that we learn to question its thought system of separation, specialness, and judgment.

(7) In applying today's idea in the shorter practice periods, the form may vary according to the circumstances and situations in which you find yourself during the day. When you are with someone else, for example, try to remember to tell him silently:

> **God is my Source. I cannot see you apart from Him.**

This form is equally applicable to strangers as it is to those you think are closer to you. In fact, try not to make distinctions of this kind at all.

This goes back to a point I made earlier about these lessons: Jesus is trying to help us generalize his teachings to *all* situations. It is not helpful if we practice this *here,* but not *there.* To do so would be to nullify everything we are learning. The emphasis on not making distinctions between strangers and those perceived to be closer to us goes to the heart of the ego's defense of *special relationships.* As he does throughout the text, Jesus is calling for the end of our specialness. *All* people are part of the Sonship of God, *without exception,* as this statement from the text explains:

> God is not partial. All His children have His total Love, and all His gifts are freely given to everyone alike.... The specialness of God's Sons does not stem from exclusion but from inclusion. All my brothers are special (T-1.V.3:2-3,5-6).

On the level of *form* we obviously cannot enjoy the same interaction with everyone, but we nonetheless need not *exclude* anyone from the love we are learning to choose as our reality. Thus we reverse the ego's emphasis on *form* rather than *content.*

(8) Today's idea should also be applied throughout the day to various situations and events that may occur, particularly to those which seem to distress you in any way. For this purpose, apply the idea in this form:

> **God is my Source. I cannot see this apart from Him.**

Jesus is reminding us again of the importance of being vigilant whenever a distressing thought crosses our minds, whether severe or mild, regardless of what we believe to be its source. When it does, we should immediately go to the Holy Spirit for help and say: "Please help me look at this differently because I am not at peace." At the end of Chapter 5 in the text, Jesus asks us to make the following series of statements when we are not at peace. They make clear that if we are not peaceful, it is our responsibility and no one else's:

> I must have decided wrongly, because I am not at peace.

I made the decision myself, but I can also decide otherwise.

I want to decide otherwise, because I want to be at peace.

I do not feel guilty, because the Holy Spirit will undo all the consequences of my wrong decision if I will let Him.

I choose to let Him, by allowing Him to decide for God for me (T-5.VII.6:7-11; italics omitted).

Thus is the defense of projection undone, and responsibility returned to the decision-making part of our minds.

Jesus concludes the lesson by saying:

(9) If no particular subject presents itself to your awareness at the time, merely repeat the idea in its original form. Try today not to allow any long periods of time to slip by without remembering today's idea, and thus remembering your function.

Jesus' purpose is obviously not to make us feel guilty, but rather to remind us we are doing the workbook because we want to learn what *A Course in Miracles* is teaching. Thus we have to be vigilant for our egos in practicing these lessons. We have already seen, and shall see again, that Jesus wants us to become aware of our *resistance* to practicing such vigilance. Only then can we choose against our fear.

LESSON 44

God is the light in which I see.

Jesus continues here his series of Level One statements: only God is true; only God is light. Everything else is an expression of the ego's darkness.

(1) Today we are continuing the idea for yesterday, adding another dimension to it. You cannot see in darkness, and you cannot make light. You can make darkness and then think you see in it, but light reflects life, and is therefore an aspect of creation. Creation and darkness cannot coexist, but light and life must go together, being but different aspects of creation.

We are so sure we are correct in what we perceive, think, and feel, which is what Jesus means by saying: "You can make darkness and then think you see in it." We are so sure we are right, but that is only because we made up the world of opposites—light and darkness—and then forgot where it came from: the nothingness of our illusory thoughts. But because we see the world, we believe it is real, and then try to get as many people as we can to confirm our perceptions and experiences, not realizing we are merely asking the blind to teach the blind.

The "light" of which Jesus speaks is not perceptual, to be clarified in the next paragraph, but is another symbol to express a characteristic of Heaven. Darkness represents the ego and its thought system of guilt, hate, and specialness; while light represents the Holy Spirit's thought system, which affirms that darkness has no effect upon reality.

(2:1) In order to see, you must recognize that light is within, not without.

When Jesus says "God is the light in which I see" he is not talking about what we see with the naked eye. Vision comes from right-minded thought, and thus we do not see light outside us. Recall Lesson 15, which I have referred to several times, where Jesus is not talking about literally seeing edges of light around objects. If you do have such an experience, realize it is nothing but a reflection of a thought of forgiveness in your mind. These lessons make it very clear that light is not external. Remember, there *is* nothing external. As we shall read in a later lesson: "There is no world! This

is the central thought the course attempts to teach" (W-pI.132.6:2-3).

(2:2) You do not see outside yourself, nor is the equipment for seeing outside you.

The "you" represents our decision maker, which is shown on the left-hand side of the chart (see p. 135). When Jesus says "nor is the equipment for seeing outside you," he is talking about the body and our sensory organs. The real seeing—vision—has nothing to do with the body and is not outside us. Vision is the result of our decision maker joining with Jesus or the Holy Spirit. In other words, Jesus is speaking about the *mind*, not the *body*.

(2:3-4) An essential part of this equipment is the light that makes seeing possible. It is with you always, making vision possible in every circumstance.

We have already discussed how in the workbook Jesus sometimes uses *God* when he means the *Holy Spirit*, and uses them virtually interchangeably, as we saw he also does with *real thoughts* and *Thoughts in the Christ Mind*. Strictly speaking it is the Holy Spirit, not God, Who makes vision possible, for the Holy Spirit is a Thought of God's light we brought with us into the dream.

(3) Today we are going to attempt to reach that light. For this purpose, we will use a form of exercise which has been suggested before, and which we will utilize increasingly. It is a particularly difficult form for the undisciplined mind, and represents a major goal of mind training. It requires precisely what the untrained mind lacks. Yet this training must be accomplished if you are to see.

Here, as well as other places in the workbook, Jesus departs from the main theme of the lesson and talks instead about our practice. It is certainly difficult to be thinking about the lesson or God throughout the day. By clear implication, Jesus is saying that we, his students, are not disciplined, and he is letting us know ahead of time that he fully expects us *not* to do the lessons as he has given them. Thus we should not feel guilty when we forget, nor does Jesus want us to deny that we forget, or deny our motivation for forgetting (which we will discuss in a moment). In fact, he frequently reminds us of the power of our minds. For example, he gently chides Helen, and indeed all of us, near the end of the text for complaining this course is too difficult to learn. After all, he says, *look what you have learned*:

> What you have taught yourself is such a giant learning feat it is indeed incredible. But you accomplished it because you wanted to, and did not pause in diligence to judge it hard to learn or too complex to grasp.
>
> No one who understands what you have learned, how carefully you learned it, and the pains to which you went to practice and repeat the lessons endlessly, in every form you could conceive of them, could ever doubt the power of your learning skill. There is no greater power in the world. The world was made by it, and even now depends on nothing else. The lessons you have taught yourself have been so overlearned and fixed they rise like heavy curtains to obscure the simple and the obvious. Say not you cannot learn them. For your power to learn is strong enough to teach you that your will is not your own, your thoughts do not belong to you, and even you are someone else (T-31.I.2:7–3:6).

Therefore, Jesus is helping us recognize not only our learning skill, but the great need to *un*learn what we have so skillfully taught ourselves: our "ancient overlearning" (T-31.I.5:4). To accomplish this undoing, great discipline of learning is required. Thus, the need for this workbook.

(4) Have at least three practice periods today, each lasting three to five minutes. A longer time is highly recommended, but only if you find the time slipping by with little or no sense of strain. The form of practice we will use today is the most natural and easy one in the world for the trained mind, just as it seems to be the most unnatural and difficult for the untrained mind.

Jesus is again telling us that we will have trouble unlearning what we have taught ourselves, and he explains why in the next paragraph:

(5:1-4) Your mind is no longer wholly untrained. You are quite ready to learn the form of exercise we will use today, but you may find that you will encounter strong resistance. The reason is very simple. While you practice in this way, you leave behind everything that you now believe, and all the thoughts that you have made up.

Jesus informs us that the problem we will encounter is our own resistance, born of the fear of losing the thoughts we made up, which, by the way, include our very selves! We have already discussed how fearfully resistant we become when in the presence of truth. The reader may recall Jesus' words in the text as to why *he* was perceived as a threat:

> Many thought I was attacking them, even though it was apparent I was not. An insane learner learns strange lessons. What you must recognize is that when you do not share a thought system, you are weakening it. Those who believe in it therefore perceive this as an attack on them. This is because everyone identifies himself with his thought system, and every thought system centers on what you believe you are (T-6.V-B.1:5-9).

Thus these lessons constitute a direct attack on our egos, seen from the perspective of the individual self desperately trying to protect its separation by defending its bodily defense against truth's incursions into the mind.

Note that Jesus is not qualifying his words. To repeat:

(5:4) While you practice in this way, **you leave behind everything that you now believe, and all the thoughts that you have made up.**

He means "*everything* that you now believe, and *all* the thoughts," not just *some* of them. That is the basis of our fear, and why everyone tries to compromise what *A Course in Miracles* is teaching, having Jesus say something he is not saying at all. He is telling you quite explicitly that if you practice as he instructs, your ego will disappear. It is therefore important to understand why you do *not* practice the specific lessons, let alone the ongoing lessons we have with each other.

Very often people ask where in *A Course in Miracles* does it say what I just said. This is one of the places, and Jesus says it in very simple English, too; no complicated sentence structure. One more time, here is the statement of the problem: "While you practice in this way, you leave behind everything that you now believe, and all the thoughts that you have made up."

We continue with yet another statement of the same theme:

(5:5-6) Properly speaking, this is the release from hell. Yet perceived through the ego's eyes, it is loss of identity and a descent into hell.

This is the idea I repeat over and over and over again: the major fear that *everyone* in this world shares is the loss of individuality or personal identity. Since we cherish this self, to expect that we would not have resistance to the workbook lessons is rather naïve.

(6:1) If you can stand aside from the ego by ever so little, you will have no difficulty in recognizing that its opposition and its fears are meaningless.

Jesus is speaking here of the decision maker, because he talks about a *you* that is not the ego, a *you* that stands aside from the ego (to the left in our chart, see p 135). As we have seen, if you stand aside from the ego you automatically stand aside with Jesus or the Holy Spirit in your right mind. It is one or the other. The *you* that has chosen the Holy Spirit, again, is the decision maker.

One other point: Jesus is talking about the ego as if it were a separate entity. But the ego is simply a thought we have made real, with which we have identified. In other words, the ego is the part of our split minds that enjoys being separated. It thus represents our opposition to the Holy Spirit's Atonement principle. In the following passage Jesus explains why he speaks of the ego *as if* it were separate from us:

> Only your [i.e., the *decision maker*] allegiance to it gives the ego any power over you. I have spoken of the ego as if it were a separate thing, acting on its own. This was necessary to persuade you that you cannot dismiss it lightly, and must realize how much of your thinking is ego-directed.... The ego is nothing more than a part of your belief about yourself (T-4.VI.1:2-4,6).

(6:2-4) You might find it helpful to remind yourself, from time to time, that to reach light is to escape from darkness, whatever you may believe to the contrary. God is the light in which you see. You are attempting to reach Him.

This also is extremely important. If we are sincere about wanting to find God and take Jesus' hand and experience his love, we must let go of our identification with the darkness. The way we reinforce and express our love for Jesus is by looking at our hatred. That again is very clear here: the way to reach the light is to escape from the darkness. But what does this mean? Since we are the ones who made darkness real by choosing it, then escaping from it means we have to change our minds. That is the role of Jesus: not to help us do what is right, but to help us *undo* what is wrong. This ensures that we automatically do, think, say, and feel what is right. It is the escape from the darkness, the undoing of the negative, the denying of the denial of truth that constitutes the journey into the light. Therefore we can say that this is not a course in the positive, but in undoing the negative. Two among a large number of passages can be cited here as evidence of this overriding emphasis in Jesus' teaching material:

> The task of the miracle worker thus becomes *to deny the denial of truth* (T-12.II.1:5).

> Why do you think you are unsure the others [the first three questions] have been answered? Could it be necessary they be asked so often, if they had? Until the last decision has been made, the answer is both "yes" and "no." For you have answered "yes" without perceiving that "yes" must mean "not no." No one decides against his happiness, but he may do so if he does not see he does it. And if he sees his happiness as ever changing, now this, now that, and now an elusive shadow attached to nothing, he does decide against it (T-21.VII.12).

The ego thought system is the denial of truth. Recognizing it for what it is allows us to say no to its negation, thus removing the ego's power as its darkness dissolves into the light.

(7) Begin the practice period by repeating today's idea with your eyes open, and close them slowly, repeating the idea several times more. Then try to sink into your mind, letting go every kind of interference and intrusion by quietly sinking past them. Your mind cannot be stopped in this unless you choose to stop it. It is merely taking its natural course. Try to observe your passing thoughts without involvement, and slip quietly by them.

To repeat, the *you* Jesus is addressing is the decision maker, the part of your mind that chooses. *Watch your mind*. When you feel guilty, when you judge your thoughts or your actions, you are making them real and opposing them. But you must look at them, which does not mean to look and then continue your unloving thoughts and actions. It means looking without judgment, realizing exactly what you are doing. That would motivate you to let them go, because you would see the pain choosing the ego is causing you. The process of looking at the ego with Jesus thus inevitably entails understanding the *cost* to us when we choose the ego instead of him, separation instead of unity, hate instead of forgiveness. When we see clearly that the choice for judgment leads to suffering and pain—the unnatural—while the choice for vision leads to peace and joy—the natural—the motivation to choose healing is strong enough to bring it about. As Jesus concludes Chapter 23: "Who with the Love of God upholding him could find the choice of miracles or murder hard to make?" (T-23.IV.9:8)

Referring to the chart (see p. 135), that is why God is on the bottom instead of the top: The thrust of the lesson and our meditation is to begin where we are on top, and then *sink down* into our minds where God is.

(8) While no particular approach is advocated for this form of exercise, what is needful is a sense of the importance of what you are doing; its inestimable value to you, and an awareness that you are attempting something very holy. Salvation is your happiest accomplishment. It is also the only one that has any meaning, because it is the only one that has any real use to you at all.

The reason "what you are doing" is so important to you is that this is the way out of hell, the way out of all pain and suffering. You need to keep reminding yourself: "I am a student of *A Course in Miracles*, and have chosen Jesus as my teacher. Moreover, I am doing the workbook because I want to escape from the hell of my life of judgment of others and myself. That is why I am the Course's student: those judgments are the source of my pain and distress, which I no longer want." Thus Jesus asks you to read these lessons conscientiously, and *think* about what they mean in terms of your goal of peace. *And then practice them.*

Jesus again turns to resistance:

(9) If resistance rises in any form, pause long enough to repeat today's idea, keeping your eyes closed unless you are aware of fear. In that case, you will probably find it more reassuring to open your eyes briefly. Try, however, to return to the exercises with eyes closed as soon as possible.

Note especially his *gentle* insistence that we become aware of our resistance, our fear of these lessons.

(10:1-2) If you are doing the exercises correctly, you should experience some sense of relaxation, and even a feeling that you are approaching, if not actually entering into light. Try to think of light, formless and without limit, as you pass by the thoughts of this world.

Jesus speaks of light as a thought in the Christ Mind, because it has no form. The reflection of light in our right minds is forgiveness, which has form because I think *I* am a person who has to forgive *you*. Again, Jesus uses the words *light* and *real thoughts* interchangeably with *right mind* and *Christ Mind*.

(10:3) And do not forget that they [the thoughts of the world] **cannot hold you to the world unless you give them the power to do so.**

This is why we are not victims of the world we see (Lesson 31), a central theme in *A Course in Miracles*. Nothing in this world can hold us, nothing can upset us unless we give it that power. A powerful passage in the text expresses this important truth:

> The secret of salvation is but this: that you are doing this unto yourself. No matter what the form of the attack, this still is true. Whoever takes the role of enemy and of attacker, still is this the truth. Whatever seems to be the cause of any pain and suffering you feel, this is still true. For you would not react at all to figures in a dream you knew that you were dreaming. Let them be as hateful and as vicious as they may, they could have no effect on you unless you failed to recognize it is your dream (T-27.VIII.10).

Why do we give that power away? Because that proves we are right and Jesus is wrong and, moreover, that his course is wrong. He teaches us here that we are responsible for our feelings of victimization. The world on the other hand, programmed by the ego, teaches us that *it* is the cause of our pain and suffering. Stated another way, the miracle teaches we are the *dreamer* of the dream, while the world witnesses to our being but dream *figures*. We shall return to this idea again and again.

Jesus closes the lesson by saying:

(11) Throughout the day repeat the idea often, with eyes open or closed as seems better to you at the time. But do not forget. Above all, be determined not to forget today.

We find in these lessons Jesus' urging us to take these lessons very seriously, to take the practice of *A Course in Miracles* very seriously. If we do not practice it day in and day out, we are not going to learn it. This has nothing to do with an intellectual mastery of the text. We cannot do these lessons properly in the end if we do not understand the text, but simple understanding is not enough. We must practice bringing the darkness of our ego's illusions to the light of the Holy Spirit's truth, and understand *why* we are doing it.

LESSON 45

God is the Mind with which I think.

(1:1) Today's idea holds the key to what your real thoughts are.

That is because our real thoughts are with God. Note in the following discussion that Jesus identifies our real thoughts with the Christ Mind.

(1:2) They are nothing that you think you think, just as nothing that you think you see is related to vision in any way.

Jesus is always giving us a little jibe, telling us that we but think we think, we but think we see. In fact, we are not thinking or seeing at all.

(1:3) There is no relationship between what is real and what you think is real.

Other words could be substituted for these. We could say, for example, there is no relationship between what God is and what the world thinks God is—so much for the theologies of the world! Returning to the workbook lesson, we see a Level One statement—there is absolutely nothing, no middle ground, between truth and illusion. Any time we think we understand something, such understanding cannot be real because we are involved only with our own thoughts, and *our* thoughts are never real. The purpose of *A Course in Miracles* is not to lead us to an *understanding* of God, but to an *experience* of His Love, for which we must escape the darkness of our guilt and hatred. The following statement from the Introduction to the clarification of terms expresses this goal of experience rather than understanding:

> A universal theology is impossible, but a universal experience is not only possible but necessary. It is this experience toward which the course is directed. Here alone consistency becomes possible because here alone uncertainty ends (C-in.2:5-7).

We can also recall this wonderful line from the text:

> You are still convinced that your understanding is a powerful contribution to the truth, and makes it what it is. Yet we have emphasized that you need understand nothing (T-18.IV.7:5-6).

(1:4–2:5) Nothing that you think are your real thoughts resemble your real thoughts in any respect. Nothing that you think you see bears any resemblance to what vision will show you.

You think with the Mind of God. Therefore you share your thoughts with Him, as He shares His with you. They are the same thoughts, because they are thought by the same Mind. To share is to make alike, or to make one. Nor do the thoughts you think with the Mind of God leave your mind, because thoughts do not leave their source.

The extremely important principle *ideas leave not their source* makes its first appearance here in the workbook, although we have already discussed it many times. Jesus mentions it again later in the lessons, and it is at the center of his teaching throughout the three books. To state it differently: This principle is the Atonement, which reflects the unchanging truth we are an idea or thought in the Mind of God, and have never left our Source. This means the separation never happened. We are thus saying that all thoughts, if they are real, have never left their Source. Even though we believe we have left God and are asleep in the dream, we can still have reflections of these thoughts. Once again, in these passages Jesus is not making a distinction between real thoughts and the reflection of real thoughts.

(2:6-8) Therefore, your thoughts are in the Mind of God, as you are. They are in your mind as well, where He is. As you are part of His Mind, so are your thoughts part of His Mind.

All is one, since *ideas leave not their source*. The mind we think we are is unreal, in contrast to the Mind of Christ, Jesus' referent here.

This is yet another example of how the language of the workbook is not, strictly speaking, theologically correct. Since forgiveness is impossible in God, as we shall see in just a moment, our forgiveness thoughts, in reality, have nothing to do with God either. More properly, forgiveness is the *reflection* of God's Thought. Read this material, therefore, as you would a wonderful poem, not a technical treatise to be analytically dissected.

(3) Where, then, are your real thoughts? Today we will attempt to reach them. We will have to look for them in your mind, because that is where they are. They must still be there, because they cannot have left their source. What is thought by the Mind of God is eternal, being part of creation.

The function of the Holy Spirit is to hold those thoughts in our minds, which, despite our mind wandering, remain in their source. Projection is a powerful and persuasive defense, yet it cannot defy the basic principle: *ideas leave not their source*. It is our learning this salvific fact that the ego continually tries to prevent.

(4:1-2) Our three five-minute practice periods for today will take the same general form that we used in applying yesterday's idea. We will attempt to leave the unreal and seek for the real.

Sentence 2 seems to say the exact opposite of the passage in Chapter 16 that I quoted earlier—"Your task is not to seek for love, but merely to seek and find all of the barriers that you have built against it" (T-16.IV.6:1)—for here the words say you should seek for truth. This is yet another indication of his inconsistent use of words. However, it is equally true that the principles he teaches never vary and are consistent, as the remainder of the paragraph makes clear. In other words, we find the truth (*the real*) by first finding the illusion (*the unreal*), and then leaving it by deciding against it. Incidentally, 4:2 is taken from the famous Hindu statement about leaving the unreal for the real. Here now is the rest of the paragraph:

(4:3-6) We will deny the world in favor of truth. We will not let the thoughts of the world hold us back. We will not let the beliefs of the world tell us that what God would have us do is impossible. Instead, we will try to recognize that only what God would have us do is possible.

The way we seek for truth and what is real is by denying the unreal, which we deny by looking at our unreal thoughts with Jesus. Again, when we look with him at our judgments, hatred, and guilt they will disappear, leaving only the truth. Indeed, the very process of *looking* is what heals. As I

discussed in the Prelude, it is *not* looking at our guilt that preserves its illusory existence. That is the function of the world and body: to keep us from looking within. Therefore, looking without guilt or judgment at our decision to be guilty undoes it, transferring its substance from a solid wall of granite—*heavy, opaque, and impenetrable*—to a *fragile veil* that has no power to keep away the light (T-18.IX.5:2-4). We shall return to this important theme repeatedly before our journey through the workbook is completed.

(5) We will also try to understand that only what God would have us do is what we want to do. And we will also try to remember that we cannot fail in doing what He would have us do. There is every reason to feel confident that we will succeed today. It is the Will of God.

Jesus is reminding us here of our purpose in doing the workbook and studying his course: what we really want to do is be an expression of God's Will, even though strictly speaking God does not have us do anything. Once again, and hardly for the last time, we see Jesus appealing to our right-minded motivation: We want to learn his lessons because they will make us feel better.

(6) Begin the exercises for today by repeating the idea to yourself, closing your eyes as you do so. Then spend a fairly short period in thinking a few relevant thoughts of your own, keeping the idea in mind. After you have added some four or five thoughts of your own to the idea, repeat it again and tell yourself gently:

> *My real thoughts are in my mind. I would like to find them.*

Then try to go past all the unreal thoughts that cover the truth in your mind, and reach to the eternal.

The way you go to the eternal is through your unreal thoughts, which you bring to the real ones of the Holy Spirit. Our chart (see p. 135) illustrates this. You find God by going through the ego system, which begins with your experience of yourself as a body. You next realize your body is a projection of the mind's unreal thoughts of separation, specialness, and guilt, which you bring to the real thoughts of the Holy Spirit. And then they are gone, leaving only the truth. This process of going through the *unreal* to the *real*—the essence of forgiveness—is powerfully described in the following passage from the text that tells of our journey through the "circle of fear" to God, with the Holy Spirit as our companion and guide:

> Yet God can bring you there [beyond all fear], if you are willing to follow the Holy Spirit through seeming terror, trusting Him not to abandon you and leave you there. For it is not His purpose to frighten you, but only yours. You are severely tempted to abandon Him at the outside ring of fear, but He would lead you safely through and far beyond (T-18.IX.3:7-9).

(7:1) Under all the senseless thoughts and mad ideas with which you have cluttered up your mind are the thoughts that you thought with God in the beginning.

These are not thoughts we normally think of as thoughts, for Jesus speaks of an expression of God's Will—Oneness, truth, and love. Even though we are unaware of them, these thoughts remain nonetheless, "held in safekeeping" in our right minds against the time we choose them, *and only them.* Jesus makes the same point in this moving passage early in the text. I quote it in its entirety.

> How can you who are so holy suffer? All your past except its beauty is gone, and nothing is left but a blessing. I have saved all your kindnesses and every loving thought you ever had. I have purified them of the errors that hid their light, and kept them for you in their own perfect radiance. They are beyond destruction and beyond guilt. They came from the Holy Spirit within you, and we know what God creates is eternal. You can indeed depart in peace because I have loved you as I loved myself. You go with my blessing and for my blessing. Hold it and share it, that it may always be ours. I place the peace of God in your heart and in your hands, to hold and share. The heart is pure to hold it, and the hands are strong to give it. We cannot lose. My judgment is as strong as the wisdom of God, in Whose Heart and Hands we have our being. His quiet children are His blessed Sons. The Thoughts of God are with you (T-5.IV.8).

(7:2-4) They are there in your mind now, completely unchanged. They will always be in your mind, exactly as they always were. Everything

you have thought since then will change, but the Foundation on which it rests is wholly changeless.

These thoughts, reflecting the Love of God, are always with us—totally unchanged. We have covered them over with senseless and cluttered thoughts, and Jesus is helping us uncover the truth that is in us. In the end we shall come to recognize that these insane thoughts are made up. Their seeming power had no effect on the truth, and of such truth is the Kingdom of Heaven remembered on earth.

(8:1-4) It is this Foundation toward which the exercises for today are directed. Here is your mind joined with the Mind of God. Here are your thoughts one with His. For this kind of practice only one thing is necessary; approach it as you would an altar dedicated in Heaven to God the Father and to God the Son.

Jesus again is urging us to take these lessons seriously and remember why we are doing them. However, we are not taking them seriously if we do not apply them, which is why our vigilance becomes so important. In the text, Jesus explains that altars are devotions:

> Both Heaven and earth are in you, because the call of both is in your mind. The Voice for God comes from your own altars to Him. These altars are not things; they are devotions. Yet you have other devotions now. Your divided devotion has given you the two voices, and you must choose at which altar you want to serve. The call you answer now is an evaluation because it is a decision. The decision is very simple. It is made on the basis of which call is worth more to you (T-5.II.8:5-12).

And so we are instructed to recognize *which call is worth more to us.* It is our practice and vigilance that will reinforce what we *truly* want.

(8:5-7) For such is the place you are trying to reach. You will probably be unable as yet to realize how high you are trying to go. Yet even with the little understanding you have already gained, you should be able to remind yourself that this is no idle game, but an exercise in holiness and an attempt to reach the Kingdom of Heaven.

We are once more asked to remember the importance of these lessons to us, being the practical and specific application of the principles of the text. The sincerity in our desire to return home will be reflected in our commitment to this ongoing practice. Thus Jesus says in the first sentence in paragraph 9:

(9:1) In the shorter exercise periods for today, try to remember how important it is to you to understand the holiness of the mind that thinks with God.

It should be apparent by now, through his continual emphasis, how important Jesus believes these lessons to be, and how important they should be to us. We shall discuss presently how this importance will be measured by our willingness to relinquish our investment in specialness.

The lesson closes with this final plea from Jesus to choose *against* ("stand aside") our ego's thoughts, and *for* his reminders of the Thoughts we share with God:

(9:2-4) Take a minute or two, as you repeat the idea throughout the day, to appreciate your mind's holiness. Stand aside, however briefly, from all thoughts that are unworthy of Him Whose host you are. And thank Him for the Thoughts He is thinking with you.

Gratitude is an important theme in *A Course in Miracles*, and one to which we shall often return. The core of this gratitude is that God has never ceased to be Who He is, despite all our insane attempts to make Him be otherwise.

LESSON 46

God is the Love in which I forgive.

This lesson is the first time we find a serious discussion of forgiveness.

(1:1-3) God does not forgive because He has never condemned. And there must be condemnation before forgiveness is necessary. Forgiveness is the great need of this world, but that is because it is a world of illusions.

As we shall see later, Jesus "likes" this first sentence so much that he repeats it verbatim in the review lesson. Forgiveness has no place in Heaven, but only in the dream that began with the condemnatory thought of sin and will end with sin's undoing through forgiveness, love's reflection. "There must be condemnation before forgiveness is necessary," which makes forgiveness an illusion since it corrects what never happened. Since God does not (because He *cannot*) recognize the illusion, He cannot correct it. There is thus no need for it in Heaven.

(1:4-5) Those who forgive are thus releasing themselves from illusions, while those who withhold forgiveness are binding themselves to them. As you condemn only yourself, so do you forgive only yourself.

Jesus is making it very clear that forgiveness has nothing to do with anyone we think is outside us. It occurs in the context of a relationship we have made real, but must recognize that what we are forgiving is a projection of the guilt we do not want, not to mention the responsibility for our distressing situation. Lessons 196-198, which we shall discuss much later in this series, elaborate on this essential point, as their titles suggest:

It can be but myself I crucify.

It can be but my gratitude I earn.

Only my condemnation injures me.

(2:1) Yet although God does not forgive, His Love is nevertheless the basis of forgiveness.

We are reminded here that forgiveness is a real and right-minded thought that reflects the real thought of love in our Christ Mind.

(2:2-3) Fear condemns and love forgives. Forgiveness thus undoes what fear has produced, returning the mind to the awareness of God.

The right mind, or forgiveness, undoes the wrong mind of fear and hate. When the right mind undoes the wrong mind, both disappear and all that remains is the awareness of God. Once again, we need to recall that *A Course in Miracles* does not teach the truth, but the *undoing* of the illusory barriers to truth; a process that allows the memory of God to dawn upon our sleeping minds, awakening us at last from the ego's nightmare world of guilt and fear.

(2:4-5) For this reason, forgiveness can truly be called salvation. It is the means by which illusions disappear.

Salvation thus has a different meaning in *A Course in Miracles*. Rather than being the plan of God to save us from our very real sinfulness, it now becomes the Holy Spirit's correction of forgiveness for our *belief* in sinfulness. It is the simple change of mind from the illusion of separation to the truth of Atonement.

(3) Today's exercises require at least three full five-minute practice periods, and as many shorter ones as possible. Begin the longer practice periods by repeating today's idea to yourself, as usual. Close your eyes as you do so, and spend a minute or two in searching your mind for those whom you have not forgiven. It does not matter "how much" you have not forgiven them. You have forgiven them entirely or not at all.

This is an expression within the dream of the *all or none* idea, what we earlier described as Level One. In our experience we do not forgive totally; we forgive a little bit here and a little bit there; we forgive this person but not another. This passage is telling us, however, that if that is our practice of forgiveness, we are not finished yet. Forgiveness has to be total, otherwise it is not real. This *all or none* idea finds similar expression in the following statement about *A Course in Miracles* itself: "This course will be believed entirely or not at all" (T-22.II.7:4).

(4) If you are doing the exercises well you should have no difficulty in finding a number of people you have not forgiven. It is a safe rule that anyone you do not like is a suitable subject. Mention each one by name, and say:

> *God is the Love in which I forgive you, [name].*

This is the first of several exercises in which Jesus asks us to identify those people we have chosen not to forgive. He assures us we shall have no trouble in identifying these special hate objects. Later on we shall be gently instructed to expand this category to include those we believe we love. An important teaching in the text is that special love and special hate are the same, being but different *forms* of the same basic *content* of separation. Thus we need to forgive *everyone*, since everyone—friend or foe—is perceived to be separate from us.

(5:1) The purpose of the first phase of today's practice periods is to put you in a position to forgive yourself.

"Forgiving yourself" is what this course is all about. I think I am forgiving someone outside me, but I am really forgiving myself. Again, needless to say, this thought is the central theme of *A Course in Miracles*. It reflects the dynamic of projection, wherein we seek to place in others the guilt we cannot accept within ourselves. Once having projected the guilt, we have no further awareness of its ongoing presence in our minds, which for all intents and purposes has been forgotten beneath the *double shield of oblivion* (W-pI.136.5:2)—the belief in guilt in ourselves (*mind*) and in others (*body*). Only by recognizing our unforgiveness of another can we be led to the unforgiveness of ourselves, and beyond that to the Atonement that links us back to the Love we never truly left.

The next few lines present various statements as suggestive of our practice for the day. These, incidentally, should not be taken as *affirmations* as is the practice of many New Age students. By this I mean that statements such as these should *not* be used to cover the ego's thought system of negativity and hate, but rather understood as symbols of the right-minded presence of correction, *to which* we bring the ego's thoughts:

(5:2–6:7) After you have applied the idea to all those who have come to mind, tell yourself:

> *God is the Love in which I forgive myself.*

Then devote the remainder of the practice period to adding related ideas such as:

> *God is the Love with which I love myself.*
> *God is the Love in which I am blessed.*

The form of the application may vary considerably, but the central idea should not be lost sight of. You might say, for example:

> *I cannot be guilty because I am a Son of God.*
> *I have already been forgiven.*
> *No fear is possible in a mind beloved of God.*
> *There is no need to attack because love has forgiven me.*

The practice period should end, however, with a repetition of today's idea as originally stated.

If we do these exercises properly, we will become increasingly able to note our ego thoughts of separation and specialness and bring them quickly to the love that embraces the Sonship as one, at the same time it undoes our thoughts of guilt, fear, and attack. This is reiterated in the lesson's final paragraph, where Jesus returns to his central emphasis of using the idea for the day, as well as its variations, whenever we are tempted to choose the ego instead of the Holy Spirit:

(7) The shorter practice periods may consist either of a repetition of the idea for today in the original or in a related form, as you prefer. Be sure, however, to make more specific applications if they are needed. They will be needed at any time during the day when you become aware of any kind of negative reaction to anyone, present or not. In any event, tell him silently:

> *God is the Love in which I forgive you.*

Jesus is asking us, once again, to be aware of any kind of negative reaction, major or minor, and then to bring these reactions *to* the suggested thoughts of the day. In this way his light can shine away the darkness in which we had sought to hide. This process requires great vigilance and diligence as we seek continually to *practice* the holy instant (T-15.IV). I am reminded of the famous joke: A lost New Yorker asks someone how to get to Carnegie Hall, the legendary concert auditorium. The response is: *Practice, practice, practice*!

LESSON 47

God is the strength in which I trust.

This introduces another important teaching that is central in the text: the contrast between our weakness and the strength of Christ in us, or between the ego's illusory power and the Holy Spirit's true power. As we read near the text's end:

> You always choose between your weakness and the strength of Christ in you. And what you choose is what you think is real. Simply by never using weakness to direct your actions, you have given it no power. And the light of Christ in you is given charge of everything you do. For you have brought your weakness unto Him, and He has given you His strength instead (T-31.VIII.2:3-7).

This lesson subtly introduces the theme of special relationships, which entail placing trust in someone or something outside us to alleviate our anxiety, or simply to make us feel good. That means we are substituting some object, substance, or relationship for the Love of God, giving power (or strength) to these special objects to bring us pleasure or alleviate pain. This choice for specialness is the substitution of weakness for strength.

(1:1) If you are trusting in your own strength, you have every reason to be apprehensive, anxious and fearful.

Trusting in our own strength means that we have made the ego thought system real. Having done so, we will feel guilty. Guilt will be projected and we will inevitably fear the punishment we believe is coming from outside us. We thus will have forgotten that the punishment we believe is forthcoming is a natural expression (really an *un*natural expression) of the guilt we feel in our minds. You can see, incidentally, how often in these lessons the dynamic of projection is discussed.

(1:2) What can you predict or control?

Everyone in this world has control issues. We always try to predict what might happen so we can be in control, thinking ahead: If I do such and such, what will the outcome be? This is mandatory if we are to survive as an ego. We have to be in control. If not, Jesus is, which means our special identity is

gone. Our need to exclude him finds its expression in the need to control what is going on around us, like the little Dutch boy who kept his finger in the dike to prevent a catastrophic flood that would destroy his village. That is our fear: if our finger slips, the waters of God's Love would rush through our defensive structure and flood our egos into nonexistence. Thus we keep our fingers of specialness and hate firmly planted in the walls of our minds, ensuring that no right-minded water of forgiveness ever gets through and washes away our self.

(1:3) What is there in you that can be counted on?

We figure a hell of a lot! We are sure that if we do not save ourselves, we are doomed. I mentioned earlier that we have constructed our lives in such a way that we were convinced from the outset that no one could be trusted; no one is dependable, and therefore the only one who could save us is ourselves. Again, we are absolutely certain we are right. However, we are not aware of the underlying thought that supports this defense: I have written my life's script so that it will prove I am all alone in the universe, and therefore I had better take care of me because no one else will! Recall that all-important line from the text:

> The secret of salvation is but this: That you are doing this unto yourself (T-27.VIII.10:1).

We *want* to be all alone, since that justifies our living all alone—trusting no one—and thus we reinforce our origin of being all alone, totally apart from our Creator and Source.

(1:4) What would give you the ability to be aware of all the facets of any problem, and to resolve them in such a way that only good can come of it?

This idea is expressed more fully in the text and manual: The Holy Spirit, not ourselves, is the only One Who can judge correctly. We read, for example:

> It is necessary for the teacher of God to realize, not that he should not judge, but that he cannot.... The aim of our curriculum, unlike

the goal of the world's learning, is the recognition that judgment in the usual sense is impossible.... In order to judge anything rightly, one would have to be fully aware of an inconceivably wide range of things; past, present and to come. One would have to recognize in advance all the effects of his judgments on everyone and everything involved in them in any way. And one would have to be certain there is no distortion in his perception, so that his judgment would be wholly fair to everyone on whom it rests now and in the future. Who is in a position to do this? Who except in grandiose fantasies would claim this for himself?... Make then but one more judgment. It is this: There is Someone with you Whose judgment is perfect. He does know all the facts; past, present and to come. He does know all the effects of His judgment on everyone and everything involved in any way. And He is wholly fair to everyone, for there is no distortion in His perception (M-10.2:1; 3:1,3-7; 4:6-10).

It is simply our arrogance as egos that leads us to believe we could possibly understand the true nature of any problem, not to mention its solution. This arrogance has ensured throughout the millennia that no problem—individual or collective—has ever truly been resolved. Thus we go from day to day, year to year, century to century, reliving the same painful experiences over and over again, with no respite from the terror of being wrong and being separated:

> Each day, and every minute in each day, and every instant that each minute holds, you but relive the single instant when the time of terror took the place of love (T-26.V.13:1).

(1:5) What is there in you that gives you the recognition of the right solution, and the guarantee that it will be accomplished?

It certainly is not us, our wrong-minded self, but our right-minded self when we choose to identify with Jesus or the Holy Spirit.

(2) Of yourself you can do none of these things. To believe that you can is to put your trust where trust is unwarranted, and to justify fear, anxiety, depression, anger and sorrow. Who can put his faith in weakness and feel safe? Yet who can put his faith in strength and feel weak?

This is what everyone's life is all about. We are frightened, anxious, depressed, angry, and sad. If not, we are not paying attention to our life's situation, which proves we are right in believing the world is a hostile, threatening, and lonely place, replete with those we cannot trust. We feel justified in thinking this is why we feel as terrible as we do, unaware that the source of these thoughts and feelings is our decision to trust the teacher of weakness, rather than the One of strength.

(3) God is your safety in every circumstance. His Voice speaks for Him in all situations and in every aspect of all situations, telling you exactly what to do to call upon His strength and His protection. There are no exceptions because God has no exceptions. And the Voice which speaks for Him thinks as He does.

Passages like these, and there are many of them in the workbook, make it sound as if the Holy Spirit is with you to tell you exactly what to do. In one sense this is true, but the focus is never really on what you do, because that is unimportant. Rather, Jesus is emphasizing how you *think* about what you do. This is where the Holy Spirit enters the picture. If you would join with His Love—meaning you have let go of the barriers that would keep you separate from Him—everything you do and say will come from love. That is what it means to be guided by the Holy Spirit. Not that He tells you specifically what to do or not to do. When your mind is aligned with His, everything coming from that mind must be His since our bodies are nothing more than a projection or extension of what is in our minds. When these are joined with the Holy Spirit, again, everything we do will be an expression of love. Our experience might be that Jesus told us this or the Holy Spirit told us that. In reality, we have simply joined with abstract love in our minds, and that love becomes the source of our specific thoughts and behavior.

The Song of Prayer specifically addresses the issue of moving beyond our need for specifics, our going so far as to ask God or the Holy Spirit for the fulfillment of our special requests. Indeed, one of the major emphases of this all-important writing is to have students of *A Course in Miracles* ask *only* for help in removing the obstacles to hearing the non-specific Voice of love. Once our egos are out of the way, we automatically *know* what to do or say.

Thus Jesus teaches in the pamphlet's opening pages:

> The secret of true prayer is to forget the things you think you need. To ask for the specific is much the same as to look on sin and then forgive it. Also in the same way, in prayer you overlook your specific needs as you see them, and let them go into God's Hands. There they become your gifts to Him, for they tell Him that you would have no gods before Him; no Love but His. What could His answer be but your remembrance of Him? Can this be traded for a bit of trifling advice about a problem of an instant's duration? God answers only for eternity. But still all little answers are contained in this (S-1.I.4).

This important teaching was underscored in a personal message to Helen, correcting her tendency to ask for *specific* words to say to a person in trouble. Here is what Jesus told his scribe:

> Remember you need nothing, but you have an endless store of loving gifts to give. But teach this lesson only to yourself. Your brother will not learn it from your words or from the judgments you have laid on him. You need not even speak a word to him. You cannot ask, "What shall I say to him?" and hear God's answer. Rather ask instead, "Help me to see this brother through the eyes of truth and not of judgment," and the help of God and all His angels will respond (*Absence from Felicity: The Story of Helen Schucman and Her Scribing of A Course in Miracles*, p. 381).

We shall return again and again to this vital point, for it points the way beyond the ego's *spiritual specialness*, one of its greatest defenses against the spiritual truths found in *A Course in Miracles* and many other spiritualities.

(4:1) Today we will try to reach past your own weakness to the Source of real strength.

This is reminiscent of Lesson 44, where Jesus helped us sink down into our minds, passing by the ego's illusions to reach the Holy Spirit's truth.

(4:2-5) Four five-minute practice periods are necessary today, and longer and more frequent ones are urged. Close your eyes and begin, as usual, by repeating the idea for the day. Then spend a minute or two in searching for situations in your life which you have invested with fear, dismissing each one by telling yourself:
> ***God is the strength in which I trust.***

Again, this is the process. The way to reach your real strength is to move past your weakness by becoming aware of your ego's thoughts. That is why there is such heavy emphasis on mind searching in these lessons. You cannot move past the darkness until you first realize that there *is* darkness. You must look at your investment in having your ego be alive and well, and then bring that investment in weakness to the strength of God within.

(5) Now try to slip past all concerns related to your own sense of inadequacy. It is obvious that any situation that causes you concern is associated with feelings of inadequacy, for otherwise you would believe that you could deal with the situation successfully. It is not by trusting yourself that you will gain confidence. But the strength of God in you is successful in all things.

Still again, we are asked by Jesus to turn away from the weakness and inadequacy of the ego's thought system to the strength of God he holds out for us. That is why he exhorts us in the text:

> Resign now as your own teacher.... for you were badly taught (T-12.V.8:3; T-28.I.7:1).

(6) The recognition of your own frailty is a necessary step in the correction of your errors, but it is hardly a sufficient one in giving you the confidence which you need, and to which you are entitled. You must also gain an awareness that confidence in your real strength is fully justified in every respect and in all circumstances.

The structure here is typical of most of the sections in the text: first you get the ego's side; then the Holy Spirit's answer. Throughout *A Course in Miracles* Jesus tells us in no uncertain terms how important it is that we look at our ego. Here he is saying we must look at our weakness, which comes from identifying with the ego. However, Jesus also teaches there is a presence of love, strength, and truth inside us, which is the basis of our looking. We become aware that the way we identify with truth and find real happiness and peace is by looking at our darkness with the expression of that truth—Jesus or the Holy Spirit—beside us. Recall that wonderful passage from the text, quoted here more fully than previously:

No one can escape from illusions unless he looks at them, for not looking is the way they are protected. There is no need to shrink from illusions, for they cannot be dangerous. We are ready to look more closely at the ego's thought system because together we have the lamp that will dispel it, and since you realize you do not want it, you must be ready. Let us be very calm in doing this, for we are merely looking honestly for truth. The "dynamics" of the ego will be our lesson for a while, for we must look first at this to see beyond it, since you have made it real. We will undo this error quietly together, and then look beyond it to truth.

What is healing but the removal of all that stands in the way of knowledge? And how else can one dispel illusions except by looking at them directly, without protecting them? Be not afraid, therefore, for what you will be looking at is the source of fear, and you are beginning to learn that fear is not real.... Do not be afraid.... to look upon fear, for it cannot be seen. Clarity undoes confusion by definition, and to look upon darkness through light must dispel it (T-11.V.1:1–2:3,8-9).

Thus we are given both sides of the split mind: the truth within, as well as instruction for the journey to that truth, which entails looking at the ego's weakness.

One more point: Looking at the ego is not enough if you do not also move beyond it to the strength of Christ. Half the lesson is not the whole. This thought is similar to the passage in the text on healing being of the *mind*, not the *body*; the removal of physical symptoms is not the issue:

Yet half the lesson will not teach the whole. The miracle is useless if you learn but that the body can be healed, for this is not the lesson it was sent to teach. The lesson is the *mind* was sick that thought the body could be sick; projecting out its guilt caused nothing, and had no effects (T-28.II.11:5-7).

Thus, "letting go of the ego" means nothing. Moreover, it is not *really* letting go if one does not identify at the same time with the gentle, defenseless, and loving strength of Christ, inherent in which is the remembrance of the Oneness of God's Son.

(7) In the latter phase of the practice period, try to reach down into your mind to a place of real safety. You will recognize that you have reached it if you feel a sense of deep peace, however briefly. Let go all the trivial things that churn and bubble on the surface of your mind, and reach down and below them to the Kingdom of Heaven. There is a place in you where there is perfect peace. There is a place in you where nothing is impossible. There is a place in you where the strength of God abides.

Again, we let go of "all the trivial things that churn and bubble" in our minds—our thoughts of specialness—by bringing them to Jesus or the Holy Spirit; no longer holding on to them for safety and defense. In other words, we no longer want the purpose they serve: preserving and protecting our separated self.

(8) During the day, repeat the idea often. Use it as your answer to any disturbance. Remember that peace is your right, because you are giving your trust to the strength of God.

And so we return to this central theme of the early lessons: the need to practice continually by bringing our disturbances to Jesus' specific answer, trusting in its strength rather than the weakness of the ego's shabby substitute for God.

LESSON 48

There is nothing to fear.

Lesson 48 is nice, short, and sweet: "There is nothing to fear." If God is the strength in which we trust, nothing in this world could ever make us afraid. The basis of fear is the principle that guilt demands punishment. If I am afraid, it is because I first see myself as guilty and weak. If I choose Jesus as the source of my strength, I am not weak or separated, and therefore not guilty. If I am not guilty, there can be no projected belief that I will be punished. Without such belief, there can be no fear. Again, it is the same process, all the time. If I want to live without fear, I must live without guilt. If I want to live without guilt, I need Jesus to help me look at it.

(1) The idea for today simply states a fact. It is not a fact to those who believe in illusions, but illusions are not facts. In truth there is nothing to fear. It is very easy to recognize this. But it is very difficult to recognize it for those who want illusions to be true.

As the text says, the only fact is God: "God is not symbolic; He is Fact" (T-3.I.8:2). The "fact"—"There is nothing to fear"—is really a reflection of God's reality. The state of fear's absence corrects the ego's fundamental thought that fear is punishment for our sin. It is this illusory fear you have to look at. You want illusions to be true because *you* are an illusion, and you want *you*—your individual identity—to be true. What makes it difficult to have an anxiety-free day is your not wanting today's lesson to be true. If it were, *you* are not true.

(2) Today's practice periods will be very short, very simple and very frequent. Merely repeat the idea as often as possible. You can use it with your eyes open at any time and in any situation.

It is strongly recommended, however, that you take a minute or so whenever possible to close your eyes and repeat the idea slowly to yourself several times. It is particularly important that you use the idea immediately, should anything disturb your peace of mind.

We can see over and over again, in just about every lesson, that Jesus is telling us to practice this thought in our everyday lives, and to bring him our concerns. In this day's exercise he is asking us to apply the thought throughout the day, *as often as possible*. Moreover, he once again urges us—"It is particularly important"—to think of the idea whenever we are disturbed; in other words, to bring the darkness of our upset to the light of his thought of love, a thought that by its very presence dispels the darkness of fear.

(3) The presence of fear is a sure sign that you are trusting in your own strength. The awareness that there is nothing to fear shows that somewhere in your mind, though not necessarily in a place you recognize as yet, you have remembered God, and let His strength take the place of your weakness. The instant you are willing to do this there is indeed nothing to fear.

When we find ourselves becoming fearful in any of the forms that fear takes—and sometimes it may not even be fear; it could be anger, depression, or sadness—it is because we chose the ego once again; in effect, telling Jesus or the Holy Spirit to get lost. That wrong-minded decision is the problem, and accepting the Correction is the solution. This simplicity of *A Course in Miracles*—one problem, one solution (W-pI.79-80)—is what makes it such a powerful and effective spiritual tool.

LESSON 49

God's Voice speaks to me all through the day.

This is a lesson from which many students of *A Course in Miracles* have derived a great deal of mileage, unfortunately going the wrong way: to hell rather than Heaven. They often take this lesson to mean that they hear the Holy Spirit tell them wonderful things—*all the time*. If we follow the thinking in these lessons, however, it is obvious that we cannot *hear* God's Voice all through the day because of our minds' constant clutter. Jesus already has explained the clutter's presence: our resistance to losing our individual and special identity. This resistance is reflected in cherishing the ego's voice of specialness in order to prevent our hearing the Voice of the Holy Spirit, as we see in this pointed passage from the text:

> You are not special. If you think you are, and would defend your specialness against the truth of what you really are, how can you know the truth? What answer that the Holy Spirit gives can reach you, when it is your specialness to which you listen, and which asks and answers? Its tiny answer, soundless in the melody that pours from God to you eternally in loving praise of what you are, is all you listen to. And that vast song of honor and of love for what you are seems silent and unheard before its "mightiness." You strain your ears to hear its soundless voice, and yet the Call of God Himself is soundless to you.
>
> You can defend your specialness, but never will you hear the Voice for God beside it (T-24.II.4:1–5:1).

While it is therefore true that God's Voice speaks to us all through the day—because the Holy Spirit is in our minds—this does not mean that we *hear* it. Pay careful attention to the lesson's words: Jesus does not say we *hear* God's Voice all through the day, but that God's Voice *speaks* to us all through the day. We are not going to listen because, again, of our resistance to losing our identity, expressed through the investment in perpetuating our specialness. That is why it is so important to read this (and all passages in *A Course in Miracles*) very carefully.

Another important point that speaks to the heart of Course students becoming confused is that we are *always* listening to an inner voice. We cannot listen to anything else! Our bodies are the vehicles (or channels) through which either the voices of the ego or the Holy Spirit "speak." Students often think that just because they hear an inner voice it must be the Holy Spirit. They unfortunately have totally forgotten about the *other* voice, which was specifically and intentionally made to drown out the still, small voice of the Holy Spirit, as we saw in the above passage. This is why Jesus emphasizes helping us remove our investment in the ego, so that we could inevitably and naturally "hear" the Voice that speaks for truth. My wife Gloria has made a similar point when she would remind students that hearing an inner voice they believe belongs to an entity "on the other side" does not necessarily mean that entity is more advanced or ego-free than they. In the end, discernment is a prime prerequisite for any spiritual seeker, no less so for students of *A Course in Miracles* who need to discern the difference between the two voices.

(1) It is quite possible to listen to God's Voice all through the day without interrupting your regular activities in any way. The part of your mind [the right mind] **in which truth abides is in constant communication with God, whether you are aware of it or not. It is the other part of your mind** [the wrong mind] **that functions in the world and obeys the world's laws. It is this part that is constantly distracted, disorganized and highly uncertain.**

This does not mean that if you are in your right mind you are not to obey the world's laws, as some students would unfortunately misconstrue this. Jesus is talking about obeying the world's laws because you *believe* they are real laws. To repeat, he is not saying, for example, that you should become an anarchist or libertarian. We read, for example, this instruction to teachers of God, his students who wish to grow beyond their ego selves:

> There is a way of living in the world that is not here, although it seems to be. You do not change appearance, though you smile more

frequently. Your forehead is serene; your eyes are quiet (W-pI.155.1:1-3).

In other words, we are not asked to look different or behave differently from anyone else. What *changes* is our attitude, or which inner teacher we have chosen to follow. When we listen to the Holy Spirit, the world becomes a classroom in which its symbols become the language through which we express His teachings. Lesson 184 discusses this in greater detail, so we will defer further discussion until then.

The issue is to obey the world's laws of illusion, not because we believe them to be true, but, again, because they are the *form* through which we express the mind's *content* of truth in a way that people can respond to without fear. An early passage in the text makes this essential point of meeting people where they are—the illusion of *form*—yet expressing the truth of the *content* of the correction, known as the miracle:

> The value of the Atonement does not lie in the manner in which it is expressed. In fact, if it is used truly, it will inevitably be expressed in whatever way is most helpful to the receiver. This means that a miracle, to attain its full efficacy, must be expressed in a language that the recipient can understand without fear. This does not necessarily mean that this is the highest level of communication of which he is capable. It does mean, however, that it is the highest level of communication of which he is capable *now*. The whole aim of the miracle is to raise the level of communication, not to lower it by increasing fear (T-2.IV.5).

It is the *content* of love that should be our inspiration and guidance, not any preconceived notions about the *form* in which that love is to be expressed. This ensures our response will be kind and non-judgmental, accepting people where they are, not where we want them to be.

(2:1-3) The part that is listening to the Voice for God is calm, always at rest and wholly certain. It is really the only part there is. The other part is a wild illusion, frantic and distraught, but without reality of any kind.

This brings to mind Plato's famous analogy from the *Phaedrus* of the charioteer and his two horses, and offers a poetic description of the right and wrong minds:

> Let it [the soul] be likened to the union of powers in a team of winged steeds and their winged charioteer.... With us men...it is a pair of steeds that the charioteer controls; moreover one of them is noble and good, and of good stock, while the other has the opposite character, and his stock is opposite. Hence the task of our charioteer is difficult and troublesome. ... He that is on the more honorable side is upright and clean-limbed, carrying his neck high, with something of a hooked nose; in color he is white, with black eyes; a lover of glory, but with temperance and modesty; one that consorts with genuine renown, and needs no whip, being driven by the word of command alone. The other is crooked of frame, a massive jumble of a creature, with thick short neck, snub nose, black skin, and gray eyes; hot-blooded, consorting with wantonness and vainglory; shaggy of ear, deaf, and hard to control with whip and goad (*Phaedrus* 246a; 253d-e).

This was an analogy that influenced Freud's view of the psyche, whereby Plato's depiction formed the basis for Freud's understanding of the *Id*, or the unconscious. That, of course, is the nature of the ego thought system: a reservoir of hatred, murder, and viciousness.

(2:4-6) Try today not to listen to it. Try to identify with the part of your mind where stillness and peace reign forever. Try to hear God's Voice call to you lovingly, reminding you that your Creator has not forgotten His Son.

Again, we can observe the implication of Jesus' urging: He asks us to recognize our call to the ego, and then choose against it in favor of our right minds, wherein dwell stillness and peace. We are encouraged to choose again, despite Jesus' awareness that our resistance is great. Yet it is early in our training, and there is still much to learn and practice.

(3) We will need at least four five-minute practice periods today, and more if possible. We will try actually to hear God's Voice reminding you of Him and of your Self. We will approach this happiest and holiest of thoughts with confidence, knowing that in doing so we are joining

our will with the Will of God. He wants you to hear His Voice. He gave It to you to be heard.

Another pep talk: God's Voice *is* within us, and patiently awaits our choice.

(4) Listen in deep silence. Be very still and open your mind. Go past all the raucous shrieks and sick imaginings that cover your real thoughts and obscure your eternal link with God. Sink deep into the peace that waits for you beyond the frantic, riotous thoughts and sights and sounds of this insane world. You do not live here. We are trying to reach your real home. We are trying to reach the place where you are truly welcome. We are trying to reach God.

Jesus wants us to be *really* clear about our purpose. However, we cannot reach God without going past the "raucous shrieks and sick imaginings" of the ego; and we cannot go past those shrieks and fantasies without looking at them. Thus, opening our minds means that our decision maker chooses the Holy Spirit's forgiveness instead of the ego's attack. We have already seen that in order to reach

God we have to set aside our identification with the ego's voice of specialness, and it is the workbook's aim to help us reach God through this process.

(5) Do not forget to repeat today's idea very frequently. Do so with your eyes open when necessary, but closed when possible. And be sure to sit quietly and repeat the idea for today whenever you can, closing your eyes on the world, and realizing that you are inviting God's Voice to speak to you.

Jesus returns to his emphasis on doing the lessons with eyes either open or closed, although his current preference in our training is our eyes shut, maximizing the experience that it is our *thoughts* that need correction. As we have repeatedly seen in the recent lessons, we are urged to apply the idea for the day as often as we can remember: "very frequently," "whenever you can." In this way, we reinforce our learning that it is the Holy Spirit's wisdom and love we truly want—found in our *minds,* not the world.

LESSON 50

I am sustained by the Love of God.

Lesson 50 differs from the preceding ones, and we shall be reintroduced to themes that will return later. Specifically, this lesson makes another statement, much clearer than the previous one, about the nature of the special relationship. The terms *special relationships* and *specialness* do not appear in the workbook at all; however, it is clear in passages like these that this is Jesus' referent.

(1) Here is the answer to every problem that will confront you, today and tomorrow and throughout time. In this world, you believe you are sustained by everything but God. Your faith is placed in the most trivial and insane symbols; pills, money, "protective" clothing, influence, prestige, being liked, knowing the "right" people, and an endless list of forms of nothingness that you endow with magical powers.

If these statements are read in the context of *A Course in Miracles* as a whole, it is obvious that Jesus is not saying we should feel guilty because we take a pill, wear warm clothing in winter, or have friends with whom we like to spend time. This passage is similar to Lesson 76 "I am under no laws but God's," which we shall discuss in due course and where we shall issue the same caveat. Moreover, Jesus is not saying we should let go of our bodily concerns. That would be confusing levels—mind and body—which he warns us about in the text (see, e.g., T-2.IV.3:8-11). We *can* overlook our bodies— physical and psychological—if we are in the real world, because at that point we *know* they are not our identity. But Jesus knows his students, and knows us well, and he wants us to be aware of the thought system on which dependencies (or special relationships) are based, and to understand the source of our trust in the things of the world. Only then can we make the meaningful choice against them. He continues with the source of these special attachments:

(2) All these things are your replacements for the Love of God. All these things are cherished to ensure a body identification. They are songs of praise to the ego. Do not put your faith in the worthless. It will not sustain you.

Again, Jesus is not saying we must give up anything that makes us feel better physically or mentally. However, he is saying we should be aware of our *dependence* on it, what in the text he refers to as *idols*. Such dependency is a statement that says God's Love is not enough; we want *more*:

> The world believes in idols. No one comes unless he worshipped them, and still attempts to seek for one that yet might offer him a gift reality does not contain. Each worshipper of idols harbors hope his special deities will give him more than other men possess. It must be more. It does not really matter more of what; more beauty, more intelligence, more wealth, or even more affliction and more pain. But more of something is an idol for. And when one fails another takes its place, with hope of finding more of something else. Be not deceived by forms the "something" takes. An idol is a means for getting more. And it is this that is against God's Will (T-29.VIII.8:4-13).

But we knew all this anyway, otherwise we would not be in the world, for no one comes here, as we have just read, unless he seeks more than the love God has offered. Be careful not to use Jesus' teaching as a reason to club yourself or others over the head. However, *do* use it as a way of reminding yourself that the journey takes you through your specialness; a journey you cannot make until you first recognize your heavy involvement in it. Lessons like this, as well as much of the text, make that abundantly clear. We shall return to this theme over and over again, for the same reason Jesus does: The journey to Heaven through hell *is* the path Jesus leads us on, and understanding the journey's contours will enable us to be led gently home.

(3) Only the Love of God will protect you in all circumstances. It will lift you out of every trial, and raise you high above all the perceived dangers of this world into a climate of perfect peace and safety. It will transport you into a state of mind that nothing can threaten, nothing can

disturb, and where nothing can intrude upon the eternal calm of the Son of God.

Jesus is reminding us our goal is to walk through this dream without fear. When we can do so, we shall realize we are not in the dream at all: the dream figure we call ourselves but reflects a thought of love with which we are now identified. Remember this is a process, and in this lesson we are presented with the journey in its entirety: where we begin, the nature of the journey—going through our specialness—and then at last the journey's end.

(4:1-4) Put not your faith in illusions. They will fail you. Put all your faith in the Love of God within you; eternal, changeless and forever unfailing. This is the answer to whatever confronts you today.

There are many lovely sections and passages in the text about not putting our faith in illusions. We read, for example, this one on *faithlessness*, putting our faith in nothing:

> It is impossible that the Son of God lack faith, but he can choose where he would have it be. Faithlessness is not a lack of faith, but faith in nothing. Faith given to illusions does not lack power, for by it does the Son of God believe that he is powerless. Thus is he faithless to himself, but strong in faith in his illusions about himself (T-21.III.5:1-4).

The opening to "Seek Not Outside Yourself" summarizes the entire section:

> Seek not outside yourself. For it will fail, and you will weep each time an idol falls. Heaven cannot be found where it is not, and there can be no peace excepting there. Each idol that you worship when God calls will never answer in His place. There is no other answer you can substitute, and find the happiness His answer brings. Seek not outside yourself. For all your pain comes simply from a futile search for what you want, insisting where it must be found. (T-29.VII.1:1-7).

Whenever we are troubled, it is because we do not believe we are sustained by the Love of God. Still closer to the truth, we do not want to be sustained by the Love of God, choosing instead to be sustained by everything else, as long as it is outside our minds. Looking at that horrid thought without judgment or guilt is the way to move beyond it to the state of true sinlessness, the innocence that is our natural Identity as God's Son.

(4:5-8) Through the Love of God within you, you can resolve all seeming difficulties without effort and in sure confidence. Tell yourself this often today. It is a declaration of release from the belief in idols. It is your acknowledgment of the truth about yourself.

The Love of God is the *content* that automatically heals all "seeming difficulties," which deal only with *form*. The ego, as we have already seen, literally made up the world of *form*—both collectively and individually—to keep us from choosing the *content* of the Atonement that ends the ego's reign in our minds. When the external problem is kept from the internal answer, the problem will never be solved, for it can but shift from one form to another. However, when brought to the truth within, it cannot help disappearing. As a later lesson on forgiveness puts it: "I will forgive, and this will disappear" (W-pI.193.13:3; italics omitted).

The reference to the idols, from which we are released, is special relationships. We invoke these substitutes for God's Love as replacements for what threatens our ego's existence, and which provide the illusion that our needs are met:

> Let not their form deceive you. Idols are but substitutes for your reality. In some way, you believe they will complete your little self, for safety in a world perceived as dangerous, with forces massed against your confidence and peace of mind. They have the power to supply your lacks, and add the value that you do not have (T-29.VIII.2:1-4).

We can therefore see that Jesus' purpose for us in these lessons is to help us recognize the idol of specialness for what it is, so we can choose against it.

Jesus asks us now to sink into consciousness, which means going deeply into our minds, an instruction we have already seen, and which our chart (see p. 135) helps us envision:

(5:1-3) For ten minutes, twice today, morning and evening, let the idea for today sink deep into your consciousness. Repeat it, think about it, let related thoughts come to help you recognize its truth, and allow peace to flow over you like a blanket of protection and surety. Let no idle and

foolish thoughts enter to disturb the holy mind of the Son of God.

The way to prevent these thoughts from disturbing your holy mind is through your recognition of them. Without such acknowledgment, they simply remain. The idea, again, is to see the "idle and foolish thoughts" of specialness in all its forms asking Jesus for help in understanding what they are, and even more importantly, what they are *for*.

(5:4-5) Such is the Kingdom of Heaven. Such is the resting place where your Father has placed you forever.

A lovely way to end this first major section of the workbook: the reminder of our ultimate goal.

This concludes the first 50 lessons, leading to the first review. We have seen how Jesus has given us an understanding of the journey, emphasizing the importance of taking seriously our study and practice of his course. This means, as we have discussed repeatedly, looking at our ego thoughts and asking Jesus' help. This process clearly implies the existence of our separated minds, split between the wrong-minded thought system of separation, guilt, and hate (the ego), and the right-minded correction of Atonement, forgiveness, and peace (the Holy Spirit). Thus are we trained by Jesus to recognize these two thought systems, asking for help to exercise our mind's power to choose the Teacher Who alone will bring us peace.

REVIEW I

Introduction

I have often spoken of the symphonic structure of *A Course in Miracles*, and usually refer to the text when I do so, but the same holds true for the workbook as well. One of the characteristics of a symphonic work, especially those written in the eighteenth and nineteenth centuries, is that the opening movement has an *exposition* that presents the different themes, a *development* section that elaborates on them, and a *recapitulation* where the composer brings back the themes, but in a new way. This is what we find in the workbook.

Lessons 1 through 60, especially, demonstrate the masterfully symphonic way Jesus has organized his material. The first fifty lessons consist of the exposition and development of the various themes, and here in the first review they return, but presented differently. He explains this at the end of the Introduction, as we shall see presently. My discussion will focus on the major themes of these early workbook lessons—the heart of *A Course in Miracles*—and the ways in which Jesus integrates them in this review.

In general, we can summarize this movement of our symphony thusly: Just as the text begins with its central theme—the first principle of miracles: "There is no order of difficulty in miracles" (T-1.I.1:1)—so do we find the workbook's central theme in these early lessons—"There is no order of difficulty in *perception*."

In the first three paragraphs Jesus instructs us how to proceed with the lessons, asking us to think about the ideas in the review "as often as possible" throughout the day:

(1:1–3:2) Beginning with today we will have a series of review periods. Each of them will cover five of the ideas already presented, starting with the first and ending with the fiftieth. There will be a few short comments after each of the ideas, which you should consider in your review. In the practice periods, the exercises should be done as follows:

Begin the day by reading the five ideas, with the comments included. Thereafter, it is not necessary to follow any particular order in considering them, though each one should be practiced at least once. Devote two minutes or more to each practice period, thinking about the idea and the related comments after reading them over. Do this as often as possible during the day. If any one of the five ideas appeals to you more than the others, concentrate on that one. At the end of the day, however, be sure to review all of them once more.

It is not necessary to cover the comments that follow each idea either literally or thoroughly in the practice periods. Try, rather, to emphasize the central point, and think about it as part of your review of the idea to which it relates.

We thus see Jesus' ongoing emphasis on thinking about, and applying these ideas throughout the day. Moreover, we note his insistence on the lesson's *content*—its "central point"—rather than its *form*. He is not seeking our literalness (i.e., compulsivity) in practicing, but our learning to generalize the lesson's message to whatever specific aspect of our day is meaningful.

(3:3–4:1) After you have read the idea and the related comments, the exercises should be done with your eyes closed and when you are alone in a quiet place, if possible.

This is emphasized for practice periods at your stage of learning.

These are two important sentences, wherein we see Jesus providing us with structured periods of meditation. In "I Need Do Nothing," on the other hand, he tells us this is not a course in contemplation or meditation (T-18.VII.4). He is certainly not against meditation, but that is not integral to the process of forgiveness. In this Introduction, Jesus indirectly cautions us about something he is more direct about in the teacher's manual ("How Should the Teacher of God Spend His Day?" [M-16]), which we have already discussed. The point, once again, is that when you have structured periods of learning or meditation, they easily become rituals and gods in their own right. In that sense they counteract Jesus' teachings on specialness. I emphasized in my lectures on the first fifty lessons that one of the principal goals of *A Course in Miracles*, well articulated in the workbook, is to have us learn to generalize. Therefore, if you can be with God, think of Jesus, or remember the lesson *only* during the structured practice periods, you are defeating their purpose. That is why Jesus specifically says "at your stage of learning." He is assuming that everyone is starting at the bottom of the ladder, and so he is essentially re-training our minds from the beginning. He is asking us to set aside everything we think we know about meditation, contemplation, prayer, and spirituality and let him teach us anew. Our teacher starts us off with structured and oftentimes simple exercises, but he does not want them to become special objects of attachment. Even though this is early in the workbook, Jesus is already issuing a word of caution about the potential misuse of these exercises.

(4:2-3) It will be necessary, however, that you learn to require no special settings in which to apply what you have learned. You will need your learning most in situations that appear to be upsetting, rather than in those that already seem to be calm and quiet.

Jesus is not saying there is anything wrong with arranging things externally in order to be comfortable when you meditate, but he does not want you to form a special relationship with your posture or breathing, the scent of your candle, the music, *A Course in Miracles*, or anything else. The emphasis should not be on modifying the external situation so you are happy, but on trying to change your thoughts so you would be *truly* happy, regardless of where you are or its conditions. Again, he is not against your doing anything that will help you relax, as long as you are vigilant for the ritualistic specialness which would act *against* your learning.

(4:4-5) The purpose of your learning is to enable you to bring the quiet with you, and to heal distress and turmoil. This is not done by avoiding them and seeking a haven of isolation for yourself.

To make this important point still again, Jesus is not saying we should not meditate and have structured periods of practice. In fact, that is precisely what this first part of the workbook has been all about. He is simply letting us know we are in the

early stages of learning, and that he is going to take us far, far beyond where we are now. We get a glimpse of this "far, far beyond" in this lovely passage from the manual for teachers, given in the context of learning to practice the justice of the Holy Spirit:

> There is no inherent conflict between justice and truth; one is but the first small step in the direction of the other. The path becomes quite different as one goes along. Nor could all the magnificence, the grandeur of the scene and the enormous opening vistas that rise to meet one as the journey continues, be foretold from the outset. Yet even these, whose splendor reaches indescribable heights as one proceeds, fall short indeed of all that wait when the pathway ceases and time ends with it. But somewhere one must start. Justice is the beginning (M-19.2:4-9).

Structured periods of practice and meditation are thus the beginning.

(5:1) You will yet learn that peace is part of you, and requires only that you be there to embrace any situation in which you are.

The idea is that we would feel peaceful not only when all is quiet around us, but also, *and especially*, when everything seems to be falling apart: when we or our families are ravaged by sickness; when anger and accusations are rampant; and when we are in the midst of guilt, anxiety, terror, and any of the feelings that are an inherent part of our lives. These are the times when we especially need to think of Jesus and what he is teaching. It would obviously make no sense from a learning point of view if we could only turn to him and find peace when we were physically quiet. Our quiet times are simply part of the training program of learning to go *inside*, so that once comfortable with this process, we can call upon peace *whenever* we find ourselves turning to the ego for help, immediately recognizing the need to change our teacher.

(5:2) And finally you will learn that there is no limit to where you are, so that your peace is everywhere, as you are.

This is the ultimate goal of learning: to *generalize* the specific lessons and situations in which we are being taught so they apply to all relationships, all situations, at all times, and in all circumstances—

without exception. If there is no world out there, which is the key metaphysical premise of *A Course in Miracles*, then the world is *inside* you. That is where peace is found. Further, if there is no world outside you, how can it affect you? That is what we need to learn, which we do through careful study and practice.

(6:1-3) You will note that, for review purposes, some of the ideas are not given in quite their original form. Use them as they are given here. It is not necessary to return to the original statements, nor to apply the ideas as was suggested then.

Note Jesus' flexibility, a model for us *not* to obsess about the *form* of these lessons, focusing instead on their underlying *content*.

The final sentence of the Introduction helps introduce what we shall be talking about as we proceed through this review:

(6:4) We are now emphasizing the relationships among the first fifty of the ideas we have covered, and the cohesiveness of the thought system to which they are leading you.

Restated, Jesus is saying that in these ten review lessons he will bring together these themes and show us how they are integrated: "the cohesiveness of the thought system." Understanding any one theme or concept in *A Course in Miracles* will automatically lead you to the others, reflecting its internal consistency. As I just mentioned, the predominant theme of these first fifty lessons is the correction of our misperceptions. We have seen again and again how much emphasis Jesus places on our learning that our thoughts determine the world we see, elaborating on the principle he gives us twice in the text: *projection makes perception* (T-13.V.3:5; T-21.in.1:1). We first look within and recognize with horror our thoughts of sin, guilt, and fear—specifically in this context, thoughts of attack and judgment—which we then project. These projections become the *cause* of the world we perceive outside us, which in our distorted experience appears as the *effect*. Thus Jesus teaches us this is a course in cause and not effect, as we have already seen (T-21.VII.7:8). In other words, this is not a course in changing the world or our behavior, but in

changing our thoughts, laden with judgment and attack.

When Jesus tells us that what we call thinking is not thinking at all, it is because we are thinking in opposition to him and God. What opposes God and His loving Oneness does not exist. Therefore, our thoughts of attack, anxiety, and judgment do not exist. Within our delusional minds, however, we most certainly think they do. We project these illusory thoughts of separation and hate, and see a world that does not exist because it comes from thoughts that are not really there. It is therefore our thinking that is the problem, from which we have to be saved. Salvation thus teaches us to correct our misthoughts, choosing the consequence of peace instead of conflict. This familiar statement near the end of the text is worth another look, to which we add an additional sentence:

> Salvation can be seen as nothing more than the escape from concepts. It does not concern itself with content of the mind, but with the simple statement that it thinks. And what can think has choice, and can be shown that different thoughts have different consequence (T-31.V.14:3-5).

Another major theme is decision, or changing our minds, and so a major thrust of these lessons is helping us realize what we are doing so that we can change our minds from thoughts of anger and judgment to forgiveness and peace. When we choose those thoughts they automatically extend, and we make the transition to what Jesus refers to as "vision." The external world does not necessarily change; indeed, many times it does not change at all. What changes is the way we perceive the world, which means the way we interpret it. Continuing with the process of forgiveness is what ultimately leads to Christ's vision, or the perception of the Holy Spirit that sees and knows the inherent sameness of God's one Son.

To summarize: The central themes—there are several subsidiary ones which we shall look at as well—are realizing the connection between our attack thoughts and the world we see; and recognizing Jesus' appeal that we change our minds and allow him to be the source of what we see, thus attaining true vision. Of the many themes of these ten review lessons, vision is by far the most important, as we shall now see.

LESSON 51

The review for today covers the following ideas:

Before beginning, let me mention something that probably has eluded almost all students of *A Course in Miracles*, certainly the non-obsessive ones. Helen had *insisted* to Jesus that each of the one-sentence introductions to the day's review be different. And you will surely be impressed to discover how many different ways Jesus can say that "the review for today covers the following ideas."

(1) (1) Nothing I see means anything.

In these early lessons Jesus emphasizes that what we see does not mean anything because what we see comes from *mis*thoughts of judgment and attack.

(1:2-5) The reason this is so is that I see nothing, and nothing has no meaning. It is necessary that I recognize this, that I may learn to see. What I think I see now is taking the place of vision. I must let it go by realizing it has no meaning, so that vision may take its place.

While Jesus does not use the term here, he points out to us that we have a split mind. We have the capacity of seeing through the vision of the Holy Spirit, but to ensure that that does not happen we cover those loving thoughts with thoughts of attack and separation. Indeed, we cannot achieve the goal of vision if we do not first recognize and understand the inherent illusory and meaningless nature of our perceptions. It is these misperceptions that we have deliberately chosen to take the place of vision, fulfilling the ego's purpose of protecting itself—really, our separated self protecting its separate identity—that prevents us from discovering the only meaning for being in this world: forgiveness.

(2) (2) I have given what I see all the meaning it has for me.

(2:2-4) I have judged everything I look upon, and it is this and only this I see. This is not vision. It is merely an illusion of reality, because my judgments have been made quite apart from reality.

This restates the teaching that the world we see is not there simply because it comes from our judgmental thoughts, which also are not there.

Remember, every thought in the ego system is a defense against the truth of the Atonement principle, which is that we never left God. Everything we perceive is a shadowy fragment of the original judgment that we separated from our Source and reality, the fundamental illusion from which all others come.

(2:5-6) I am willing to recognize the lack of validity in my judgments, because I want to see. My judgments have hurt me, and I do not want to see according to them.

Jesus is appealing to our sane, rational minds to understand that what we are doing with our thoughts, and therefore with the perceived world, hurts us: "My judgments have hurt me." The ego has set up its defensive system as a huge gap between our attack thoughts and the pain that is their effect. This gap is represented by the world of time and space, its purpose being to enable us to feel justified in attributing our pain to "things beyond [us], forces [we] cannot control" (T-19.IV-D.7:4). That, of course, is the wonder of projection from the ego's point of view. We wind up feeling assured that we are not responsible for the pain that results from our choosing against God and His Love: others, our bodies, or the world are the cause of our distress—anyone or anything *but* ourselves.

Thus the idea of these lessons is to bring the *effect* to the *cause*, so we can realize it is our judgments alone that have hurt us. In so doing we restore to awareness the power of our minds to decide our own destiny: happiness or misery, peace or conflict.

(3) (3) I do not understand anything I see.

(3:2-4) How could I understand what I see when I have judged it amiss? What I see is the projection of my own errors of thought. I do not understand what I see because it is not understandable.

This is the beginning of humility. We are always so sure we are right: what I see is what I see, what I hear is what I hear, and my understanding of a situation is what I say it is because *I* say it is. If we are skillful enough, we get a multitude of people to agree with us. That is not sanity, but collective *insanity*! In French this is known as *folie à deux*: a delusion shared by two people. But it could just as easily be ten, hundreds, thousands, millions, if not billions, for we all share the same insanity. We therefore cannot truly understand anything, nor go to anyone else for true understanding. If at any point we feel specialness, judgment, or separation, we should not trust anything we conclude based on those feelings; we will inevitably be wrong.

(3:5-8) There is no sense in trying to understand it. But there is every reason to let it go, and make room for what can be seen and understood and loved. I can exchange what I see now for this merely by being willing to do so. Is not this a better choice than the one I made before?

The way in which we attain vision is by the simple willingness to do so. Over and over we see Jesus appealing to the power of our minds to *choose*: vision or judgment, happiness or misery, peace or pain. What makes it possible for us to choose differently is becoming aware that we do indeed have the power to make this choice, and this power resides in our minds, not in the world or body.

(4) (4) These thoughts do not mean anything.

(4:2) The thoughts of which I am aware do not mean anything because I am trying to think without God.

This is the bottom line. Representing God is the Holy Spirit, Jesus, or the thoughts of these lessons. If we are not thinking in harmony with these thoughts—i.e., if we are holding on to grievances, attack thoughts, or specialness needs in any way, shape, or form—we are *not* thinking, and anything that results from not thinking must also be non-existent. Remember, cause and effect are never separate. Illusions can merely breed further illusions.

(4:3) What I call "my" thoughts are not my real thoughts.

The reason is that they are "my" thoughts. Jesus wants us to learn that whenever we say "this is mine" or "this is me," and whenever we speak of "my" thoughts, perceptions, or body, everything that

follows will be wrong because it would be based upon separation and specialness. At the ontological beginning, the ego said to God: "This is mine. This is *my* self, not yours. I am no longer part of you and I am right!" This attitude is always wrong because the Sonship of God is one, and there can be no true distinction among the seemingly different Sons. The belief in personal possession or special identity is the cover for the impersonal and non-special Self that we share with all, *as* All.

(4:4-5) My real thoughts are the thoughts I think with God. I am not aware of them because I have made my thoughts to take their place.

Jesus repeatedly tells us we have made our own thoughts to replace the thoughts we think with God, and we have done so because we want to be an "I." We cherish the first person *singular* and the first person possessive *singular*. It is not "our," the ego tells us, but "mine."

(4:6-8) I am willing to recognize that my thoughts do not mean anything, and to let them go. I choose to have them be replaced by what they were intended to replace. My thoughts are meaningless, but all creation lies in the thoughts I think with God.

Again, Jesus is reminding us that we have a choice, and he encourages us to make that choice to have *our* thoughts be replaced by *God's* thoughts—His Son as He created Him.

(5) (5) I am never upset for the reason I think.

(5:2) I am never upset for the reason I think because I am constantly trying to justify my thoughts.

Once we make the decision to be an individual and a first person possessive singular, we constantly try to justify that existence. This is the role of the face of innocence: It is not my fault, and I gather together as many people as possible to justify the perception of myself as a victim. This is never difficult to do, by the way, because the vastness of the world supplies an almost endless number of potential objects for our projections. Moreover, what makes it interesting is that we *all* seek to justify our face of innocence, thereby ensuring that we continue to exist as separated individuals *but that others will be responsible for the sin.* Therefore, it is they who will be punished for the sin that is no longer found in us.

(5:3-7) I am constantly trying to make them true. I make all things my enemies, so that my anger is justified and my attacks are warranted. I have not realized how much I have misused everything I see by assigning this role to it. I have done this to defend a thought system that has hurt me, and that I no longer want. I am willing to let it go.

Students doing the workbook for the first time usually do not pay careful attention to what they are reading. However, if they continue studying *A Course in Miracles* over many years and read the workbook much more carefully, which I strongly recommend, they will be astounded at what Jesus is actually saying; statements such as we have just read being prime examples.

Jesus here is putting words in our mouths, hoping we shall keep them there: We are now deciding we are glad we were wrong, and even happier to realize there is someone else within us who is right. This involves letting go of our anger, judgments, and arrogance; our devotion to specialness; and ultimately our individuality. We need to withdraw our investment in using others as reinforcement for our defense of projection, putting them either in the category of special love or special hate—objects with whom we seem to join, or from whom we seem to separate. Either way, our ego's need to demonstrate its innocence is fulfilled through attack and judgment, making others guilty of the sins we have projected onto them, magically hoping we can escape punishment through this insane and magical dynamic. Now we can happily say we choose otherwise.

LESSON 52

Today's review covers these ideas:

As discussed above, we find here the continual weaving of themes from the early lessons. In this set Jesus introduces forgiveness.

(1:1) (6) I am upset because I see what is not there.

(1:2-8) Reality is never frightening. It is impossible that it could upset me. Reality brings only perfect peace. When I am upset, it is always because I have replaced reality with illusions I made up. The illusions are upsetting because I have given them reality, and thus regard reality as an illusion. Nothing in God's creation is affected in any way by this confusion of mine. I am always upset by nothing.

This is an example of why we cannot study this course, let alone practice it, without understanding its underlying metaphysics. That is not necessarily a requirement for those just starting out with *A Course in Miracles*, but as we go along we see how its underlying metaphysics is present all the way through. Thus, if the world out there comes from our thoughts, which do not exist, the world must not exist either. It therefore makes no sense to be upset by it.

The truth is that we fear reality because it represents the end of our delusional thought system of separation, which includes the insane idea we can and do exist apart from God. It is thus our egos that fear the decision for reality. That is why Jesus teaches in the text that we "are not really afraid of crucifixion. [Our] real terror is of redemption" (T-13.III.1:10-11). However, the ego teaches that reality is to be feared because of what we did to it; namely, separated from its love, thereby destroying it. Thus we deserve to be punished for our sin. However, the Holy Spirit's Atonement principle is that we *never* separated from God, and therefore there is nothing to fear. Nothing happened—"Not one note in Heaven's song was missed" (T-26.V.5:4)—and without the belief in sin, there can be no fear of punishment. The ego's thought system of sin, guilt, and fear is made up. Nothing, therefore, can only lead to nothing, to paraphrase King Lear's outburst.

(2:1) (7) I see only the past.

(2:2-4) As I look about, I condemn the world I look upon. I call this seeing. I hold the past against everyone and everything, making them my enemies.

Once again we see that if we understood the Course's metaphysics, we would quickly realize why these lines are true. We began our existence as individuals by making God our enemy, and then, as one Son, projected that thought, making up a world of billions and billions of fragments. But the ontological thought came with us, and exists in each individual fragment. Thus the prevalence of *one or the other* in our thinking and experience: If I am to exist, everyone else must be killed. We people our world with many special love partners, however, so that our ultimate goal is not apparent. Nevertheless, we hold the past against everyone and everything, making them our enemies. And what is the past? Sin. We sinned in the past, projected it out, and now see it in everyone else. What we think we see, therefore—a world of separation and sin—is not really there at all, and thus is not *seeing*. Our arrogance in all this lies in that we really believe we think, see, hear, and especially that we understand.

(2:5-7) When I have forgiven myself and remembered Who I am, I will bless everyone and everything I see. There will be no past, and therefore no enemies. And I will look with love on all that I failed to see before.

It is not only that I *will* bless everyone, I *must* bless everyone, because if there is only God's blessing within my mind, that is all I can ever see. Again, if I realize I am a child of God, I am not separate from Him. Thus, there is no sin, and without sin there is no past. Obviously, then, there is nothing to project. What remains is the blessing of love on all things, for we have blessed ourselves with the thought of forgiveness.

(3:1) (8) My mind is preoccupied with past thoughts.

(3:2-3) I see only my own thoughts, and my

mind is preoccupied with the past. What, then, can I see as it is?

Vision is impossible as long as I believe I am separated and special, as long as I think that I count, am important, am wonderful, and on and on and on—the *me, myself and I* syndrome. These are but ways of asserting that I exist and, moreover, that I demand to be treated with the dignity I deserve. Needless to say, hidden in back of this is that I want you *not* to treat me this way, because then my ego is home free: I have become the eternal victim, and you the eternal victimizer. I get to keep my ego's cake of separation, eat, and enjoy every guilty morsel, too.

(3:4) Let me remember that I look on the past to prevent the present from dawning on my mind.

If we read this carefully we can recognize a clear statement of purpose: "Let me remember that I look on the past *to* prevent the present from dawning on my mind." There is a purpose for our holding on to the past and our attack thoughts. That is what keeps the present, the holy instant, and Jesus' love from "dawning on my mind." In the presence of his love we can no longer exist as special and hate-filled individuals. That is the fear: losing our special identity.

(3:5-6) Let me understand that I am trying to use time against God. Let me learn to give the past away, realizing that in so doing I am giving up nothing.

Again, we see the purpose behind our world of time and space. The ego uses its linear time—*past, present*, and *future*—as the way of reinforcing its underlying thought system of *sin, guilt*, and *fear*. In this way, the Everything of God is prevented by the nothingness of the ego from being remembered.

(4:1) (9) I see nothing as it is now.

(4:2-4) If I see nothing as it is now, it can truly be said that I see nothing. I can see only what is now. The choice is not whether to see the past or the present; the choice is merely whether to see or not.

We cannot see the past, because there is no past, no sin, no separation. Thus what we think we see—which includes what I remember happening in the past and whatever I am seeing now—is a projection

of our sinful past on to others. Consequently, what we are seeing is not there at all, and that characterizes our insanity.

(4:5) What I have chosen to see has cost me vision.

That is precisely why I have chosen to see it! The vision of Christ sees the Sonship as one, in which there are no special, important people. We are all the same. This *sameness* of purpose reflects the *Sameness* of God's one Son. Perception originated in the need to defend against knowledge, which is remembered through Christ's vision.

(4:6) Now I would choose again, that I may see.

Note the recurring emphasis on the power of our minds to choose. Even if we are not yet ready to make this choice—vision still being too frightening—we can at least recognize the possibility of choice, and forgive ourselves for not yet being able to make it.

(5:1)) (10) My thoughts do not mean anything.

(5:2-5) I have no private thoughts. Yet it is only private thoughts of which I am aware. What can these thoughts mean? They do not exist, and so they mean nothing.

My thoughts mean nothing because they are "my" thoughts. They are based on separation and exclusivity, and so are based on the exact opposite of Heaven's Oneness, our *non-specific*, and thus *non-private* reality.

(5:6-7) Yet my mind is part of creation and part of its Creator. Would I not rather join the thinking of the universe than to obscure all that is really mine with my pitiful and meaningless "private" thoughts?

Importantly, Jesus says "all that is really mine," not what I *think* is mine, which are but a few scraps of specialness. What is *really* mine are the gifts of Heaven: love, eternal life, real freedom, and perfect oneness.

Obviously Jesus does not think very much of our individuality, and he implores us not to think very much of it, either. The problem is that we value it much more than we ever thought we did. As we work seriously with *A Course in Miracles*, it becomes clearer and clearer how much we do value our individuality, how much we do have serious authority problems, and how we do not want anyone to tell us anything other than what we believe is true. We need to be aware of this arrogance without judging ourselves; to realize that, yes, this is where my thoughts are coming from, and they are just a silly mistake.

It is apparent as one reads through *A Course in Miracles*, not just these lessons, that Jesus is persistently consistent in presenting the truth to us, and does not judge us for our illusions. He makes fun of us occasionally, but his attitude is certainly not punitive. He simply says: "Will you please recognize that you are wrong and I am right. As long as you continue to think otherwise, you will not be happy. I am not the one who will punish you; *you* will punish you. I wait patiently for you, but why delay your happiness?" As he asks us twice later in the workbook: "Why wait for Heaven?" (W-pI.131.6:1; W-pI.188.1:1)

LESSON 53

Today we will review the following:

We see here a direct connection pointed out to us between our thoughts and the world, even though Jesus has made this connection before.

(1:1) (11) My meaningless thoughts are showing me a meaningless world.

(1:2-4) Since the thoughts of which I am aware do not mean anything, the world that pictures them can have no meaning. What is producing this world is insane, and so is what it produces. Reality is not insane, and I have real thoughts as well as insane ones.

Our thoughts of individuality, sinfulness, specialness, etc., have produced this world. Therefore, since the cause of the world is my insane thoughts, then the world, as the effect, must be equally insane. *Cause* and *effect* are never separated, for they are one. Reality, however, is not insane, despite the ego's protestations to the contrary. It tells us God is insane, vengeful, and angry, yet "[He] thinks otherwise" (T-23.I.2:7). As he did in the first fifty lessons, Jesus explains that we have a split mind, containing unreal thoughts of hate, and real thoughts of love. It remains for us to choose which ones we shall make real for ourselves. He tries to help us realize how miserable and unhappy we become when we choose the unreal thoughts of attack, judgment, and specialness. It is that misery that will ultimately impel us to choose again:

> Tolerance for pain may be high, but it is not without limit. Eventually everyone begins to recognize, however dimly, that there *must* be a better way. As this recognition becomes more firmly established, it becomes a turning point (T-2.III.3:5-7).

(1:5) I can therefore see a real world, if I look to my real thoughts as my guide for seeing.

This is the world of vision, the *inner* world in which there are no thoughts of separation or judgment; the world of thought that is beyond the dream of hate, wherein we are able at last to see the dream for what it is. From there it is only an instant longer until God reaches down and lifts us to himself, the

last step in our journey, as we see depicted in this lovely statement:

> And then your Father will lean down to you and take the last step for you, by raising you unto Himself (T-11.VIII.15:5).

We shall return to a discussion of the real world later.

(2:1) (12) I am upset because I see a meaningless world.

(2:2-7) Insane thoughts are upsetting. They produce a world in which there is no order anywhere. Only chaos rules a world that represents chaotic thinking, and chaos has no laws. I cannot live in peace in such a world. I am grateful that this world is not real, and that I need not see it at all unless I choose to value it. And I do not choose to value what is totally insane and has no meaning.

In "The Laws of Chaos" Jesus puts the word "laws" in quotation marks, signifying they are not really laws because they make no sense; the only *true* laws are the laws of God. Jesus does not do so here, but the meaning is the same: "chaos has no laws."

Before we can elect *not* to value what is "totally insane," we first have to accept that the world *is* totally insane. What helps us realize this is that the world makes us totally unhappy. Our specialness desires—even when they are fulfilled and gratified—do not make us happy and do not bring us the peace of God. They bring us the peace of the ego, but not Heaven's peace. The ultimate reason our insane thoughts are so upsetting is that they remind us of our original insane thought, which we believe will lead to our punishment. In the ominous words of the ego, depicted in this powerful passage from the manual, we read (and tremble!) about the effect of our insane thought of separation, placed in the context of magic thoughts, recognized in another and/or in ourselves:

> They [magic thoughts] can but reawaken sleeping guilt, which you have hidden but have

not let go. Each one says clearly to your frightened mind, "You have usurped the place of God. Think not He has forgotten." Here we have the fear of God most starkly represented. For in that thought has guilt already raised madness to the throne of God Himself. And now there is no hope. Except to kill. Here is salvation now. An angry father pursues his guilty son. Kill or be killed, for here alone is choice. Beyond this there is none, for what was done cannot be done without. The stain of blood can never be removed, and anyone who bears this stain on him must meet with death (M-17.7:2-13).

Forgiveness allows us to examine the destructive insanity of such a thought system, helping us accept it for what it is; a recognition for which we can only be deeply grateful, as its miracle leads beyond insane magic to the pure sanity of eternal life.

(3:1) (13) A meaningless world engenders fear.

(3:2-5) The totally insane engenders fear because it is completely undependable, and offers no grounds for trust. Nothing in madness is dependable. It holds out no safety and no hope. But such a world is not real.

The only reality is Heaven, which is totally dependable because it is certain: There is only God. This world, as we all have experienced it, is not dependable. It was made to be so. That is what lets us know that the world and our experience of it are not real. Once again, it is our guilt, born of the belief in sin, that leads us to expect certain punishment and to trust no one. The best we can do is protect ourselves from certain attack by utilizing various defenses, which serve only to maintain the separation that established the need for defenses in the first place. Thus the vicious cycles of guilt and attack, and attack and defense, continue and continue and continue. They will always continue, until their fundamental premises are exposed to the truth.

(3:6-8) I have given it the illusion of reality, and have suffered from my belief in it. Now I choose to withdraw this belief, and place my trust in reality. In choosing this, I will escape all the effects of the world of fear, because I am acknowledging that it does not exist.

Again, it is essential that we make the connection between our suffering (the *effect*) and our thoughts of judgment, attack, and specialness (the *cause*). We do not escape the world of fear by use of our armaments—attempts to control, manipulate, and seduce. We control the world only by realizing there is no world to control. What does need to be controlled, however, are our thoughts, as Jesus gently admonished Helen, to repeat an earlier quote: "You are much too tolerant of mind wandering" (T-2.VI.4:6). Most of the time there is nothing we can do about the uncertain world, but we certainly can do something about our uncertain thoughts. And we must, for they serve a vitally important purpose. They keep us here, holding intact our individuality, self-concepts, and very existence. Recognizing the purpose of our thoughts enables us to exert the power of decision to change the ego's goal of separation to the Holy Spirit's goal of Atonement. By changing the ego's underlying purpose we are able to escape its effects of pain, anxiety, and fear.

(4:1) (14) God did not create a meaningless world.

(4:2-6) How can a meaningless world exist if God did not create it? He is the Source of all meaning, and everything that is real is in His Mind. It is in my mind too, because He created it with me. Why should I continue to suffer from the effects of my own insane thoughts, when the perfection of creation is my home? Let me remember the power of my decision, and recognize where I really abide.

You can see how Jesus returns over and over to the core symphonic themes of these lessons: reality, illusion, and the power of our minds to choose between them. The point here is extremely important, because the problem is that we have forgotten that we have such power to choose. The ego set up its series of defenses so we would never remember that we have a mind, let alone a mind that can choose. Thus were the body and brain made to keep our minds hidden from us, replaced by the mindless state of living in a body that is governed by a brain that thinks it thinks, but in reality only carries out the thoughts of the unconscious mind. These thoughts are but two: the ego belief that the meaningless has triumphed over the meaningful; and the Holy Spirit's Atonement that the ego thought is unreal because it is outside the Mind of God. Thus it has no effects. Despite my feverish dreams to the contrary, I remain at home in God, held in memory in my right mind by the Holy Spirit. Now I can remember and choose again.

(5:1) (15) My thoughts are images that I have made.

(5:2-4) Whatever I see reflects my thoughts. It is my thoughts that tell me where I am and what I am. The fact that I see a world in which there is suffering and loss and death shows me that I am seeing only the representation of my insane thoughts, and am not allowing my real thoughts to cast their beneficent light on what I see.

This points out a crucial dimension of anyone's work with *A Course in Miracles*. Many of its students tend to deny they see a world of suffering, loss, and death. Instead they proclaim the world is really wonderful—part of God's or Jesus' plan; moreover, the new millennium will bring healing everywhere it is needed, bathing us all in light. The problem with looking through such rose colored glasses is that if we do not recognize the insanity, pain, and suffering of the world, we will never recognize their source in our minds. *The only way we can return to the insanity in our minds is by recognizing the insanity we perceive.* If we stubbornly, arrogantly, and self-righteously insist that everything is wonderful—e.g., this is a wonderful world,

replete with wonderful happenings; this is a wonderful course Jesus gave us—we will never realize that what we are seeing outside is a defense. Rather than see the hateful world we made, we cover it over and make it into something pretty. It is not a pretty world because it was made from a most *un*-pretty thought! Once more, the only way we can get to our thoughts and change our minds about them is to see their effects, which, again, is the cruel and vicious world in which we live.

(5:5-7) Yet God's way is sure. The images I have made cannot prevail against Him because it is not my will that they do so. My will is His, and I will place no other gods before Him.

Jesus again appeals to the power of our minds to choose: between illusions and the truth. The final sentence is taken from the first commandment in the Book of Exodus (20:3), the basis for part of the discussion in Chapter 10 in the text (see especially T-10.III-V). The point there, as well as here, is that the ego's gods of separation, sickness, suffering, and death have no power over the Son of God, who remains as God created him. God remains God, and no wild imaginings can erect another to take His place, except in dreams. Thus our will has never ceased to be one with His, and we remain at home, where God "would have us be" (T-31.VIII.12:8).

LESSON 54

These are the review ideas for today:

(1:1) (16) I have no neutral thoughts.

In this lesson Jesus focuses almost exclusively on the power of our thoughts. The reason we have no neutral thoughts is that our thoughts have the power to make up a world such as the one in which we live: a world of pain, suffering, and death; a world in which God appears to be absent. Our thoughts can be just as powerful on the right-minded side, however, in their power to undo the ego. The ego's thoughts have no effect in Heaven, of course, but within the dream they have tremendous power; thus the focus in *A Course in Miracles* on the power of our minds; specifically on the power to choose.

(1:2-4) Neutral thoughts are impossible because all thoughts have power. They will either make a false world or lead me to the real one. But thoughts cannot be without effects.

These statements are reinforced by a statement Jesus makes in the text: "All thinking produces form at some level" (T-2.VI.9:14). Our thoughts have extraordinary effects. They can make the world of specialness in which we live, or help us attain the real world by the complete undoing of the ego's world. The problem is that because of our defensive structure, including the power of denial, we almost never experience the effects of our thoughts. Consequently, we are not aware we have thoughts, because we are not aware we have a mind.

(1:5) As the world I see arises from my thinking errors, so will the real world rise before my eyes as I let my errors be corrected.

The real world, which is the end product of forgiveness, is the state of mind in which all ego thoughts have been undone. It is not something that is specifically chosen, but rather is the natural state of the guiltless mind when the ego's thought system of guilt has been chosen against.

(1:6-8) My thoughts cannot be neither true nor false. They must be one or the other. What I see shows me which they are.

This is another statement of that important

theme, *one or the other*. We do not have Heaven *and* hell, or hell *and* Heaven. They are mutually exclusive states. This is the underlying metaphysical premise of *A Course in Miracles*, the cornerstone of its thought system: There is God, and there is nothing else. If we believe there is something else, we are believing there is no God. Again, the way we know which thoughts we have chosen in our minds is by vigilantly paying attention, with Jesus beside us, to our perceptions of the outer world. They will reflect to us our decision for Heaven or hell, truth or falsity.

Now Jesus returns to the idea he had stated previously:

(2:1) (17) I see no neutral things.

(2:2-6) What I see witnesses to what I think. If I did not think I would not exist, because life is thought. Let me look on the world I see as the representation of my own state of mind. I know that my state of mind can change. And so I also know the world I see can change as well.

We can see how Jesus repeatedly returns to this theme. The beauty of this review is in the succinct manner in which Jesus weaves together the major themes of the first fifty lessons. And this is a crucial one: "Let me look on the world I see as the representation of my own state of mind." We recall these parallel lines from the text:

> [The world is] the outside picture of an inward condition (T-21.in.1:5).

> [Perception] is the outward picture of a wish; an image that you wanted to be true (T-24.VII.8:10).

We cannot change the world but we can indeed change our minds. Certainly, "the world I see can change as well." This does not mean, however, that the outside world can change, but rather *the way that I see it* will change. Keep in mind that perception is never of facts, it is always an interpretation of what we call facts; an interpretation of either the ego or the Holy Spirit. When Jesus talks about "the world that I see," he is not talking about a world outside: *There is no world outside*. The world is nothing but a projection or extension of the thoughts in our minds. It is essential, therefore, that we recognize the direct connection between the world and our thinking, otherwise we will never be able to do anything to change our thoughts.

Before we move on, note the allusion in 2:2—"If I did not think I would not exist"—to Descartes' famous dictum: "I think therefore I am (*Cogito ergo sum*)." However, while the great 17th century philosopher used this statement to prove his *real* existence, Jesus ultimately employs it to demonstrate the presence of our *illusory* existence, stemming from our *illusory* thoughts.

In paragraph 3 Jesus introduces the thought of *oneness*—in Heaven as God's one Son, as well as within the split mind. God's Son is One, whether He is called Christ or the separated Son of God:

(3:1) (18) **I am not alone in experiencing the effects of my seeing.**

(3:2-4) If I have no private thoughts, I cannot see a private world. Even the mad idea of separation had to be shared before it could form the basis of the world I see. Yet that sharing was a sharing of nothing.

Even though it "was a sharing of nothing," that does not mean we do not believe it. These statements nicely reflect the idea that despite what the world looks like—i.e., even in its dream of separation—the Son of God has remained one. That is why forgiveness is the central teaching of *A Course in Miracles*: In forgiving you, I reflect that you and I have no separate interests, for we share the same need to awaken from the dream of separation, guilt, and hate. That begins the process of reversing the ego's fragmentation. As the text emphasizes: If I forgive you perfectly, behind you stand thousands more, and behind each one stands yet another thousand (T-27.V.10:4). This means that if I forgive you perfectly, I have forgiven the Sonship—there *is* only one Son.

(3:5-7) I can also call upon my real thoughts, which share everything with everyone. As my thoughts of separation call to the separation thoughts of others, so my real thoughts awaken the real thoughts in them. And the world my real thoughts show me will dawn on their sight as well as mine.

This tells me my function: It is not to heal others, nor to change or teach them in the conventional way. My function is to remind you that the choice I have made in the holy instant is the same one you can make. A passage in the manual for teachers wonderfully summarizes this for us. We have quoted it already, but its relevance certainly deserves additional mentions:

> To them [those who are sick] God's teachers come, to represent another choice which they had forgotten. The simple presence of a teacher of God is a reminder. His thoughts ask for the right to question what the patient has accepted as true. As God's messengers, His teachers are the symbols of salvation. They ask the patient for forgiveness for God's Son in his own Name. They stand for the Alternative. With God's Word in their minds they come in benediction, not to heal the sick but to remind them of the remedy God has already given them. It is not their hands that heal. It is not their voice that speaks the Word of God. They merely give what has been given them. Very gently they call to their brothers to turn away from death: "Behold, you Son of God, what life can offer you. Would you choose sickness in place of this?" (M-5.III.2).

However, the process works the other way as well: My separation thoughts call to the separation thoughts in you. The expression of my decision for the ego—judgment, attack, anxiety, and fear—tells you that you are right in believing you are separate, because I am demonstrating that you are. My anger confirms you are right, as does my special love and dependency. You want me to confirm that you are right, just as I want you to do the same for me. These are the "secret vows" we make with each other to reinforce our insanity, as Jesus explains in the text, again in the context of sickness:

> This is the secret vow that you have made with every brother who would walk apart. This is the secret oath you take again, whenever you perceive yourself attacked. No one can suffer if he does not see himself attacked, and losing by attack. Unstated and unheard in consciousness is every pledge to sickness. Yet it is a promise to another to be hurt by him, and to attack him in return.
>
> Sickness is anger taken out upon the body, so that it will suffer pain. It is the obvious effect of what was made in secret, in agreement

with another's secret wish to be apart from you, as you would be apart from him. Unless you both agree that is your wish, it can have no effects (T-28.VI.4:3–5:3).

Yet, again, Jesus is also telling us we can reinforce right-mind thinking in each other:

> Whoever says, "There is no gap between my mind and yours" has kept God's promise, not his tiny oath to be forever faithful unto death. And by his healing is his brother healed.
>
> Let this be your agreement with each one; that you be one with him and not apart. And he will keep the promise that you make with him, because it is the one that he has made to God, as God has made to him. God keeps His promises; His Son keeps his (T-28.VI.5:4–6:3).

Thus, when I choose Jesus as my teacher instead of the ego, and I release my grievances through forgiveness, I am teaching there is a right-minded thought in you as well, and in that moment I have become a healing symbol for you. I do not have to say anything, nor preach to you. Indeed, *I* do nothing. Moreover, the *you* may be someone who died twenty years ago. Since minds are joined, forgiveness has nothing to do with bodies. *You* as a thought and *I* as a thought are still united. Whenever I choose to let go of my grievances against you, I am sending a clear message that says: "Awaken from the dream of death." Delivering that message is our only function.

(4:1) (19) I am not alone in experiencing the effects of my thoughts.

(4:2-3) I am alone in nothing. Everything I think or say or do teaches all the universe.

"All the universe" is the universe of the Sonship in my mind, joined with everyone else's. There is only one mind, and I can think, say, or behave from the Holy Spirit or my ego. Thus Jesus reiterates his teachings on oneness—spirit *and* ego.

(4:4-6) A Son of God cannot think or speak or act in vain. He cannot be alone in anything. It is therefore in my power to change every mind along with mine, for mine is the power of God.

This does not mean I can literally change your mind for you. I can serve as an example of one who has changed his mind for himself, thereby realizing

that that "self" is all of us. Likewise, Jesus cannot do it for us. He can be our teacher and model, showing us there is another choice we can make, but he cannot choose for us. Jesus explained this to Helen early on in the scribing, and therefore to all of us, in the context of her asking him to take her fear away. His answer was a foreshadowing of all he was to teach in *A Course in Miracles*, for he emphasized the power of Helen's mind to choose fear or against it, and that he could not, and certainly would not remove that power from her mind by making the choice for her:

> You may still complain about fear, but you nevertheless persist in making yourself fearful. I have already indicated that you cannot ask me to release you from fear. I know it does not exist, but you do not. If I intervened between your thoughts and their results, I would be tampering with a basic law of cause and effect; the most fundamental law there is. I would hardly help you if I depreciated the power of your own thinking. This would be in direct opposition to the purpose of this course. It is much more helpful to remind you that you do not guard your thoughts carefully enough (T-2.VII.1:1-7).

(5:1) (20) I am determined to see.

(5:2-3) Recognizing the shared nature of my thoughts, I am determined to see. I would look upon the witnesses that show me the thinking of the world has been changed.

The witnesses we look upon are the witnesses we send out. This is an implied reference to "The Attraction of Guilt" in the "Obstacles to Peace" (T-19.IV-A.i). We send out messengers of love or fear, and what we send out we see outside us, which become the witnesses that show what we have chosen. If we are angry or upset, stubborn or having a temper tantrum, that tells us we have sent out messengers of guilt, fear, hatred, and certainly separation. It is these external witnesses we make real in our perception, seeing them outside rather than in our selves. Another passage in the text illustrates the important role our perceptions play in healing. By observing the witnesses in the world I perceive, I am taught to see them as reflecting a decision I made in my mind. Only then can I exercise the mind's power to change this decision:

Damnation is your judgment on yourself, and this you will project upon the world. See it as damned, and all you see is what you did to hurt the Son of God. If you behold disaster and catastrophe, you tried to crucify him. If you see holiness and hope, you joined the Will of God to set him free. There is no choice that lies between these two decisions. And you will see the witness to the choice you made, and learn from this to recognize which one you chose (T-21.in.2:1-6).

(5:4-5) I would behold the proof that what has been done through me has enabled love to replace fear, laughter to replace tears, and abundance to replace loss. I would look upon the real world, and let it teach me that my will and the Will of God are one.

Thus will we know which choice we made by paying careful attention to what we perceive around us. We cannot be reminded too often that perception is not an objective fact, but always an interpretation. When *A Course in Miracles* teaches us to look at what we perceive, Jesus is not speaking of looking out and seeing a desk or a book, a tree or a person. Rather, we are being instructed to look at the *way* we perceive objects, people, and situations. In other words, do we perceive proof of the Atonement principle, or proof of separation? Again, what we perceive will reveal to us what our minds have chosen. Perceptions of love or calls for love reflect the decision to accept the Atonement, and this unequivocal choice ushers in the real world and the happy remembrance of the unity of God and His Son.

LESSON 55

Today's review includes the following:

(1:1) (21) I am determined to see things differently.

Jesus is now appealing directly to the power of our minds to choose.

(1:2) What I see now are but signs of disease, disaster and death.

In deference to Helen, I like to point out alliteration when it appears. Note the three d's: *disease, disaster, and death*. Again, it is important we perceive disease, disaster, and death all around us, *not* love, hope, and joy, for there is none. Indeed, the world was made *not* to be a place of love, hope, or joy. If we do not recognize this, we will have no motivation for changing our mind. We will believe in our arrogance that we have already changed it by virtue of our having perceived light instead of darkness, love instead of hate, life instead of death. We believe what our egos have programmed us to believe, which is why we need to question the value of having chosen the ego as our teacher.

(1:3-5) This cannot be what God created for His beloved Son. The very fact that I see such things is proof that I do not understand God. Therefore I also do not understand His Son.

This at least is a good initial step, because if we think we are looking on a world of light, peace, and joy, we will believe we understand God, Jesus, and, unfortunately, his course. Acknowledging that what we see "are the signs of disease, disaster and death" is the beginning of the humility that reaches to Wisdom. We begin by denying the ego's thought system of denial, and gradually, step by step, we are led by Jesus to understand that spirit and ego are mutually exclusive states, and so are love and hate, life and death, joy and pain. To make one real is to deny the other.

(1:6-7) What I see tells me that I do not know who I am. I am determined to see the witnesses to the truth in me, rather than those which show me an illusion of myself.

Once having learned to tell the difference between *form* and *content*, we call upon our new Teacher to help us see truly, the vision of Christ that

reminds us who we are—along with our brothers—as God's one Son.

(2:1) (22) What I see is a form of vengeance.

(2:2-3) The world I see is hardly the representation of loving thoughts. It is a picture of attack on everything by everything.

This is the same point Jesus was making earlier, saying the world we see represents an attack on "everything by everyone." There are no exceptions. If we think we see a loving world, we will believe there are only loving thoughts within and so we will not look at the *un*loving ones. By our not looking, the unloving thoughts remain buried in our minds, and whatever is buried has the terrible habit of finding its way out—the dynamic of projection—and attacking everyone else. Because we are not aware that the source of our attack is our minds' unloving thoughts, we will not be aware that we are the ones who did this. We will actually think that because we think we have only loving thoughts, our attacks and judgments of others are loving, too. That is why it is important to see the world for what it is and recognize its source. Only when we look with Jesus at the *un*loving thoughts in our minds and forgive them, will we realize that underneath the unloving thoughts and concealed by them are the loving ones we have always had.

(2:4-6) It is anything but a reflection of the Love of God and the love of His Son. It is my own attack thoughts that give rise to this picture. My loving thoughts will save me from this perception of the world, and give me the peace God intended me to have.

The unloving nature of the world is again unmistakably depicted in Jesus' words: "It is anything but a reflection of the Love of God and the love of His Son." The last sentence is carefully phrased: "My loving thoughts will save me from this perception of the world." The problem is the *perception*. It is not the world. Disease, disaster, and death do not exist out there, because *there is no out there*. They exist in a mind that is filled with guilt, hatred, and terror. Therefore it is the *perception* that has to be changed, not the world: "Seek not to change the world, but choose to change your mind about the world" (T-21.in.1:7). Our perception is changed by first bringing it back from its projected form to its source, the *mind.* Only then, as we have already seen, can we exercise the mind's power of decision and choose the loving thought of the Atonement instead of the unloving thought of separation.

(3:1) (23) I can escape from this world by giving up attack thoughts.

(3:2-5) Herein lies salvation, and nowhere else. Without attack thoughts I could not see a world of attack. As forgiveness allows love to return to my awareness, I will see a world of peace and safety and joy. And it is this I choose to see, in place of what I look on now.

One could not ask for a more explicit statement of salvation. We are not saved from the world or from some abstract sense of sin, but from our own thoughts. To escape the horrors of the world—Hamlet's "slings and arrows of outrageous fortune" —one need only look with Jesus at our horrifying thoughts. Joined with his gentle laughter at the silliness of the ego's thought system of attack, we watch its thoughts slowly dissolve into their own nothingness. Looking out, we perceive only "peace and safety and joy," the world of forgiveness given form.

(4:1) (24) I do not perceive my own best interests.

(4:2-3) How could I recognize my own best interests when I do not know who I am? What I think are my best interests would merely bind me closer to the world of illusions.

I do not know who I am because *I* think "*I* am," with the emphasis on the *I.* I actually think there is an "I" here, therefore I do not know who I am. How, then, could I possibly know what is best for me? What we think is best is always some glorification, gratification, or anything that will preserve our illusory identity as an individual "I."

(4:4) I am willing to follow the Guide God has given me to find out what my own best interests are, recognizing that I cannot perceive them by myself.

That we cannot do this without help is an extremely important theme throughout *A Course in Miracles.* There is no way we can do this without the Holy Spirit's or Jesus' help. Humility says: "I do not know, I do not understand, but thank God there is Someone in me who does, and thank God He is right and I am wrong." That is why Jesus says that he needs us as much we need him (T-8.V.6:10): he cannot help us *unless* we ask him to. We see this "collaborative venture" (T-4.VI.8:2) expressed in the statement we have already seen in its full context: "Together we have the lamp that will dispel it [the ego's thought system]" (T-11.V.1:3). Jesus cannot accomplish this without us, and we certainly cannot accomplish it without him!

The next set emphasizes the important theme of purpose, which, to state it again, is not emphasized as much here as it is in many other places in *A Course in Miracles.*

(5:1) (25) I do not know what anything is for.

(5:2-3) To me, the purpose of everything is to prove that my illusions about myself are real. It is for this purpose that I attempt to use everyone and everything.

Everything we think, and everything we see in the world has the purpose of proving we are right. That is the very reason for having made the world in the first place: What God did we can do even better. There are no exceptions in this *either-or* thought system. Just as holiness and love do not make exceptions on the side of love, specialness does not make any exceptions, either. We either love or hate, forgive or attack; but there is no in between: If my self is real, then my Self is not; and, to the ego's dismay, *vice versa.* As a much later lesson puts it: "Let me not forget myself is nothing, but my Self is all" (W-pII.358.1:7).

(5:4-6) It is for this that I believe the world is for. Therefore I do not recognize its real purpose. The purpose I have given the world has led to a frightening picture of it.

I have used the world to fulfill my purpose of proving I am right; i.e., that the illusion about my individuality is the truth. This means I killed God so I could exist. However, in my right mind I understand how I have used the world to fulfill the purpose of making attack real and justified. If I am to exist, everyone has to be sacrificed to my selfish desire. If I am trying to do it to you—since everyone out there is part of the dream I made up—I know you are trying to do the same thing to me. This inevitably produces a world of fear, not safety, for our guilt can only cause a world of perceived punishment and death. But now I gladly choose otherwise.

(5:7) Let me open my mind to the world's real purpose by withdrawing the one I have given it, and learning the truth about it.

Here, too, it is clear that Jesus and *A Course in Miracles* cannot do it for us, but can only remind us we have to withdraw our beliefs about the world. We need to open our minds by withdrawing the purpose we gave to the world. In other words, again, we have to say (and mean!) that we were wrong. Only then can we recognize the world's true purpose of forgiveness, the pathway that leads us home through the power of our mind to decide *for* God instead of *against* Him.

LESSON 56

Our review for today covers the following:

(1:1) (26) **My attack thoughts are attacking my invulnerability.**

(1:2) How can I know who I am when I see myself as under constant attack?

I have to see myself as under constant attack because I am attacking everyone else. That is why the lesson is entitled: "My attack thoughts are attacking my invulnerability." I am truly invulnerable as God's Son, but in identifying with the ego I see myself as vulnerable, because guilt demands punishment and I feel victimized by God's counterattack. If I believe everyone else is going to attack me, I cannot be as God created me—innocent and invulnerable. Thus, the ego reasons to me, if it can prove that God's Son *is* truly vulnerable—the purpose of the body—then how could I be God's Son? This reasoning is clearly presented in the following passage from "What is the Body?" to which we shall return much, much later in this series:

> For the Son of God's impermanence is "proof" his fences [bodies] work, and do the task his mind assigns to them. For if his oneness still remained untouched, who could attack and who could be attacked? Who could be victor? Who could be his prey? Who could be victim? Who the murderer? And if he did not die, what "proof" is there that God's eternal Son can be destroyed? (W-pII.5.2:3-9)

(1:3) Pain, illness, loss, age and death seem to threaten me.

Again, it is essential to realize we are living in a world of pain, illness, loss, age, and death; a world deliberately chosen by our egos to prove that its thought system of separation is right and the Holy Spirit's Atonement is wrong.

(1:4-5) All my hopes and wishes and plans appear to be at the mercy of a world I cannot control. Yet perfect security and complete fulfillment are my inheritance.

Jesus once again is showing us we have a split mind, and that we can choose whether we will see ourselves as living in a state of constant terror, fear, and vulnerability, or in a state of constant safety. It is not true that we are, again, "at the mercy of things beyond [us], forces [we] cannot control" (T-19.IV-D.7:4), for the truth is that our "Self is ruler of the universe" (W-pII.253).

(1:6-8) I have tried to give my inheritance away in exchange for the world I see. But God has kept my inheritance safe for me. My own real thoughts will teach me what it is.

It cannot be said often enough that in order for us to access our real thoughts, we first have to let go of our unreal ones, which we cannot do without knowing they are there. We learn this happy fact by understanding that the world we perceive is the one we made, and is therefore unreal: a projection of our unreal thoughts of separation and guilt. Our true inheritance is as a beloved and treasured Child of God, not the ego's child of guilt and fear. As Jesus concludes "The Treasure of God":

> What God has willed for you *is* yours. He has given His Will to His treasure, whose treasure it is. Your heart lies where your treasure is, as His does. You who are beloved of God are wholly blessed (T-8.VI.10:1-4).

(2:1) (27) **Above all else I want to see.**

(2:2-6) Recognizing that what I see reflects what I think I am, I realize that vision is my greatest need. The world I see attests to the fearful nature of the self-image I have made. If I would remember who I am, it is essential that I let this image of myself go. As it is replaced by truth, vision will surely be given me. And with this vision, I will look upon the world and on myself with charity and love.

Jesus always comes back to the same central ideas: Our perceptions reflect our self-image—child of God or child of the ego—and vision corrects the vicious and fearful misperceptions of the ego, reflecting our Identity as spirit. Vision thus *undoes* the ego's thought system. As we are taught in the text: The ego always speaks first (T-5.VI.3:5), and the Holy Spirit is the Answer:

The ego speaks in judgment, and the Holy Spirit reverses its decision, much as a higher court has the power to reverse a lower court's decision in this world. The ego's decisions are always wrong, because they are based on the error they were made to uphold (T-5.VI.4:1-2).

With vision replacing judgment, we look out on a unified world of peace and love, regardless of what our physical eyes behold.

(3:1) (28) Above all else I want to see differently.

(3:2-3) The world I see holds my fearful self-image in place, and guarantees its continuance. While I see the world as I see it now, truth cannot enter my awareness.

The projected world's purpose is to keep my fearful self-image in place. This foreshadows an important statement in Part II of the workbook, speaking of our unforgiving thoughts:

> An unforgiving thought is one which makes a judgment that it will not raise to doubt, although it is not true. The mind is closed, and will not be released. The thought protects projection, tightening its chains, so that distortions are more veiled and more obscure; less easily accessible to doubt, and further kept from reason. What can come between a fixed projection and the aim that it has chosen as its wanted goal? (W-pII.1.2)

Thus do our projections enable the ego to protect its self-concept of separation and hate, since that concept is now perceived to be external to the mind that is its source. This is the self-concept that says I am an individual, an individuality I purchased at the cost of sin. This sin must be punished, and therefore I deserve to be afraid. Nothing really has changed except that now I believe I am not the source of the fear, which has its source in something outside me. Certain of what I see, I never question my perception. Without my perception being questioned, my condition of fear and pain cannot be answered by the Holy Spirit.

(3:4) I would let the door behind this world be opened for me, that I may look past it to the world that reflects the Love of God.

The one who opens the door for us is Jesus, but we must *let* him do it, by asking his help to bring our illusions of attack to his truth of forgiveness. This real world of complete forgiveness reflects God's Love, which waits just beyond the door held open by Jesus:

> Christ is at God's altar, waiting to welcome His Son.... The door is not barred, and it is impossible that you cannot enter the place where God would have you be.... You can refuse to enter, but you cannot bar the door that Christ holds open. Come unto me who hold it open for you, for while I live it cannot be shut, and I live forever (T-11.IV.6:1,3,5-6).

(4:1) (29) God is in everything I see.

(4:2-4) Behind every image I have made, the truth remains unchanged. Behind every veil I have drawn across the face of love, its light remains undimmed. Beyond all my insane wishes is my will, united with the Will of my Father.

As in lessons one through fifty, Jesus emphasizes the nature of our right minds. The wrong mind is filled with thoughts of attack: disease, suffering, death, murder, and judgment. He helps us realize that these thoughts are covering something else. However, the fact that he tells us this does not mean we need not go through the work of choosing the *something else*, but at least now we are aware of what it is we choose between. It is not that I choose *kill or be killed*—do I kill you or do you kill me?— I choose miracles *or* murder (T-23.IV.9:8). This passage tells us there is another thought system in our minds, awaiting our choice. It also implies there is a *purpose* inherent in our having chosen attack over love: the wish to preserve our identity— chosen in separation and forged in hate—by proving we are right and God is wrong. Thus we chose to live in darkness, and believed it to be real *because we believed it.*

(4:5-6) God is still everywhere and in everything forever. And we who are part of Him will yet look past all appearances, and recognize the truth beyond them all.

Jesus reassures us that the "outcome is as certain as God" (T-2.III.3:10), for we shall surely make the right choice—as any good Platonist would— between appearance and reality. Our fervent attempts to the contrary, we remain as God created us, powerless to change the resplendent truth about ourselves. Thus do we see a world reflecting back to us the radiant reality of God's Love.

(5:1) (30) God is in everything I see because God is in my mind.

(5:2-5) In my own mind, behind all my insane thoughts of separation and attack, is the knowledge that all is one forever. I have not lost the knowledge of Who I am because I have forgotten it. It has been kept for me in the Mind of God, Who has not left His Thoughts. And I, who am among them, am one with them and one with Him.

Held for us by the Holy Spirit is the memory of the knowledge that we never truly separated ourselves from God. Early in the text Jesus says that "to lose something does not mean it has gone. It merely means that you do not remember where it is" (T-3.VI.9:3-4). The same is true here: Even though we have lost the knowledge of who we are and have forgotten our Source, it does not mean His Love is not fully present in our minds. Such reassurances are replete in *A Course in Miracles*. Here are two of them:

> The Father keeps what He created safe. You cannot touch it with the false ideas you made, because it was created not by you. Let not your foolish fancies frighten you. What is immortal cannot be attacked; what is but temporal has no effect (T-24.VII.5:1-4).

> You can lose sight of oneness, but can not make sacrifice of its reality. Nor can you lose what you would sacrifice, nor keep the Holy Spirit from His task of showing you that it has not been lost (T-26.I.6:1-2).

What remains is the acceptance of Jesus' certainty, which points to our mind and the memory of the Oneness that created us one with Him.

LESSON 57

Today let us review these ideas:

(1:1) (31) I am not the victim of the world I see.

(1:2-9) How can I be the victim of a world that can be completely undone if I so choose? My chains are loosened. I can drop them off merely by desiring to do so. The prison door is open. I can leave simply by walking out. Nothing holds me in this world. Only my wish to stay keeps me a prisoner. I would give up my insane wishes and walk into the sunlight at last.

We find this compelling because we feel we are victims. If this is a world we made, which is what Jesus has been teaching us from the beginning, the world is not the problem. *The fact that we made it is the problem*—"How can [we] be the victim of a world that can be completely undone if [we] so choose?"

We have to be willing to admit we have been wrong about everything. What makes us believe we are right is our experience of being victimized by everything else. Remember, the "everything else" is not only others' bodies, but our own as well. The body is exclusively outside the mind, the source of our true identity.

The analogy to a prisoner walking into the sunlight refers to Plato's famous Allegory of the Cave in *The Republic*. It is worth summarizing—albeit briefly—as Jesus makes more specific reference to it in the text.* The allegory is set in a cave, where prisoners are chained in such a fashion that they can see only the interior wall of the cave, unknowing of the opening behind them, through which stream the sun's rays, casting shadows onto the wall, of the passers-by along the road that runs past the mouth of the cave. Thus the prisoners believe that the shadows are the reality, since they know of nothing else. One of the prisoners (representing Plato's esteemed teacher Socrates) is freed and, turning around and making his way to the light, begins to understand the difference between appearance and reality. Returning to teach his companions the truth, he frees them, only to meet with murder at the hands

of those still fearful of truth's light. Here, then, are the two specific references in the text:

> Prisoners bound with heavy chains for years, starved and emaciated, weak and exhausted, and with eyes so long cast down in darkness they remember not the light, do not leap up in joy the instant they are made free. It takes a while for them to understand what freedom is. (T-20.III.9:1-2).

> Eyes become used to darkness, and the light of brilliant day seems painful to the eyes grown long accustomed to the dim effects perceived at twilight. And they turn away from sunlight and the clarity it brings to what they look upon. Dimness seems better; easier to see, and better recognized. Somehow the vague and more obscure seems easier to look upon; less painful to the eyes than what is wholly clear and unambiguous. Yet this is not what eyes are for, and who can say that he prefers the darkness and maintain he wants to see? (T-25.VI.2)

Thus we recognize we have been our own jailors, and now can make the only sensible decision available to us: leave the darkness for the light. Our chains of guilt and attack were simply the unwillingness to open our eyes and *see*, and now we choose vision. The next paragraph repeats the lesson:

(2:1) (32) I have invented the world I see.

(2:2-3) I made up the prison in which I see myself. All I need do is recognize this and I am free.

That is why Jesus keeps saying this is a simple course. All we need do is realize we made this up; that the world is an hallucination (T-20.VIII.7)—everything we think is hurting us is not true. The key to unlocking this illusory prison of darkness has always been in our minds. Now at last we have the teacher and path that help us realize this joyous fact is indeed so.

---

* The interested reader may also consult my discussion in *Love Does Not Condemn*, Second Edition, pp. 327-30.

(2:4-8) I have deluded myself into believing it is possible to imprison the Son of God. I was bitterly mistaken in this belief, which I no longer want. The Son of God must be forever free. He is as God created him, and not what I would make of him. He is where God would have him be, and not where I thought to hold him prisoner.

This is a theme that becomes prominent later in the workbook: Lessons 94, 110, 162, and Review VI. If we are as God created us, everything the ego and its world have taught us is false. Their "light" deceived us, and once we recognize it was *self*-deceiving we can do something about it by choosing differently, leaving the world of darkness forever and returning the world of light—"where God would have us be"—to our awareness.

(3:1) (33) There is another way of looking at the world.

(3:2-3) Since the purpose of the world is not the one I ascribed to it, there must be another way of looking at it. I see everything upside down, and my thoughts are the opposite of truth.

In order to be able to look at the world "another way," a key statement in *A Course in Miracles*, we need the humility to admit we are wrong. It is always helpful to be vigilant, to realize how stubbornly we insist we are right, not only in the blatant ways of believing the separation is real, but in the subtle and everyday ways of being so certain our perceptions of others are correct.

(3:4-6) I see the world as a prison for God's Son. It must be, then, that the world is really a place where he can be set free. I would look upon the world as it is, and see it as a place where the Son of God finds his freedom.

Clearly the reference here is not to the world itself, but to our *perceptions* of the world; and even more to the point, the *purpose* we have given it. If we have given the world the purpose of imprisoning us, it will do so. If, on the other hand, we have given it the purpose of forgiveness and release, we are free. We shall return to this important theme presently. For now we can remember that the shift in purpose entails a shift in teachers, therein shifting our perception of the world from a prison of guilt to a classroom of forgiveness.

(4:1) (34) I could see peace instead of this.

(4:2-4) When I see the world as a place of freedom, I realize that it reflects the laws of God instead of the rules I made up for it to obey. I will understand that peace, not war, abides in it. And I will perceive that peace also abides in the hearts of all who share this place with me.

This refers to the real world, which we shall discuss in much greater depth later. Suffice it to say for now that it reflects the oneness of reality by enabling us to see all members of the Sonship—*without exception*—as sharing the common goal of leaving the prison house of war for the place of peace that abides in *all* people. Thus we shift our purpose from guilt to peace, imprisonment to freedom.

(5:1-2) (35) My mind is part of God's. I am very holy.

(5:3-5) As I share the peace of the world with my brothers, I begin to understand that this peace comes from deep within myself. The world I look upon has taken on the light of my forgiveness, and shines forgiveness back at me. In this light I begin to see what my illusions about myself kept hidden.

This is also an important theme, especially in the manual (e.g., M-in.1-3): Teaching others is how we learn. The more I let go of my grievances against you, teaching there is another way of thinking, the more I reinforce that idea in myself. In this light of forgiveness I see what my illusions kept hidden. As we have seen, forgiveness consists of joining with Jesus, our together holding the lamp that shines in the darkness of our minds, exposing the ego's illusions to the light of truth (T-11.V.1). Forgiveness lifts the veils of the ego's defensive system, allowing us to see the love that is really there. By withdrawing the projections of guilt's darkness from you, I reflect the willingness to withdraw my investment in the darkness in me. Thus do illusions give way to the light of truth, and peace dawns upon a mind that had heretofore believed in conflict.

(5:6) I begin to understand the holiness of all living things, including myself, and their oneness with me.

This is what lies underneath the ego's belief we are children of separation, specialness, guilt, and fear. It is this constellation of unholiness that has become the cover for our inherent holiness as children of love; a holiness shared by *all* "living things," including ourselves. We can therefore equate unholiness with separation, and holiness with oneness.

LESSON 58

These ideas are for review today:

This next series of lessons is about our holiness, the other side of our minds that is kept hidden by the ego and the unholiness of its thought system.

(1:1) (36) My holiness envelops everything I see.

(1:2) From my holiness does the perception of the real world come.

When we make the internal shift and identify with Jesus' love instead of the ego's hate, his love extends through us. We may perceive the exact same world—the dream in *form* does not necessarily change—but now it is perceived through the love that is within ourselves. This marks the birth of true compassion. We do not feel sorry for people's bodies, but for the real source of their pain: the belief they are orphaned and will never return home. In that compassionate vision are *all* people recognized as sharing the same suffering.

(1:3-5) Having forgiven, I no longer see myself as guilty. I can accept the innocence that is the truth about me. Seen through understanding eyes, the holiness of the world is all I see, for I can picture only the thoughts I hold about myself.

This is a succinct summary of forgiveness: We first shift our perception so that by looking differently at another's sin—recognizing it is but a projection of a belief about ourselves—we accept the illusory nature of the ego's thought system of separation and attack. This allows the innocence of the Atonement to return to our awareness and then become the basis of our new perception of the world.

Innocent or true perception is all-inclusive, as we now see:

(2:1) (37) My holiness blesses the world.

(2:2-5) The perception of my holiness does not bless me alone. Everyone and everything I see in its light shares in the joy it brings to me. There is nothing that is apart from this joy, because there is nothing that does not share my holiness. As I recognize my holiness, so does the holiness of the world shine forth for everyone to see.

We are not only one in the ego thought system, we are also one in the Holy Spirit's. With this recognition, born of our new perception, is the ego's belief in separation undone by the vision of Christ that embraces the Sonship (and thus the world) with its holiness. If our vision is not all-inclusive, it is not vision. By excluding even one part of the Sonship, the Whole is excluded as well, and so we can never remember we are God's Son. That is why Jesus gives us these words as a reminder:

> To your tired eyes I bring a vision of a different world, so new and clean and fresh you will forget the pain and sorrow that you saw before. Yet this a vision is which you must share with everyone you see, for otherwise you will behold it not. To give this gift is how to make it yours. And God ordained, in loving kindness, that it be for you (T-31.VIII.8:4-7).

(3:1) (38) There is nothing my holiness cannot do.

(3:2-3) My holiness is unlimited in its power to heal, because it is unlimited in its power to save. What is there to be saved from except illusions?

We are not saved from the world, nor from some terrible fate, and we do not save the world for other people. We are saved from our misthoughts, the mistakes coming from having chosen the ego instead of the Holy Spirit. That has nothing to do with the world, but everything to do with our illusory thoughts. Again, it is a salvation that heals as *one*, because there is only *one* illusion in *one* Son.

(3:4-6) And what are all illusions except false ideas about myself? My holiness undoes them all by asserting the truth about me. In the presence of my holiness, which I share with God Himself, all idols vanish.

Again and again we see Jesus returning to this central point: Our misperceptions are caused by the *one* misperception of ourselves—we are not as God created us. When this *one* misthought is healed, all the ego's mistaken images—the idols of specialness—are undone as well: *one* problem, *one* misperception of unholiness; *one* solution, *one* vision of holiness.

(4:1) (39) My holiness is my salvation.

(4:2-3) Since my holiness saves me from all guilt, recognizing my holiness is recognizing my salvation. It is also recognizing the salvation of the world.

Jesus' symphonic theme continues, in an almost endless series of wonderful variations. The *one* problem of guilt disappears in the *one* solution of holiness, which causes all problems to disappear as well. Thus is my perception of myself healed and saved, as well as my perception of the world, which has never left its source in my mind.

(4:4-5) Once I have accepted my holiness, nothing can make me afraid. And because I am unafraid, everyone must share in my understanding, which is the gift of God to me and to the world.

The source of *all* fear is our having chosen the unholiness of our separate individuality instead of the holiness of the oneness of God's Son. Since minds are joined, acceptance of my holiness reminds others to make the same choice. This does not mean that everyone *will* make that choice now. However, it does mean that in my holiness I recognize the choice has *already* happened because the separation has been undone. *When* that choice is accepted throughout the Sonship is only a matter of time.

(5:1) (40) I am blessed as a Son of God.

(5:2-8) Herein lies my claim to all good and only good. I am blessed as a Son of God. All good things are mine, because God intended them for me. I cannot suffer any loss or deprivation or pain because of Who I am. My Father supports me, protects me, and directs me in all things. His care for me is infinite, and is with me forever. I am eternally blessed as His Son.

All loss, deprivation, and pain arise because we have forgotten who we are. That is the problem, without exception, which is why there is no order of difficulty in miracles (T-1.I.1:1). When we drop Jesus' hand and take the ego's instead, we are automatically in pain. Following the ego's strategy to protect our wrong decision, we put a gap between the cause of the pain and our experience of it, and think we understand its source—the world, our special partner, our bodies, our food, or whatever—and thus are never able to recognize the real cause in our minds. When we at last come to our senses and realize our mistake, we return to the thought of Atonement that reflects our true Self, an Identity that is perfectly safe because It is beyond all thoughts of pain and loss. Awakening from the ego's dream of suffering, we are home with the God we never truly left.

LESSON 59

The following ideas are for review today:

In Lesson 59 we again find the theme of who we are as God's Son, and the wonderful and wondrous effects of coming to understand and accept its truth.

(1:1) (41) God goes with me wherever I go.

(1:2-7)) How can I be alone when God always goes with me? How can I be doubtful and un-sure of myself when perfect certainty abides in Him? How can I be disturbed by anything when He rests in me in absolute peace? How can I suffer when love and joy surround me through Him? Let me not cherish illusions about my self. I am perfect because God goes with me wherever I go.

It is not that God literally walks with us. Rather, Jesus teaches that God is with us because His Love is in our minds, which is where we are. It is this Love—our Self—that is the basis for undoing the thought of separation: the home of all illusions of suffering and pain.

All that is needed for this Love to return to awareness is calling upon the power of our minds to choose, one of *A Course in Miracles*' most impor-tant themes, to which we now turn:

(2:1-2) (42) God is my strength. Vision is His gift.

(2:3-6) Let me not look to my own eyes to see today. Let me be willing to exchange my pitiful illusion of seeing for the vision that is given by God. Christ's vision is His gift, and He has given it to me. Let me call upon this gift today, so that this day may help me to understand eternity.

We always have a choice about the thought sys-tem with which we identify, made possible once we remember that our feelings of dis-ease and distur-bance emanate from the mind's mistaken choice, and from nowhere else. Thus do we exchange the ego's misperceptions for the vision of Christ, exclu-sion for unity, separation for forgiveness, and time for eternity.

(3:1-2) (43) God is my Source. I cannot see apart from Him.

(3:3-7) I can see what God wants me to see. I cannot see anything else. Beyond His Will lie only illusions. It is these I choose when I think I can see apart from Him. It is these I choose when I try to see through the body's eyes.

Again, all misperceptions stem from the illusory belief we can be apart from God; the Idea of God's Son, which we are, can leave its Source. Thus does our thought of separation give rise to a world of separation, which we believe is there because we believe we see it. The body's eyes have now re-placed vision, a substitution that remains in place until we change our minds.

(3:8-9) Yet the vision of Christ has been given me to replace them. It is through this vision that I choose to see.

A Course in Miracles has as its purpose the change in mind that allows *vision* to replace the ego's *seeing*. This vision cannot come unless we make a choice that says: I have been thinking and perceiving wrongly. I know there is another way, because there has to be another way of feeling. I am not happy, and want to be at peace. I therefore let go of my investment in being right. Thus does our de-sire for true peace and happiness become the moti-vation for choosing vision to replace illusions.

(4:1) (44) God is the light in which I see.

(4:2-4) I cannot see in darkness. God is the only light. Therefore, if I am to see, it must be through Him.

As the text reminds us: "Vision [or light] or judg-ment [darkness] is your choice, but never both of these" (T-20.V.4:7). We choose one or the other, and in our right-minded choice is all the world made free.

(4:5-7) I have tried to define what seeing is, and I have been wrong. Now it is given me to under-stand that God is the light in which I see. Let me welcome vision and the happy world it will show me.

I have to realize I have been wrong about everything I see, and everything I think I understand. How often does Jesus remind us of this happy fact; happy indeed when we are not identified with the ego's stubborn insistence that it is right and God is wrong. This happy acceptance of the truth is the birthplace of our humility, leading to Christ's vision that blesses the world along with me.

The lesson closes with a return to the thought of Oneness, which undoes the world because it undoes the separated mind:

(5:1) (45) God is the Mind with which I think.

(5:2-4) I have no thoughts I do not share with God. I have no thoughts apart from Him, because I have no mind apart from His. As part of His Mind, my thoughts are His and His Thoughts are mine.

Remember, the ego system is born of the idea that our thoughts are our own, God's thoughts are His, and never the twain shall meet. Not only that, we tell God what His thoughts are. This insane arrogance forms the basis of the second law of chaos (T-23.II.4-6), wherein God becomes as insane as we:

> The arrogance on which the laws of chaos stand could not be more apparent than emerges here. Here is a principle that would define what the Creator of reality must be; what He must think and what He must believe; and how He must respond, believing it. It is not seen as even necessary that He be asked about the truth of what has been established for His belief. His Son can tell Him this, and He has but the choice whether to take his word for it or be mistaken (T-23.II.6:1-4).

The insanity of such a belief is easily corrected once we recognize its sheer madness. The clouds of separation quickly disperse in this return to sanity, and we rejoice in the Oneness of Love that has never been changed, and which remains as the Thought of our Self, at one with the Sonship and the Mind of God.

LESSON 60

These ideas are for today's review:

This final lesson returns to forgiveness, the central theme in Jesus' symphony of love and truth.

(1:1) (46) God is the Love in which I forgive.

(1:2-3) God does not forgive because He has never condemned. The blameless cannot blame, and those who have accepted their innocence see nothing to forgive.

The fact that God does not forgive becomes the basis for our forgiveness in the dream. Forgiveness is necessary only as the correction for condemnation. When judgment of ourselves is withdrawn, our judgment of others is withdrawn as well: the *idea* of judgment can never leave its *source*. We are thus asked by Jesus to accept our past mistakes, thereby accepting the light-filled innocence that rests in peace just beyond the darkness of our belief in sin. With condemnation gone, nothing remains to forgive.

(1:4-6) Yet forgiveness is the means by which I will recognize my innocence. It is the reflection of God's Love on earth. It will bring me near enough to Heaven that the Love of God can reach down to me and raise me up to Him.

That is the problem: We do not want to be lifted up to Heaven, for then our individuality disappears. Recognizing our innocence allows us to realize how sinful and guilty we believed we were, because we wanted to be apart from God. Seeing the pain that has resulted from such a belief, we can make the choice for sanity. No longer afraid of God's *last step*, which ends the process that our decision to forgive our brother began, we allow His Love to lift us back from earth to Heaven.

Another important theme in these five lessons, not to mention throughout *A Course in Miracles*, is that we do not forgive on our own, as we now see:

(2:1) (47) God is the strength in which I trust.

(2:2-3) It is not my own strength through which I forgive. It is through the strength of God in me, which I am remembering as I forgive.

I am not the one who forgives you. I can only ask the Holy Spirit for help in looking at you differently, because the way I am looking at you now is not making me happy. The bottom line is recognizing there are painful effects of my choosing to be right, selfish, and special. I thus lay aside the weakness of my petty strength, choosing instead the strength of Christ that is restored to my awareness through forgiveness.

(2:4-6) As I begin to see, I recognize His reflection on earth. I forgive all things because I feel the stirring of His strength in me. And I begin to remember the Love I chose to forget, but which has not forgotten me.

The problem again is simply that we have forgotten. Yet forgetting is active. We have chosen to forget because we wanted to remember the weakness of our individuality instead of Christ's strength. However, forgetting our Identity did not destroy it. Our Self merely waited for us to change our minds, effected by our change of perception: from judgment to vision, weakness to strength.

Paragraph 3 returns us to the real world:

(3:1) (48) There is nothing to fear.

(3:2-4) How safe the world will look to me when I can see it! It will not look anything like what I imagine I see now. Everyone and everything I see will lean toward me to bless me.

Once we choose the place of perfect safety in our minds, represented by Jesus, the world we experience outside will be its mirror. It cannot *not* be that way, since *ideas leave not their source*. The beauty of this forgiven world is reflected in this lovely passage from the text:

> Can you imagine how beautiful those you forgive will look to you? In no fantasy have you ever seen anything so lovely. Nothing you see here, sleeping or waking, comes near to such loveliness. And nothing will you value like unto this, nor hold so dear. Nothing that you remember that made your heart sing with joy has ever brought you even a little part of the happiness this sight will bring you. For you

will see the Son of God. You will behold the beauty the Holy Spirit loves to look upon, and which He thanks the Father for. He was created to see this for you, until you learned to see it for yourself. And all His teaching leads to seeing it and giving thanks with Him.

This loveliness is not a fantasy. It is the real world, bright and clean and new, with everything sparkling under the open sun. Nothing is hidden here, for everything has been forgiven and there are no fantasies to hide the truth (T-17.II.1:1–2:3).

Recalling this beauty will help us choose again when we are tempted to make real the ego's ugly world of specialness.

Note the usage of "everyone" and "everything" in 3:4 to describe our vision. If anyone or anything is excluded from the light of safety, all the world is plunged in darkness, the shadow of our mind's darkened thoughts of guilt.

(3:5-6) I will recognize in everyone my dearest Friend. What could there be to fear in a world that I have forgiven, and that has forgiven me?

This is the vision of Christ, in which the entire Sonship is perceived through the eyes of holiness. Not one aspect of the Son is excluded, and with separation gone, so is all fear, which had been the inevitable result of our belief in sin and guilt. This vision is nicely captured in the opening lines in Helen's very first poem, "The Gifts of Christmas":

> Christ passes no one by. By this you know
> He is God's Son. You recognize His touch
> In universal gentleness. His Love
> Extends to everyone. His eyes behold
> The Love of God in everything He sees.
> *(The Gifts of God,* p. 95)

With such love beside and within us, fear is impossible; its place taken by the love forgiveness brings.

(4:1) (49) God's Voice speaks to me all through the day.

(4:2-3) There is not a moment in which God's Voice ceases to call on my forgiveness to save me. There is not a moment in which His Voice fails to direct my thoughts, guide my actions and lead my feet.

As I had mentioned when we did Lesson 49, this does not mean we *hear* His Voice all through the day; it simply means He is *calling* to us throughout the day. This is the Call we fervently and ferociously try to conceal—the purpose of the world we have made; the purpose of our specialness thoughts of attack, judgment, and desire. These are easily set aside when we decide we no longer wish to hear the ego's raucous shrieking. The stunning yet gentle silence of God's Voice returns in the instant we wish to hear its sound, and *only* its sound. Thus does God's sweet song of love extend all through the dream, guiding our thoughts, words, and deeds.

(4:4-5) I am walking steadily on toward truth. There is nowhere else I can go, because God's Voice is the only Voice and the only Guide that has been given to His Son.

There is nothing else. Any other pathway we choose is nothing and leads nowhere, because it comes from a voice that does not exist. The loveliness of this recognition is described in these beautiful closing paragraphs in "The Real Alternative," which reminds us that as a Thought of God we have never left our Source; the road back to Him undoes the road that never existed in reality:

> He has not left His Thoughts! But you forgot His Presence and remembered not His Love. No pathway in the world can lead to Him, nor any worldly goal be one with His. What road in all the world will lead within, when every road was made to separate the journey from the purpose it must have unless it be but futile wandering? All roads that lead away from what you are will lead you to confusion and despair. Yet has He never left His Thoughts to die, without their Source forever in themselves.
>
> He has not left His Thoughts! He could no more depart from them than they could keep Him out. In unity with Him do they abide, and in Their Oneness Both are kept complete. There is no road that leads away from Him. A journey from yourself does not exist. How foolish and insane it is to think that there could be a road with such an aim! Where could it go? And how could you be made to travel on it, walking there without your own reality at one with you?
>
> Forgive yourself your madness, and forget all senseless journeys and all goal-less aims.

They have no meaning. You can not escape from what you are. For God is merciful, and did not let His Son abandon Him. For what He is be thankful, for in that is your escape from madness and from death. Nowhere but where He is can you be found. There *is* no path that does not lead to Him (T-31.IV.9-11).

And finally, the symphonic movement that is this review ends with a return to its central theme; the cycle of love concluding with the love and wisdom with which it began:

(5:1) (50) I am sustained by the Love of God.

(5:2-4) As I listen to God's Voice, I am sustained by His Love. As I open my eyes, His Love lights up the world for me to see. As I forgive, His Love reminds me that His Son is sinless.

And who is His Son? I am. Since we are all one, when I realize my sinlessness I realize everyone is sinless, too. It cannot *not* be, if God's Love *is* His Love.

(5:5) And as I look upon the world with the vision He has given me, I remember that I am His Son.

Jesus ends this movement of his symphony with the attainment of our ultimate goal. The way we reach the vision of the real world is by paying careful attention to the external world, so it can teach us that the *outside* mirrors the *inside*. The pain of our experience as bodies, interacting with other bodies, becomes the motivation to cry out for the other way, the other Teacher. Thus we come to change our minds, choose the Holy Spirit's Thought as the source of our seeing, and look out upon a world through Christ's vision. The real world greets our sight, and we finally remember Who we are as God's one Son, gladly exclaiming these words from Part II of the workbook:

Be glad today! Be glad! There is no room for anything but joy and thanks today. Our Father has redeemed His Son this day. Not one of us but will be saved today. Not one who will remain in fear, and none the Father will not gather to Himself, awake in Heaven in the Heart of Love (W-pII.340.2).

Thus we end this heavenly movement with a happy thought of Oneness, the thought that ends the nightmare dream of illusion and joyfully awakens us to the remembrance of our Father's Love.

Complete Index of References to *A Course in Miracles*

TEXT

TEXT (continued)

TEXT (continued)

TEXT (continued)

TEXT (continued)

TEXT (continued)

TEXT (continued)

TEXT (continued)

TEXT (continued)

TEXT (continued)

TEXT (continued)

TEXT (continued)

TEXT (continued)

TEXT (continued)

TEXT (continued)

TEXT (continued)

TEXT (continued)

WORKBOOK FOR STUDENTS

WORKBOOK FOR STUDENTS (continued)

WORKBOOK FOR STUDENTS (continued)

MANUAL FOR TEACHERS

MANUAL FOR TEACHERS (continued)

CLARIFICATION OF TERMS

PSYCHOTHERAPY: PURPOSE, PROCESS AND PRACTICE

THE SONG OF PRAYER

* *

THE GIFTS OF GOD

THE GIFTS OF GOD (continued)

THE GIFTS OF GOD (continued)

* *

ABSENCE FROM FELICITY

APPENDIX

On Doing the Workbook
Excerpts from "The Workbook of *A Course in Miracles*:
Its Place in the Curriculum • Theory and Practice"

CONTENTS

1. The Place of the Workbook in the Curriculum of *A Course in Miracles*

One of the major mistakes many students of *A Course in Miracles* make, often occurring relatively early in their work but just as often extending beyond that, is to confuse the workbook with the Course itself. Many years ago, my wife Gloria and I did a ten-city speaking tour of Australia, and very often people would tell us how they had been working with the Course for two, three, or four years. Through subsequent conversations with them, it became obvious that they really had very little understanding of what the Course was saying. We discovered that what they meant by saying they had been students was that they had done the workbook, and they somehow thought that was the Course. Quite frequently over the years as well, we have heard people say, "Oh, I know about *A Course in Miracles*; I did it last year," and what they typically meant was that they did the workbook.

The workbook is not *A Course in Miracles*. It is simply one part of the curriculum, and is certainly not the Course's theoretical teaching. Right at the beginning, Jesus says that studying the text is necessary to make the workbook lessons meaningful. If you want to know what *A Course in Miracles* says and what it teaches, then the text is where you need to go, not the workbook. I will give numerous examples to illustrate that. In fact, up until the time the Course was published, whenever Helen, Bill, and I would speak about the text, we would always refer to it as "the Course," and the workbook we simply called "the workbook." I remember sitting with Helen on her couch just prior to the Course's publication and saying to her that we really could not do that anymore, because the three books were clearly labeled "text," "workbook," and "teachers' manual." It was always clear to us, however, that the heart of the Course's teaching was found in the text. If you want to know what the workbook is saying in terms of presenting *A Course in Miracles*, then you must first understand what the text is saying. That does not mean you have to work with the text before working with the workbook. The end of the teachers' manual makes it clear that it does not matter which book you do first (M-29.1).

Thus, just as a cautionary note, do not confuse what the workbook says with what *A Course in Miracles* teaches. The purpose of the workbook, as the Introduction states, is "to train your mind to think along the lines that the text sets forth" (W-in.1:4). The workbook is the mind-training program. Often I like to refer to it as the laboratory. You may recall that in college when you took a course in chemistry, biology, or physics, there were classes taught by the professor who gave homework assignments, and then there were laboratory sessions that were part of the course itself. These lab sessions were where you put into practice what you had learned in the classes. The lab in itself would not be sufficient to teach you the subject matter of the course. It was an integral part of the course, but it was not a substitute for what the professor taught or the textbook presented. Similarly, it would be a mistake to isolate the workbook from the text. There are several places in the workbook, including the Introduction, where Jesus makes it clear that the workbook is the application of the theoretical principles presented in the text (see, for example, W-pI.39.1,2; W-pI.132.5:3,4; W-pI.161.6:2).

One of the important points the text helps us to understand, implied in the workbook but not specifically stated there, is that part of the ego's plan to keep us separated from God and our true Identity as Christ is to convince us we are mindless. If we are mindless, then we obviously do not know we have a mind, and since the ego rests in the mind, as does the Holy Spirit, we have no way of accessing the problem (the belief in the ego thought system), and certainly no way of gaining access to the solution (the Holy Spirit's forgiveness) that undoes the problem.

The purpose of the workbook, then, is to train us to know that we do have a mind, and that our thoughts are important. Most important of all is that we have a choice. This is one of the most important themes of *A Course in Miracles*, a major theme throughout the text, and the basis for the workbook: we have a choice whether to listen to the voice of the wrong mind (the ego), or to listen to the Voice of our right minds (the Holy Spirit). Thus, one of the major purposes of the workbook is to train our minds to think that way and understand we have a choice. Without the background and the theory the text provides, the exercises of the workbook will make no sense. Again, this does not mean that we cannot do the workbook as a learning exercise. In fact, we are urged to do that whether we understand what the workbook is teaching or not, but we will not benefit from the full curriculum of the Course without understanding that the intellectual context of the workbook is the text.

2. Cautions and Guidelines

The Use of Language: Form and Content

There are a number of cautions I would like to mention at the beginning, which, if not heeded, can lead students astray, resulting in their misunderstanding what the Course is teaching. One caution has to do with the workbook's use of language. As you may have heard me say other times, Jesus is not always consistent in his use of language. Words are used one way in one part of the Course, and another way in other parts. He is always strictly consistent, of course, with the content or meaning, but the forms in which this content is expressed are not always consistent.

This is particularly true in the workbook. One clear example is that often when Jesus uses the term *God* he really is speaking of the Holy Spirit. One of the clearest examples of that is in Lesson 193, "All things are lessons God would have me learn." At the beginning of that lesson, Jesus makes it very clear that God does not teach, and does not know about learning because learning occurs only within a split, dualistic mind. God is a Mind of perfect unity, and our Identity as His Son as Christ shares in that perfect Oneness. Therefore there is no teaching or learning in Heaven, which means there could be no teaching or learning in this world coming from God. What Jesus really means in that lesson is that all things are lessons the Holy Spirit would have us learn, because it is the Holy Spirit Who is consistently, in all three books, referred to as our Teacher. God is not our Teacher. Again, our Creator does not know about teaching and about His Son needing to learn.

The two earlier lessons, "God is in everything I see" and "God is in everything I see because God is in my mind" (W-pI.29, 30), are not lessons in pantheism or that God is present in our split mind. It is the *purpose of God* that is in our split mind, as Lesson 29 makes clear. This purpose, which is held there by the Holy Spirit, is that we forgive. That then becomes another way of understanding that everything we perceive in this world can serve the holy purpose of reminding us of Who we truly are and that we are really not here at all, even though the lesson itself says "God is in everything I see because God is in my mind."

There are many other examples of this in the workbook. Another lesson specifically says we should ask God to tell us what to do (W-pI.71.9), even though a later workbook lesson says that God does not know what we ask, for He does not hear our prayers (W-pI.183.7). In the section from the teachers' manual "What Is the Role of Words in Healing?" (M-21), Jesus again makes it very clear that God does not hear words, because words were made to separate us from Him. What makes us understand each other, what makes words *words* is the fact that we live in a dualistic world. In Heaven there are no words because there is only one "sound," if you will; the "sound" of Love that has no sound, form, or melody. God does not know about words, hear words, or answer prayers because to do so would make the illusion real.

Why, then, does Jesus tell us we should ask God? Why does he spend all of Part II of the workbook, Lessons 221 through 360, giving us prayers to say to God the Father, even though he tells us elsewhere that the Creator does not even know about us? The answer is that *A Course in Miracles* is speaking about listening to the Holy Spirit, Who throughout the Course is described as God's Voice. Notice that never is the Holy Spirit called the Voice *of* God. He is always called the Voice *for* God. Jesus was very clear about that with Helen (a few times Helen miswrote Voice *of* God) because God does not have a voice. It is the Holy Spirit Who is described as the Voice that speaks *for* God, even though He is not God's Voice literally. Nonetheless, we are repeatedly called upon, especially in the workbook, to ask God for help. And again, in Lesson 71 we are asked specifically to ask our Father what we should do, and then silently wait for His answer.

In other words, we should not take what the Course says literally in terms of form, because if we do, we will find so many inconsistencies that we will be tempted to throw the book away. We need to learn that Jesus was not hung up with form. That, among other things, drove Helen crazy, because she was very much concerned with form. Everything had to be just right and consistent. It was quite clear to her that this was an ego thing, and that was not how *A Course in Miracles* was meant to be.

In summary, then, on the level of form, you can find dozens upon dozens of inconsistencies and conflicting statements, but not on the level of content. It is extremely important that you be aware of this when you work with the workbook. If you are starting out with the Course and beginning with the workbook, the chances are that you are not going to notice this or even think about it. But as your work with the Course deepens over years, it will probably become clear to you that its words should not always be taken literally. Many of these statements are to be taken as metaphors and, specifically, metaphors that are meant to meet us in the dualistic world we think we inhabit. This leads me to the next important point, the Holy Spirit, which will lead us more into the theory of the Course.

The Holy Spirit: Friend, Not Enemy

One of the key elements in the ego thought system—the element, in fact, that directly leads to the making of the physical universe—is that the Holy Spirit is our enemy, not to mention the One for Whom He speaks. This belief is the inevitable result of our guilt, which comes from the belief that we have sinned against our Creator, having stolen His reality, power, and Mind; indeed, have stolen His very life. All this has rendered the Almighty lifeless, meaning that our existence has been built on His moribund corpse. Sin is all about our having committed this horrific act, with guilt the equally horrific result. This in turn set into motion the terrifying thought that now God will rise from the grave and destroy us. The fourth and final obstacle to peace is the fear of God, the fear of His wrath that the ego tells us is inevitable. To avoid that wrath, we left the mind and made the cosmos in which to hide. The thought of sin is buried in our minds, and the purpose of the world and body is to protect us from this thought that means our certain destruction. Mindlessness, therefore, is the ego's premier defense and its salvation.

Experiencing ourselves in this world as physical and psychological beings, we are not in touch with the devastating thought that rests in the bottom of our minds. The ego tells us that if we ever go within, a maniacally vengeful God will be there, ready to pounce and destroy us, taking back the life we stole from Him. This means that we will no longer have life, which is the meaning of death in the ego system: punishment for sin.

To avoid this horrific end, we made the world and made ourselves mindless. The thought that underlies our identification with this world, our investment in it and preoccupation with the body as sick or well, happy or sad, is the terror that if we return to the mind, divesting from the body, God will get us for He is our eternal Enemy. The Holy Spirit, therefore, must also be our enemy since within our dream of separation, He speaks for God. This insane thought upholds the universe and our existence within it.

An essential part of the mind-training program, therefore, is to teach us there is another way of looking at the Holy Spirit. We have first to be taught that there is indeed a Holy Spirit, a loving Presence of God's Love in our minds. It is helpful to think of God's Voice as the memory of our Source that we took with us into our dream when we fell asleep and began to dream the terrible nightmare of sin, guilt, and fear: stealing from God, being overwhelmed by our self-hatred, and fearful of the punishment we believe will come from Him. The correction for this horror is the memory of Who we truly are as God's Child. Yet this memory has been buried in the mind, as has the thought of sin, guilt, and fear. And so we have to be taught that there is a mind, and that it contains the thoughts of separation *and* Atonement, that Thought being the Holy Spirit's forgiveness.

Since the workbook is the mind-training vehicle of the Course, an essential part of the workbook is to teach us that there is indeed a Holy Spirit present within us, and that He is our Friend and not our enemy. Not only is the Holy Spirit our Friend, but

His Source, God Himself, is our Friend. It is always helpful to keep in mind that Jesus, our elder brother, speaks to us as if we were little children because spiritually we are. No matter how old we think we are chronologically, or mature socially, physically, and psychologically, on a spiritual level we are barely infants. Lovingly and gently, then, our teacher speaks to us on the level we can understand.

The key thought that anchors us in this world of illusion is that if God ever finds us He will destroy us; if the Holy Spirit finds us He will deceive us; if we take Jesus' hand he will lead us to oblivion. This is why we need a mind-training program that teaches that They are all our Friends; indeed, our only Friends. Therefore, there is the emphasis in the workbook on speaking to the Holy Spirit. Recall Lesson 49, "God's Voice speaks to me all through the day." If you were raised in the Jewish tradition, you were taught that the last time God spoke was to the prophet, Malachi. If you were brought up as a Protestant or Catholic, you were taught that the last time God really spoke was when He "wrote" the Bible. There may be some special people who, by virtue of their specialness, feel that God speaks to them, but then He does not speak to anyone else.

In light of this, one of the purposes of the workbook is to teach us that this is not the case. God does not play favorites for there is no specialness in Heaven, unlike this world that was born of specialness. God speaks to all of us the same way because we are all the same. We are all one with Him. A major focus of the workbook is to have us recognize that there is indeed this Presence of the Holy Spirit in our minds, a loving Presence, a Presence that cares about us. Just as an older brother would comfort a younger sibling who is terrified of a wrathful parent, so Jesus comforts us, his beloved siblings, who are also terrified of a wrathful Parent. Yet it is a wrathful Parent we made up, and so he teaches us, as an older brother would teach a younger brother or sister: "Don't be upset. Daddy is not angry with you. He loves you. Daddy is not going to punish you, which means that you can place your future in his hands. You can ask Daddy what to do and He will tell you. You can ask Daddy's Voice what to do, and He will tell you." And so on. Again, there are many places in the Course where Jesus makes it clear that God does not even know about us, but that is not helpful to those just starting to make their way home.

One very impressive aspect of *A Course in Miracles* is that it is written on many different levels at the same time. No matter where we are on the spiritual ladder of Atonement, at the beginning or near the top, we will find something in it that will help us. The teachings in the Course that God does not know about our individual existence, let alone speak to us, that He does not know about a world that does not exist—all these belong near the journey's end. Most of us are not close to that, and therefore we need a teaching that meets us where we are on the ladder.

To reiterate, while there is nothing in *A Course in Miracles* that dictates when one should do the workbook, in general the idea is that students do the workbook relatively early in their work with the Course. This is not an absolute rule, and if you feel personally guided to do it differently, or to do it upside down or backwards, that is what you should do. Nonetheless, I think it safe to say that because of how the Course is written, including the training exercises, the workbook typically should be done at a reasonably early stage in one's journey with the Course.

It must be recognized that there is a strong emphasis in the Course on seeing God and the Holy Spirit as involved with us, that our Teacher sends us situations or people, or sends us to people, even though in reality He does no such thing. Since everything is in our minds, meaning there is literally no world outside our thoughts, one of the central thrusts of the early lessons, why would the Holy Spirit do things in the world? Yet Jesus says that in many places, especially in the workbook, because that is frequently our experience. Yet our unconscious egos have us believe that the Holy Spirit's activity in the world is punitive because of our guilt, and so we need a correction on that level that tells us: "Yes, the Holy Spirit is involved in your life, but it is a loving involvement. He is your Comforter, Friend, and Teacher, and He will not hurt you." It would not be helpful to us spiritual children, in a perpetual state of terror, even if we are unaware of it, to be told that the Holy Spirit is not involved in our world at all. That would terrify us even more. Imagine yourself as a small child being told by your older brother, Jesus, "It is not that Daddy is not angry at you; Daddy does not even know about you." Because this would not be a comforting statement, Jesus for the most part does not say that to us.

On occasion he does, but this is not the central focus of his teaching. When we are ready to hear the pristine, non-dualistic truth, we will suddenly realize what this course is really saying.

The Workbook Is Not the Course

This leads to another caution, which I mentioned at the beginning. Because the workbook is usually done relatively early in one's work with the Course—and we can define "relatively early" as from one to twenty-five years—one is apt to confuse the workbook with the Course. One is apt to think that because "God's Voice speaks to me all through the day" (W-pI.49), I *hear* God's Voice all through the day, forgetting the sobering line in the teachers' manual that says that "very few can hear God's Voice at all…" (M-12.3:3); forgetting, too, the important teachings we find much more in the text than in the other two books, that the Holy Spirit is not involved with effects (for example, T-27.VIII.9). He is not involved with the world, but with our thoughts. People are prone to work only with the workbook because it is easier to read and its message tends to be more positive than that of the text. There is, for example, nothing in the workbook on special relationships or the laws of chaos, and very few references to murder or hate. It is the text where these black-and-blue passages are found.

In summary, students often make the mistake of thinking the workbook is the heart of *A Course in Miracles*, while it is simply a one-year training program. At the end of the workbook are these disconcerting words, "This course is a beginning, not an end" (W-ep.1:1). It can be tempting to believe that when day 365 comes, the heavens will open up in welcome and the Holy Spirit will descend and place a medal on us proclaiming that we are now an advanced teacher of God and should go forth to save the world. And then we are disappointed to find that nothing happens.

One final observation: as a one-year training program, the workbook does not have to be done more than once, unless of course your internal guidance so directs you. Moreover, having "done it once" does not mean you cannot read it more than once. It is an extraordinary book, and is certainly worth reading and rereading. I should also note that the introductions are an important part of the workbook's pedagogy: the introduction to the workbook itself, as well as the introductions to the review lessons, and in Part II. In these introductions, Jesus speaks to us more directly about the nature and purpose of the workbook, and how to avoid falling into certain traps.

The Workbook: A Mind-training Program

Returning to the idea that the workbook is a mind-training program, we need to recognize that the mind that Jesus is retraining knows practically nothing. He continually refers to us as little children because little children do not understand the world. Contrary to many New Age teachings, Jesus does not see children as wise, quasi-angelic beings who are exemplars of wisdom, blessedness, and innocence. Quite the opposite. He sees children as demanding creatures needing to be taught, for they do not recognize the illusory nature of the world. Throughout his course, Jesus is the elder brother who teaches his very small siblings the nature of reality, distinguishing it from illusion. But as any loving teacher or brother, he teaches at the level we can understand, and so he talks to us *as if* there were a Holy Spirit or loving Father Who is directly involved with our physical lives. Identified with the ego, we do believe They are involved with us, but as a cruel Parent or Teacher Who would punish and destroy us. This is why this thought has to be gently corrected before it can be replaced. It upholds our stubborn insistence that the world and body are reality. It explains why so much of the Course, and the workbook in particular, is pitched at that level.

I cannot say this often enough: *this is a mind-training book*. Its purpose is to train our minds to think differently. Since we have thought wrongly about God, the role of the Holy Spirit, and ourselves, we need a correction. One more time, this is why Jesus speaks about God and the Holy Spirit as being specifically involved with us, but this is not the overall teaching of *A Course in Miracles*, which is found in the text. With very few exceptions, we do not find in the workbook the blood-curdling passages that describe the ugly nature of ego thought system.

I am stressing this point so that you will not confuse your work with the workbook with your work with *A Course in Miracles* as a whole. This is a lifetime's work, and as you read the text and plumb the depths of its teachings, as your experiences of forgiveness increase, you begin to get a glimpse of Jesus' true message, which is far more than you thought at first. So please do not take the workbook all by itself. It is a brilliant book, form and content, but it is not the sum and substance of the Course's teachings.

The Workbook As a Projective Test

Another aspect of the workbook that is helpful to see is that it is like a projective test. Projective tests are administered by psychologists to subjects or patients who are asked to project their own thoughts and perceptions onto various objects. The most famous of these is the Rorschach ink-blot test, a series of ten ink blots devised by the Swiss psychiatrist Herman Rorschach in the early twentieth century. His idea was to better understand how his patients perceived themselves and the world, and their relationship to it. His original monograph remains the best presentation of the test. Rorschach was not interested in studying pathology, but in how people in general perceived. He made hundreds of ink blots, and ultimately chose the ten he thought would work the best for his purpose. Some cards were black and white, while others had color. They were all essentially formless, and Rorschach was actually more interested in *how* the stimuli were seen (content), rather that *what* was seen (form).

The core idea of projective tests, therefore, is to present subjects with a stimulus and then see their responses. By analyzing these responses, the psychologist has a better idea of the subject's thought process. My point here is that we can look at our reactions to the workbook in the same way. The greatest value of going through the workbook exercises has nothing to do with the specific mind-training part of it, although that is clearly important. The true healing lies in our ability to monitor our responses to these exercises, as I will now explain.

The Compulsive Approach

We find that many students strive to do the workbook perfectly: "I am going to be the best Course student ever. I will do the workbook perfectly, obeying it to the letter. When Jesus says I should think of God six times an hour, I will do it!." Some students even purchase wrist alarm watches, the purpose being that when the hour strikes twelve or whatever, they will not forget to do their workbook lesson, totally missing what the workbook's mind training is about. Its purpose is to train our minds to *want* to think of God, to see Him and the Holy Spirit as our Friends so that we would want to spend time with Them, be with Them, and go to Them when we are in trouble. Yet our minds are not trained like that. To use an alarm to remind you defeats this purpose because you are actually circumventing this training.

Supporting this need to be perfect is the idea, whether conscious or not, that Jesus is sitting in Heaven with a score card keeping track of us, noting how many times we forget his holy word. We have to do his workbook perfectly so he will not be angry at us. This means we have fallen prey to the underlying thought I mentioned earlier, that God, the Holy Spirit, and Jesus are angry. Why? Because we are miserable sinners, having turned our backs on Their Love. And so, here is this holy book given us by Jesus, and we stand in terror that we are going to betray it, as we did God in the original instant. We will forget the holy sentence of the lesson's title, perhaps even forget there is a lesson. Many people who pride themselves on having good memories suddenly realize they have the beginnings of dementia because they cannot even remember one sentence. They can remember dozens of telephone numbers, but when it comes to five, six, or seven words, their minds are a blank.

It is this great fear of failing Love once again that leads many students to strive mightily to do the lessons perfectly. When you catch yourself falling into this trap, remember that the hidden premise is that you are a terrible sinner, and guilt is teaching you that if you are not careful, God will get you. To forestall His wrath, you strike a bargain with Him, which is nothing less than the specialness bargain we all made with our angry Father: if we behave correctly, are good little boys and girls (for example, do Jesus' workbook perfectly), He will see our goodness and innocence, have mercy and not punish us. This is what underlies the need for students to be perfectionists when it comes to the workbook.

We can see, then, how the workbook can be very useful as a projective technique or device. Watch yourself interact with the workbook, wanting to do it without mistake. Interestingly, many people come to the Course from fundamentalist or other strict religious backgrounds, where they were taught that if you do not perform God's rituals, He will punish you. Whether you were raised Jewish, Protestant, or Catholic, the idea was that if you did not do what God, the Bible, your rabbi, minister, or priest told you to do, God would be angry. Many people leave all that because they realize its insanity—that God does not think that way. Then they come to *A Course in Miracles* and transfer their old training and do the very same thing. They see the workbook as a series of rituals that must be performed religiously. Yet Jesus makes it very clear that ritual is not his focus. The workbook is indeed highly structured, but it is not meant to be approached as ritual or simply another series of *shoulds*.

Another form of this dynamic is deciding you will not move on to Lesson 2 until you do Lesson 1 perfectly. Many, many years ago, within the first year of the Course's publication in fact, a group of people who were working with the Course came one evening to my home to ask me questions. Among them was a very sincere and studious young man who proudly proclaimed to the group, including me, that he had been working with the workbook 28 days and was still on Lesson 1, but that he was going to get it absolutely perfect. Again, this misses the point of the mind training. It is that same mentality: "I have to get it just right." I assure you that if you could do Lesson 1 perfectly, you would not have to do the other 364 lessons and you would not have to study the text. You would not have to do anything with this course. Remember again that the workbook is meant for people starting out on the journey. Jesus is assuming we are very small children who are new to the ways of salvation, and so he is not expecting us to be perfect. He

makes it very clear in the workbook how undisciplined our minds really are.

Therefore, you do not have to do the lesson perfectly. As a general rule, I suggest that if you get through a day and feel that you did not do the lesson justice, you could perhaps spend another day or two, maximum, on that lesson and then move on. If by the third day or so you are still experiencing difficulty, the chances are there is a deep resistance in you. The worst thing you can do at that point is to fight against it. Simply assume there is something in that lesson that is frightening you and causing the block. The best thing, then, is to move on to the next lesson. Whatever that block is, you can be sure it will surface again, not only later in your work with the workbook, but years later in your work with the Course. You do not want to fight against this, and you do not have to do it perfectly.

Another issue that arises in this context is that we sometimes wonder whether a lesson is having any effect when we do not feel anything as we are doing it. There really is no way of ascertaining if it is helping us or not, because we are the last persons in the world who would know. This is what Jesus means in the text when he says, "Some of your greatest advances you have judged as failures, and some of your deepest retreats you have evaluated as success" (T-18.V.1:6). It is best not to try to evaluate your own work. Just do the best you can. What you want to learn from doing the workbook is that salvation is not a big deal, and that its undoing is soft and gentle. Otherwise you run the risk of making the error of the ego very real.

The Haphazard Approach

The other side of the coin has to do with people being totally haphazard with the workbook, skipping over lessons, doing a lesson any way they want to, or simply forgetting the lesson entirely. This is also an expression of fear and guilt. Compulsive people want to be perfect so that God will not be angry at them and will forgive them. The opposite side to the same coin of guilt is the magical hope of students that by forgetting about the workbook, God will forget about them: the same thought of sin, guilt, and fear of God's punishment, but in a different form. Therefore, the hope is that if they could put a fog around themselves in the workbook, not only will it protect them from the workbook's threat to their ego, but from God as well.

Not Judging Oneself

Again, what is most important is to watch yourself do the workbook without judgment, seeing how quickly you forget. When Jesus says to think of God every hour, watch how many hours go by without your thinking of Him. When he says to think of God six minutes every hour, watch how quickly those times go by without even a thought of the goal of your salvation. When the lesson says to start a day by spending fifteen minutes with God, note without judgment how quickly you allow the world to "be too much with you," "causing" you to forget, or if you don't, seeing how you watch the clock, waiting for the fifteen minutes to end.

If you could think of God throughout the day, I assure you *A Course in Miracles* is not for you; you are way beyond it. As a student of the Course, you should begin with the premise that God is the last Person you want to think of, the Holy Spirit is the last One you want to be your Teacher, and Jesus certainly is the last person in the world you ever want to connect with, because if you really wanted him to be with you all the time, he *would* be with you all the time. You would experience his love constantly, allowing this love to extend through you to everyone, without exception. And again, you would not need his course. Jesus is not expecting us to welcome him with open arms, nor to welcome his text or workbook. And he is certainly not expecting us to really believe that we are the one Child of the Father Who loves us. If we truly believed all this, we would not even be here.

Unresolved Issues with God, the Holy Spirit, Jesus

Remember, the thought that underlies the physical universe and our seeming existence in it is that God is going to catch up with us, dooming us to annihilation. If we believe God will get us, we certainly believe that the Holy Spirit is God's general, dispatched into the battleground of our minds to destroy us. The Holy Spirit's lessons, therefore, are not what we want to devote our time to, nor is He the One we want as our Teacher.

That is why we need a mind-training program that will discipline us to think differently, learning that we have a choice between seeing the Holy Spirit as our enemy or Friend. But we have to be taught that because we do not believe it. We can say that the purpose of the workbook is to teach us what we do not know. If you take a class in college, and on the very first day you tell the teacher that you do not have to read the assignments or attend the lab because you know everything, the teacher would be justified in asking what you are doing in the class. Well, Jesus would be justified in saying the same thing. If you believe that you can hear the Holy Spirit just like that, I assure you that you do not need this course, whose purpose is to help you understand how terrified you are of your Teacher, how much you hate Him because He represents the Love you believe you sinned against. Before you can get beyond this to the Love that you both have and are, you first must look at your ego thoughts about yourself, the Holy Spirit, and God. The workbook, then, is the help that begins this process of unlearning the ego thought system.

To say this another way, we need to observe ourselves in relationship to the workbook and see how we act out our specialness issues, just as we do with the people with whom we live and work. There is no difference. Practically everyone in the Western world, including most people who work with *A Course in Miracles*, has unresolved issues with Jesus. That is one reason his identity as the author of the Course is so manifest—it allows us to project onto him so we may let go of our guilt. In other words, almost everyone has an authority problem with Jesus. It would have to be that way because the world is the expression of our authority problem with God, to wit: "Who is the author of my reality: God or me?" If it is God, my ego is out of business and its thought system of separation is a lie. But if I am the author of my reality, that puts God out of the picture. It is one or the other. To escape from this idea that we usurped God's place on the throne is why we made this world, which becomes the embodiment of the authority problem. What follows from this is that if Jesus is a symbol in the Western world of God's Love, and we as students of the Course believe this course came from him, it stands to reason that we will act out with the author of the Course exactly what we act out with the Author of our reality.

There are a number of different ways in which we act out our authority problems. One is to kill the authority, and we have all done that in one way or the other. We might work with the Course and challenge what it says and argue with it. Or we may take what the Course says and change it. That is a more subtle way, so that the Course does not say what it says; it says what *we* say it says. If the authority says, "Do this workbook lesson and think of God five minutes of every hour," we can manifest our authority problem by not doing it five minutes of every hour, but four and a half, or two and a half, or skipping a few hours. This thumbs our noses at the authority, saying, "I will not submit to you. Don't tell me what I should do with my day." This obviously places us in great conflict, because there is another part of us that obviously respects the Course's authority, otherwise we would not be studying it. In turn, this puts us in conflict with ourselves in the sense that the part of us that truly knows this world is not our home also knows that we cannot leave this world without help, and that Jesus, specifically his course, represents that help. There is thus a part of us that wants that help, and a part that is at the same time terrified of that help.

We all share this conflict, and can learn to identify the conflict within ourselves by seeing how we deal with the workbook.

Another expression of the authority problem is to do exactly what the authority wants you to do. This is the aforementioned compulsive who will do the workbook perfectly. In this case, there is still the part that hates the authority, but is terrified of him. We hate him because he is stronger, more powerful, and wiser. There is another part of us that is even more afraid of the fact that he will punish us if we do not do the right thing, and therefore we had better do what he says. That is when *A Course in Miracles* becomes a religion, and we simply transfer all the rituals that we learned as children onto the workbook, which now becomes like the Bible, setting forth the rituals that should govern our lives.

Again, seeing how we deal with the workbook can be a kind of projective test to help us see how we deal with Jesus, the Holy Spirit, God, and indeed all authority figures.

The "Proper" Way of Doing the Workbook

Q: You have mentioned all the different ways of dealing with the workbook, but you haven't said anything at all about the normal or proper way to do it.

A: The "proper" way of doing the workbook is to do it exactly the way you do it: as a fully developed ego, which is what we are, and rather than being ashamed of it, to simply observe it in action. Everyone has an authority problem. If we did not, we would not be in this world. In the text, Jesus says the authority problem is "the root of all evil" (T-3.VI.7:3), which is another way of saying it is the root of all sin. Everyone here is in competition with God, as Lesson 13 points out. There is no normal way of doing the workbook because no one here is normal. Normal people do not do the workbook because normal people do not come into this world. And so, the "normal" way is to do the workbook as it says, and then watch how you try to bend the rules. We may be too afraid to break the rules, but surely there can be nothing wrong with bending them, we say to ourselves. But that little bending is enough of a little gap to maintain distance between

ourselves and God. There are actually very few rules in the workbook, but one of them is not to do more than one lesson a day. How tempting it can then be to do two a day.

Many, many years ago Gloria and I were visiting Bill Thetford and Judy Skutch in California, and we attended a weekly Course meeting. At some point a young woman very proudly told the group that she had found a way to do the entire workbook in one day. She took the 365 lessons and divided them by the number of hours and minutes in the day, and proceeded to do the entire workbook in twenty-four hours. I still remember the stunned silence in the room. Bill kept his head down. I kept mine down, too, but peeked a look at him at one point, as he did with me. No one said anything. The poor lady was in such a rush to reach salvation that she did not read the very first page that says not to do more than one lesson a day.

That is an extreme example, but we can catch ourselves doing something similar, if not in form, certainly in the content of bending the rules. We need to realize that that is just another way of saying to the authority, "I'll give you some of my day, but not all of it." Again, if we are doing the workbook sincerely, the chances are pretty high that we believe Jesus or the Holy Spirit gave the Course to us, and that it did not come from an earthly source. It means that we have enough respect for it that we choose to devote time and energy to it so as to learn from its greater wisdom. But we need to watch ourselves attempt to make deals with this greater wisdom, as we have done with God.

Every formalized religion has done the same thing. Having a ritual is a way of saying to God, "I will make a bargain with You. I will read Your holy book, perform the rituals You demand, and in exchange You will love me and welcome me back home." This special bargain is what we do with *A Course in Miracles*, too. Once again, we need to watch how we try to deviate from the workbook instructions, and then ask ourselves why we would want to put ourselves in opposition to Jesus and argue with him. Why do we want to think, for example, that we can write a better workbook than he? We need to see this dynamic in ourselves, but *without judgment*.

To summarize, the normal way to do the workbook is to be as ego-based as you are with everything else, but to observe this without judging yourself. Lesson 95 is an excellent description of how one should do the workbook. If you could truly say to Jesus, "I am trying to be sneaky, to withhold from you, and to prove to you that I know better than you. Yet I know you will not condemn me for it," that would be a wonderful way of beginning the process of learning what forgiveness is: our sins against God have had, and still have, no effect. Thus, you could "sin" all the time with this workbook, and at the same time learn that your sins against Jesus and his course have no effect. That is the "proper" way of doing the workbook.

And so, the real value of the workbook is found in being able to do it "sinfully," but to know that you are not being punished. Jesus is not sitting in judgment of you, and even though you may not have that image consciously, the chances are very high that this image of him underlies how you are doing his workbook.

Q: Are you saying that if I have gone through 230 lessons and then stopped, that if I pick it up at some future point and finish it, I will still get the merit badge at the end?

A: Not only that, you will get the merit badge at the beginning because it is not earned, but accepted. That is what the workbook will help you understand. Remember what I have been saying, one of the important focuses of the workbook as a mind-training program is to teach us that the Holy Spirit and Jesus are our Friends, and that God is a loving Creator, not an enemy. The idea is to go through the workbook as a "sinner," which is the only way we can go through it because if we were sinless we would not be here. I mean sin, of course, in the context of the belief that we are separate from our Source. If we can go through the workbook and not experience condemnation, guilt, and fear, we will have learned the wonderful lesson of forgiveness, which is the Course's only purpose. The love in our minds that the ego had concealed, would then be freed to guide us in our study and practice.

The workbook does not seem to say this, because you do not have to understand that idea in order to do the lessons. But it is important to be able to forgive yourself for not doing the workbook perfectly, just as it is important to forgive yourself for reading a passage in the text, get to the end of it and forget every word you read. It is so important, then, to be able to say, "Yes, that is what my ego would do. It is terrified of what I am reading, and so it causes a screen to fall so that I do not see." One more time, the idea is not to try to do this perfectly, because if you could do it perfectly you would not need it. Just observe yourself in action trying to make bargains with Jesus.

Q: I knew that I was messing up, and I even messed up with the workbook cards. So I kept telling myself, "I am not guilty, this is not sinful," but that did not help. So I kept watching, messing up, and forgiving, over and over again.

A: Good. Understand that this course is terrifying you, and say to yourself: "I am terrified of learning that I was wrong and the Holy Spirit was right. I do not want to change my mind, because a part of me is beginning to understand that mind-changing means letting go of judgment, anger, specialness, and self-importance, and I am not ready to do that."

Watch yourself defend against losing all that by forgetting what the workbook is, forgetting the lesson or lesson card. Simply recognize where all this is coming from and that it is not a sin. That is the crucial idea: you can do whatever you want with Jesus and he does not get angry or condemn you for it. You can mess up doing the workbook, but can then forgive yourself for having done so. The messing up came from fear, not sin. And your ego should be terrified. This thought system is the most terrifying thing in the world because it means the end of the world—literally. As you begin to realize this, there will of course be fear, and with fear comes resistance, denial, projection, and all the other defenses.

Being Addicted to the Workbook

One further point about doing the workbook: Very often what happens to students after they have done the lessons for the year is that they suddenly feel a sense of emptiness. As a result, they want to do the workbook again. They do it a second year and they feel the same emptiness, and they want to do it still again. Before you know it, they have become addicted to the workbook. Now you might say it is better to be addicted to the workbook than to cocaine, but it is the same addiction to guilt—only the form is different. The addiction is saying there is something missing in me and I need to fill the lack from the outside. While there is of course nothing inherently wrong about doing the workbook over and over for forty years, it would help to step back and watch yourself go through the addiction process that says if you do not have your morning fix, something will go wrong. This would simply mean there is something in the workbook you have not paid attention to, confusing form and content, behavior and mind.

To repeat, there is nothing wrong in doing the lessons again if that is what makes you feel better. Remember, though, there is a period when cocaine feels good, too. Any time you feel you cannot live without this—whatever the "this" is, even this holy book—you are involved in a special relationship. That is why there is this very important passage in Lesson 189: "Forget this world, forget this course, and come with wholly empty hands unto your God" (W-pI.189.7:5). The purpose of the Course is to have the Course become obsolete. That is not going to happen right away, but that is its purpose. Nothing is wrong should you find yourself addicted to the Course, but be aware that you are addicted to it, and you know you are addicted to it if you cannot go without it. *A Course in Miracles*, as three books, is still something external. Its purpose is to have the external three books teach you what is internal, and then to have you rely on what is internal: the Love of God through Jesus or the Holy Spirit.

You thus need to watch yourself become addicted to the Course. You do not necessarily have to stop the addiction, but do be aware of it. All that is required of any student is to do the workbook once. This is not to say that as you work with *A Course in Miracles* over many years, you will not be inspired by certain lessons or prayers that you find yourself going back to over and over. These wonderful passages and prayers that provide inspiring help when you need them are one of the lovely dividends of the Course. These are not the problem. The problem is the need that borders on addiction, where you believe that without the Course something would be lacking inside you.

To reiterate, the purpose of *A Course in Miracles* is to train us to know that we can be in touch with the Holy Spirit twenty-four hours a day. Its three books offer us a pathway that trains us to become aware of His Presence all the time. Feeling His Love throughout the day, we need nothing else. That is the difference between a teacher and an advanced teacher of God. The teacher of God, as explained in the section in the manual "How Should the Teacher of God Spend His Day?," is someone who still needs structure and ritual. The advanced teacher no longer requires such help because the Holy Spirit *is* the structure and ritual, as it were.

You may think that there is nothing wrong with being addicted temporarily until you are ready to give it up. The problem—and this is the case with any addiction, which is what specialness is—is that you do not know it is specialness, and so you do not know you are addicted. In other words, you can work with this course, and because it is such a "holy" book and you do it faithfully every day, year in and year out, you no longer are aware of the dependency. You are not aware you cannot give it up. However, it is quite another thing to be able to say,

"Yes, I am addicted because I am afraid of being on my own." This is different because it is honest. The problem enters when you think you are doing something holy, when it is just another form of the ego's specialness.

Certainly, as part of the process, people should form a special relationship with the Course. Despite what I said a moment ago, it *is* better than cocaine, *as long as you are aware of the addiction*. Then you can move through it to the love that is beyond the defense. Anyone who has been a psychotherapy patient knows that. A typical part of the treatment is where the patient forms a strong transference to the therapist. If that projection remains, however, no healing can occur, for the line has been blurred between reality and fantasy. But if the therapist helps the patient move through the dependency to become autonomous, the transference is healed as is the patient. It is the same thing here. The Course's purpose is to have Jesus help us become dependent on him, seeing him as our teacher instead of the ego. At the end of the journey we realize he is no longer our teacher because we have become him. That happy day comes when we are near the end, but for now we need to see our special relationship with Jesus and the dependence on him and his course. The challenge is to know it is temporary and not a permanent arrangement.

I want to expand briefly on this idea of the temporary nature of our relationship with Jesus or the Holy Spirit. When we are steps away from accepting the Atonement and attaining the real world, we recognize that the Holy Spirit is not separate from us. Just as we had believed we were our ego, now we know we are the Holy Spirit, because He is only a Thought, the memory of God's Love. If we remember that we *are* God's Love and His Love is one, how could we be different from the Voice that tells us so? That is what Jesus means when he says that he is the manifestation of the Holy Spirit (C-6.1:1). There is no difference between him and the Holy Spirit except that Jesus is the name we give to the Holy Spirit in form, and perceive him as someone who actually lived as a body.

Returning to our special relationship with Jesus, if he is the symbol (or manifestation) in our world of God's Love, and it is that Love we hate and fear because we believe it is in competition with us, we are going to hate him, too, which is why the world has always hated him. Therefore, it should come as no surprise that people have special relationships with Jesus. Some of the forms are outright hate; other forms are more subtle and we call them love. We need to become aware of these aspects of specialness, and the Course is a most helpful way of doing that. That is why Jesus says he needs us to forgive him (T-19.IV-B.6). One of the essential by-products of working through *A Course in Miracles* is that we will heal our relationship with Jesus. He does not mention himself very often in the workbook, but if the Course has come from him, then clearly he is the one speaking to us in the lessons.

As I have been saying, watch yourself relate to and interact with the workbook. What you are really doing is interacting with the *teacher* of the workbook. The holy relationship with the Course comes in recognizing that its words are your teacher, and the Holy Spirit or Jesus are the embodiments of that teaching. Their purpose is to teach you to remember Who you are; to teach you how to become comfortable with your ego and to forgive it; to lead you through pain and terror to the love and peace that is beyond the ego. When you attain that love and peace, you no longer need *A Course in Miracles*.

We need to recognize the important difference between form and content. What we want from the Course is not its form, but the content of its teaching message. As we learn and increasingly identify with its message of forgiveness, we will need the form of the Course less and less. We learn not to make the Course special. Even saying it is from Jesus does not make it special, because we ultimately want to learn he is not special either, otherwise we will be caught in the same trap that has ensnared the Churches for centuries. A holy relationship with the Course as opposed to a special one means that we relate to it as a means toward the end, not as the end. That is why Jesus says those "blasphemous" words I quoted before, "Forget this world, forget this course..." (W-pI.189.7:5). He says in the text that the aim of any teacher is to make himself dispensable (T-4.I.6). That includes him, the greatest teacher.

It is essential that we not skip steps, a point we will come back to again and again. We do not want to dismiss the Course before we have really learned it, and we do not want to dismiss Jesus as our teacher before we have learned everything he can teach us. Returning to what I said earlier, that is the danger of working only with the workbook, because the workbook often makes the process sound so easy. Over and over again in the lessons Jesus says, "This is a special day" or "This is the day you are going to make it." Then you turn the page and realize, "My God, I haven't made it. And not only have I not made it, but Jesus knew I would not make it because the lessons are continuing." It is important to understand that his view of time is much different from ours. When he says, "This day you will make it," he is talking about attaining the holy instant, which we can attain any day, any moment, and that blessed time extends into forever.

It is very easy, if we do not understand the text and have it as a background, to exclaim, "I have made it. I am a teacher of God. Look at me. I can channel, heal, and do all these wonderful things." If we work sincerely with the text, I guarantee that this mistake will not happen. That is why I have been saying that the workbook is not the teaching of *A Course in Miracles*. The text contains the teaching. If we work with the text and really understand it, we cannot fall into that trap, for we will realize that the workbook is a series of mind-training exercises that will help us begin the process of applying the text's teaching in our everyday lives.

One student said that the value of the workbook for her is that it helped her get in touch with the ancient memory, and she wondered whether she were right in concluding that she was doing the workbook correctly. Such an experience is of course wonderful, but the problem enters in if she does not generalize that experience so that it is integrated in her life. Moreover, she would need to sidestep the temptation to attribute that experience to doing the workbook. Generalization is a major theme of the workbook, and if done correctly, the workbook, in addition to the study of the text, would enable students to be in touch with that memory all the time. That way we would avoid the dependency on the workbook that would prevent us from generalizing such a beautiful experience.

Again, there is nothing wrong in having those kind of experiences, because doing the workbook could very well lead to them. But it is essential to see those experiences as the beginning, not the end,

and then generalize to every aspect of our life. This would help us to understand that the memory is within us, that the memory of Who we are as God's perfect Child is within us, not outside and only in certain special people. The workbook, in one sense, has fulfilled its purpose if it has helped us get in touch with that. But this purpose is obviated if all we learn is that the only way to get in touch with that ancient memory is by reading these holy words. In the same way, therapists would have failed if their patients leave their office every week and feel wonderful, and then for six other days feel terrible, only to return next week and say how great they feel talking to them. Therapists want their patients to generalize those positive transference feelings to all situations, all the time. Jesus wants the same thing for us as we work with his course.

Students sometimes express the feeling that the workbook makes them feel loved, like a little child who is being praised and encouraged by its mother as it is learning to walk. That is a good point because the workbook does make you feel good, and it is important that we feel good in relation to ourselves and to God, as this corrects how absolutely rotten we feel about ourselves and our relationship with our Creator. However, we are not aware of that. Many passages in the text do not make us feel good, for we are asked to really look at the ego. In painstaking detail, Jesus exposes the ugly and terrifying picture of the ego's thought system of hate.

But this is not the purpose of the workbook. In general, it provides us with experiences that make us feel good by reminding us that God is not angry, nor is Jesus or the Holy Spirit. These are extremely important steps, albeit early ones. To be told that God does not know about us, as I said earlier, is not helpful. It is a terrifying statement because if God does not know about us, we do not exist. And so before we are ready to look at that horrifying thought and move beyond it, we need first to think of God as Someone Who loves us. Learning that we are not miserable sinners is what begins to undo the thought system that underlies the universe and our existence within it.

3. The Theory Underlying the Lessons

A helpful preparation for beginning the lessons is to have a grounding in the theory on which the workbook rests. This would provide a more meaningful context for what the lessons are saying, both as a teaching on the level of form, as well as what they are leading us toward. This would be another way of speaking of the workbook's mind training, but will be more specific in terms of the theory that underlies the lessons.

The theoretical framework that the workbook reflects is that God's Love is already present in our minds, but covered over by the ego's thought system. Thus, all we need do is remove the interferences to that Love. As one lesson says, "Your part is simply to allow all obstacles that you have interposed between the Son and God the Father to be quietly removed forever" (W-pI.189.8:3). In other words, the Course's focus is not on God or finding love, but on removing the obstacles, and the workbook is specifically geared toward helping us do that. The workbook, reflecting what is discussed in much greater detail in the text (see T-19.IV), also explains these obstacles. A chart will help us trace the flow of the undoing process. I should mention that this chart is different from the one I frequently use, for it is upside down. The reason is that the workbook is upside down, in the sense that the typical movement we find depicted in the text is that God is on top and the separation is the ladder that leads us away from Him until we hit bottom. This means that the Atonement process goes from bottom up, wherein we make our way up the ladder the separation led us down (T-28.III.1:2). In the workbook, the process of forgiveness is usually described as going the other way, with God at the bottom and the ego's layers of defense placed over Him and His memory.

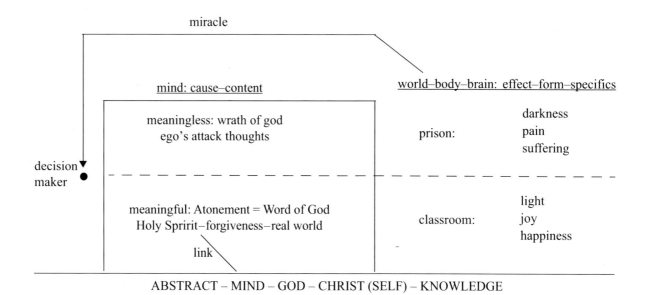

ABSTRACT – MIND – GOD – CHRIST (SELF) – KNOWLEDGE

Therefore, we begin at the bottom with God and Christ, our real Self. Several important lessons contrast our ego self with the Self that is our Identity as Christ. The unity of Father and Son is the truth that is Heaven. Very little is said in the workbook about how the separation began, which is also the case in the text. Suffice it to say that we had the separation thought, which then appeared to separate us from our Source as well as our true Self, giving rise to the separated mind. In *A Course in Miracles*, the Holy Spirit is described as the Voice that speaks for God, the memory that came with us into our dream that recalls to us Who we are as Christ. As our Teacher, the Holy Spirit's principal message is forgiveness, which culminates in the attainment of the real world.

When the Son of God seemed to fall asleep and began his dream, two voices spoke to him. The first is the ego's thought of separation, answered by the Holy Spirit's principle of the Atonement that says that the separation never happened. By choosing to believe in the lies of the ego, we sought to cover over this Voice with the ego's thought system of attack. In the early lessons, Jesus refers to the ego's attack thoughts as meaningless, while the Holy Spirit's Thoughts of forgiveness are what alone are meaningful within the dream. This calls into play an important term that is never mentioned as such in the Course, but which is indirectly referred to throughout: the part of the split mind that chooses between these two voices. We call it the *decision maker*, which we usually characterize by a blue dot or black dot on the printed chart.

One of the key ideas, especially in the early workbook lessons, is the relationship between these two thought systems and the world. Attack thoughts, when projected from the mind, give rise to the world, which we then experience as a prison. Three words that are prominent in the workbook (as well as the text) to describe our experience in the physical world are *darkness*, *pain*, and *death*. When the Atonement Thought of the Holy Spirit is expressed in the world, our lives here are seen as classrooms that reflect the light of His Presence. The world, then, becomes a place of joy and happiness because of its purpose of helping us awaken from the dream.

A principle that is absolutely essential to understanding *A Course in Miracles* is that there is no difference between what is in the world and what is in the mind, the world being simply a shadow that reflects the mind's thoughts. The important lesson, "My thoughts are images that I have made" (W-pI.15), describes how the images of what we perceive and experience in the world come from our thoughts. They are one and the same. Krishnamurti made this idea the cornerstone of his teaching: the observed and the observer are one, what is seemingly outside is the same as what is inside. The illusion of the world is that there is a difference, that the world outside is separate from us. Reading the early lessons carefully, you will be astounded to find the Course's metaphysics clearly laid out. At first blush

these lessons appear very simple, but they are anything but that.

Jesus makes it clear in the workbook that we do not need to understand anything he is saying. All he asks is that we do what he says, not that we necessarily believe him. As we advance in our work with *A Course in Miracles*, we may find ourselves reading the workbook a few times, and probably will be very surprised, as I just said, to find the metaphysical wisdom in those early lessons; again, that our inner and outer worlds are one and the same.

In trying to change our perceptions of other people and heal our relationships, the focus is on changing what we perceive to be outside us, as bodies. The reason is that we believe there really are people outside us who have to be forgiven. In reality, what we perceive outside is nothing but a split-off thought within the mind. This means that we end up forgiving ourselves, another major theme of the Course. However, since we believe we are separated bodies relating to other separated bodies, this experience is where we need to begin, which is why *A Course in Miracles* is written the way it is, including the Holy Spirit and God being treated as if They were separate People Who do things for us. Once again, since we are like very small children who do not understand the difference between reality and illusion, Jesus does not demand that we share his level of understanding. He teaches us *from* his level of understanding, but his teaching comes in a form we can accept at our own level of believing we are bodies.

It is only when we understand that there is no difference between the outer and inner worlds, body and mind, that we can also understand that in forgiving someone we perceive to be outside ourselves, we are really forgiving a part of the mind of which we were not aware. As we have observed, the rationale behind the workbook is to train our minds to understand that we have a decision-making mind. We all believe we are "out here," which means we are mindless bodies. What we consider to be our thoughts are not our thoughts at all (see Lesson 45). In fact taking two separate sentences and making them one, we have this statement: "The thoughts you think you think are not your real thoughts." This is because the thoughts we think we are thinking are really coming from our brain, which is part of the body, and so these are not thoughts at all. The real thoughts are only two: the ego's guilt (which includes thoughts of sin and attack) and the Holy Spirit's forgiveness. There are no others.

What we think are our thoughts are "out here." Therefore, we need a spirituality that reminds us that what we perceive outside is a reflection or projection of what is inside. With this understanding, our focus returns to the mind, where we become aware that we have a choice between two thoughts or teachers. We need this mind training because we have forgotten the truths the Course articulates. This includes the content of our attack thoughts, which are projected as our external attack thoughts. This content of the mind is that we believe we attacked God, and now believe He is on the counter-offensive and will attack us back. The ego has convinced us that this madness is true.

Freud came close in terms of understanding that what seems to be conscious is a projection of what is unconscious, but he never got beyond the brain to the mind. The real meaning of the unconscious, as *A Course in Miracles* would teach, is that unconscious thoughts involving the body are not the problem. For example, something terrible happened to me as a child and I will never look at it again, thus repressing it. Now it is in my "unconscious," and surfaces every once in a while but I do not know where it is coming from. However, that is not what is truly happening. There are no unconscious thoughts in the brain. What we consider to be these unacceptable and frightening thoughts are only reflections of a mind that is rooted in *the* ego thought that we attacked God, stole His life and left Him for dead, raising ourselves in His place. But He will surely find us and get even. It is this horrific thought that is the real meaning of the unconscious, it being totally out of our awareness.

This is not so clearly spelled out in the workbook, but is in the text, which is why you should not mistake the workbook for the Course itself. The workbook, as I have been saying, will not give you the sum and substance of the Course's teaching. It is not meant to. It is the Course's thought system—the ego and its undoing by the Holy Spirit—that is why people have so many problems with it. We are unconsciously terrified that if we practice what Jesus is teaching us, our attention will leave the world of bodies and return to the mind, the home of God's wrath. This helps us understand, which the workbook does not really explain, why there is a

world: to provide a hiding place so our maniacal Father will never find us. In other words, we would have to look at the real source of our anxiety and pain, which is the mind's decision for guilt. This has nothing to do with the world at all, but only with the anxiety that comes from the belief that God will destroy us if He ever finds us; the fear that comes from our guilt telling us we deserve to be annihilated for the terrible and sinful thing we did.

Of course the ego is no one's fool. It knows that in our being so afraid of it, we are not only preserving it by believing in it (how can you fear what does not exist?), but also by denying the Holy Spirit's solution. The ego therefore makes up this idea that we have attacked God so that we will become so fearful of the Holy Spirit's Presence that we will run into a world and believe we are actually there in bodies. The purpose of this is not really to keep us from our guilt, because guilt is an illusion (the Atonement principle: no separation, no sin, no guilt). The ego's true purpose is to keep us from the mind's choosing the Holy Spirit as its Teacher. This is the reason Jesus places such emphasis on our developing a relationship with the Holy Spirit, learning that He is our only Friend, One Who loves and comforts us. This corrects the mistaken belief that the Holy Spirit is the enemy. This insanity led us to deny His loving Presence in the mind, Its place taken by the wrath of God, now experienced in His punitive Voice.

As long as we believe we have attacked God and stolen His treasure, we will believe He will punish us. In turn, anyone who represents God will be seen as an enemy, whether we are talking about the Holy Spirit, Jesus, or *A Course in Miracles*. Whoever the person was who lived two millennia ago, known to the world as Jesus, we can better understand through the lens of the Course why the myth of crucifixion arose, and why what could only have been a loving message was crucified with him. Our world thus became a smokescreen to hide the guilt, which the world merely reflects: "The world you see is the delusional system of those made mad by guilt" (T-13.in.2:2).

I conclude by bringing back one of the workbook's most central points: there is no difference between what is outside (the world) and what is inside (the mind).

4. The First Fifty Lessons

We can say that the first fifty lessons in the workbook are similar, at least in one major respect, to the fifty miracle principles that open the text. Their similarity lies in that they are both like great Wagnerian preludes, which contain many of the themes in the music drama to follow. The fifty miracle principles, which in brief and succinct fashion describe the characteristics of the miracle and how and why it works, sow the seeds for what the rest of the text will amplify. In like manner, we could say that these first fifty lessons contain the seeds or themes that will be elaborated on in the succeeding lessons.

In these first fifty lessons, thus, we have a wonderful summary of *A Course in Miracles* itself, reflecting its basic theory. On the metaphysical level, these lessons teach that the world is an illusion, being simply a thought that has not left the separated mind. They describe the attack thoughts of the ego and the purpose of its thought system of self-preservation, as well as how we undo this thought system through forgiveness. Finally, the lessons tell us what it means to be a teacher of God, an instrument of the light of Heaven that now shines through us.

As a kind of reprise of the major themes of the prelude, I will briefly review what is on the chart. Our true reality and Identity is Christ, the extension of God's Love that is our real Self. We took with us into the dream of separation the memory of God's Love and our Self. This memory is the Holy Spirit and His principle of Atonement. The ego counters this Thought by building up clouds of illusion and guilt, which fill our mind with attack thoughts that seem to drown out the Voice that reminds us that the light of Christ still shines in us. To ensure that our decision maker never chooses the Holy Spirit and remains with the ego, the ego removes its thought system of sin, guilt, and fear by projecting it into the world. The world then becomes nothing more than the "pictorial representation" of the mind's thoughts of attack, guilt, and vengeance (W-pI.23.3:2).

When we recognize there is "another way"—there are but two choices in the mind instead of one, and we can choose the Holy Spirit—we then look out on a world that has been transformed into a classroom instead of a prison, a classroom in which we both learn and teach the lessons of forgiveness. Even though the term *teacher of God* does not appear in the workbook (it appears only in the manual), the concept of the teacher of God does. Lesson 37, "My holiness blesses the world," is a nice description of what it means to be a teacher of God. When we remove the obstacles in our mind, the love-filled light of Jesus or the Holy Spirit shines through us. It is the holiness our minds have chosen that blesses the world, simply by being what it is.

5. Passing Through the Clouds of Guilt

The specific focus of my comments here is the process of going through the clouds (of guilt), which Jesus talks about specifically in Lessons 69 and 70. Indeed, he tells us there that he is the one who will help us through them (W-pI.70.9:3-4). Following this, I will focus on what it means to be a teacher of God, an extension of the Holy Spirit's Love and light in the world. This is one area that can be particularly tempting for students to get trapped in, because they tend to confuse form and content. Finally, as I have emphasized previously, the idea of not getting caught in rituals and structures is central to the process of the workbook lessons. There are some passages later on in the workbook that deal specifically with these areas as well.

Lessons 68 through 72 contrast the ego's plan for salvation through guilt and attack with God's plan for salvation through turning within and forgiving. Referring to the chart, we can see that the ego's plan for salvation, which is the ego's plan to save itself, consists in first making thoughts of guilt and attack real in the mind, and then projecting this content, leaving us to deal with the guilt and attack that is now perceived to be outside us. Our focus becomes riveted in the mindless world of bodies, the culmination of the ego's strategy. God's plan for salvation, really the Holy Spirit's, is the miracle's return of attack thoughts from the world to the mind, there to be looked at without judgment and thus released. The ego's plan has us look outside; the Holy Spirit's correction brings us inside.

Lesson 69 uses clouds to symbolize the ego's interference to truth. In the exercise in paragraph 4, we are asked to "try to let go of all the content that generally occupies [y]our consciousness." Even though the workbook at this point does not explain this process, the way we let go of the content that generally occupies our consciousness (attack thoughts, grievances, etc.) is to look at them without judgment. To say this one more time, the workbook should not be taken as a substitute for the text, because the process as expressed here sounds so easy, saying that all we have to do is close our eyes, think of our grievances, let them go, and then we will find ourselves basking in the light of Heaven. We all know that in practice this is not that easy. The danger comes in thinking that it is, because then we will believe we have let the ego go when we have not done so at all. What we have done is bury our attack thoughts in the mind, and from there they will inevitably surface in very unloving ways.

Taking the abortion issue as an example, many people who claim to be acting in the name of love and life really end up attacking, if not murdering, in defense of their belief. This is projection at work. The guilt in the mind that we think has been undone because we are on the side of truth, love, and God is not looked at, and so is denied or repressed. Inevitably, then, the guilt will come up again and be projected. This is what explains how well-meaning people can fight cruel and nasty wars in the name of love and truth. It certainly explains why Christians throughout the centuries have been able to wage war in the name of the Prince of Peace. They were simply unaware of their hidden thoughts of guilt and attack, the breeding ground for projection, attack, and war.

Jesus next asks us to think of our minds "as a vast circle, surrounded by a layer of heavy, dark clouds. You can see only the clouds because you seem to be standing outside the circle and quite apart from it" (W-pI.4:2-3). Jesus is borrowing an image he first used in an important passage in the text, which is much more complicated (T-18.IX.5-8). When we compare the two passages, we again see how the workbook is not meant to be a substitute for the text. To help illustrate the ideas expressed in these passages, I have composed another diagram:

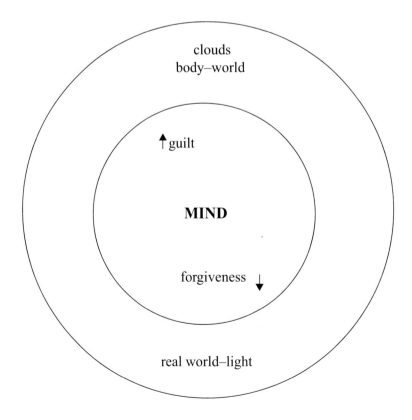

We are now told that the split mind is surrounded by a circle of clouds. Specifically, the clouds are our investment in the world of specialness and our pre-occupation with the body. The "dark clouds" are the ego thought system that is projected out. Interestingly, the workbook does not speak of the projection as the body or world, as does the text. There, a critical distinction is made between the guilt in our mind and the projections of guilt onto the body and world, a distinction that is not necessary for the exercise. Remember, Jesus has told us that it is not necessary to understand what he is talking about. All we need do is what he asks of us. For the purpose of the exercise, we need but get past the clouds and return to the mind. The discussion in the text helps us understand the nature of the process, that the cloud of guilt is really in the mind. From there the guilt is projected onto the world, which then assumes the function of the cloud to obscure the light in our decision-making minds and keep us from choosing it.

When we are "standing outside the circle," we do not see the mind, implying we are identified with the body. The idea, of course, is that the light is in our mind, but when we are outside it, all we see are the clouds, and therefore we "can see no reason to believe there is a brilliant light hidden by the clouds. The clouds seem to be the only reality. They seem to be all there is to see." We all know that when we are in the midst of an attack of depression or anxiety, or feel pain, there is nothing else that is real to us. God is the furthest thing from our mind, unless He is a magical Deity to Whom we pray to get us out of the mess we made. The real, loving God remains a total void because all we know are the clouds. When we are involved with any kind of situation in the world which we believe is important, we cannot be aware of the light shining in the mind. The world of clouds compels our attention, becoming a powerful preoccupation and distraction device, which of course is its purpose. God seems like a myth, Jesus a non-existent being, and forgiveness absolutely impossible. There is no one in the world who does not know what this is like, because it is what being here is all about.

Once we see the clouds as the only reality, we are not going to try to get past them, because we do not have a clue about there being anything beyond them. That is precisely the purpose of the clouds of guilt, projected as the clouds of bodily problems and concerns that conceal the mind's clouds of guilt. We can see in all of this the mighty purpose served by the workbook, and *A Course in Miracles* in general: to remind us that there is indeed a light that shines in the mind, and that there is indeed another way, something more in our minds than guilt, another purpose in the world besides survival and minimizing the pain of living in the imprisoning body that suffers and dies.

Let us turn now to the comparable passage in the text. My purpose in this is twofold: not only to elaborate on the lesson's message, but also to show how the workbook is not a substitute for the text, which provides an in-depth treatment of the relationship between mind and body, and how guilt acts to conceal the light. This passage appears in the second half of the "Two Worlds" in Chapter 18. The basis for this material is the discussion, one of the most important in the Course, about the world literally being made to conceal the guilt in the mind.

For the purpose of this diagram, guilt is depicted as being in the top part of the mind and forgiveness in the lowest. The purpose of the world is to conceal the mind's guilt. Remember that the ego is always afraid we will return to our minds and choose the Holy Spirit's forgiveness instead of its guilt. Just as guilt was made to cover the Holy Spirit in our minds, the world serves the purpose of covering the guilt. The world is now seen as the shadow of our guilt, except we do not know where or even what the guilt is. All we believe in are the shadows. This is similar to Plato's Allegory of the Cave, where the prisoners see only the shadows on the interior wall of the cave, and because their chains prevent them from turning around, they do not know that there is a source of light behind them, that there are real figures walking back and forth along the road outside the cave. All they see are the shadows on the interior wall, and therefore mistake these shadows for reality, a confusion that was one of Plato's major themes. Jesus does the same thing in his course, although the extent of the confusion he describes extends beyond Plato. The point is that the world is the shadow of our guilt, but we think the shadow figures are real.

To round out the picture, we can see that just as guilt is projected onto the world, becoming clouds that obscure the light, forgiveness extends into the world, an extension that ultimately becomes the real world reflecting the light of Christ. In terms of the chart, the ego has us move upward from the mind to the world, while the Holy Spirit has us move from the world to the mind, allowing His Love to extend itself to the world.

This, then, is the gist of the passage from the text. In the two preceding paragraphs, Jesus established the image of the clouds and said that if we are standing on earth looking up at the clouds, we might see all manner of images in them, reminiscent of our earlier discussion of Rorschach's ink blots. About the clouds Jesus says, "it is easy to see a whole world rising. A solid mountain range, a lake, a city…" (T-18.IX.7:1-2). This does not make what we are seeing real, however. He also says that the clouds may seem to be solid, but they do not have the power to stop even the fall of a button (T-18.IX.6:4). He continues the image in paragraph 8:

> So should it be with the dark clouds of guilt, no more impenetrable and no more substantial. You will not bruise yourself against them in traveling through. Let your Guide [the Holy Spirit] teach you their unsubstantial nature as He leads you past them, for beneath them is a world of light whereon they cast no shadows. Their shadows lie upon the world beyond them, still further from the light. Yet from them to the light their shadows cannot fall (T-18.IX.8).

Clouds seem to have the power to destroy the sun, but all they do is obscure it. In and of themselves, the clouds have no substance. They are not solid, although they may appear to be, which is recognized by anyone who has flown, observing how the plane flies beyond the cloud bank to where the sky is brightly lit with the sun. Jesus is using the same image here. He is asking us to go through the clouds of guilt and realize their substanceless nature.

The next step:

> This world of light, this circle of brightness is the real world, where guilt meets with forgiveness. Here the world outside is seen anew, without the shadow of guilt upon it. Here are you forgiven, for here you have forgiven everyone. Here is the new perception, where everything is bright and shining with innocence, washed in the waters of forgiveness, and cleansed of every evil thought you laid upon it (T-18.IX.9:1-4).

To summarize the process: We go through the clouds of the world realizing they are but shadows of the cloud that is the mind's guilt. Letting Jesus take us by the hand, as it were, we go through guilt to forgiveness, which means we look at our guilt without judgment. We bring guilt to forgiveness, darkness to light, illusions to the truth. On a practical level, this translates to when we feel overwhelmed with ego thoughts, we bring our guilt, anger, specialness, depression, and anxiety to Jesus or the Holy Spirit. We look at these thoughts with Them, which means we do not judge ourselves. In this way our guilt is forgiven, and when it is forgiven it disappears. Nothing then remains but the light of forgiveness. Identifying with that light perfectly is the state of mind known as the real world. From that perspective we look out on the same world, no longer through the eyes of guilt that led to experiencing the world as hostile or threatening, but through the eyes of forgiveness, the vision of Christ. The light of this vision shines through us, informing all our perceptions, whether we are in a beautiful natural setting or a death camp.

Returning to Lesson 69 in the workbook, we find the same process we just saw described in the text, although the presentation is not as complicated:

> After you have thought about the importance of what you are trying to do for yourself and the world, try to settle down in perfect stillness, remembering only how much you want to reach the light in you today,–now! Determine to go past the clouds. Reach out and touch them in your mind. Brush them aside with your hand; feel them resting on your cheeks and forehead and eyelids as you go through them. Go on; clouds cannot stop you (W-pI.69.6).

Near the end of Lesson 70, Jesus makes the process much more personal:

> Now we will try again to reach the light in you, which is where your salvation is. You cannot find it in the clouds that surround the light, and it is in them you have been looking for it. It is not there. It is past the clouds and in the light beyond. Remember that you will have to go through the clouds before you can reach the light. But remember also that you have never found anything in the cloud patterns you imagined that endured, or that you wanted (W-pI.70.8).

Expressed here is the important theme I have been stressing. To reach the light we must first deal with the darkness. We cannot skip over steps. We must go through the clouds. This is where Course students can get caught, which happens, as I have been saying, when they work only with the workbook. They will not understand the process of healing. We do not simply jump from where we are, in the world, to the Light of Christ. We first go through the clouds of guilt, which means we look at our specialness and all other ego issues. This is where resistance comes in, where fear is exacerbated, and where we find the source of the temptation to change the Course to meet our needs.

Importantly, we do not have to do this if we do not want to. We do not have to deal with the ego, and there are many other spiritual paths that do not ask this of us. There is nothing wrong with any of these approaches. If that is the path that we resonate to, we need to follow it. Yet we should not confuse *A Course in Miracles* with these other pathways. This is not a course in simply going to the light, but going through the darkness. We forgive the darkness of our guilt, learning not to be afraid of it. With the ego allies of guilt and fear gone, nothing is left but the light.

Moreover, we do not have to search for the light or go to it, because the light is there. If we have to search for it, we are telling ourselves it is not there. Rather, we want to search for the darkness, for the dark thoughts in our minds so we can forgive them. This is not to suggest extensive analysis. The dark thoughts are found simply by watching how we interact with the world through constant judgment, and then we bring these judgments to the guilt-ridden mind that is their source. By looking at these judgmental thoughts without judging them, attacking them, or feeling guilty about them, we cause

them to lose their power. And then they will disappear into the gentle light of our forgiveness.

We all can relate to the last sentence: "But remember also that you have never found anything in the cloud patterns you imagined that endured, or that you wanted." If we are honest with ourselves, we will recognize that when we attain a goal we have set for ourselves, we feel it is never enough. Perhaps it is enough for that day, but it will not be enough the next day, or week or month. We always need more. Nothing in this world satisfies or fulfills us totally and permanently.

We must truly accept this. It is one thing to pay lip service to what Jesus says, sweetly nodding as we say, "Yes, yes, yes, what you are saying is true." It is quite another thing to understand fully what he means, and to be clear with ourselves, not only in terms of the obvious ways in which the world has failed us, but also in terms of the subtle ways that things we have sought in the world have not satisfied us. In practically all of us there is a lingering hope, usually unconscious, that there is still some aspect of specialness that will give us what we want, something in the world that will make us feel good about ourselves. This is another example of confusing form and content, believing that something from the outside world (form) will supply the lack we experience within our minds (content).

Jesus concludes with this most comforting and reassuring offer of his help:

> Since all illusions of salvation have failed you, surely you do not want to remain in the clouds, looking vainly for idols there, when you could so easily walk on into the light of real salvation. Try to pass the clouds by whatever means appeals to you. If it helps you, think of me holding your hand and leading you. And I assure you this will be no idle fantasy (W-pI.70.9).

Questions

Q: Jesus doesn't actually say here that we have to look at the clouds.

A: True. The idea of looking appears later in the workbook, but it is extremely important in the text. The point I have been making is that we do not get the complete theory or the full process of forgiveness

from the workbook. That is why this sounds so easy and why so many people are tempted to work only with the workbook and set the text aside. We cannot let go of the clouds if we do not look at them because, as the text explains, it is our not looking at them that allows them to remain. Denial is one of the most primitive and powerful of all defenses.

Taking Jesus' hand means looking at our anxiety, anger, depression, and guilt with him, but without judgment. If we are looking and also hoping he will take it all away from us, we have made it real, which means we have not truly looked, but judged. We are not seeing because we see what is not there. This is an extremely important point. If we hold to the idea that Jesus will take the problem from us, we are saying there is a problem. Yet there is no problem, only the mind's belief there is. Looking with Jesus means realizing that whatever we are feeling has no effect on his love for us. That love and our mind's peace are alone what matters to us. Indeed, they alone are truth within the illusory world of separation.

The separation fallacy began with the idea that the Son's attack thought on God, his need to usurp God's place on the throne and make it his own made it impossible for God ever to love him again. Thus, the great Judaeo-Christian myth of Adam and Eve ends with God banishing the two sinners from the Garden (Heaven), placing an angel with flaming spears at the gate, ensuring they never get back in. What a wonderful expression of the ego thought system! It is essential to realize that to ask Jesus to take a problem away is to make it real, which once again, in the words of the early workbook lessons, means we are not seeing because we are seeing something that is not there.

As I have been emphasizing, the early workbook lessons are incredible in terms of what they are teaching. Jesus means literally that when we see a problem outside us, we are not seeing, because there is nothing there but an hallucination. Walking with him means to see through his eyes. The phrases "turning it over to him," "passing through the clouds of guilt," and "taking his hand" are expressing this process of looking at our ego thoughts, and not giving them power to interfere with our love for Jesus and his for us. In this way we replicate the original Atonement principle that our attack thoughts against God had no effect: "…not one note in Heaven's song was missed." Nothing happened. This does not mean that we are to deny our terror, pain, depression, or guilt. We look at whatever we are experiencing, but without blaming ourselves or others. Then they disappear. This may seem like a fine point, but it is crucial. It is what separates *A Course in Miracles* from practically every other spiritual path I know: we are not asked to deny the ego, but asked to look at it without guilt, recognizing its purpose. What enables us to look without judgment is taking Jesus' hand, which is why he makes the gentle recommendation: "imagine that I am taking you by the hand as you pass through the clouds of guilt, and I assure you this is no idle fantasy."

Q: Would it be accurate to say that we are supposed to look at our ego and love it?

A: You can give it a little tickle and look at it in a loving way; not that you embrace it, but rather look at it and say, "This means nothing." You want to look at it and no longer give it any power. You do not want to love it: guilt is not lovable; murder is not lovable. You could reach the point where you can say that a murderous thought is silly because it is not going to get you what you want; in fact, it will deprive you of what you truly want: the peace of God. But I would not go so far as to say that it is lovable.

Q: I thought that if I didn't do that I would be judging it and therefore giving it a reality that it does not have.

A: If you are loving it, you are also giving it a reality it does not have. You do not love something that is not there. You love something that you believe *is* there. When you say it is silly, what you are really saying is that it was silly of me to believe that this thought had any power over God's Love.

Q: Could we say that we have to forgive the ego?

A: Yes, you could, but you are really forgiving yourself, the decision maker, for having chosen the ego. The ego is absolutely nothing. You forgive yourself for having put *nothing* in the place of *everything*, and then building a world of *nothing*, which seems to be *something*, to conceal the *nothing* that is the defense against the *Everything*.

Q: Does the ego also present us with good things? You talk about the ego, its attack, anger, and pain, and I can relate to that. But doesn't the ego also have nice stuff that fools us and paints a pretty picture of the world? After all, the world is not all pain and suffering; it has beautiful trees and lovely sunshine. Isn't that the same as ego?

A: Absolutely. That is the distinction between special hate and special love. Special hate refers to things, people, and settings we find objectionable. Special love refers to things, people, and settings we find pleasurable. The ego works the same way. We can get as addicted to a beautiful sunset, lake, or country setting as we can be repulsed by the ugliness of nature or the cruelties of war.

Q: What happened to the nice part of me that I thought was kind of fun? That is the hardest stuff to reconcile.

A: There is no question about that, but to address that adequately would require another workshop. The most insidious forms of specialness are those that seem to be so positive—gratifying, loving, and kind. Those are much more difficult to deal with. In Lesson 12, for example, Jesus says that "a 'good world' implies a 'bad' one, and a 'satisfying world' implies an 'unsatisfying' one" (3:6). We are always into opposites, opposite sides of the same coin of separation and duality.

Q: So then is this also something that we would look at with Jesus or the Holy Spirit?

A: Yes. We realize that we believe our peace depends on the day being gorgeous and our being in a beautiful setting, and without that, we would not have a good day. We need to look at this with Jesus because we are saying that his love is not enough; a beautiful lake or sunset is needed to make us happy. This does not mean, of course, that we cannot enjoy the peaceful nature scene, but that we realize they are substitutes for the Love of God, rooting us in the world instead of experiencing the love in our right minds. And then not feeling guilt because madness has been our choice. What does help is to see the beautiful forms as symbolic reminders of love's beauty in the mind, the love we truly want above all else and can choose as our reality.

Q: When we really believe that nothing can separate us from God's Love, the lessons of the Course are over?

A: Correct. Then you no longer need *A Course in Miracles*. As I have been saying, I think it is naïve of students to believe they can do this in a relatively short period of time. The fear of loss of self is too great.

Lesson 95: How to Do the Workbook

I turn now to another way Jesus provides to help us get through these clouds of guilt, which means looking at our sins and forgiving them. I return to something I discussed earlier, the way Jesus asks us to do his workbook and how we choose to do it. I had emphasized that *the* way to do the workbook is to fall flat on your face with it, to forget about God, to forget the lesson, to make the mistakes we all make—but to look at all this without judgment, without feeling you have to make up your lost time with a particular exercise, without feeling that you have to fool Jesus or other people, or that you have to be the perfect workbook student.

My comments will be in the context of Lesson 95, "I am one Self, united with my Creator," which I also mentioned before. What is interesting about this lesson is that in the middle of it Jesus departs from the lesson's theme, and speaks instead about how to do the workbook. The lesson, among many others, contrasts the grandeur of the Self that God created with our version of ourselves, described in this lesson as "a ridiculous parody on God's Creation; weak, vicious, ugly and sinful, miserable and beset with pain." (2:1). Jesus begins with this, and then shifts to comments about how one deals with our lapses in memory. This discussion in turn becomes the segue back to the lesson's theme.

And so, in the fourth paragraph Jesus talks to us about how to do the workbook. He tells us that our minds are still relatively untrained and undisciplined, and therefore we need structure. Here we are, three months into his workbook, and we are told that we are not meditating properly, that our minds are still wandering. What is helpful about this is that almost always the mind will wander; yet Jesus lets us know that he is aware of this and we should not feel guilty. The content underlying this message is: "I know you are a 'miserable sinner'; I know your ego does not care about me or God, but We love you. Do not hide from me the fact that you are not thinking of me, that you place the idols of the world above me and the lessons, that you seek to usurp my place in your mind and life with special things that are trivial. I know you are doing this, and it is all right. None of that has any power, except in dreams."

This is extremely important, for it is how we will see, both in form and content, that Jesus is underscoring the message of his course: "I love you, the Holy Spirit loves you, God loves you, nothing has happened to change that happy Fact." Not only is this the message in terms of the meaning of everything, but the very form of his giving us this message says the same thing. We do not have to pretend with him. We do not have to be a spiritual giant who sits and meditates, and then watches the world disappear as the mind is flooded with light and love. He is telling us, "I know this is not what happens, and that is okay. My love for you remains the same." If we get that message just once, we have learned the Course and do not need it anymore. It says that our perceived sin against God has not affected His Love, and if it that is true, the sin does not exist and is not a cause of anything. Without sin there is no justification for guilt, and no need to project the guilt into the future and fear punishment. The entire ego thought system disappears with the simple statement, "It does not matter what you do; my love for you has not changed."

Jesus is telling us not to fool him or ourselves. We merely have to be aware of our lack of mental discipline and consequent need for mind training. If we are not aware of this, how are we going to forgive our lapses? This means our sin will stay buried, only to surface in our projections. The danger is that we will think we have done something when we have not. In the New Testament, Jesus repeatedly is seen as chastising the Pharisees. In one dreadful scene, he calls them "a generation of vipers." I am not saying that Jesus actually said this, but taking those incidents as instructive, we can understand the biblical Jesus saying to them that their mistake was in believing that if they kept the letter of the law, they were keeping its spirit. The Pharisees were the branch of Judaism that adhered strictly to the teachings of the Old Testament (the letter of the law), and therefore believed they were spiritually superior to other Jewish groups. In essence, Jesus was telling them they were obeying the forms of love (i.e., special love), but missing its content.

Once again, the danger is that the hatred concealed by the form stays buried in the mind, resurfacing later in very ugly ways. The bloody history of Christianity unfortunately attests to this.

Therefore, Jesus is saying here that we should never feel guilty because we go through long stretches of time forgetting about him and the daily lesson. He tells us: "I know you will forget. You have this curriculum so that your mind can be trained to remember. Do not feel guilty because you are sinning." Naturally, he does not see our forgetting as sinful, but we do. Forgetting his words and turning our backs on his presence is a reminder of what we accuse ourselves of having done with God, and we all re-enact, over and over again, that ontological instant of horror. Remember, this world is proof to our insane minds that we killed off God, convinced that we could build a better world than His; that, in fact, we could be God. As I mentioned earlier, this is the germ of the authority problem: I have defeated the authority. I have usurped His place on the throne. I am God.

The purpose of *A Course in Miracles* is to remind us how pygmy-like we are spiritually. We are very little children, very far from the spiritual giant of our fantasies. Jesus gently lets us know this, and we need to stop fighting him and trying to pretend we are something we not. Rather, we should acknowledge, "Yes, this is what I am, but it is not a sin." This honesty lets his love back in. If we insist that we do not have an ego, or have just bare traces of it, we are going to believe we do not need him. This is exactly what the ego wants, that we be our own author: "I don't need Jesus or the Holy Spirit because I can do it by myself. In fact, I have already done so." We thus effectively see to it that we never get the help we need, and mire ourselves still deeper in the ego's morass of guilt and fear.

And so our teacher says to us: "You are still a little child, and therefore you need this structure, but when you grow up you will not need it anymore." He makes a similar point in "How Should the Teacher of God Spend His Day?" from the manual (M-16). He talks there about advanced teachers of God never having to ask, "How should I spend my day?" because the Holy Spirit's Love guides them. Until we reach that point, however, structure is very necessary. Remember again, the workbook is a one-year training program that usually is done near the beginning of one's work with the Course. That is why its structure is so important.

Questions

Q: According to the Course, then, is the essence of meditation just simply looking at the ego and not going off into the light, or doing the things that would give me a high?

A: Right. This is not a course in achieving a spiritual high. Just the opposite. It is a course in helping us realize how low we are, and then to look at that low with Jesus. That is what will raise us up. In the context of the Course's process, meditation would mean looking at the low with him, just as forgiveness is looking at the ego with him. When we really understand that, it will make perfect sense to us, and will also make our life incredibly easy. We will no longer have to fight to do something, like meditate: "Today I was going to get it right. But I meditated for fourteen and a half minutes, and in the last thirty seconds I blew it." We need not struggle with forms or even content. We merely look at our egos without judgment.

To expand on this, we can say that the goal of *A Course in Miracles* is not that we have no ego thoughts, that we never get sick, or that we are never guilty, angry, or fearful. Its goal for us is that, after a while, we would automatically respond to these thoughts or actions by looking at them with Jesus. Then they will disappear. If we think we must approach it differently, we will be setting a standard we will never reach. If we say that we need to go through a day without a single ego thought, our ego will be rampant because we are implying that the ego is real and terrible, and salvation means that we will be free of it. This merely gives it a reality and strength it does not have.

The goal of the Course is that we have all the ego thoughts we want, but look at them with Jesus or the Holy Spirit, no longer giving them power to take Their Love from our minds. How could these thoughts not disappear then? That is the importance of these lines from the manual, "Do not despair, then, because of limitations. It is your function to escape from them, but not to be without them" (M-26.4:1-2). This refers to the limitations of the body, and what we escape from is the burden of guilt we placed upon them, whether the limitations

be physical or psychological. Our function is not to be without these, to transcend the physical or psychological laws we have made. Our function is to look at these and our identification with them, but without guilt and judgment. That is how we negate them, exemplifying "the proper use of denial" (T-2.II.1:12). The improper use of denial has us believe that guilt is so fearful we will never look at it again. Jesus helps us deny that the mind's guilt has any power over God's Love.

As I discussed earlier, getting yourself an alarm clock to be sure that you practice exactly as Jesus instructs you misses the whole point. The idea is not to literally spend five minutes of every hour with Jesus or with the workbook lesson. The idea is that you would *want* to; but even more to the point, the idea is to be aware of how much you do *not* want to. If you use an alarm clock, you are short-circuiting the process, because then you are not allowing yourself to see how much you do not want to learn your lessons, and are therefore pre-empting the forgiveness process. Also involved, as I mentioned earlier, is thinking that if you get an alarm clock to remind you to do the exercise, you will be in Jesus' good graces because he will put a check-mark on your chart in Heaven each time you "remember."

This leads you to getting caught up with numbers rather than with the content. This is not a course in *quantity* but *quality*. This is another common error, and has been there almost from the Course's publication in 1976. People become excited about the growing number of students, from hundreds to a couple of thousand, tens and hundreds of thousands, even a million or more. The excitement comes from believing that the large number of people studying the Course means something. They do not realize they have merely gotten caught in the ego trap of making the world of multiplicity real: if there are enough bodies that study *A Course in Miracles*, the world will be saved.

In the 1970s there were people who sent copies of the Course to the Carter White House and to the Vatican. The idea was that if we can get people in power to be students of the Course, and they then broadcast it to the world, the world would be saved—*as if there were a world that needed saving.* This is the mistake, which is why we cannot meaningfully work with this course if we do not understand its metaphysics. When Jesus says "There is no world!" (W-pI.132.6:2), he means it literally. Note the exclamation point! Since there is no world, how could what does not exist be saved? It is the world of the mind that has to be saved. The world does not need great Course teachers, nor does it need great books written on it. The world does need people who live the Course, and putting it into practice has nothing to do with worldly events or activity. We shall return shortly to what it really means to be a teacher of God.

And so this is not a course in the multiplication of students, because once you get caught in that (numbers are solidly in the ego system), you obviously are involved in the world of duality. There is only one number in the entire universe—one. In the teachers' manual there is a question, "How Many Teachers of God Are Needed to Save the World?" (M-12). The answer is one. While that "one" could be seen as Jesus (or anyone else who transcended the ego), its underlying meaning is that Jesus represents the one Christ. Only one teacher is needed to save the world, because there *is* only one teacher for there is only one Son, not billions. Our job is simply to do our part to save the one Son, which means that we heal our mind of thoughts of guilt, which is the acceptance of the Atonement. It does not matter if the President, the Pope, or anyone else has a copy of *A Course in Miracles*. All that matters is that *you* have a copy, and that you work with the Course and do what it says and learn its lessons.

Q: In reference to numbers, does that mean that getting the Course into the media is not helping?

A: Who is to say if it is helping or not? The point that I was making is that if you are a student of *A Course in Miracles* and become happy because it is in the media, there is something wrong. Whether it is in the media or not should be no one's concern. What people suffer from is thinking somehow this is their course. It is not. This is Jesus' course, and I assure you that he does not care if it is in the media or not because he does not know about the media. There is no carefully orchestrated plan that is going to see to it that this gets into the White House and to every world capitol, into all the churches and synagogues, etc. He does not have agents in each of these places who are going to do his work. It is not like that. He would be insane if he had such a plan because it would be making the world real.

There is only one plan: the acceptance of the Atonement. If *A Course in Miracles* gets into the media, the Vatican, or Congress, it does. So be it. But of what interest is that to you, me, or anyone else? Our concern should only be to accept the Atonement. How could the other matter if there is no world and the decision-making mind is everything? Once you think it does matter, you have been caught in believing the world is real. This subtle trap is so easy to fall into, but is easily avoided if you keep on your bathroom mirror, written in indelible crayon: "There is no world!"

If there is no world, then what or whom are you going to save? Whom are the media going to report to if there is no world? That does not mean you deny what you do or what your physical life or classrooms are. It just means that when you find yourself getting concerned or depressed because something is not happening publicly with the Course, or you get exalted and exuberant because it is, you realize you have trapped yourself into believing there is something out there that has to be saved. There is no one out there who needs *A Course in Miracles*, because there is no one out there! There is, however, someone in here who does need *A Course in Miracles*—our decision-making minds.

Q: Shouldn't we be gleeful that the Course is spreading, and should we not be upset that it is being altered or compromised by some people?

A: That is the same mistake. If you are concerned that the Course is being altered, you are saying there is something outside you that has power. Even assuming that you are right, that there is someone out there who is compromising the Course, remember that everyone will have a different understanding of who is compromising what. So, you may be correct, but if you are upset, you are saying the person has committed a sin, and now you, on your shining white horse with *A Course in Miracles* blazing in the air, are going to ride into town and burn the heretics because you know the truth. We get caught in this mistake all the time. Your only concern should be with yourself, whether you are choosing the ego or the Holy Spirit as your teacher.

The other part of this issue is why you would be surprised that people would compromise the Course; people compromised God right at the beginning. It is possible, nonetheless, to describe errors without judging the students, without making a big deal about it. That is the crucial thing. Remember that in his course, Jesus says very clearly that for two thousand years Christians have compromised what he has taught. Those are not his exact words, but he is very clear that Christians have made many, many mistakes. Never, though, do you get the feeling that he is judging. He is simply saying, "This is the way it is. What is so unusual about that? The whole world is a compromise."

Generalization

In paragraph 8 of Lesson 95, Jesus moves the discussion into generalization, where it becomes obvious that he is not talking just about the particular workbook lesson, but a much larger theme. Here are two extremely important sentences: "The Holy Spirit is not delayed in His teachings by your mistakes. He can be held back only by your unwillingness to let them go." The immediate reference is to the mistakes we make with the workbook. But we can generalize that to mean that the Holy Spirit is not hindered by *any* of our mistakes. The problem, however, is not the mistakes themselves. It is our unwillingness to let them go by feeling guilty, or by justifying or rationalizing them, making up stories to support the error. Again, the problem is not the mistake, that we forget to think of God five minutes on the hour, or that we condemn instead of forgive. The problem is that when we forget, we hold on to the mistakes by feeling guilty or projecting the blame onto someone or something else. This, then, is the same thing I have already mentioned: the problem was not the *tiny, mad idea* of being separate from God, but taking it seriously. Calling the *tiny, mad idea* a sin is taking it seriously. Calling it a *tiny, mad idea* and saying it is silly—"It is a joke to think that time can come to circumvent eternity...." (T-27.VIII.6:5)—is calling it a mistake. As the Course repeatedly says, sins are punished, mistakes are corrected.

Therefore, we want to unlearn the original mistake we made by calling the mistake a sin, instead of simply saying it was a *tiny, mad idea* that had no effect. We unlearn by repeating the error, over and over, but now looking at it differently. One expression of this mistake is failing to do the lesson the way we are "supposed to," as if there were a "supposed to," as if there were a right way of doing the workbook. Remember, the "right" way of doing the workbook is to do it "wrong," and then to forgive yourself for having done so. That is something else you should put on your bathroom mirror: "The right way to do the workbook is to do it wrong and then forgive yourself for it." Put "There is no world!" first, though, because that is more important.

To restate this essential point, the Holy Spirit is held back not by mistakes but "only by your unwillingness to let them go." That is guilt's purpose, and why there is such tremendous emphasis in the Course on guilt. Guilt is what takes the mistake, freezes it, and calls it a sin. When you simply look at it gently without judgment and smile at it, it disappears. Not looking at it is the unwillingness to let it go in order to preserve our separated self.

In one beautiful passage in *The Gifts of God* (p. 118), the prose poem Helen had taken down, Jesus asked her to give him the ego's gifts, her guilt and fear, and in exchange he would give her the gifts of God. This, of course, is for all of us as well. We come to him with clenched fists, tightly holding onto our sin and guilt. Jesus implores us to open our hands and realize there is only empty space within, into which he now would be free to place his gifts of love. The idea is not that we have to be perfect; it is that we forgive ourselves for not being perfect, for our "lapses in diligence," our "failures to follow the instructions for practicing the day's idea."

What he is asking of us is not that we give him our love, but that we give him our sin, guilt, and attack thoughts. We do not have any love we can give him; if we did, we would be just like him. We give him our guilt and then he takes it away. It is not that he literally takes it from us; it is simply that when we open our hand, the guilt is gone. The clenched fist reflects our belief that there is something there to hold and cherish: sin. Guilt keeps it clenched, and projection protects it; but when we open our hand we realize there is nothing there, and then his love automatically takes its place. Our doing the workbook the way he asks us to in Lesson 95 is what accomplishes this.

In another important passage in paragraph 8 of Lesson 95, Jesus instructs us further about being tolerant of our weakness so that it does not delay our learning: "If we give it power to do this, we are regarding it as strength and are confusing strength with weakness." Generalizing, we can say that we, the decision-making mind, give the ego power to delay our return home; in fact, we give the ego power to tell us that we are not home in the first place. We give other people's egos power as well. What undoes this power and strips it away, making the ego impotent, is simply looking at it and saying it cannot interfere with God's Love for us or ours for Him.

In paragraph 10, Jesus shifts the focus to the larger issue, taking us back to the principal theme of the lesson:

> Let all these errors go by recognizing them for what they are. They are attempts to keep you unaware you are one Self, united with your Creator, at one with every aspect of creation, and limitless in power and in peace. This is the truth, and nothing else is true.

Our teacher is saying that all our attempts to fail this course are deliberate. It is not accidental that we forget the workbook lesson. It is not accidental that we drop his hand and pick up the ego's instead. It is not accidental that we keep attacking people or ourselves, finding grievances to upset us rather than letting them go. All of these are attempts to keep the clouds of guilt and attack firmly in place, so much so that we will not hear the Holy Spirit's Voice remind us that we are one Self united with our Creator, as the title of the Lesson states. These ego thoughts attempt to keep the ego alive and well, and occur in things both trivial and consequential. They are all the same. Jesus is telling us here again not to be afraid of making mistakes, and not to try to be perfect. We need not prove that we love him. We merely have to accept his love rather than the ego's guilt.

The idea in all this, to come back again to the core principle, is not to confuse form with content. The content of the workbook is the retraining of the mind. The form is everything he is asking of us. But he is not interested in the form; only the content is important. We cannot retrain our mind if we do not know we have one, let alone know what is in it—the ego's viciousness, fear, anger, and resistance. In sum, doing the workbook is a wonderful way of bringing to the surface all these defenses against God's Love so we may let them go.

Review III—Introduction

I would like to read the Introduction to Review III, paragraphs 2 and 3, as they reflect some of the ideas we have been discussing:

> We understand, of course, that it may be impossible for you to undertake what is suggested here as optimal each day and every hour of the day. Learning will not be hampered when you miss a practice period because it is impossible at the appointed time. Nor is it necessary that you make excessive efforts to be sure that you catch up in terms of numbers. Rituals are not our aim, and would defeat our goal.
>
> But learning will be hampered when you skip a practice period because you are unwilling to devote the time to it that you are asked to give. Do not deceive yourself in this. Unwillingness can be most carefully concealed behind a cloak of situations you cannot control. Learn to distinguish situations that are poorly suited to your practicing from those that you establish to uphold a camouflage for your unwillingness.

Jesus is again telling us that he knows we will not be able to do exactly what he says. Sometimes, incidentally, people will leave their families and jobs for a whole year so that their practice sessions will not be interfered with by the mundane and trivial things normal people deal with every day. They think they will then be able to do the workbook perfectly. If there are people who have not done that, there certainly are those who wish they could and envy those who can. What they fail to realize is that their everyday life and responsibilities are the perfect place, the perfect classroom in which to practice their daily lessons of forgiveness. It is important to remember that Jesus is not interested in numbers; he does not count how many times we fall short in our practicing. It is not necessary to set aside special times to do the workbook or to arrange special settings. Recalling our earlier discussion, this is not a course in traditional meditation. We are not even asked to focus on God. Rather, we are asked to *learn* how to think of God all the time, which really means becoming increasingly aware of how much we do *not* think of Him, or even want to think of Him. We need to become aware of the interferences and not judge them. That is when they will begin to fall away.

Years ago, I was working with contemplative sisters who had regularly scheduled prayer times each day. Some days, because of responsibilities or emergencies, they were not able to pray at those specific times. They would tell me that just before they went to bed they would quickly make up all the missed prayer periods. This is what Jesus is talking about, except he is not talking about prayerful nuns. He is certainly not excluding them; indeed some of his best friends are nuns, even ex-nuns! What he is saying is that we do not have to make up what we missed, as if he were standing in Heaven with a score card. He asks only that we be honest with ourselves, echoing his appeal in the text: "Be very honest with yourself…for we must hide nothing from each other" (T-4.III.8:2). Moreover, he is asking us to be honest with him: "Do not be deceived by the fact that very often you will skip a practice period, not because you had an emergency that required your time and attention, but because you did not want to spend time with me. Be honest with yourself. Of course you do not want to spend time with me, for that would exclude your ego. And since I do not take it personally, nor do I judge it, you should not either." We need to discern whether we really cannot do the lesson, or simply do not want to do it and are just pretending we cannot.

The idea is to generalize these instructions for the practice periods to everything we do. This is another reason it is helpful for us to truly accept that Jesus and the Holy Spirit do not do things in the world, nor are They interested in what goes on in it. To be involved in the world would make the world real, and further, it would confuse form with content. Their exclusive concern is with our choice to identify with the love that is in our minds. When we can look without judgment at how much we have identified with the guilt, fear, and attack thoughts in the mind, they all disappear. What remains is the love that flows through us by itself. That is what it means to be a teacher of God, which brings us to the final theme of our discussion of the workbook.

6. On Being A Teacher of God

Although the term *teacher of God* does not appear in the workbook, as I mentioned earlier, Jesus nonetheless talks about it in Lessons 153 through 157, among others, such as Lesson 37 that I referred to above. There are a number of places in the text where this same idea is expressed with regard to the miracle, forgiveness, and salvation (T-16.II.1; T-22.VI.9; T-27.V.1). In each of these, Jesus teaches that our only function is to choose the miracle or forgiveness, while their extension is not our responsibility.

My earlier comments regarding the issue of involvement in the Course's life in the world come to mind here. Our function is simply to accept the Atonement for ourselves, which is learning to choose between the miracle and a grievance, forgiveness and attack. Once we make the right-minded choice, which we do whenever we look at our ego thoughts without judgment, the love that is reflected by our decision automatically extends through us. It does not matter whether one is giving classes or writing books on *A Course in Miracles*, is a bricklayer, psychotherapist, head of a family, teaching school, or fixing a pipe. Whatever one is doing would automatically be the instrument through which the love of Jesus in our minds would flow, *and it is this love that heals, not the forms in which it is expressed.*

And so our focus should not be what we do with the form, but only in making room for truth. Jesus tells us this near the end of the workbook: "We are concerned only with giving welcome to the truth" (W-pII.14.3:7). Our job is to know truth, not to teach or extend it. And we come to know truth by making room in the mind by releasing our guilt when we forgive. This allows truth to extend through us naturally. That is why Jesus had told Helen very early in the scribing that these words meant for her were to be kept in the Course: "Ask me which miracles you should perform." In other words, "Do not do things on your own. Do not be a do-gooder. Let me be the do-gooder. Just choose me and be with me, for this will free my love to guide you in what to say and do in terms of people you will help." This is the meaning of "Trust not your good intentions. They are not enough" (T-18.IV.2:1-2). It is the well-intentioned people who focus on saving the world. This is not a course in being well-intentioned. It is a course in realizing how evil our intentions frequently are, yet once we look at these with Jesus' love beside us, they disappear, allowing his love to joyously flow through us.

We turn now to Lesson 155, an extremely important lesson to which I refer quite often, especially its opening paragraph. That paragraph—the whole lesson, in fact—alerts us to the common ego trap of attempting to appear holy, of wanting everyone to know how wonderfully advanced we are as teachers of God. That inevitably involves making judgments about the forms and behaviors of the teacher of God, such as the license plates an advanced teacher should have, to use an extreme example. That is the aforementioned confusion of form and content, to which Jesus calls our attention. It should also be noted that in this lesson Jesus is actually talking about *advanced* teachers, as he does in the ten characteristics of God's teachers in the teachers' manual.

(W-pI.155.1:1-4) There is a way of living in the world that is not here, although it seems to be. You do not change appearance, though you smile more frequently. Your forehead is serene; your eyes are quiet. And the ones who walk the world as you do recognize their own.

"You do not change appearance." You do not behave differently, talk, dress, or eat differently. Indeed, you typically look like everyone else, the only difference being that you smile more frequently because you are peaceful. This is because you "step back and let Him lead the way." *You* do not lead the way. *The Holy Spirit* leads the way. You step back and look at your ego with Him, not taking it seriously and giving it power to affect you. This lifts the burden of guilt and pain from you, leaving only a gentle smile. With guilt gone, all that is left in your mind is the love of Jesus, and that is what comes through you. It is essential to realize that there is nothing you need do for that love to come through. Your job is simply to step back and look at the interference of your ego. He does the rest.

A recurring theme, appearing in the text but much more frequently in the workbook, is that Jesus, the Holy Spirit, and Christ need our bodies. One expression of this comes in Lesson 154 "I am among the ministers of God":

> We practice giving Him [the Holy Spirit] what He would have, that we may recognize His gifts to us. He needs our voice that He may

speak through us. He needs our hands to hold His messages, and carry them to those whom He appoints. He needs our feet to bring us where He wills, that those who wait in misery may be at last delivered. And he needs our will united with His Own, that we may be the true receivers of the gifts He gives (W-pI.154.11).

Apart from "will," referring to our mind's right-minded decision, everything that Jesus mentions here—voice, hands, and feet—refers to our bodies.

Another expression of this theme occurs in the Introduction to the Fifth Review, where Jesus says:

> Let this review be then your gift to me. For this alone I need; that you will hear the words I speak, and give them to the world. You are my voice, my eyes, my feet, my hands through which I save the world (W-pI.rV.9:1-3).

Still another reference comes in the last paragraph of the summary called "What Is the Second Coming?" in Part II of the workbook, where the Second Coming is the subject:

> Pray that the Second Coming will be soon, but do not rest with that. It needs your eyes and ears and hands and feet. It needs your voice. And most of all it needs your willingness (W-pII.9.5:1-4).

The *Second Coming* is the Course's term for the end of the Atonement, the final awakening of the Son wherein the fragmented Sonship is reunited. The passage makes it clear that the Second Coming (or Holy Spirit) needs not only our body but our willingness, which reflects the mind's shift in identification from the ego to the Holy Spirit.

There are many other references of this nature in the Course. Their significance stems from the way they help us understand that Jesus is not against the body, and that even though he tells us there is no world, only an insane belief in it as an attack on God, he does not condemn it. He uses the world because we believe in it, and shifts its purpose to a classroom through which he can communicate his message. He needed Helen's body, for example, so that this non-specific message could take form. He needed her mind's decision to let his love come through her body in order to take down his words. The source or the content of the Course is abstract love. The words are its form.

What made Helen holy was not her scribing *A Course in Miracles*, but that she had the willingness to unite with Jesus. That same holiness is in everyone, which is why when people would try to put Helen on a spiritual pedestal for doing this "holy work," she would consistently tell them that what she did they could do. This idea of willingness is a major theme in the Course, especially in the text, where it is spoken of as a "little willingness" (see T-18.IV). We simply need the little willingness to drop the ego's hand and take Jesus' instead. This means looking at our ego and not taking it seriously. When we do that, we identify solely with the Love of God, which we now know is what we are. Then that Love will automatically come through us and be manifest in the world.

The world and its images are nothing but projections or extensions ("pictorial representations") of what is in our minds. If what is in our mind is the Thought of Love, then everything we do and say would manifest that Love. As I observed earlier, this is why Jesus tells us he is the manifestation of the Holy Spirit (C-6.1:1). When he appeared on this earth, he looked like everyone else as a body. However, what came through him, what his body reflected, was Heaven's resplendent love. *This* is what made him different. His mind was totally at one with the Love of Christ, and so everything he said and did reflected that. The Holy Spirit used Jesus' voice, eyes, ears, hands, and feet, through which He gave that message. Jesus' message is exactly the same today, and so in the Course he asks that we become his manifestation. Since he is no longer in a body and does not speak words, he needs *our* bodies—voice and words—through which he can convey to others his non-specific message of God's Love, the Atonement principle that says that the separation from God never happened, and so we are not separate from each other.

Students are very prone, as I have been saying, to making the mistake of identifying with the form: "I want to be a holy person; I want to teach *A Course in Miracles* just as you do," as if there were something holy about delivering a lecture. What is holy is the love that hopefully informs the lecture, not the lecture itself. What makes you a teacher of the Course is not the ability to expound on what it teaches, simply repeating a series of concepts, but the love with which you teach. Clearly, then, you are not the teacher, for it is the love of Jesus through you that teaches. Therefore, the idea is not to get caught in the form, but to identify as

much as possible with the love that is your identity. Again, it is your acceptance of this love that makes you a teacher of God.

Moving to the second paragraph of Lesson 155, we see a continuation of Jesus' teachings on how we become his teachers:

(W-pI.155.2) The world is an illusion. Those who choose to come to it are seeking for a place where they can be illusions, and avoid their own reality. Yet when they find their own reality is even here, then they step back and let it lead the way. What other choice is really theirs to make? To let illusions walk ahead of truth is madness. But to let illusion sink behind the truth and let the truth stand forth as what it is, is merely sanity.

Anyone who comes into this world is trying to protect his or her self-image as a separated self, the world and the body being the means of demonstrating that. In that sense, the world is a hiding place in which to avoid our own reality. The teacher of God "let[s] illusions sink behind the truth and let[s] the truth stand forth as what it is, merely sanity." As teachers of God, we realize we can be in the world and yet not of it; live in the world as bodies, and yet know that the Holy Spirit is within us as minds, that we are children of God and not the ego. Our ego has stepped back, meaning that the "you"—the decision-making mind—who has identified with the ego has stepped back, and therefore love is the reality and leads the way. Everything we do will then emanate from that reality. Jesus is reminding us that we are tempted to bring the truth to the illusion, rather than the illusion to the truth. The lesson is to look at the illusion and not be afraid of it. Only then can it recede and be replaced by the truth.

In the fourth and fifth paragraphs of this lesson, Jesus sets forth three different ways of being in the world: The first comprises people who believe that the world is evil or sinful, and must be avoided. The second consists of those who believe that the world is valuable, and who are intensely attached to it because it is the means of attaining contentment and happiness. The third is the middle path, that of the (advanced) teacher of God. These are the ones who walk with Jesus and not the ego. Their behavior and appearance will be be like everyone else's, but there will be a peace about them for it is love that comes through, not guilt or specialness.

(W-pI.155.4-5) If truth demanded they give up the world, it would appear to them as if it asked the sacrifice of something that is real. Many have chosen to renounce the world while still believing its reality. And they have suffered from a sense of loss, and have not been released accordingly. Others have chosen nothing but the world, and they have suffered from a sense of loss still deeper, which they did not understand.

Between these paths there is another road that leads away from loss of every kind, for sacrifice and deprivation both are quickly left behind. This is the way appointed for you now. You walk this path as others walk, nor do you seem to be distinct from them, although you are indeed. Thus can you serve them while you serve yourself, and set their footsteps on the way that God has opened up to you, and them through you.

Those who believe the world is evil are seeing in it the projection of their own sin, but no longer perceived as theirs. They see the form of sin outside themselves, resulting in their belief that the world is a bad place. This is often a temptation for people who work with the Course, as they think that when Jesus says the world is an illusion, he is really saying the world is sinful. If you feel you have to retreat from the world or its responsibilities, from being normal, you are saying the world is bad, unholy, or unspiritual. Once you say that, you have made it real, and in doing so, you have made real as well the thoughts of separation and guilt that the world represents.

This was the Gnostic error. The Gnostics, a philosophical school that thrived in the early Christian centuries, almost unanimously taught that the world is not real, that God did not create it, the God of both Old and New Testaments was the ego God (though they did not use that term), and that the true God was beyond that. Convinced of this, many of them—not all—fled from the world, believing that involvement with it was sinful, believing that because the world was the effect of the inferior God, to get involved with it in any way was to fall into the clutches of this false deity. Valentinus was among the very few Gnostic teachers who escaped that trap.

People who work with *A Course in Miracles* often get caught in the same snare. Its critics sometimes base their judgments on the grounds that it is Gnostic. However, they do not realize that it is Gnostic in one area but not the other. The Course does of course teach that God did not create the world, but it does not condemn the world or counsel its students not to be involved with the body. As the text says:

> The body was not made by love. Yet love does not condemn it and can use it lovingly, respecting what the Son of God has made and using it to save him from illusions (T-18.VI.4:7-8).

1) This first way of being in the world is based on the belief the world is bad, and so must be given up. The problem is that there is another part of us that is attracted to the world, meaning we would have to sacrifice what we are attracted to: God says I should not be involved with the sins of the flesh; therefore I must separate myself from the bodily sins, the pleasures of sex, food, clothing, a comfortable bed, etc. Thus the problem is in the world, leading us to avoid it all cost. This leaves us with the conflict of believing that God is asking us to give up something we really want, a wonderful way of demonstrating that the world and the thought system that made it are real.

The idea of sacrifice and loss flows from this conflict of renouncing the world while still believing in its reality. The notion of sacrifice has played a prominent role in almost all the world religions, both East and West. But in this lesson, Jesus is telling us that this is not how he wants us to be. He makes the same point in the section "I Need Do Nothing" (T-18.VII), where the context is those who spend a lifetime in contemplation, sacrifice, and fighting against sin. He explains that this approach will work in the long run because its goal is God, but it will take a very long time. The way he offers us in his course is much shorter because it does not first make the error real, and then seek to overcome it. It simply looks at the error and says it is not the truth.

Again, many students of *A Course in Miracles* are tempted to go in that direction, born of the now-familiar error of confusing form and content, and so seek to change their behavior. Students then affirm "I trust my brothers who are one with me"; "In my defenselessness my safety lies"; "A healed mind does not plan," and express these "affirmations" by modifying how their bodies live, often placing their lives or the lives of their loved ones in danger, to wit: I won't lock my car or home, I won't plan for the future, I will drop all insurance policies because I am an advanced teacher of God and beyond such worldly concerns." There is a magical hope that by changing what is external (behavior), we are changing what is internal (the mind). All that happens, however, is that the guilt within stays there, but now barricaded even more firmly. Our behavior may have been modified, but the mind has not changed.

The world's thinking, therefore, is that by changing behavior we can change our self. *A Course in Miracles* teaches the opposite, that by changing our self—i.e., the mind—our world will change, or certainly our experience of it will change. The idea is not to focus on changing the outer. Remember that the inner is the cause of the outer, not the other way around.

To reiterate this central point, the major interference to our development as teachers of God is confusing form with content. This is a course in content only, not form. The passages in the text that deal with special relationships have as their purpose helping us to resolve this confusion. In a veiled criticism of Christianity (Catholicism, especially), Jesus points out the confusion of form and content in establishing ritual as the Will of God, that one shows one's love of the Creator by obeying the laws He set up. The thrust of Jesus' critique is that it is not the ritual or form that is important, but the content. This confusion is evident in the ritual of communion (the Eucharist), where the Catholic Church teaches that the faithful become one with Jesus by joining with his transubstantiated body. This is why he tells us in the Course that it is his mind he wants us to join with, not his body.

The issue, once again, is the mistaken belief that by modifying our external life we will have a corresponding change in our internal life. We carry this out by adopting behaviors in the world that we judge to be spiritual, as we just saw ("I place my future in God's hands") or by adopting behaviors that enable us to avoid the world we have judged to be such a sinful place.

This is why this lesson is so important. In essence, Jesus is telling us to be normal, to look and act like everyone else, but do everything with him instead of the ego. As I often say, one of the most important points to keep in mind when you work with the Course is not to forget to be normal; do not try to be different or separate from others.

One final point about this first way of being in the world: Once we label certain behaviors as spiritual or unspiritual, we are saying there is a hierarchy of illusions; for example, having insurance policies is bad, not having them is good; having locks on doors is bad, not having them is good. To say things in the world are good or bad obviously presupposes a world. Moreover, once we assert that something is spiritual, the opposite must be true as well; and if we assert that anything is unspiritual, its opposite must be true. This means we are in duality. By separating the world into holy and unholy people, spiritual and unspiritual activity, we perceive a pictorial representation of the mind's duality: God-ego, victim-victimizer, holy-unholy. We take that insane thought, project it into the world, and see duality and opposition everywhere.

2) The second form of living in the world, which Jesus also warns us against, has to do with people who believe the world is valuable. Typically, these are the ones society calls materialistic, devoting themselves to acquiring cars, money, and possessions of all kinds, along with striving for fame, prestige, and adulation. The world, then, is a good place if it gives them what they want. Yet, Jesus tells us that having "chosen nothing but the world…they have suffered from a sense of loss still deeper, which they did not understand." In other words, after getting what they want, people will feel that it is not enough; something is still missing. Since the ego loves comparisons, there is the nagging belief that someone else has more, which merely intensifies the drive to acquire more. They react to this distress by striving to get more and more and more, sensing at the same time that they will never have enough. Ultimately, this second group bases its value as persons on the quantity of external possessions, or being esteemed by others. What has truly happened is that the sense of emptiness in the mind has been filled, not with the Love of God—that is what they fear—but with the love of money and things, and other bodies who will worship at the shrines of specialness.

3) The middle path, however, "leads away from loss of every kind, for sacrifice and deprivation both are quickly left behind.… You walk this path as others walk, nor do you seem to be distinct from them, although you are indeed" (W-pI.155.5:1,3). What makes you different as an advanced teacher of God

is that you now walk with Jesus or the Holy Spirit and not with the ego, which simply means that your external behavior and form will be the same as everyone else's, but there will be a peace about you, you will smile more frequently, and only love will come through you. There will be genuine compassion and concern not for one group versus another, but for *all* people. There will be no exceptions in anything you see, do, or feel. You will recognize that everyone is both victim and victimizer, for we all suffer from the tremendous mountain of guilt coming from believing we have actually destroyed Heaven, run away from home, and will never find our way back.

What is also distinctive about this middle road is that once you identify with the peace of God and Jesus' love, you will experience that state of mind as perfectly natural and not out of the ordinary. There will therefore be no need to boastfully announce your "advanced state" to others, for example. The Holy Spirit teaches through contrast (T-14.II.1), and you will recognize this natural state by seeing that you no longer react to situations as you once did. Your peace will be unmistakable and you will feel the difference, as will those who live and work with you.

Finally, you will serve others not by doing good works in the world, but by reminding them of what you have remembered. There is nothing wrong in helping others in the world as long as you know that you are not the helper and have no investment in the world's reaction. You do not confuse form (behavior) and content (thought). The subsection "The function of the teacher of God" in the manual for teachers is a wonderful presentation of this important aspect of being a teacher of God. Jesus refers there to how, as a teacher of God, we would help people who are sick, but obviously this is meant to extend to everyone, not just those who are physically ill.

(M-5.III.2:2-3,6-12) The simple presence of a teacher of God is a reminder. His thoughts ask for the right to question what the patient has accepted as true.... They stand for the Alternative. With God's Word in their minds they come in benediction, not to heal the sick but to remind them of the remedy God has already given them. It is not their hands that heal. It is not their voice that speaks the Word of God. They merely give what has been given them. Very gently they call to their brothers to turn away from death: "Behold, you Son of God, what life can offer you. Would you choose sickness in place of this?"

All we do as a teacher of God is remind—not by words, but by the mind's peace that extends through us into the world. This is the reminder to others that they can question the way they have been believing, feeling, and behaving: The anxiety and pain we feel comes always from a choice we made that we have taken as a given, and have forgotten how to question; our anger seems to be a reality, and our guilt something we were born with. All this is what we must now question.

To the mindless who have forgotten they have a mind, our peace is a way of saying there is another choice. In Jesus' words, "They stand for the Alternative." Our function is not to heal the sick, not to do something external that will make people feel better. Our bodies may end up doing just that, but in truth the healing will be done through us. And we will know the difference when we have no investment in the other person being happy or healed, or some situation changing because of us. We will know we have done it with the Holy Spirit rather than the ego when our self-image does not change because of the wonderful work we are doing, and all the people who tell us how wonderful we are. In other words, we know that the love and peace of Jesus are all that we want, all that we have, and all that we are, and there is nothing else. Therefore, whether the other person tells us how wonderful we are is irrelevant; whether another person gets up from the sick bed and walks because of us is irrelevant. This does not mean that things like this will not happen; it just means that they are irrelevant to our inner peace and true healing.

What helps is not having healing hands or saying holy words, whether from the Bible, *A Course in Miracles*, or any other book: "They merely give what has been given them. Very gently they call to their brothers to turn away from death: 'Behold, you Son of God, what life can offer you. Would you choose sickness in place of this?'" This does not mean that we visit a person in the hospital with the teachers' manual in hand and read from it. I know that sounds funny, but I assure you there have been Course students who have done precisely that. Again, this is only and always about content (mind), never the form (body). Having gotten our egos out of the way, love and peace will naturally be reflected in our behavior and demeanor. Our right-minded thinking will speak to the fact that it is in the other person as well, since minds are joined. Just as we chose to have Jesus be with us, this person's decision-making mind can also choose to be present to his love.

(M-5.III.3:1-2) Not once do the advanced teachers of God consider the forms of sickness in which their brother believes. To do this is to forget that all of them have the same purpose, and therefore are not really different.

Here again we see the theme, presented over and over again in the workbook, that everything is the same. This is the reason for the strong emphasis in the early lessons' instructions that we not specifically exclude any object in the day's practicing because everything is the same. Jesus teaches us this profound message in seemingly simple instructions. He is teaching us not to be taken in by form. That is what I meant earlier in my caution about numbers and quantity. It does not matter how many people study *A Course in Miracles*. It does not matter if there is only one person studying the Course—you—because within our particular dream, we *are* the only ones studying it, and that should be our only focus. Since our minds are truly one, the love that unites us automatically extends to embrace every mind. Yet this extension, in the mind or world, is not our concern. It happens automatically and naturally without our need to make it so. Being an advanced teacher of God is therefore the easiest thing in the world because we do not do anything. Everything is done through us. Our sole responsibility is to focus on the interference, and with the Holy Spirit beside us, to let it go.

What can be confusing, to return to this earlier theme, are those passages in the workbook that suggest that God is involved with our world, and that what we do with our bodies is important. Consider Lesson 71, which would have us say to Him: *"What would You have me do? Where would You have me go? What would You have me say, and to whom?"* This can easily foster the magical thinking that if we simply say that prayer, all will be well for we will be told—by God Himself!—what to do, etc. It is for this reason I keep urging students not to take out of context what is said in the workbook. Identified

with bodies, we cannot help but have a magical view of God or Jesus. We repress our secret belief that God is the wrathful Enemy, and cover it with the fantasy that our Father will make everything wonderful for us. But because we really believe God is our Enemy, Jesus corrects us by saying that our Father is our Friend Who is concerned with us as persons. Thus we read in Lesson 194 "I place the future in the Hands of God":

> God holds your future as He holds your past and present. They are one to Him, and so they should be one to you. Yet in this world, the temporal progression still seems real. And so you are not asked to understand the lack of sequence really found in time. You are but asked to let the future go, and place it in God's Hands (W-pI.194.4:1-5).

Jesus is saying that there is no time, only an illusion in which past, present, and future are one. However, we cannot comprehend this because we still believe time is real, and so he is not asking us to understand there is no future. He simply asks us to trust that God loves us. It is the older brother talking to his little siblings, knowing it would not be helpful to tell the little ones, "Don't bother asking Daddy; he does not even know who you are." The helpful correction is to say, "You can trust Daddy; he is not angry at you." That is the message: God is not angry. He does not seek to punish, but merely to love. Nothing has happened to interfere with His Love.

Jesus does not convey that message by giving us an extensive discourse on sin, guilt, and fear, and on time being made as a defense against that fear. What is helpful at this point is to correct the mistake that says we cannot trust God because He is wrathfully punitive. And so we can trust our Father, placing our future in His Hands, even though Jesus also lets us know that there is no future, saying in effect: "Because you believe there is a future, I will talk to you that way. It is not the form of what I am saying that is true, but the content." This is similar to his saying that God misses us, and is lonely and incomplete because we left Him. From the Course's perspective, this is rank heresy. Yet, that *is* what Jesus says. Why? Not because the words are literally true, but because their content is, being that Jesus teaches us his message of love in a way we can understand without fear. The ego would tell us that God is glad

His Son is gone, and good riddance to him, too! Instead, Jesus tell us that our Father is lonely because we ran away from home. In yet another passage we are told that God weeps over us. Lovingly, Jesus uses symbols to convey the truth, which is that God loves us, and our perceived sins against Him have had no effect.

In Lesson 192 "I have a function God would have me fill," Jesus refers to God when he really means the Holy Spirit, Who alone knows about forgiveness:

> It is your Father's holy Will that you complete Himself, and that your Self shall be His sacred Son, forever pure as He, of love created and in love preserved, extending love, creating in its name, forever one with God and with your Self. Yet what can such a function mean within a world of envy, hatred and attack?
>
> Therefore, you have a function in the world in its own terms. For who can understand a language far beyond his simple grasp? (W-pI.192.1:1–2:2)

Jesus makes it clear that he knows this world is a place of "envy, hatred and attack," being a representation of the *thought* of envy, hatred and attack. It is therefore more meaningful for him to talk to us about how to undo this thought than to speak of a Love we cannot understand and that we are its extension.

We thus have another clear statement of why Jesus talks to us the way he does in the Course. Since we are like little children, more often than not he speaks to us that way, for "who can understand a language far beyond his simple grasp?" What is not beyond our grasp is this: "You have a loving Father in Heaven Who acts like a person. He thinks, feels, and weeps; He misses you, and is lonely and incomplete without you; He talks to you and you can pray to Him. Finally, in His great Love for you, He has a plan to undo the ego." In other words, Jesus talks to us as if God has a body, because believing we have a body, God must have one, too.

Yet Jesus also gives us passages in the Course to help us understand that God is abstract, not specific, that He does not have a body and does not know about the world, that He does not understand words and does not hear prayers, and so on. If these statements are put side by side, it seems as if he is contradicting himself. If we see the spiritual journey in terms of a ladder, however, we can then understand that many of Jesus' statements are directed toward the bottom of the ladder, some to the middle, and some to the top. Understood that way, they are not contradictory at all. We must always think content or purpose, not form. And so we read that forgiveness is not from God:

> Forgiveness represents your function here. It is not God's creation, for it is the means by which untruth can be undone. And who would pardon Heaven?... Forgiveness gently looks upon all things unknown in Heaven, sees them disappear, and leaves the world a clean and unmarked slate on which the Word of God can now replace the senseless symbols written there before (W-pI.192.2:3-5; 4:1).

Forgiveness is unknown in Heaven. It does not touch truth at all, because truth is beyond all the world's illusions. The "untruth" that conceals truth is what has to be undone. "Forgiveness gently looks on what is unknown in Heaven": all our attack thoughts—hate, sin, specialness—and the projections of those attack thoughts in the world. Recall these important lines: "Forgiveness...is still, and quietly does nothing.... It merely looks, and waits, and judges not" (W-pII.1.4:1,3).

The importance here is understanding that Jesus is not talking about our doing great and wondrous things in the world. He does not care about numbers of students or converting the world to *A Course in Miracles*. He is simply teaching us that forgiveness looks at what is unknown in Heaven, and then gently watches it disappear. It must disappear because we looked at it gently. If we looked harshly, which is how we usually look at the world of the ego—through the eyes of guilt, fear, and judgment—it becomes even more solidified in our minds because we have made the ego's thought system real. As we continue to read, study, and practice the Course, we will see how often this idea appears of not making the ego real.

Once again, "Forgiveness gently looks upon all things unknown in Heaven, sees them disappear...," and at that point the world is left clean. In this context the world is the mind, because the outer and the inner are the same. Without the ego, the mind is left with only the Word of God, the Atonement principle that reflects the Holy Spirit's Love. This is Jesus' home, the right mind that is freed of thoughts of sin, sacrifice, and attack. God's healing Word replaces "the senseless symbols written there before." Our bodies, then, become classrooms of learning:

> Forgiveness is the means by which the fear of death is overcome, because it holds no fierce attraction now and guilt is gone. Forgiveness lets the body be perceived as what it is; a simple teaching aid, to be laid by when learning is complete, but hardly changing him who learns at all (W-pI.192.4:2-3).

The body, made to be a limitation and an attack on love—an instrument of guilt, suffering, pain, and death—is now transformed into a teaching aid. It is not good or bad, holy or unholy, but neutral, freed to serve the holy purpose of forgiveness. Again, the body is not holy in itself, but merely serves the mind's holy purpose. This is what it means to be an advanced teacher of God. We are not the Word of God, but have allowed it to speak through us. Our job is simply to choose against the barriers to the truth, having at last given welcome to it. What remains is the shining Word that is the resplendent love of Jesus, which naturally and effortlessly extends through us.

7. Summary and Closing

To conclude, I would like to make some summary statements of our discussion. A major purpose of the workshop from which this excerpt is taken, was to help people understand the nature of the workbook, as well as foster an appreciation for its importance and place in the curriculum of *A Course in Miracles*. The humbling effect of such appreciation would help students see how much can be missed when they work with the Course, that it takes more than one, two, or ten readings to begin to fully understand its purpose and what wisdom is contained in it.

This profound thought system is not saying what we think it is saying. On one level, its message is that God loves us, we are not separate from Him, and we are all one, but there are dozens and dozens of spiritualities, ancient and contemporary, that say something very similar. What makes this course different and such a powerful learning tool is that it emphasizes the need to look at the ego thought system. Because Jesus says the ego is illusory does not mean we should not pay any attention to it. Just the opposite, in fact. We must pay careful attention to it because *we* believe it is real. Again, it is humbling to become aware of how much we resist truly understanding the meaning of these words, let alone putting them into practice.

If you reread the workbook, I guarantee that you will see it differently. And then, if you reread the text, you will certainly see it differently as well. It takes many, many years of study and discipline to be able to put into practice its teachings. It is not easy to look at the ego and have it disappear. Once again, if it were that simple, none of us would be here. We find ourselves in this world because we do not want to look at the ego. That is why this is a course in mind training, of realizing we are minds and not bodies.

I have frequently quoted Helen as saying that *A Course in Miracles* was for five or six people. Obviously this was a symbol rather than a literal number, though at times she was tempted to actually count. But what Helen was really expressing is the recognition that this is a very difficult course and not for the masses. Religions or spirituality that are aimed at large numbers of people do not spend an inordinate amount of time, as does the Course, talking about the murderous and vicious hate of our special relationships. And very few Western spiritualities speak of the illusory nature of the world and the profound implications of this non-dualism for our everyday living, that we are not so much to pay attention to the world; but to our thinking about it. Our focus, therefore, is not on changing what is outside, the form; it is on changing our thoughts, and even more to the point, on looking with Jesus at the ego's ugliness so we can finally realize it is not ugly at all. It is simply a silly thought that we once took seriously.

Again, this is a most challenging course and it should be approached with respect. This most assuredly does *not* mean that we should treat it as a holy book, surrounding it with flowers, incense, and the like. It does mean, however, that we should approach it with a humility that says: "I do not know anything, and want to be taught, and this is the vehicle I believe will help me, with the teacher who will help me learn it." We then would realize that if this is our spiritual path, we are more than willing to spend the rest of our lives taking the journey with Jesus, which means walking the path of our ego, but not walking alone. When we walk the path of our ego with him, the path will change. That is what he means by vision, when we suddenly hear birds chirping, brooks gurgling, and see flowers bursting forth from the earth. These are of course but symbols to denote how beautiful the world will appear to us because we have identified with the beauty within.

Being with Jesus is the most beautiful experience in the world, and when that beauty is a part of us, we will look out on a world of beauty, even if the world of form is as ugly and vicious as before. But feeling the beauty and love within, that is what we will see outside: *projection makes perception*. That is what it means to be a teacher of God who is advancing toward the goal of awakening from the ego's nightmare of separation. Through the mind-training program of the workbook, Jesus helps us not to underestimate our investment in, and identification with the ego. Thus we walk with him through the snares of illusion, but with open eyes that now see the truth behind appearances, the love beyond the fear, and the light that has never stopped shining midst the darkened clouds of guilt.

As a close, I will read the lovely page from Part II of the workbook entitled "What Am I?" (W-pII.14). The whole second part consists of these wonderful lessons and prayers to God. After each group of ten, there is a page with a question, which then is answered, all 14 of which serve as a wonderful summary of the themes of *A Course in Miracles*. The final one is the answer to the question, "What Am I?" We are told several times in the Course that this is the fundamental question we should ask. The ego, of course, gives us the answer: you are a sinful, guilty person, which you then will deny, making a world that seems to tell you that you are something else. The true answer, of course, is the Holy Spirit's: you are God's true and only Son. This page is a beautiful expression of this truth. It closes with an inspiring rendering of what it means to be a teacher of God, living in the world of illusion. It does not refer to holy works we would do, or all those we would convert. Rather, it expresses the simplicity of being a messenger who demonstrates to the world the love that Jesus in his course has taught us.

What Am I?

I am God's Son, complete and healed and whole, shining in the reflection of His Love. In me is His creation sanctified and guaranteed eternal life. In me is love perfected, fear impossible, and joy established without opposite. I am the holy home of God Himself. I am the Heaven where His Love resides. I am His holy Sinlessness Itself, for in my purity abides His Own.

Our use for words is almost over now. Yet in the final days of this one year we gave to God together, you and I, we found a single purpose that we shared. And thus you joined with me, so what I am are you as well. The truth of what we are is not for words to speak of nor describe. Yet we can realize our function here, and words can speak of this and teach it, too, if we exemplify the words in us.

We are the bringers of salvation. We accept our part as saviors of the world, which through our joint forgiveness is redeemed. And this, our gift, is therefore given us. We look on everyone as brother, and perceive all things as kindly and as good. We do not seek a function that is past the gate of Heaven. Knowledge will return when we have done our part. We are concerned only with giving welcome to the truth.

Ours are the eyes through which Christ's vision sees a world redeemed from every thought of sin. Ours are the ears that hear the Voice for God proclaim the world as sinless. Ours the minds that join together as we bless the world. And from the oneness that we have attained we call to all our brothers, asking them to share our peace and consummate our joy.

We are the holy messengers of God who speak for Him, and carrying His Word to everyone whom He has sent to us, we learn that it is written on our hearts. And thus our minds are changed about the aim for which we came, and which we seek to serve. We bring glad tidings to the Son of God, who thought he suffered. Now is he redeemed. And as he sees the gate of Heaven stand open before him, he will enter in and disappear into the Heart of God.

Please see our Web site, *www.facim.org*, for a complete listing of publications, including multiple media types.

Foundation for A Course in Miracles®
(961) 296-6261 • fax (951) 296-5455